89-0923

WITHD

POLITICS AND PRODUCTIVITY
The Real Story of Why Japan Works

Edited by
CHALMERS JOHNSON
LAURA D'ANDREA TYSON
JOHN ZYSMAN

WITHDRAWN

A RESEARCH PROJECT OF THE BERKELEY ROUNDTABLE
ON THE INTERNATIONAL ECONOMY (BRIE)

BALLINGER PUBLISHING COMPANY
A Subsidiary of Harper & Row, Publishers, Inc.

International Standard Book Number: 0-88730-350-1

Library of Congress Catalog Card Number: 88-31238

Printed in the United States of America

Library of Congress Cataloging-in-Publication Data

Politics and productivity : the real story of why Japan works / edited
   by Chalmers Johnson, Laura D'Andrea Tyson, John Zysman.
      p.   cm.
   "A research project of the Berkeley Roundtable on the International
Economy (BRIE)."
   Includes bibliographies and index.
   ISBN 0-88730-350-1
   1. Industrial productivity—Japan. 2. Industry and state—Japan.
I. Johnson, Chalmers A. II. Tyson, Laura D'Andrea, 1947-   .
III. Zysman, John. IV. Berkeley Roundtable on the International
Economy.
HC465.I52P65   1989
338.952—dc19   88-31238
                                                         CIP

CONTENTS

LIST OF FIGURES

LIST OF TABLES

ACKNOWLEDGMENTS

The editors wish to thank the Ford Foundation, and David Packard for financial support that made this book possible.

PREFACE
The Argument Outlined

Laura D'Andrea Tyson
John Zysman

From the vantage of traditional economics, Japan has made very serious policy errors. It has, for example, protected its domestic economy against foreign competition and intervened in specific industrial sectors and in the affairs of particular firms. Perhaps its capacities and resources have been so great that it has succeeded despite its policy errors. Or perhaps, as this book suggests, traditional American economic and political conceptions about the dynamics of international trade and domestic development are flawed and must be reconsidered in view of Japan's spectacular development success.

Japan's emergence as an industrial powerhouse poses a broad powerful challenge to the United States. For years the challenge has been most visible in competition in specific industrial sectors. From low-wage, labor-intensive apparel through shipbuilding, steel, and automobiles to technology-intensive semiconductors, Japanese industry has established positions in the U. S. and world markets. More troubling, in those same sectors, American firms have lost market share at home and abroad. The challenge from Japan is intellectual as well as economic.

The problems of specific industries reflect a broader challenge. Stories of industries and firms troubled by foreign competition confirm and texture readings of the trade and productivity data: American firms are having difficulty matching their competitors abroad. The staggering trade deficits of the 1980s have accumulated into a substantial national foreign debt. The huge trade imbalance cannot be explained simply as a consequence of the surging dollar value in the early 1980s.[1] The recent substantial decline of the dollar has not produced the expected return to trade equilibrium. Rather, more fundamentally, rates of growth and productivity of Japanese firms have steadily outstripped not only American rates but those of the other advanced industrial economies as well. The American rates have been near the bottom of the league. At one time the disparity could be attributed to an effort at industrial catch-up, but this is no longer the case. The U.S. productivity advantage has largely disappeared. Most troubling, perhaps, is that our eroding trade position in manufacturing comes at a moment of seemingly basic innovation in the machines and know-how that constitute manufacturing practice. Indeed, we are now re-equipping our factories with imported capital equipment. It is no longer simply a matter of our competitors catching up with us in what we do, but of new industrial practices emerging abroad that are not being matched here. If we cannot keep pace at this juncture, we could find ourselves beginning a long, cumulative economic decline that ultimately threatens our national wealth and power.

Certainly Japan continues to obtain technology wherever it is available and to translate it into commercial advance, as the United States itself did for so long. However, now talk has begun of a new, "technoeconomic" paradigm emerging in Japan, a new trajectory of technology development. That trajectory emerged from a pattern of industrial catch-up shaped by policies of import substitution and export promotion. As Japan reaches industrial maturity in a broad range of industries, its government is exerting substantial efforts to build a Japanese position in advancing technologies. Agencies such as the Ministry of Trade and Industry (MITI), which have become familar names in policy discussions in the United States, are involved. So, also, are less well-known agencies such as the Science and Technology Agency and the Ministry of Health. A generation from now, Japan will almost certainly have created its own mechanisms for advancing the technological frontiers in a range of domains. Now the continuing pace of productivity increase suggests that Japan may indeed be on a growth trajectory different from that of the United States.

As Japan ascends, America frets about its decline. The relative competitive positions of Japan and the United States are changing.

For the first twenty-five years of the postwar period, America was indeed a hegemon. It had the capacity to shape the international system, forcing others to play by its rules. Its domestic economy was little affected by economic policy choices abroad. In trade and finance America had the resources to make the side payments and absorb the costs required to assure international economic stability. It could offer access to its market as an instrument of security policy, sustain a high dollar, and permit others to devalue to bring their trade balances in line. Interdependence was for others; the United States was at the center of the system. America's capacity to ignore international pressures, its place as a hegemon, ended with the floating of the dollar in 1971. We had to change the international rules to accommodate our own domestic needs. American foreign commercial and financial policy had to attend to the short-term needs of the domestic economy rather than pursuing the longer term objective of assuring system stability. Yet America was still dominant. The new rules still reflected its wishes. In the years since 1971, the international position of the American economy has sharply eroded. America's ability to impose its preferences in the face of opposition from the other advanced countries has weakened. America no longer dominates the international economy. Yet the United States remains economically preeminent; it is the strongest and largest single economy in the world.

The shifting patterns of trade and the emergence of new lines of technological development force new tasks on the United States. If the United States is to remain even preeminent, it must respond to them quickly and effectively. The purposive and successful domestic as well as trade strategies of our competitors will force the United States to adjust. We are discovering that there are different ways of organizing capitalism. It is not a matter of whether the United States can or should imitate its competitors. The task will be for the United States, in its own way, to develop new capacities that are equal to its new challenges. This will not be easy because America's economic and political institutions have evolved in the twentieth century in a manner that suits its once dominant position, not in a manner that suits the increasingly competitive international environment.

We cannot respond to our problems unless we can identify them. The Japanese success and the emergence of new forms of industrial organization and manufacturing pose an important intellectual challenge. They stretch the limits of traditionally and simply interpreted economic theory. Often this provokes a kind of denial. There have been many efforts to examine the patterns of growth in Japan to demonstrate that state influence has been less important than generally understood or has been counterproductive. There have been attempts to show that Japan's policies of import substitution and protection targeted at specific industries did not matter or did not work. Such efforts try to reshape the case to fit the theory.

This book considers instead assumptions and analyses that reconcile theory with the reality of successful state intervention. Proposed here is a new analytical framework for understanding Japan's development strategy and the implications for Japan's growing prowess in international markets. This framework is based on the view that although Japan is an advanced capitalist democracy, the institutions of capitalism that it has built in the context of its unique experience with industrialization differ fundamentally from those encountered in American capitalism.

In the Japanese variant of capitalism, markets are emphasized as a source of growth rather than of short-run efficiency, and a primary role of government is to supply incentives to promote growth through markets. The perspective motivating Japanese policy is explicitly dynamic and explicitly developmental. From this perspective, the competitive advantage of a nation's producers in world markets is created by policy rather than given by immutable resource and technological endowments. Moreover, in a dynamic world, temporary policies to create competitive advantage for domestic producers can have long-term effects that are difficult to reverse.

Part I of the book develops these basic ideas about the institutions and objectives of Japanese capitalism. Its chapters provide an analytical rationale for a key feature of Japan's development strategy: the targeting of industries on the basis of their perceived potential for economic growth and technological change.

The first chapter, by Giovanni Dosi, Laura D'Andrea Tyson, and John Zysman, examines the effects of this targeting strategy on Japan's growth and trade performance. This strategy has had long-term beneficial effects on Japan's competitive position in world markets. To understand these effects, it is necessary to abandon the static assumptions of international trade theory, even the so-called new trade theory, and to adopt a dynamic model in which national patterns of production and trade specialization at a moment in time can affect a nation's growth and technological trajectory over time.

The authors distinguish three kinds of efficiency: Ricardian efficiency (the allocation of resources according to their effects on current economic conditions), growth efficiency (the allocation of resources according to their effects on economic growth), and Schumpeterian efficiency (the allocation of resources according to their effects on the pace and direction of technological change). Japan's policy choices clearly were dominated by considerations of growth and Schumpeterian efficiency in a self-conscious way. The authors demonstrate that under conditions of imperfect competition and rapid technological change, a targeting strategy based on these criteria can generate higher levels of economic welfare over time than can a market strategy based on Ricardian efficiency. The authors conclude that Japan is at the forefront of a new technological trajectory and that it would not be there without the interventionist targeting strategy that gradually but definitely guided Japan's industrial structure toward those sectors having the greatest growth and technological potential. Policy affected where and how much investment occurred, what kinds of skills and technological learning took place, and by its influence on the production profile of the economy, policy ultimately affected the pace and direction of technological innovation and diffusion.

The second chapter, by Stephen S. Cohen and John Zysman, argues that America's huge trade deficit with Japan cannot be understood simply as a product of price increases caused by a changing exchange rate. Certainly price increases accentuated and accelerated the problem, but at its core the difficulty is that Japanese manufacturing appears to have taken off on a distinct trajectory. It is not simply a matter of American firms catching up to Japanese practice, but more profoundly a matter of changing direction as well.

Cohen and Zysman argue that an erosion of manufacturing capacities has contributed substantially to America's trade problems. The difficulty lies not in machines and technology, but in strategies for automation and the goals American firms seek to achieve through production innovation. Mass production and administrative hierarchies created the basis for American industrial preeminence in the years after World War II. There is substantial evidence that American firms have been unable to adopt or adapt to the production innovations emerging abroad. Those innovations constitute the creation of a distinct technoeconomic paradigm built around flexibility rather than simply volume production. The distinctly different responses of the American and Japanese economies to a quite similar economic shock, the rapid and extreme rise in the value of the nation's currency, suggest that they are on distinct technological trajectories. That hypothesis is supported by a look at the direction of manufacturing innovation.

Part II of the book focuses on the interplay between government and market institutions in Japan. Chapter 3, by Tyson and Zysman, examines the influence of government policy on industrial outcomes in a logical sequence with institutions and policy structuring markets and market dynamics, market signals driving corporate strategy, corporate strategy shaping production strategy and innovation, and corporate strategy and policy interacting to create long-term competitive advantage in world markets. Despite formal changes in Japan's policies, the basic logic of protection and promotion of targeted activities remains, and the basic patterns of Japanese trade—in particular, distinctively low import penetration rates in manufactured goods—remains unaltered. The authors conclude that the Japanese market is characterized by a moving band of protectionism; the targets of policy and the forms of policy have changed over time, but the restrictive effects of policy on the access of foreign producers to Japanese markets in important emerging and declining industries persist.

Government policy or outright discrimination is only part of the story of market access in Japan. Foreign firms find the Japanese market very difficult to penetrate. Ronald Dore has remarked that there is a natural immunity to imports that comes from "a dense web of 'relational contracting'."[2] Economic relations are embedded in social or organizational connections that tend to make it difficult for outsiders to participate or that slow down and raise the cost of entry. "Imports penetrate into markets and where there are no markets, only a network of established 'customer relationships', it is hard for them to make headway."[3]

These networks are significant and varied. Distribution channels, as is widely noted, are arcane. Webs of suppliers linked to dominant companies abound. Firms depend on close and long-term ties to a small number of suppliers rather than seeking the best price at any moment from a large set of bidders. These long-term "business relationships" do not embody guarantees, but a set of mutual efforts to work through problems rather than walk away from them. They also imply privileged access to attempt new sales or new lines of cooperation, access built on previous trust that would be unavailable to outsiders. There is also an element of reciprocity. Suppliers may be expected to reciprocate to their major customers, particularly if those customers can themselves be suppliers.

All societies consist of business networks and webs of social connections. What apparently distinguishes Japan is the extent and often formal character of those ties. One of the crucial elements of this web is the *kieretsu*, the networks of businesses around trading companies or banks. Chapter 4, by Michael Gerlach, depicts the formal structure of these fluid organizations and speculates on their significance in shaping trade flows. Gerlach argues that densely linked and strongly preferential trading systems, such as those found in the Japanese *keiretsu*, are likely to be impervious to fluctuations in exchange rates or to government liberalization efforts. Thus, even when the government reduces policy barriers to market access in Japan, foreign firms continue to confront barriers that stem from the long-term contractual relationships among Japanese firms.

Part III contains case studies of how the interaction between government institutions and market institutions shapes competitive outcomes in specific industries and product lines. Some argue that the targeting of industrial activities is a thing of the past in Japan, but these chapters indicate that policies of promotion and protection essential to this strategy remain firmly in place in the high-technology areas of telecommunications, semiconductors and semiconductor equipment, and aerospace.

Chalmers Johnson, who introduced the notion of Japan's "developmental state" in his 1982 book *MITI and the Japanese Miracle*, examines its workings in the telecommunications industry. A developmental policy is a political creation, and the political victory and its bureaucratic and policy manifestation must continuously be recreated. Johnson's chapter demonstrates that the essential elements of promotion and insulation remain firmly in place in the telecommunications sector. From an international and comparative vantage, the round of reshuffling in the structure of the telecommunications industry that has altered the formal arrangements and the internal dynamics of the system leaves the developmental arrangements untouched. Michael Borrus has labeled the process developmental re-regulation—the forms of policy and organization change, but the core objective of creating advantage in global markets remains.[4] As one senior official remarked, "Even with (the policy changes at issue) we are confident of defeating foreign capital."[5] Johnson argues that the politics of reregulation are driven by the struggle for bureaucratic advantage between MITI and the Ministry of Post and Telecommunications. The Liberal Democratic party's policy councils have played a crucial role in shaping the outcome of the initiatives launched by these ministries. The bureaucratic conflicts open the policy arena to political influence. Foreign pressures have not reshaped the system but have been used as weapons in the interbureaucratic struggle. The developmental thrust has not been eliminated, but we should be clear that it is rooted in political choice and in institutions that evolve and change.

Chapter 6, by Jay S. Stowsky, explores U.S.-Japanese competition in the semiconductor production equipment industry. Stowsky argues that equipment development and manufacturing prowess in the semiconductor industry are tightly linked, representing a capability embodied in people and organized in firms but not readily tradable across national boundaries. Stowsky's major thesis is that with regard to both the generation of learning in production and the appreciation of economic returns from such learning, the U.S. semiconductor equipment and semiconductor industries are structurally weak relative to the Japanese industries. The Japanese industrial model involves higher levels of concentration of both chip and equipment suppliers and greater quasi-integration between them. In part, this is the result of the *keiretsu* form of organization discussed in Gerlach's chapter. But policy, too, has been important. The government-sponsored very-large-scale integration (VLSI) project in Japan encouraged a cooperative approach among producers, allowed the overall development costs of a successful semiconductor industry to be shared, and provided an institutional context in which semiconductor device and equipment firms could work together to organize a production system geared toward the constant introduction and refinement of new production technologies.

The final chapter, by Richard Samuels and Benjamin Whipple, explores Japan's efforts to begin to establish its own position in the aircraft industry through the development of advanced fighter planes. Their interpretation of the FS-X (Fighter-Support/Experimental) program is at odds with conventional understandings that emphasize continued Japanese dependence on American technology. Inevitably, Japanese efforts to establish position in advanced technology sectors must extend to their own defense. The question is not whether but when and what form the defense effort will take. Samuels and Whipple provide evidence on this question. We, the editors, expect that Japanese defense efforts will be organized differently from those in the United States, in particular that there will be more use of existing commercial technologies more rapidly incorporated into final systems. This may come to represent a substantial challenge to the procurement process in the United States.

NOTES

1. Elizabeth Kremp and Jacques Mistral, "Commerce Exterieur Americain: d'ou vient, ou va lé deficit?" *Economie Prospective Internationale* 22 (Paris: Centre d'Etudes Prospectives et d'Informations Internationales, 1985).
2. Ronald Dore, *Flexible Rigidities* (Stanford, Calif.: Stanford University Press, 1986), p. 248.
3. Ibid.
4. Michael Borrus, François Bar, Patrick Cogez, Anne Brit Thoresen, Ibrahim Warde, and Aki Yoshikawa, "Telecommunications Development in Comparative Perspective: The New Telecommunications in Europe, Japan and the U.S.," Working Paper 14, Berkeley Roundtable on the International Economy, University of California, Berkeley, May 1985; and Michael Borrus and François Bar, "From Public Access to Private Connections: Network Policy and National Advantage," Working Paper 28, Berkeley Roundtable on the International Economy, University of California, Berkeley, September 1987.
5. See note 69 of Chapter 5.

DEFICITS, EQUILIBRIA, AND TRAJECTORIES

1 TRADE, TECHNOLOGIES, AND DEVELOPMENT
A Framework for Discussing Japan

Giovanni Dosi
Laura D'Andrea Tyson
John Zysman

From the traditional analytical perspective of economics Japan has done many things wrong. During the first two decades of its postwar development, perhaps longer, Japanese markets were formally closed to the penetration of foreign goods and capital. The Ministry of International Trade and Industry (MITI), with the help of the Ministry of Finance and other government organizations, acted as gatekeeper to the Japanese market, limiting the access of foreigners and targeting industries and firms for promotional policies.[1] Capacity expansions and reductions in various industries were often planned firm by firm, and numerous and growing violations of Japan's antitrust law were left unchecked. Cartels and other informal mechanisms for market-sharing and risk-sharing among domestic producers were overlooked or actively encouraged by Japanese policymakers convinced that under certain conditions, "controlled" competition was preferable to market competition. Foreign direct investment was precluded, and the import of foreign technology was strictly controlled by MITI, which acted as an intermediary between domestic firms and foreign suppliers of technology, often to the benefit of the former and the disadvantage of the latter. Interest rates were held below market-clearing levels, and credit was allocated to targeted firms and activities at preferential rates, while nonpriority borrowers were credit-constrained. Exports were promoted not by simple reliance on the "correct" exchange rate but by a variety of tax, credit,

3

and protectionist policies that raised the returns to exports to Japanese producers. In targeting industries for preferential policy, Japanese policymakers overrode notions of comparative advantage in favor of such ill-defined criteria as the dynamic or technological potential of a particular economic activity.[2]

Today policies like those adopted in Japan are routinely attacked by the International Monetary Fund (IMF) and the World Bank, the two most influential international organizations advising countries on development strategy.[3] Few would deny, however, that Japan has been a spectacular success story in economic development. What are we to conclude from the apparent contrast between Japan's economic success and its often flagrant and self-aware violations of the nostrums of traditional economic thinking? Did Japan succeed despite these violations or would it have done even better if its policymakers had accepted the contemporary collective wisdom of traditional economic thought? Alternatively, does Japan's economic success and the distinctive policy and institutional choices on which it appears to rest indicate that traditional thought must be reconsidered?

A key feature of Japan's development strategy is the targeting of industries on the basis of their perceived potential for economic growth and technological change. Japan's actions appear motivated by a Schumpeterian perspective, the notion that competition in the form of new products and processes is the real engine of growth over time. Price competition, the kind of competition that is the focus of most economic analysis, is deemed less important in driving long-term national development than traditionally thought, although such competition has mattered critically in specific sectors once technology has been developed and mastered. Moreover, under conditions of technological change and the imperfections in price competition to which it gives rise, there can be no priori assumption that economic welfare is better served by "free" market signals than by government targeting policies that "distort" such signals. Most important, under such conditions, even temporary policies can have permanent long-term effects. When increasing returns exist in an industry, many market outcomes are possible, and policy measures introduced at one moment can have self-reinforcing effects over time. Japan's promotion and protection of its semiconductor industry in the 1970s is a significant determinant of the strength of its industry in international markets today.

Most of the industries in which Japan has been most successful and in which the international competition between the United States and Japan is now strongest are characterized by rapid technological progress in both product and process. When technological change is a key determinant of market outcomes, standard economic models that treat such change as exogenous are a poor guide to understanding the dynamics of market competition and the effects of policy on such competition. Yet such models continue to serve as the foundation for economic policymaking in the United States and continue to inform the policy prescriptions of most economists.

Certain critical issues must be addressed to develop such a model and to understand the rationale behind Japan's targeting strategy and the reasons for its developmental success. Because the focus of interest is the strength of Japan's industry in international markets, we begin with a brief survey of trade theory, contrasting the traditional theory of comparative advantage with the so-called new trade theory. Fundamentally, the new theory presents the analysis of trade when the assumption of perfect competition is abandoned. It explores how competition and government intervention in imperfect markets create a strategic logic to trade. Once the classical assumption of perfect competition is dropped, it is easy to demonstrate that there are many theoretical circumstances under which government targeting can have a long-term beneficial effect on national economic welfare.[4]

The "new" trade theory, while more appropriate to the imperfectly competitive conditions characteristic of most trade flows among the advanced industrial countries, is mostly static in its orientation.[5] It is concerned with the once and for all effects of policy on trade outcomes and economic welfare. It does not examine how national patterns of trade and production specialization at a moment in time can affect a nation's growth and technological trajectory over time.

Because we are interested in such dynamic effects, we introduce two new notions of economic efficiency—growth efficiency and technological efficiency—and we use them to evaluate Japan's development strategy. Japan's technoeconomic paradigm is unique. Its government's targeting of industries on the basis of their growth and technological potential and its unique institutional and organizational strengths for promoting such industries are the foundations of Japan's dramatic competitive success in world markets.

TRADITIONAL TRADE THEORY

Until the late 1970s, international trade theory was dominated by the concept of comparative advantage. This concept implies that nations trade to take advantage of differences in their productive capabilities. Formally, it implies that countries tend to export in sectors in which they have a comparative production advantage relative to their competitors and to import in sectors in which they have a comparative production disadvantage. According to the theory of comparative advantage, even a country with an absolute production disadvantage, in the sense of higher domestic costs of production for all traded commodities, gains from trade by exporting those goods in which its production disadvantage is least.

In formal standard models of comparative advantage, production is assumed to exhibit constant returns to scale.[6] Both increasing returns in the traditional sense and learning-curve economies are excluded. Markets for tradable products are assumed to be perfectly competitive, and trade is assumed to occur under full-employment conditions. Under these assumptions, trade arises only to the extent that countries differ in tastes, technology, or factor endowments. Ricardian models of trade explain comparative advantage in terms of a single key factor of production, such as labor productivity or natural resource endowments, or in terms of technological differences. The Heckscher-Ohlin variant of comparative advantage theory assumes the existence of two or more factors of production—usually labor and capital—and argues that countries tend to export goods embodying their relatively abundant factors and to import goods embodying their relatively scarce factors. Whichever type of comparative advantage model is adopted, the same general welfare implication applies: free trade results in welfare gains for trading partners.

During the last decade, the standard models of comparative advantage based on traditional constant-returns, perfect-competition assumptions have been supplanted to some extent by new models that emphasize increasing returns and imperfect competition.[7] The new models seem much more appropriate to trade in manufactured products. In many manufacturing sectors the assumptions of constant returns and perfect competition are obviously unrealistic. The new models recognize a powerful motivation for trade: Countries specialize and trade not only because of underlying differences in tastes and resource endowmnets, but also because of increasing returns that lead to the geographical concentration of production of each good. To the extent that trade is driven by economies of scale and dynamic learning, trade occurs under imperfectly competitive conditions. This is hardly surprising because most trade in manufactured goods occurs in industries that economists usually think of as oligopolistic.

At first glance, the view that trade is inherently of mutual benefit to trading nations is not challenged by notions of increasing returns and imperfect competition. Under increasing returns, trading countries can specialize in the production of different goods, achieving the cost economies of increased scale of production while maintaining or increasing the diversity of goods available. In addition, trade may actually reduce the market imperfections that would be associated with a closed economy by subjecting producers to more competition in world markets with a larger number of competing producers. Thus the new models seem to confirm the welfare implications of the more standard models: trade is a good thing with mutual gains for all.

A closer look at this argument, though, shows that with increasing returns and imperfect competition, free trade is not necessarily and automatically the best policy. Trade without barriers and government policies of promotion that distort markets may improve national welfare. However, government policy to strengthen the competitive position of domestic producers in world markets may generate higher levels of national welfare than would result from free trade.

In recent years, the "new" trade theory literature has concentrated on conditions under which government policy of intervention and promotion may actually improve national welfare. Two conditions give rise to this result. First, industries that are imperfectly competitive tend to generate high returns (excess profits or quasi-rents)—in other words, the resources employed by these sectors earn higher returns than those available in the rest of the economy. Under this condition, national welfare may be improved by government policy to win larger market shares for domestic producers in world markets and hence a larger share of world profits for the domestic population. If the world computer industry is a high-profit, high-wage industry, then national protectionist and promotional policies that capture a large share of the world computer industry for domestic producers and workers may improve national welfare at the expense of competitors abroad.

Such policies act to shift the world pool of returns in a high-return industry from one set of national producers to another and are thus inherently "beggar thy neighbor" policies. The new trade theory literature often refers to this rationale for government policy as a "profit/rip-off" rationale. National policies that target the successful, high-return export industries of other nations for development are sometimes understood from this vantage point.

Government policies of promotion to improve national welfare can be justified by the second condition. Standard notions of externalities or spillover effects define this condition. Simply put, certain industries may be more important than others because they generate benefits for the rest of the economy, and government policies to promote or protect them can improve welfare by fostering these spillover effects. In fact, the proposition that protectionist or promotional policies can improve national welfare when an industry generates external economies is part of the conventional theory of trade policy. In a sense there is nothing really new about this branch of the new trade theory. What the new literature has done is to strengthen the case for welfare-improving policy by focusing on externalities resulting from the research and development activities of high-technology industries and by linking the analysis of externalities to the analysis of the imperfectly competitive market conditions inherently characteristic of such industries.[8]

High-technology industries are likely to generate positive externalities because of the knowledge generated by their research and development activities and because the benefits of this knowledge cannot be completely appropriated by the private agents who pay the costs for the generation of such knowledge. It is useful to distinguish three different kinds of knowledge generated by research and development and innovation: (1) knowledge, such as production process knowledge reflected in firm-specific learning curves, which can be internalized within a firm and is therefore largely appropriable; (2) knowledge of product design that once generated can often be captured by competitors through "reverse engineering"; and (3) knowledge that spreads beyond the innovating firm but not necessarily easily beyond national or sometimes even regional boundaries.[9] This third kind of knowledge is often embodied in people and spread through social and academic networks. Both the second and third kinds of knowledge generate benefits that are not completely appropriable by the innovating agent. In industries experiencing rapid technological progress, firms routinely take one anothers' products apart to see how they work and how they are made, and at least in the United States, firms routinely raid one another's R&D talent and the knowledge they embody. The third kind of knowledge may be largely appropriable within a given set of national or regional boundaries, but not by the agents responsible for footing the R&D bill that gave rise to the knowledge.

When knowledge is not completely appropriable, the social returns to R&D investment activities are likely to exceed the private returns. This is the standard externality argument in support of policies to promote improvement in national economic welfare.[10] It applies equally to both domestic industries and those involved in international trade. As long as the externalities resulting from such policies are international in scope—in other words as long as the knowledge fostered by such policies flows across national boundaries as easily as within them—each nation stands to benefit from the policies of its trading partners. A technological breakthrough sponsored by government policy in Japan benefits U.S. producers just as it benefits Japanese producers. The bottom line is that the resulting knowledge has the potential to benefit everyone regardless of national boundaries. In contrast, there is a conflict of interest if knowledge spills over within a country but not between countries.

The potential for national conflicts of interest in the support of high-technology industries becomes even more pronounced once one recognizes that such industries are never perfectly competitive. Investment in knowledge inevitably has a fixed-cost component: once a firm has improved its product or technique, the unit cost of that improvement falls as more is produced. The result is dynamic economies of scale that undermine perfect competition and eliminate a basic premise of the free-trade argument. Indeed, since each piece of new knowledge must be different from previously produced knowledge, the assumption of homogeneous products on which perfect competition rests must be largely invalid for markets based on technological competition. Under these circumstances, government policies that promote the R&D activities of high-technology industries may win a larger share of the world returns from such industries for domestic producers and workers and at the same time generate externalities primarily for domestic producers and only secondarily for foreign ones.[11]

In other words, both "profit/rip-off" and externality rationales for policies to target high-technology industries may exist in certain circumstances. As an illustration, a targeting policy to promote the Japanese computer industry may generate technological knowledge from which both Japanese and American firms may benefit, but the policy may also increase the share of the Japanese producers in world production and returns at the expense of the share of American producers.

The new trade theory literature provides theoretical conditions under which government policies to promote industries or activities because of their strategic characteristics can improve national economic welfare relative to the free-trade outcome. This conclusion has provoked some heated debates among economists about the wisdom of such policies.[12] First, there is a debate about the feasibility of evaluating whether an industry is strategic or not: how to measure the extent of increasing returns and the nature of imperfect competition or the extent of externalities? Even with the most sophisticated tools currently at our disposal, such measures are empirically very difficult and subject to large errors.[13] Second, there is a debate about how one evaluates whether a proposed policy will do more harm than good, especially when its effects on other industries or activities not targeted by policy are considered. Uncertainty is a feature of all economic policy, but it becomes even more important when the key issue is how a policy will affect firms in an imperfectly competitive industry. For example, as Paul Krugman notes, the effects of a protectionist trade policy or an R&D subsidy depend crucially on whether firms behave cooperatively or noncooperatively, whether they compete by setting prices or outputs, whether there is a sort of "winner takes all" game or, conversely, whether benefits of research strategies are shared also by competitors.[14]

Unfortunately, it is both theoretically and empirically difficult to predict which form of behavior is most likely. If, as many models indicate, the effect of an interventionist policy is to encourage uncooperative behavior and the entry of new firms, then the national benefits of intervention may be dissipated by competition, which drives excess profits to zero in the world market or which passes the benefits of national R&D policies to foreign consumers in the form of lower prices. Furthermore, to determine whether strategic policy improves welfare or not, the government must understand its effects not only on the targeted industry, which is difficult enough, but also on other industries.

Finally, there is a debate among economists about how widespread and important strategic activities are. If competition in world industries rapidly drives excess profits to zero, learning spreads quickly and costlessly across firms and countries, and market prices are good indicators of social returns both now and in the future, then there are few strategic activities that can benefit from market-promoting policies, according to one argument. If, instead, large excess profits in particular industries or activities can persist for long periods of time despite competition and prices are poor indicators of social returns now or in the future, then the scope for welfare-improving policies can be quite broad. It was the latter perspective that motivated Japanese developmental policy during the postwar period, while the former perspective is clearly the basis of policymaking in the United States.

THE LIMITS OF THE OLD:
THE NEED FOR THE NEW

The new trade theory pushes the limits of traditional economic thought about the welfare effects of government policy, but it still reflects many of the assumptions and foundations of such thought. Inherently static in orientation, the theory is centrally concerned with the problem of the optimal allocation of existing resources. Its models examine the once and for all gains to be obtained by different patterns of resource allocation, a market-determined one and a policy-driven one. Typically, these models show that under certain stringent conditions, a policy-induced outcome may induce a once and for all improvement in economic welfare, due in the last resort to better terms of trade that the domestic economy enjoys with the help of policy.

The rationale behind Japanese developmental policy has different intellectual roots. Japanese policymakers have been critically concerned about the links between current resource allocation decisions and the future evolution of the economy. In the words of a MITI official, "optimal resource allocation from a long-term dynamical viewpoint cannot be accomplished by the market mechanism alone . . . this is an area in which industrial policy can—and should—play a useful role.[15] It is this perspective that led Japanese officials to abandon the theory of comparative advantage as a guide to policy and to target industries and technologies that in their view had the greatest potential to promote rapid economic growth and development over time. It is impossible to understand this perspective within the confines of the new trade theory. An inherently dynamic analytical framework is needed.

To develop one we first draw a distinction between Ricardian or allocative efficiency on the one hand and growth efficiency and Schumpeterian efficiency on the other. The allocation of resources among industries and activities in response to current measures of social profitability and under conditions of non-increasing returns is generally Ricardian efficient, in the sense that it maximizes or at least improves current economic welfare. In the case of market imperfections and externalities of the types discussed above, the realization of Ricardian efficiency may require government intervention. In the presence of increasing returns, there are in theory many possible points of Ricardian efficiency. Multiple outcomes are possible and which outcome is realized depends in part on government policy.

Consider the example of two countries that each can undertake production in two possible industries (say aircraft and computers), each of which has large set-up costs or some other source of increasing returns.[16] Given current market conditions, a possible Ricardian efficient arrangement would be for one country to produce all of one commodity, earning the returns for its domestic population, the other to produce all of the other. The countries could then trade to arrive at their preferred consumption mix to the benefit of both.

There are, however, two possible arrangements. Which commodity is produced in which country is indeterminate. And when the two countries differ in size or the two industries differ in their potential for future demand growth or future technological change, the two possible outcomes can have different welfare consequences in both the short run and the long run. Furthermore, the outcome will be sensitive to the initial conditions of competition between the countries.

More concretely, the early history of market shares, in part the consequence of small past events and chance circumstances and in part the consequence of past government policy, can determine which solution ultimately prevails, that is, which country produces what. In short, with increasing returns and imperfect competition, market outcomes that are Ricardian efficient in the sense that they maximize current economic welfare are themselves path-dependent. History as well as contemporary indicators of social profitability affect the outcome.

The allocation of resources among industries and activities can be evaluated not only according to its Ricardian efficiency but also according to two other performance criteria:

1. Its growth efficiency or its effects on long-term rates of growth of economic activity
2. Its Schumpeterian efficiency or its effects on the pace and direction of technological change.

These two criteria clearly dominated Japanese economic policymaking in a self-conscious way. Japanese industrial policy targeted industries and activities that appeared to the Japanese planners to have the greatest future growth potential and the greatest technological potential over the long run (see Chapter 3). As Freeman argues in his insightful book on Japanese technology policy, "MITI saw as one of its key functions the promotion of the most advanced technologies with the widest world market potential in the long run."[17] Under conditions of imperfect competition and technological change, an allocation of resources that is Ricardian efficient—in other words, efficient by current market indicators—may not be efficient in the growth or Schumpeterian sense.

OF EQUILIBRIA AND TRAJECTORIES

The future growth and technological development of a nation is affected by the composition of its industries and activities, in other words by its current allocation of resources. As a result of its past economic history, each country must be understood to be on a distinct developmental trajectory. National development trajectories rest on the existing composition of production (the production profile of the existing economy) and on the paradigms of how to develop and exploit technology, which in turn are shaped by the market positions confronting a nation's private and public economic actors and by the institutional structures that constrain their strategies.

If the dynamic potential of economic activities differs, then a national specialization at a given moment, which is efficient in terms of a given set of market indicators, may not maximize economic welfare in the long run. If private agents and policymakers allocate resources according to these indicators, the future development trajectory of the economy may be adversely affected. A nation may realize an efficient allocation of resources to specialize in those industries and activities in which the opportunities for growth and technological development are least. In this case there can be a real conflict between short-term Ricardian efficiency and longer term dynamic efficiency.

A consequence of this perspective is that the outcome of strategic trade conflicts is not simply a matter of the one-time gains or losses that result when one government's policy allows its firms to gain a dominant position in global markets to the disadvantage of its trading partners. What may be at stake are future gains and losses in terms of each nation's dynamic potential. A nation's current competitive successes and failures in international trade will affect the areas in which technical skills will be accumulated, innovation undertaken, and economies of scale reaped. And the growth and technological potential of different areas are not the same. In short, different industries and activities may be strategic not only in the static ways suggested by the new trade theory but also in terms of their dynamic potential for future growth and technological change.

GROWTH EFFICIENCY AND
DEVELOPMENT TRAJECTORIES

Growth efficiency is essentially a demand-side idea. It rests on a Keynesian assumption that an economy's growth depends on the growth of demand for its products. This assumption in turn rests on the implicit assumption that there are always unutilized resources that can be mobilized to meet growing demand. In other words, economic growth is primarily constrained by demand growth, not by supply capabilities. This is likely to be the reality in most modern economies. Yet this reality runs counter to the assumptions of trade theory, even the new trade theory. These theories assume the aggregate level and rate of growth of economic activity to be unaffected by trade. The growth efficiency idea, in contrast, considers how trade outcomes may affect growth over time by influencing patterns of national specialization. Countries may specialize, as a result of trade, in industries with different growth potential in world markets.

When the world is a Keynesian one, the growth efficiency of a particular pattern of production and trade specialization depends in part on the income elasticities of demand for different products in world markets—that is, on how fast the demand for particular products increases as world income grows. The idea is that the faster the demand for a nation's products increases in world markets as world income grows, the faster that economy will be able to grow, all other things being equal. Since products differ significantly in their income elasticities, a pattern of specialization in goods with high income elasticities of demand generates more rapid growth prospects for a nation's products in world markets and is therefore superior according to the growth efficiency criterion. Seen from this perspective, other things being equal, a nation with a large percentage of its output and exports in apparel, a product with a low income elasticity of demand, has less attractive long-run growth prospects than a nation with a large percentage of its output and exports in telecommunications equipment, a product with a high income elasticity of demand. It is exactly this kind of thinking that led the Japanese to target industries whose products were perceived to have high income elasticities as a foundation for rapid economic growth. Similar choices have been adopted and defended by a variety of developing countries around the world.

Economists tend to attack this kind of reasoning because it overlooks the role of relative prices in the demand for a nation's exports in world markets. A nation may be highly specialized in the production and export of goods with low growth potential on the income side. Nonetheless, if the relative prices of its products fall over time, demand for its goods can continue to grow rapidly. Actually, this argument has two parts. First, if the relative price of the goods produced by the nation fall in world markets over time, world demand might shift toward such products as a result of price-driven substitution in world consumption patterns. This first line of reasoning rests on the assumptions that the price elasticities of demand for traded products in world markets are relatively large and that the possibilities of price-related substitution in consumption are quite broad.

Given what we know about patterns of world demand, these are questionable assumptions. Second, even if the pattern of world demand does not change, a nation may win a growing share of a declining world market, if it becomes a more price competitive producer in that market, either through devaluation or other cost-cutting means. This line of reasoning implies that a nation may be forced to accept the welfare loss of declining terms of trade—falling prices of its exports relative to the prices of its imports—to stimulate world demand for its exports. This is hardly an attractive long-term growth strategy. Moreover, it is probably not workable. Even as the advanced countries compete among themselves in technology-intensive products and products requiring sophisticated manufacturing, they are pressured by producers from the newly industrializing countries, whose low costs rest on low wages. A strategy of defending or expanding market against traditional competitors by lowering costs simply may bump into a new set of competitors entering the global market. Indeed, from a long-term perspective, the view of the classical economists about the evolution of consumption patterns may be a more realistic starting point for planning a long-term development strategy. The claimed view is that consumption patterns are relatively stable over time, evolving gradually under the influence of relative prices, income growth, changes in income distribution, and social and institutional factors.

Let us accept the idea that sectors differ in their long-run growth potential, and for the reasons suggested here. It still remains to demonstrate that there may be possible conflicts between an allocation of resources that is Ricardian efficient in the short run and one that is growth efficient in the long run. One might be tempted to speculate that if private agents knew that different products had different income elasticities and that these different elasticities determined the demand potential of different products over time, they would make business decisions incorporating such knowledge. If so, an allocation of resources that was optimal by current market signals, in other words a Ricardian allocation, would also necessarily be optimal for long-run growth potential.

Why might current market signals fail to yield an allocation of resources that maximizes an economy's growth potential? One possibility, of course, is the existence of capital market imperfections or constraints. Firms or would be entrepreneurs may be able to raise funds for investment in industries that offer high rates of returns over relatively short periods of time but unable to raise funds for investment in industries that offer returns that are both uncertain given existing world market conditions and recoverable only over the long run. If national capital markets are "impatient" and risk averse, then it may be difficult to invest in risky, long-term projects despite their long-term growth potential.

Imperfect product markets, moreover, make it impossible to reconcile fully the future risks and returns on current investment in uncertain and emerging industries and technologies. Under conditions of nondecreasing returns there is simply no way that markets can relate the varying future growth efficiencies of various industries to relative profitability signals facing individual producers. Basically, this argument is a variant of the infant-industry argument. Because of increasing returns, current market signals can be misleading indicators of future profitability. Consequently, government policies to promote a domestic industry with high future growth potential can improve economic welfare over the long run. Without such policies, producers may well find it profitable to produce goods that a decreasing number of people on world markets may want to buy. The reader may think as extreme examples of the growth consequences of patterns of short-run specialization in such "inferior" products as jute, mechanical typewriters, or black and white television sets, as compared to the growth consequences of specialization in such income-dynamic products as synthetic fibers, word processors, and color televisions. As this analysis makes clear, limited price-induced substitution between products and patterns of demand that are largely determined by product-specific income elasticities may well imply a painful trade-off between short-term allocations of resources that are Ricardian efficient and those patterns of production that could yield comparatively higher rates of macroeconomic growth.

As a resource-poor country, Japan's growth potential was seen by Japanese planners to be constrained by its ability to sustain huge imports of resources over time. Japan needed to develop a production base that could generate huge exports of industrial products over time without requiring declines in Japan's terms of trade. Products that appeared to have high income elasticities of demand in world markets seemed to be the most promising avenue of development over the long run. Yet at any moment, given current world market conditions, Japanese producers might have found it more profitable to allocate resources to other products that were efficient in the Ricardian sense. If the markets for all products were perfectly competitive, a condition not realized because of the prevalence of increasing returns in many industries, especially those with high income elasticities of demand in world trade, then producers would have been able to move easily from one line of production to others as the growth potential of different products changed over time. As it was, a decision not to develop an industry with high growth potential at a given moment of time was not easily reversible. Failure to break into a high growth potential product at one point in time increased the costs of doing so at a later date.

Before leaving this discussion of growth efficiencies, it is important to note one additional way in which the composition of a nation's output can affect its potential for growth over time. As the new trade theorists have pointed out, imperfectly competitive industries can generate excess returns, and government policy can influence the distribution of these returns among countries. In static models, policies to win a larger national share of world returns in such industries have a once and for all effect on national income and welfare. But if higher returns earned today finance higher national investment rates and more R&D, there may be dynamic effects as well. Such effects may be especially important in high-technology industries. While investments in physical capital goods are often financed by borrowing, using the physical capital as collateral, expenditures on R&D are not for the most part collateralizable investments.[18] If firms confront difficulties in raising external capital to finance their R&D investment, then their R&D activities may be constrained by their current returns, and higher returns resulting from a targeted government policy may result in a higher R&D effort to improve their competitive position tomorrow. This insight helps to explain why Japanese semiconductor firms were able to mount a huge R&D and investment drive in the late 1970s while the efforts of their American competitors paled by comparison. As the Japanese firms captured a growing share of the world market from American producers and as the profit margins of Japanese firms were bolstered by the dramatic appreciation of the dollar, Japanese producers were able to finance massive R&D investments in both process and product innovations that allowed them to surpass the technological levels of their U.S. competitors. Meanwhile, U.S. firms with declining profits and even losses in some cases were unable to raise sufficient internal and external funds to mount a sustained R&D response to the growing Japanese challenge.

The idea that the excess returns resulting from a strong opposition in a high-technology industry may affect the technological dynamism of that industry over time goes back to Schumpeter.[19] According to Schumpeter, the dynamism of capitalism depends largely on competition based on new products and processes rather than on price competition. And competition in new products and processes both results in and depends on imperfect competition. Without the lure of excess returns, there will be no incentive to innovate, and with innovation and the market imperfections it creates, the excess profits required as an incentive to innovate will exist. Although Schumpeter made his arguments at the industry level, they can be applied to the national level as well. Nations that support the competitive success of their high-technology industries in world markets can strengthen the incentives to innovate by domestic producers. The result may be greater technological dynamism and more rapid economic growth over the long run.

DEVELOPMENT TRAJECTORIES AND TECHNOLOGICAL DYNAMICS: THE MEANING OF SCHUMPETERIAN EFFICIENCY

Economic development is fundamentally a product of technological change. To understand different national development trajectories, we need to understand the process of technological change. Yet traditional economic models provide little help in understanding this process.

Formal economic theory treats technology as unchanging. Or, more precisely, the ways technology changes are conceived as largely independent of the current allocation of resources. In this sense, technological change is largely exogenous to economic models and analysis. Traditional studies of economic growth, for example, usually find that a significant share of growth is attributable to technological development, but they treat the technology component of growth as exogenous or unexplained.[20] If technology is a central determinant of growth, however, how can we have of theory of growth without a theory of technological change?

A quite different view emerges from studies of the process and history of technical change. These studies indicate that technology is not a set of blueprints given by scientific advances that occur independently of the production process but often a joint output of the production process itself.[21] The pace and direction of technological innovation and diffusion are shaped by production and market position. Technological knowledge is not simply information that can be bought or sold, but often a subtler set of insights that develop only in conjunction with production. From this perspective, technological knowledge is not disembodied knowledge that can be purchased like a pattern for a sweater or a supercomputer, but rather it is rooted in the activities of design and production.

An obvious implication is that different mixes of production today mean different technological opportunities and different technological capabilities tomorrow. According to this view, within each technology and each sector the technological capabilities of firms and countries are generally associated with the actual process of production in the same or closely related activities. The pattern of technological change is not exogenous but is shaped by current patterns of resource allocation and production.

Moreover, at any moment technological opportunities vary across products and industries. As a consequence, a firm's or a nation's current specialization in production will affect its potential for future technological dynamism. Together, these insights suggest that the present allocation of resources can have a powerful effect on the direction and rate of technological advance over time.

In short, technological change is a path-dependent process in which the past affects the future scope of learning and innovation.[22] An implication is that there may be trade-offs between an allocation of resources that is Ricardian efficient and one that yields greater technological dynamism over the long run. To understand this line of argument better, it is necessary to examine the process of technological change in greater detail.

Technology involves a fundamental learning aspect, often characterized by tacit and idiosyncratic knowledge and by varying degrees of cumulativeness over time. To argue this point, it is necessary to distinguish between scientific and technological knowledge, although in practice this distinction may sometimes be difficult to draw.[23] Scientific knowledge establishes a set of basic theories, principles, and premises from which technology can be built. Scientific knowledge is close to the notion of blueprint information that often characterizes discussions of technology in the traditional economics literature. Scientific knowledge can quite often be precisely specified and easily communicated in a common language. Moreover, the institutions of scientific development are international and the flow of information across national borders is extensive.

Technological knowledge, in contrast to scientific knowledge, is often local in nature in the sense that what is learned depends on the past history of technological, manufacturing, and marketing successes and failures. Technological skills, competences, and organizational capabilities are all usually incrementally developed, drawing on previous strengths and experiences. As a consequence, technological knowledge is often more difficult to communicate across national borders than scientific knowledge. The transfer of a basic scientific insight from one national community of scholars to another may be quite straightforward, while the transfer of production technology may be quite difficult, as numerous case studies of technology transfer suggest.

Technological knowledge and indeed the intellectual paradigm required to translate new technical possibilities into innovative products and processes flow through communities as much or more than through markets. Consequently, national and sometimes even regional communities generate distinctive technological directions and trajectories.

From this perspective, an important part of technological knowledge does not flow easily across national borders. Such knowledge accumulates in firms in the form of skilled workers and proprietary technology and difficult to copy know-how. It accumulates in communities in such diverse forms as suppliers, repair services, and networks of know-how. It accumulates in nations in the skills and experiences of the work force and in the institutions that train workers and diffuse technology. As Jay Stowsky notes in Chapter 6, such "local" or nontraded knowledge is precisely the kind of knowledge that is often the most important during the initial development phase of a new product or process, knowledge that can escape the confines of a single plant or firm into regions or communities but that cannot be fully embodied in the product that is finally produced and sold. Because such knowledge is embedded in the experiences and skills of the firms and people involved in the innovation process, it does not flow easily or quickly across national borders.

Again, the processes of technological change and diffusion are rooted in existing production activities and in the linkages among sectors. Whether analyzed through the optic of spillovers and externalities, the optic of linkages, or other optics, the nature of linkages among sectors matter. Differences in the existing production base represent constraints and opportunities for technological development in the future.

If technological knowledge is a joint output of production so that the pace and direction of future technological change is affected by the current pattern of production, and if such knowledge is local in nature, then the current pattern of a nation's production and trade specialization can have a powerful effect on its future technological trajectory. And if, as seems evident, different activities or industries differ in their technological potential, nations with different current patterns of specialization will have different long-term growth and technological prospects.

This seems like a strong argument for national policies to target those industries and activities with the greatest technological potential, and clearly this was an argument used by the Japanese planners. But the validity of such an argument depends on a prior demonstration of why market signals may fail to yield optimal outcomes under such circumstances. Why, in short, may there be a trade-off between patterns of resource allocation that are Ricardian efficient in the short run and those that are Schumpeterian efficient in the long run? The answer to this question is found in the spillovers and imperfections inherent in the process of technological change.

Technological knowledge always involves some form of increasing returns for three reasons. First, there are usually significant setup costs or sunk costs involved in the creation of such knowledge, as a result of which there are static economies of scale in production utilizing this knowledge. Second, there are usually significant learning effects or dynamic economies of scale in the use of such knowledge. For both reasons, the value of such knowledge is likely to increase with the scale of production. Third, given the cumulative nature of technological knowledge, the probability of successfully innovating, with some search effort, is likely to depend also on the past innovative performance of individual firms and countries.

The scope for increasing returns to technological knowledge becomes even broader in light of the spillovers likely to exist between knowledge generated in one industry and the rest of the economy. Technological knowledge generated by a single activity can thus result in increasing returns in that activity and in other activities throughout the economy. As the history of technological change indicates, technological knowledge generated in one activity can have profound and unexpected spillover effects elsewhere. At its origin, the production of bicycles drew on technological knowledge from the production of shotguns. Innovations in food processing, even processes that do not involve any chemical inputs, draw on continuous chemical processes. Technological knowledge gained in the production of automobiles and airplane manufacturing promoted innovation in machine tools and vice versa. Beer companies in Japan are currently drawing on their fermentation expertise to enter the biotechnology business. Technological complementarities, sometimes called "untraded" interdependencies, and information flows that do not correspond to the flows of products represent a structured set of technological spillovers or externalities that form a collective asset of groups of firms or industries.

As Nathan Rosenberg, a noted economic historian of technological change remarks:

> The ways in which technological changes coming from one industry constitute sources of technological progress and productivity growth in other industries defy easy summary or categorization. . . . The transmission of technological change from one sector of the economy to another. . . . has important implications for our understanding of the process of productivity in an economy. Specifically, a small number of industries may be responsible for generating a vastly disproportionate amount of the total technological change in an economy.[24]

In the presence of increasing returns and spillover effects, the market cannot signal to private agents the unintended outcome of their collective behavior. To put it differently, markets cannot deliver information about or discount the possibility of future states of the world whose occurrences are themselves externalities resulting from the interaction of the present decisions of behaviorally unrelated agents. Under such circumstances, there may be trade-offs between Ricardian efficiency and Schumpeterian efficiency. And under such circumstances policies to target activities and industries with the greatest potential for generating technological knowledge of widespread applicability throughout the economy may improve economic welfare over time. In spirit, this argument is similar to the argument of the new trade theory that policies to promote industries with technological spillovers may be welfare-improving. But the perspective here is a more dynamic one. It builds on the notion that the whole trajectory of national technological change is influenced by current patterns of resource allocation. From this perspective, the potential gains from policy intervention are not once and for all but affect the entire future trajectory of growth and technological progress. Such intervention, even if temporary, can have permanent effects on the future course of economic development.

SCHUMPETERIAN EFFICIENCY, TECHNOLOGICAL DYNAMISM, AND POLICY

Even if the arguments suggested here are correct, they may be questioned as a rationale for government policy. Markets at least signal present efficiencies. Future dynamic gains, precisely because they cannot be signaled and are inherently uncertain, represent a sort of policy gamble. Neither the market nor policymakers, no matter how clever, can definitely determine whether a given industry or technological activity is a certain foundation for future growth or technological progress. Therefore, policies to target industries or activities in pursuit of growth or Schumpeterian efficiency are as likely to fail as market signals. Dynamics may matter to future economic welfare, but knowing that is not sufficient for the formulation of welfare-improving policy measures.

Our response to this line of argument is twofold. First, we believe that at any moment of time the future social benefits of certain technologies are clearly evident. Yet because these benefits are far in excess of the privately appropriable benefits available to individual economic agents, investment in such technologies is likely to be too small to be socially optimal. We call such technologies "strategic-transformative" technologies, because they promise to radically transform the products and production processes of a wide range of sectors that employ them and thus to have a profound effect on the competitiveness of national producers in a wide variety of world markets.[25] Today such technologies broadly include microelectronics technologies, new materials, superconductivity, and biotechnologies.

Second, investments in transformative technologies can be self-fulfilling prophecies. If the initial investments are not great enough to get private producers to start down the relevant learning curves, the potential benefits of dropping prices and the extended use of such technologies in a variety of economic activities. Or to put it differently, in the absence of policy, new technologies may not displace old ones at a socially optimal rate. The current productivity advantages of established technologies may win out over the future advantages of newer technologies, even though the former advantages may be much smaller than the latter. Determined policy efforts to pay front-end development costs or create initial markets may encourage firms to gain the knowledge to capture the benefits of the learning curve.

In recent years, Japanese targeting policies have concentrated on high-technology industries, including semiconductors, computers, and telecommunications. The Japanese view these industries, like steel and shipbuilding in the past, as providing the infrastructure on which the future competitive success of a variety of sectors depends. A policy of promoting R&D and growth in these new infrastructural activities is viewed as generating beneficial effects throughout the economy. These industries provide inputs for production throughout the economy and they enjoy both static and dynamic increasing returns. Policies to promote these industries can result in lower cost inputs for a variety of user industries whose expansion in turn can feed back into still lower costs for these inputs. This virtuous interdependence between the high-technology industries and downstream users gives rise to a true externality-creating process, in which private increasing returns in the high-technology industries result in social increasing returns in downstream user industries.[26]

Finally, it should be noted that the high-technology industries are strategic not only because of their linkage and knowledge externalities, but also because they are characterized by imperfect competition. Take the case of new materials and biotechnology. Assume, as appears to be the case, that both technologies in a mature phase will require lower cost inputs and less energy than comparable current technologies. An energy- and resource-poor nation such as Japan can reap substantial collective gains from a switch from the traditional to the new technologies. The national import bill and dependence on external sources of raw materials and energy would both be reduced. Consequently, commercial advantage in specific sectors aside, there are substantial social externalities or spillovers that make it rational to use policy to promote investment in these technologies. These investments may also permit Japanese firms to have a distinct advantage in commercializing these technologies, in gaining advantage in the design of products implementing their possibilities, and in reaping a large fraction of world profits from these and related activities.

TECHNOLOGICAL TRAJECTORIES, PLASTICITY, AND NATIONAL SETTINGS[27]

An important lesson about the nature of technological development, about the character of trajectories, lies in the process by which market positions freeze after periods of fluidity. The possibilities at the beginning of a technical transition are broad, but they narrow over time. Know-how accumulates around a technology. As the investment builds around the products that are succeeding in the market, alternative technical solutions become economically less attractive. Funds for experimentation in these areas dry up. Continued development therefore tends to follow lines already established.

The development of automobile engines is illustrative. One way of increasing fuel efficiency is to make cars lighter. One of the heavier components of the car is the engine. Engines could be made lighter by substituting aluminum for iron. But aluminum, though lighter, is not as durable, as strong, or as easy to manipulate in engine manufacturing processes. The technological question became whether to try to make aluminum stronger or to reduce the amount of iron in an engine to make it lighter. Iron won out in mass production cars not because of its inherent properties, but because automobile engineers had much greater knowledge about it and experience with it.[28]

The direction of technological development is not determined a priori by inherent technical characteristics or by any economic advantage that will accrue to all producers.[29] Instead, it is inherently uncertain. It depends in critical ways on chance, social conditions, corporate strategy and choice, and government policy. Take government as a case. Regulations influence the direction of private investment, and public investment shapes the economic infrastructure. Because both government policy and corporate strategy vary in different nations, the direction or technological development also differs from nation to nation. At any moment the state of science, engineering, and know-how defines what is perceived to be the national "technical possibility set." But they do not define which options in the set of possibilities are exploited.

Innovations emerge from complex interaction among three factors: market demands as expressed in prices, needs that might be satisfied but are not yet expressed by buyers and sellers in the marketplace, and new additions to the pool of scientific or technical knowledge. Technology is not plastic, shaped to our will. Not all things are technically possible, but technology in the long run has no internal autonomous logic that inevitably dictates its evolution or use. Technological development does not drive society as it evolves, rather technology itself is also shaped by social development. Moments of radical shifts in technology, periods of transition, are periods when political choice can exert some control over technology. Technological and social development are interactive, shaped by and shaping each other.

This line of reasoning leads us to several conclusions. If technological development is inherently uncertain, then the most conservative national or firm strategy for assuring the success of development is to spread one's bet.[30] The best analogy is to covering the table at the roulette wheel. Some might see this as a form of redundancy. We would argue that it is not. A spare tire is redundant, but it is essential if there is a flat tire. A second phone line provides a capacity if the first one is in use. Both are identical to the apparatus they replace. They are quite literally redundant, or extra, under ordinary conditions. Bets on a roulette wheel, however, are not identical; each is valuable precisely because it is different from the others. In terms of static efficiency, the extra or unused efforts would be duplications, wasted effort. In dynamic terms, the extra options are essential to guarantee success.

Technology managers have often recognized this. Indeed, the Polaris submarine development program built multiple bets into the program at critical technological junctures.[31] The biggest technical uncertainty was whether the missiles could be fired from below the surface, and different projects were undertaken to solve the firing problem.

The multiple bets that technological development requires are not placed evenly around the table. Instead, they cluster in two areas, according to two principles. First, research and development bets are historically rooted. They reflect the past development of the firm and the national economy and tend to follow the direction of past work. The resources available for tackling the next round of technical problems reflect what comes before. Technology has history. Second, the needs to which the technology is being applied differ in each national community, and so the technological tasks vary. The implications of these two principles around which technology bets cluster on the roulette table are significant.

If we accept these two principles, we are led to a range of conclusions. When a technology is in its infancy, and still fluid, the line of its technical evolution is inherently uncertain. This is not to say all things are possible, but rather that more than one direction of development is possible. An emphasis can be put on making steel stronger or lighter. The pace and direction of development are matters of decision. The direction a technology takes will depend partly on circumstance and individual choices. The directions of effort and evolution are set by the cluster of technology bets. The outcomes, the winners among competing possibilities, emerge when the sunk investment and differential learning become so great that radical alternatives are too pricy.[32] Broad market acceptance of a new technology, for whatever reason—be it public relations or real performance—excludes new possibilities. After positions freeze, a radically new technology will not be developed unless it is so attractive that producers and users are willing to walk away from their investments in earlier technologies and, often, new entrants emerge. If the gains from new technical approaches look marginal, they will be ignored; if gains look potentially important but slow to develop or very risky, they may never be captured.

Technological development is shaped by the community in which it occurs. A trajectory of technological development is an expected outcome of a particular national community.[33] During ordinary times, when national differences produce only small branches off the main trunk of technological evolution, the ability of society to shape technology is not nearly as visible as the powerful constraints that mature technologies have set for society. Alternate routes—the roads not taken—are hidden in the past. In periods of transition, however, the direction of technology itself—its branches, not its twigs—is affected by the clustering of bets. The direction in which investment develops will be heavily influenced by where the bets are placed. That placement will depend on the needs of the national community and the resources built up during its previous development. Thus, the "bet placer," be it a company or a nation, actively shapes technological development. As the new branches grow, they block others from emerging.

National context, by setting the cluster of bets, shapes technology. Computer technology for example, could grow along several different lines in the next years. The line that wins out will reflect the historical contours and current needs of its community of origin. By blocking other options, the winning route is imposed by sustained investment on other communities. Because the winning and then dominant technological route reflects, at least in part, the historical roots and national options of a specific community, it gives at least an initial advantage to the innovating country. The technology emerges from and plays to the national strength of the innovating country. The winning technology always imposes its own constraints, and once set, it can shape the patterns of trade. Technology becomes a binding parameter; it does not begin as one.

We start to have the basis of a notion of technological trajectory. Learning curves and cumulative problem-solving expertise, technological linkages, and nationally rooted technological developments all create the basis for firms in one nation to surge to advantage in world markets together.

MARKET TASKS, TECHNOLOGICAL CAPACITIES, AND THE EMERGENCE OF NEW PARADIGMS

Let us reconsider this notion of technological trajectory and national communities using a quite different kind of language. In this section we examine tasks, market and technological problems, and the capacities of firms and nations to solve them.

There is an established literature that treats the process of technological evolution at the firm level through the optic of "search" and discovery. Different industry structures influence the "search rules." Differences in firm organization influence these rules. The general conjecture is that given any level of technological competence and the techniques of production that a firm can master, its specific organizational structure and strategies affect both its level of efficiency and the rates and direction of its innovation, and thus the patterns of its competitiveness over time.[34]

There is also a literature on the influence of the institutional structure of the economy on the patterns of government policy.[35] In the same fashion that an industry structure establishes a set of constraints and opportunities for firms within a sector, the options in an economy as a whole are affected by both market and institutional structures. The result is that distinctive patterns of economic response and policy characterize different nations.[36] Countries tend to respond in defined manners, in a few similar ways, to a wide range of problems. The solutions vary less than the problems. When the solution fits the problem there is a policy success, but it is hard to build a solution if the problem requires an approach outside the bounds established by the structure of the political and economic system. Consequently nations, like firms, embody defined capacities. Their search for solutions is limited, like that of firms, by their structure and capacities.

Let us apply this logic to the problem of technology development and trade competition. Nations, Christopher Freeman argues, represent "systems of innovation." That is, they represent a set of institutions that create resources and direct them toward specific problems and solutions.

> When Britain opened up a major "technological gap" in the first industrial revolution, this was related not simply to an increase in invention and scientific activities . . . but to novel ways of organizing production, investment and marketing and novel ways of combining invention with entrepreneurship. When Germany and the United States overtook Britain in the late nineteenth and twentieth centuries, their success was also related to major institutional changes in the national system of innovation, as well as to big increases in the scale of professional research and inventive activities. In particular both countries developed new ways of organizing the professional education of engineers and scientists and of organizing research and development activities as specialized departments within firms, and employing graduate engineers and scientists.
>
> Similarly today, when Japan is opening up a new "technology gap," this is related not simply or even mainly to the scale of research and development, but to other social and institutional changes.[37]

A national technology system represents an institutional capacity for certain tasks and distinctive weaknesses for others. A technology system, though, is not just a set of resources available for innovation and development. It is also an approach to technology and how it is used. Periodically, a cluster of new technologies and a new approach to technology, a "technoeconomic paradigm," emerges.[38] Certainly, the vast bulk of innovations are incremental or marginal changes in an existing product or process in response to market opportunities and pressures. Sometimes there are more radical innovations that are "discontinuous events and in recent times . . . usually the result of a deliberate research and development activity in enterprises and/or in university and government laboratories.[39] Such radical innovations may serve to launch new products or so substantially improve the cost and quality of established products as new markets emerge.

More rarely, there are "far reaching changes in technology . . . [that affect] one or several sectors of the economy as well as giving rise to entirely new sectors." These are what we have labeled as transformative technologies. They are clusters of technologies, "based on a combination of radical and incremental innovations together with organizational innovations." For example, today such clusters of innovations include synthetic materials, petrochemical innovations, injection molding and extrusion machinery, and their application.

Freeman argues that some changes, some clusters of innovations, are so powerful "that they have a major influence on the behavior of the entire economy." At issue in these cases is not simply a set of innovations, but in fact an entire way of viewing the use and application of technology.[40] The expression *technoeconomic paradigm* implies a process of economic selection from the range of the technically feasible combinations of innovations, and indeed it takes a relatively long time for a new paradigm to diffuse through the system. Such a paradigm involves a new set of best practice rules and customs, new approaches to how to relate technology to market problems, new solutions to established problems. The notion of a major industrial transition, of a second industrial divide, of a shift from "Fordist to flexible" manufacturing that has become a fad in some debates points to just such a shift in technological paradigm.[41] A radical shift in perspective opens distinctly new possibilities for productivity and competitive advantage. The reality of such a shift is reflected in literature as diverse as left-wing social commentary and the *Harvard Business Review.*

New paradigms change and create national development trajectories. Such new "paradigms" do not emerge simply from a clustering of technological breakthroughs. Rather the technological breakthroughs may require a new definition and perception of a problem. Consequently, the emergence of a new technology, such as information and communications technology, does not in itself create a new paradigm. Microelectronics can be used to reinforce established mass production strategies or to implement new flexible strategies. There are certainly costs or constraints attached to the technologies themselves; they are not so flexible or plastic that they can be shaped by conception and demand to any shape and social use. The properties of specific technologies may make certain lines of development or use more difficult and others more attractive.

Nonetheless, we postulate that the emergence of a new paradigm must be understood as an interplay between the community and the technical frontier. It is not by accident that nations propelling themselves into industrial prominence do so riding new sectors and new paradigms. Germany in the late nineteenth century, America in the midtwentieth century, and now Japan in the late twentieth century are all examples.

CONCLUSIONS

In the Japanese variant of capitalism, markets have been emphasized as a source of growth rather than as a source of short-run efficiency, and a primary role of government has been to supply incentives to promote growth through markets. The perspective motivating Japanese policy has been explicitly dynamic and explicitly developmental. Japanese policymakers have chosen to target industries for promotion on the basis of their perceived potential for economic growth and technological change. In the words of this analysis, they have emphasized growth and Schumpeterian efficiencies over short-run or Ricardian efficiency in their choice of industrial targets. Their targeting strategy has had long-term beneficial effects on the competitive position of Japanese producers in a variety of critical industrial sectors in world markets. To understand these effects, it is necessary to abandon the static assumptions of international trade theory, even the so-called new trade theory, and to adopt a dynamic model in which national patterns of production and trade specialization at a moment in time can affect a nation's growth and technological trajectory.

Today Japan appears to be opening up a new technology gap over its major industrial competitors. It has developed a new technology system based on a cluster of new transformative technologies and a new approach to using them. The evidence suggests that the world is at the beginning of something akin to a third industrial revolution based on the productive capabilities of these new technologies and that Japan is at the forefront of developing and using them to competitive advantage in a variety of sectors. In contrast to the mass production strategies characteristic of the second industrial revolution, this new revolution is based on flexibility in production organization. As the chapters in this book indicate, several features of the Japanese institutional structure, including the nature of industrial organization and the linkages between small and large firms, the unique system of labor-management relations, and the cooperative nature of research and development activities promoted by government policies, make Japan especially well suited for the kind of flexibility required to use the new production technologies to full advantage.

The basic argument of this chapter is that Japan would not be at the forefront of this new technological trajectory without the interventionist targeting strategy that gradually but definitely guided Japan's industrial structure toward those sectors with the greatest growth and technological potential. Policy affected where and how much investment occurred, what kinds of skills and technological learning took place, and by its influence on the production profile of the economy, policy ultimately affected the pace and direction of technological innovation and diffusion.

If our argument is correct, then it suggests the need to reconsider traditional notions of the appropriate role of government and markets in economic development and to examine alternative institutional forms of capitalism. The American model of capitalism, which is the model that permeates traditional economic thought, is clearly not the only model of capitalism nor does it appear to be the most promising one from a developmental point of view. What Americans and others may learn from Japan is how to design a set of economic institutions, based on capitalist rules, that are more conducive to rapid growth, high productivity, and rapid technological change than the institutions characteristic of contemporary American capitalism. During periods of radical change in technoeconomic paradigm and the terms of international competition, such as the one the world is witnessing today, old skills and old institutions, successful under earlier conditions, may be ill suited to new tasks.

Our argument has a sobering implication for those who believe that the huge trade imbalance between the United States and Japan is simply a matter of adjusting macroeconomic imbalances in both countries and finding the "right" exchange rate. As history demonstrates, there is a persistent tendency for a strong technical leader country to run trade surpluses over long periods of time. Such surpluses reappear repeatedly despite currency adjustments and other measures designed to "restore trade equilibrium." At the same time there is a persistent tendency for "weaker" countries to encounter recurrent balance-of-trade constraints on growth, resulting in stop-and-go cycles of growth and slowdown, accompanied by a gradual decline in the value of their currencies and in their relative standards of living. If Japan has actually set out on a new development trajectory that has greater growth and technological potential than that of the United States, then neither currency realignments nor coordinated macroeconomic policies that return both economies to the conditions prevailing at the beginning of the 1980s will eliminate the huge trade imbalance between them.

NOTES

1. For this perspective on Japanese policy, see T. J. Pempel, "Japanese Foreign Economic Policy: The Domestic Bases for International Behavior," in Peter Katzenstein, ed., *Between Power and Plenty: Foreign Economic Policies of Advanced Industrial States* (Madison: University of Wisconsin Press, 1978).

2. For a detailed discussion of the policy patterns summarized here, see Chapter 5. See also Chalmers Johnson, *MITI and the Japanese Economic Miracle* (Stanford, Calif.: Stanford University Press, 1982) and Kozo Yamamura, *Policy and Trade Issues of the Japanese Economy* (Seattle: University of Washington Press, 1982).

3. For a discussion of standard IMF policy prescriptions, see John Williamson, *The Lending Policies of the International Monetary Fund* (Washington, D.C.: Institute for International Economics, August 1982); for a discussion of standard World Bank policy prescriptions, see The World Bank, *World Development Reports* for 1983, 1984, and 1985 (published for the World Bank by Oxford University Press).

4. By policies to improve national economic welfare, we mean efforts to improve the overall position of the entire community rather than policies to shift income from one part of the community to another. Rent-seeking policies, by contrast, are intended to permit one group to capture economic gains at the expense of others.

5. For a discussion of the "new trade theory," see Elhanen Helpman and Paul Krugman, *Market Structure and Foreign Trade* (Cambridge, Mass.: MIT Press, 1985); Paul Krugman, ed., *Strategic Trade Policy and the New International Economics* (Cambridge, Mass.: MIT Press, 1986); and Paul Krugman, "Is Free Trade Passé?," *Economic Perspectives* 1, no. 2 (Fall 1987): 131–44.

6. For a complete description of the standard models of comparative advantage see, for example, John Williamson, *The Open Economy and the World Economy* (New York: Basic Books, 1983).

7. There have been many contributions to the new trade theory. In addition to the references cited in note 4, see also, James Brander and Barbara Spencer, "Export Subsidies and International Market Share Rivalry," *Journal of International Economics* 18, no. 1 (1985): 83–100, and Anthony Venables and M. Alastair Smith, "Trade and Industrial Policy under Imperfect Competition," *Economic Policy* 3, no. 1 (October 1986): 621–72.

8. See, for example, James Brander and Barbara Spencer, "International R&D Rivalry and Industrial Strategy," *Review of Economic Studies* 50 (1983): 707–22.

9. This threefold distinction was suggested by Paul Krugman in "Strategic Sectors and International Competition," in Robert M. Stern, ed., *U.S. Trade Policies in a Changing World Economy* (Cambridge, Mass.: MIT Press, 1987).

10. There is a fascinating and compelling application of this argument in a study of the computer industry in Kenneth Flamm, *Targeting the Computer: Government Support and International Competition* (Washington, D.C.: Brookings Institution, 1987).

11. An analysis of firm-specific assets that may yield quasi-rents to particular producers is in David Teece, "Profiting from Technological Innovation: Implications for Interaction, Collaborating Licensing and Public Policy," *Research Policy* 16, no. 6 (December 1986): 285–305.

12. For an overview of these debates, see James Brander, "Shaping Comparative Advantage: Trade Policy, Industrial Policy and Economic Performance," in Richard G. Lipsey and Wendy Dobson, eds., *Shaping Comparative Advantage* (Toronto: Prentice-Hall, 1987).

13. For evidence on the empirical difficulties involved, see the various empirical applications of the new trade theory presented in Robert Feenstra, ed., *Empirical Research in International Trade* (Cambridge, Mass.: MIT Press, 1988).

14. Krugman, "Is Free Trade Passé?."

15. Director General S. Fukukawa of the International Trade Administration Bureau of MITI is quoted in Christopher Freeman, *Technology Policy and Economic Performance: Lessons From Japan* (London: Pinter, 1987).

16. This illustration is adapted from W. Brian Arthur, "Self-Reinforcing Mechanisms in Economics," Working Paper 11, Stanford University, Center for Economic Policy Research, Stanford, Calif., September 1987. See also W. Brian Arthur, "Competing Technologies and Lock-in by Historical Events: The Dynamics of Allocation Under Increasing Returns," Stanford University, Center for Economic Policy Research, Stanford, Calif., 1985 and Paul A. David, "Narrow Window, Blind Giants and Angry

Orphans: The Dynamics of Systems Rivalries and Dilemmas of Technology Policy," Working Paper 10, Stanford University, Center for Economic Policy Research, Stanford, Calif., 1986 (Paper presented at the Conference on Innovation Diffusion, Venice, Italy, March 1986).

17. Freeman, *Technology Policy and Economic Performance*, p. 35.

18. Joseph E. Stiglitz, "Technological Change, Sunk Costs, and Competition," unpublished paper prepared for a conference at the Brookings Institution, Washington, D.C., December 1987.

19. Joseph Schumpeter, *Capitalism, Socialism and Democracy* (New York: Harper, 1942).

20. As an illustration, see Edward Dennison, *Why Growth Rates Differ: Postwar Experience in Nine Western Countries* (Washington, D.C.: Brookings Institution, 1967).

21. See, for example, Giovanni Dosi, Christopher Freeman, Richard R. Nelson, Gerald Silverberg, and Luc Soete, eds., *Technical Change and Economic Theory* (London: Frances Pinter, and London and New York: Columbia University Press, forthcoming), and Giovanni Dosi, *Technical Change and Industrial Transformation* (London: MacMillan, and New York: St. Martin's Press, 1974).

22. See Arthur, "Competing Technologies." See also the chapters by W. Brian Arthur; Giovanni Dosi and L. Orsenigo; and Gerald Silverberg in Dosi et al., eds., *Technical Change and Economic Theory.*

23. On such a distinction, see also Partha DasGupta and Paul A. David, "Information Disclosure and the Economics of Science and Technology," Stanford University, Center for Economic Policy Research, Stanford, Calif., April 1985.

24. Nathan Rosenberg, *Inside the Black Box: Technology and Economics* (New York: Cambridge University Press, 1982), pp. 74–76.

25. This term and notion has been used widely in our work. See, for example, Stephen S. Cohen and John Zysman, *Manufacturing Matters: The Myth of the Post-Industrial Economy* (New York: Basic Books, 1987), and Laura D'Andrea Tyson, "Competitiveness: An Analysis of the Problem and a Perspective on Future Policy," in Martin K. Starr, ed., *Global Competitiveness: Setting the U.S. Back on Track* (New York: W.W. Norton, 1988).

26. This type of virtuous interdependence is discussed in greater detail in Krugman, "Strategic Sectors and International Competition."

27. Excerpted from Cohen and Zysman, *Manufacturing Matters*, pp. 94–97.

28. William J. Abernathy, *The Productivity Dilemma: Roadblock to Innovation in the Automobile Industry* (Baltimore: Johns Hopkins University Press, 1978).

29. Charles F. Sabel, *Work and Politics: The Division of Labor in Industry* (New York: Cambridge University Press, 1982), p. 32. Sabel's work implies but does not directly develop this position.

30. Richard Nelson points out that "It is important to recognize the essential uncertainties which surround the question—where should R&D resources be allocated—in an industry where technology is advancing rapidly. There generally are a wide number of ways in which the existing technology can be improved, and at least several different paths toward achieving any of these improvements. Ex ante it is uncertain which of the objectives is most worthwhile pursuing, and which of the approaches will prove most successful. Before the fact, aviation experts disagreed on the relative promise of the turboprop and turbojet; those that believed in the long-run promise of commercial aircraft designed around turbojet engines were of different minds about where to go forward with a commercial vehicle. Whether and when computers should be transistorized was a topic on which computer designers disagreed; later the extent and timing of adoption of integrated circuit technology in computers was a subject which divided the industry. . . . The uncertainty that characterizes technological advance in high technology industries warns against premature unhedged commitments to particular expensive projects, at least when it is possible to keep options open. The divergences of opinion suggest that a degree of pluralism of competition among those who place their bets on different ideas, is an important, if wasteful, aspect of technological advance." See Nelson, *High-Technology Policies: A Five-Nation Comparison* (Washington, D.C.: American Enterprise Institute for Public Policy Research, 1984).

31. Harvey Sapolsky, *The Polaris System Development: Bureaucratic and Programmatic Success in Government* (Cambridge, Mass.: Harvard University Press, 1972).

32. See Nelson, *High-Technology Policies*, and Sapolsky, *The Polaris System Development.*

33. Charles Sabel suggests in his imaginative book, *Work and Politics*, that technological development is a product of choice. He argues that case when talking about this transition: "by the end of the 1980s it is likely that comparable stories, different in substance but with equally uncertain ends, will be told for each of the advanced industrial countries. The reindustrialization debate in the United States, the wave of new-liberalism in Great Britain and nationalization in France, and the discussion of democratization and social ownership of large firms in Sweden are surely just the first signs of an epochal redefinition of markets, technologies, and industrial hierarchies. The outcomes will depend on the daring and imagination of trade unions, industrialists, and politicians, and on the ideas of different social classes about how they want to work and live. But as soon as a new system, however shaky, is in place, the scientific thinkers on the Right will tell you everything everywhere, down to the last detail, was determined by the pursuit of efficiency. Scientific thinkers on the Left will say that each group's inevitable pursuit of its interest, determined by its place in the division of labor, is the real explanation. Both will agree that

ideas of dignity and honor, the political programs they inform, and the conflicts to which they give rise were only foam on the wave of history. If you have been persuaded by the book you have just read, you will not believe them." (p. 2.)

34.   For a broad discussion of how a firm's organizational structure and strategies affect its innovativeness and competitiveness, see Richard Nelson and Sidney Winter, *An Evolutionary Theory of Economic Change* (Cambridge, Mass.: Belknap, 1982); See also David Teece, "Technological Change and the Nature of the Firm," in Dosi et al., *Technical Change and Economic Theory.*

35.   See, for example, John Zysman, *Governments, Markets and Growth* (Ithaca, N.Y.: Cornell University Press, 1982), and Katzenstein, ed., *Between Power and Plenty.*

36.   Zysman, ibid., and *Innovation Policy in France: A Report for the OECD* (Paris: Organization for Economic Cooperation and Development, 1986).

37.   Freeman, *Technology Policy and Economic Performance*, p. 31.

38.   Ibid., p. 63.

39.   Ibid. See also Christopher Freeman, John Clark, and Luc Soete, *Unemployment and Technical Innovation: A Study of Long Waves in Economic Development* (London: Frances Pinter, 1982).

40.   Freeman, *Technology Policy and Economic Performance*, p. 64. See also Giovanni Dosi, "Technological Paradigms and Technological Trajectories," *Research Policy* 11 (1982): 147–62; Richard Nelson and Sidney Winter, "The Search for a Useful Theory of Innovation," *Research Policy* 6 (1977): 36–66; and Carlota Perez, "Microelectronics, Long Waves and World Structural Change: New Perspectives for Developing Countries," *World Development* 13, no. 3 (March 1985).

41.   Note that when even the film industry begins to be discussed in these new terms, more than a set of technological changes is occurring. Certainly an academic fad is in motion. However, that intellectual fad also seems to be at work in industry as well.

2 DIVERGING TRAJECTORIES
Manufacturing Innovation and American Industrial Competitiveness[1]

Stephen S. Cohen
John Zysman

The growing debate on American competitiveness and productivity has focused attention on manufacturing and manufacturing innovation.[2] The scale and composition of the trade deficits of the past few years are the most prominent indicator that the competitive position of the American economy is weakening.[3] The debate is about why the deficits have developed and what they mean. The position here is that much of the problem lies in an erosion of American manufacturing skills and capacities. Put differently, the trajectory of technological development that carried the United States to industrial dominance has been challenged by a distinct model, a distinct paradigm that has put some of our most important competitors—particularly Japan—on a distinct technological trajectory. If our position is correct, traditional economic remedies cannot in themselves reverse the decline in America's position in the international economy.

The huge trade deficits of the 1980s were driven by sharp increases in the value of the dollar that priced American goods out of world markets and made imports a bargain. The inflow of funds to finance the budget deficits pushed the exchange rate up. Consequently, some economists argue, the problem is fundamentally one of mistaken domestic macroeconomic policy. The process that created the trade deficits is reversible; reduce the budget deficit, thereby reducing demand for foreign borrowings to finance it and thereby reduce the trade deficit. This established view that is built from static

39

equilibrium perspective of traditional trade theory is not so much wrong as it is limited and limiting.

Fifteen years ago the traditional remedy suggested by traditional theory worked; devaluation rapidly reversed trade flows. This time, however, it has not, at least not as expected. Since 1985 the dollar has lost about half its value against the yen, but the trade deficit has stubbornly refused to follow suit. Only at the end of 1987 was a monthly decline first registered: the deficit fell to $13 billion, itself a record just a few months earlier. Certainly there is some price for the dollar at which imports would wane and exports surge—if people had confidence that the exchange rate advantage would last. But balancing its external trade account is not a nation's only economic objective. All nations, even the poorest, eventually do. The trick is to do it with high and rising incomes: that is the definition of national competitiveness.[4] A permanently falling dollar translates into a continually more impoverished America. Clearly something new is affecting America's position in the international economy. What is it?

Certainly, we have new competitors. The most important are Japan and Asia's newly industrializing countries. Japan's trade pattern is different from those of other advanced economies, for which intrasectoral trade has been the key to open trade. Japan uniquely has tended not to import in those sectors in which it is a major exporter.[5] Moreover, the currencies of the Asian newly industrializing countries with whom we run major trade deficits have not risen against the dollar to the extent the yen and European currencies have.

Most important, the United States once had dominant positions in product and production. We made products others could not make or could not begin to make competitively. Consequently, high wages and a high dollar did not displace us from markets. That situation has changed; indeed we are no longer on the dominant technological trajectory. In more technical terms, the price elasticities of American imports and exports have changed.[6]

In the past two years the soaring yen has confronted Japan with a currency shock similar to the one the United States faced in 1981. A comparable percentage rise in the dollar flattened U.S. industrial investment and created massive trade deficits. But despite a doubling of the yen against the dollar, and a set of special emergency measures aimed at increasing imports, the Japanese increased investment in production and have sustained a trade surplus.

Why are the U.S. and Japanese responses to massive currency movements so different? The contrasting behavior of the two economies in analogous situations suggests different efforts and capabilities to respond to economic challenges through innovation in manufacturing.[7] In the language of the argument in the first chapter of this book, it suggests distinct technological or developmental trajectories.

Determined Japanese firms attempt to increase productivity and flexibility and introduce new products as a means of defending market position. Certainly many Japanese firms have absorbed yen increases, often out of exceptional profit margins that resulted from a combination of U.S. quotas on imports and Japanese production advantages. And some costs are reduced as a strengthening yen lowers import costs of raw materials and components. Several years ago major firms announced that they would remain competitive from a Japanese production base even if the yen rose to 120 to the dollar, whereas in some segments of electronics the principal Japanese firms could remain competitive with the yen at 90 to the dollar.[8]

We must not lose perspective. Not all Japanese producers are that good, and not all production activities lend themselves to such dramatic improvements. Japanese firms are also moving production offshore, although their capacities for production innovation remain great. There are some differences from the American experience even here. There is little belief in Japan that moving offshore to produce in a cheaper labor environment is a viable long-term solution. Moreover there is a greater tendency for Japanese producers to retain control of the production rather than simply subcontract from local producers.

Yet another view of the trade deficit is that the problem is not one of American firms, which know perfectly well how to produce and compete, but of America as a production location.[9] The inference, quite at variance with the argument advanced here, is drawn from data on the export performance of American multinational corporations. Between 1966 and 1977 American multinational corporations increased their share of world exports, maintaining it through 1983 while the American national share dropped. There are major problems with the inferences drawn from the data. First, much of the data represents automotives and aeronautics. Despite the high exports automotives generate from various countries, however, the competitive positions of Ford and General Motors have weakened since 1966. Nor are sales of military aircraft the best indicators of economic efficiency. Boeing, the dominant company in commercial aircraft, operates less as an American multinational than as an American domestic producer that exports substantially. This correction aside, America's competitive position in commercial aircraft is weaker now than it was in 1966. Airbus has become a major competitor; Japan is building an aircraft industry, in part as a subcontractor to Boeing, while established European companies and upstart Brazilians produce short-range and specialty craft.

But most important, in these and other sectors, what does it mean that American multinationals export so much from diverse locations? Those export numbers could be as much a sign of weakness as of strength. They could indicate decisions to manufacture components, subsystems, and even final products in various cheap-labor locations abroad and export them back to the mother company in the United States. (Perhaps the company has failed to innovate in manufacturing and no longer has the skills to produce competitively in high-wage locations.) The U.S. consumer electronics industry exhibited that kind of busy export performance as it was being sliced down by Japanese competitors who operated from a base that included rapidly rising wages, rapidly rising productivity, and a trajectory of innovation in production that proved decisive.

In sum, inferences drawn from the export performance of American multinational corporations do not undermine our proposal that there is an important link between America's falling competitiveness and our difficulties in manufacturing innovation.

ORGANIZATIONS AND USE OF PEOPLE

At the core, American difficulties in sustaining manufacturing innovation lie not in machines and technology but in organizations and the use of people in production, in the strategies for automation and the goals of production innovation. The problem is not with our robots or our local area networks, but with understanding how to exploit their productive promise. In the first part of the century, American firms built the model of advanced production. They established an approach to production and innovation that gave us the capacity to respond to the tasks of the first part of this century. What went wrong? How did we fall from our position of leadership?

Here we must simplify a very complicated story.[10] In the late nineteenth and early twentieth century, the United States developed an industrial structure that projected this country into global economic preeminence. That structure rested on two fundamental innovations: mass production and the hierarchical, multidivisional corporation. Mass production began in the early nineteenth century with production of interchangeable parts for guns; with Henry Ford's production of automobiles it became the model of how to produce in an advanced economy. It meant volume production of standardized products for a relatively homogeneous market. Volume allowed the specialization of tasks, both for machines and people. Moderately skilled workers, moreover, could produce sophisticated products.

The organization of people and machines turned on an underlying concept of how to produce. The concept was variously labeled Taylorism, for the management of people, or Fordism, for its market and production strategy. There was very much a paradigm of production, a defined conception of how to exploit technology in the marketplace. The hierarchical but multidivision corporation, likewise, emerged in the United States to permit administrative control of complex activities on a continental scale.[11] A theory of management, likewise, emerged to explain this approach and make it operational.

During World War II and in the years that followed, the American system of management and production conquered the world. At home, the system defined the lines along which technological advance would proceed, and technological advance steadily improved the system's performance. Despite new technologies and new industries developing during the past forty years, the basics remained entrenched until challenged by foreign competitors using different approaches.

Why, then, did the system freeze? First, many sectors such as automobiles and steel became stable oligopolies with only marginally increasing demand and high barriers to entry. These structures tended to divert competition from production costs or basic technological development to marginal product, process, and style changes. Also, complex social structures have resilience and inertia. The production structure developed elaborate systems of labor relations and comparably complex systems of management training, recruitment, organization, and reward. Massive forces had structured themselves around the basic design of that production system. Changing it would mean changing them. Finally, there was the inescapable fact that the system worked. It won the war; it won the peace. It was successful beyond any precedent or any contemporary comparison, and it could be steadily improved.[12] The mass production paradigm was not going to change without outside pressure. Suddenly we were vulnerable to innovation from abroad.

INNOVATION FROM ABROAD

The innovations that emerged from abroad took two forms. One involved nationally distinct government policies for managing advanced industrial economies, policies that favored investment over consumption and allowed government's direct participation in the protection and promotion of industrial development. The second, the central part of our story in this chapter, came in manufacturing and more broadly in the organization of production. During the postwar period, the gap between America and its allies closed. Yet while attempting to imitate American practice, firms and governments abroad established distinct manufacturing systems that suited their economic circumstances and social settings. Later, as world markets changed, and as technology gaps among advanced nations narrowed, the newly established models of production proved to have significant advantages.

Emblematic of these production innovations are code words such as "just-in-time production" and "quality circles," which at once suggest and obscure concrete changes in the way goods are designed and produced. The innovations in the best firms extend beyond the shop floor to the nature of the product, beginning with a design concern for manufacturability and extending to a corporate strategy in which anticipated economies of scope can justify investments in new technologies that are difficult to justify through more traditional criteria but that figure in the firm's strategic positioning against its competitors. Put differently, American production strategies stayed fixed while our competitors implemented statistical process control and reorganized factories to take full advantage of NC machine tools.

NEW PARADIGMS OF PRODUCTION

At present only limited systematic evidence exists to demonstrate that production organization differs sharply between countries, that a distinctly new paradigm of production has emerged. For now we find only clues drawn from narrower research projects. First we look at two images of production, one from Japan and the other from Italy. We use the word "image" intentionally, because the images are more suggestive than the models, which are robust and complete. From Japan emerges the picture of the high-volume, automated factory operating through the night with no lights and no workers. The Japanese are not simply copying American production with less expensive capital or even pushing the American model of mass production to its logical conclusion. Something quite different is happening: flexible automation was created. For example, as part of a general reorganization of production, Japanese producers have reduced inventories and improved materials flows as well as altering quality control processes and substantially reducing labor content.

The important outcome is that the relation between production and corporate strategy is altered. Manufacturing becomes a competitive weapon. The evidence is overwhelming that low cost has not been the only or the most important advantage of Japanese production innovations. The Japanese did not invent the color television, the videotape recorder, or the semiconductor. But they developed designs and manufacturing systems that created decisive competitive advantage. It was not Japanese advances in the design of microchips, but in the yields of the production systems, that have made them the largest microchip producers and exporters in the 1980s. Equally important have been their innovations in the organization of production, which permit them to introduce new products rapidly and constantly to improve and adapt the workings of that system. Honda defended its market position in motorcycles in Japan by abruptly introducing an entire new product line. The product cycle from design to production for Honda automobiles is faster than any foreign rival's.[13] American producers, in contrast, typically do not make production innovations incrementally. They tend to jump from one production plateau to another; change is slower and riskier.[14] Japan's flexibility has developed from continuous production innovation, often with internal design of equipment and a skilled work force able to understand and implement the continuous changes. Advanced production technologies are not an alternative to skilled workers. It is the capacity to manage the continuous evolution of the production system, and not merely the ability to operate an automated factory, that is the competitive meaning of postindustrial manufacturing.

Japan is not the only source of production innovation. In Italy networks of small firms have developed a different approach to innovative production organization, that of flexible specialization. Using modified traditional technologies, communities of small firms have established themselves as world-class producers in sectors such as textiles, apparel, and machine tools. These horizontal networks involve shifting combinations of cooperation and competition, with today's collaborators being tomorrow's competitors. Flexible specialization, as Charles Sabel and Michael Piore call it, becomes possible. Similar networks of world-class machine tool firms are found in Germany as well, suggesting that the model is not purely Italian.

The horizontal model of Italy and the vertical or Japanese model differ greatly from one another. Yet they share some common features. One of these is to limit inventories. The need for inventories is radically reduced, not just because some inventories are pushed back to suppliers, but because all producers in the chain learn to modify production to limit their own inventory needs. A second common element is a network of small suppliers tied to common tasks by market relations and direct, hands-on contact rather than by administration and bureaucracy. Those fluid networks give flexibility to small and large companies alike. Some of the networks are vertical, with tiers of suppliers linked to large firms such as Fiat and Benetton in Italy or Toyota in Japan. Others are horizontal networks. These steps toward vertical disintegration of production were not created deliberately. Rather, in Japan and Italy hordes of small producers survived, in part through political protection, into the late twentieth century. As a result, small firms account for more manufacturing in Japan and Italy than in other advanced countries. The networked system was created as producers, large and small, sought ways of competing in national and global markets in the twentieth century. The pattern differed from that established under American conditions. The networks proved more flexible and resolved problems that traditional administrative integration could not.

Rapid expansion in Japan, and in a less steady way in Italy, permitted capital investment and the introduction of new machines, and in the effort to catch up to more established technologies forced interative production innovation. Introducing new machines opens the possibility of production reorganization but does not ensure it.[15] Nor do new production systems ensure increased productivity. Indeed, new production systems rarely function perfectly when introduced and initially may lower productivity. Yet rapid growth generated not only investment in new machines, but also new approaches to manufacturing, new organizations to implement them, and new strategies to gain advantage from them.[16] The innovations that initially were ways of competing in a world in which America's allies were laggards became unexpectedly the basis of advantage.

FLEXIBILITY IN MANUFACTURING

Basic approaches to manufacturing are changing. An effort is being made to create the concepts and language to examine and discuss these changes, and flexibility is the key word.[17] Traditional mass production is inherently rigid. It rests on volume production of standard products or components with specialized machines dedicated to specific tasks. Now the notion is to apply a set of more general-purpose tools to produce a greater range of products. Importantly, the bulk of manufacturing has involved batch production that was difficult to automate. Now new approaches and programmable equipment open batch production to increased automation and reduce some of the cost difference between batch and series production.

Flexibility, a firm's ability to vary what it produces, rests on organization. The same machines can be used in rigid or flexible automation. Technology itself is channeled and formed by the conceptions of those who would use it. However, flexibility is an imprecise objective as much as a description, and has come to mean not one, but a variety, of ways to adjust company operations to shifting market conditions. Static flexibility suggests that a firm has the ability to adjust operations at any moment to changes in the mix of products the market is demanding. If one product is not selling, production can be oriented quickly to another. It implies adjustment within the confines of established products and a fixed production structure. This notion is captured in the distinction between economies of scale and economies of scope. Economies of scale is the notion that the cost of producing a single unit declines as volume increases. Economies of scope are gained not in the volume production of a single good, but in the volume production of a set of goods.[18] Scope and scale often move together: large-scale plants may be required to realize flexibility. The advantages of scale do not disappear. Very expensive production lines make possible the volume production of a variety of products. In some industries, such as semiconductors, the cost of a basic production line has risen steadily even while application and user-specific products have become possible. Economies of scope are created by standardizing processes to manufacture a variety of products.

Dynamic flexibility, in contrast to static flexibility, means the ability to increase productivity through improvements in production processes and product innovation. The capability to change quickly in response to product or production technology—to put ideas into action quickly—is the central notion. In a period when automation technologies permit new production strategies, dynamic flexibility is crucial.[19] There is a fundamental and new approach to the ties between manufacturing and strategy, to the lines of technological development. As Jaikumar points out, making flexibility and responsiveness the mission of manufacturing "flies in the face of Taylor's view of the world which for 75 years has shaped thinking about manufacturing."[20]

THE INFRASTRUCTURE OF
U.S. PRODUCTION

Is American industry capturing the possibilities of new technologies, or is it caught in an increasingly obsolete production paradigm? The evidence, which by its nature is fragmentary, comes in two forms. The first is a large set of industry and firm case studies of international competition and production organization. These cases are more than anecdotes, for taken together they represent a substantial share of the economy and tell a consistent story, a story of slow and partial adjustment. In steel American firms import from Japan production know-how that was based on an earlier Austrian innovation. In automobiles American firms struggle to match the cost and quality performance that has enabled Japanese firms to capture a large, permanent share of the American market. In both sectors the recent drop in the dollar's value has closed the gap in final costs but has not placed American firms on a competitive trajectory of technology development.

The semiconductor industry recently was shocked to discover that its seeming technological advantage was vulnerable to production developments in Japan. The production tools that embody know-how and innovation—machine tools in metal bending industries, automatic looms and jet spinners in textiles, photolithographic and ion implantation equipment in semiconductors—increasingly are imported. One offshore producer of apparel argues that, on paper, the economies permit him to bring production back to the United States, but the required skills and infrastructure no longer exist. They can be found in cheap-labor locations. It is not simply that a set of firms or sectors are in difficulty, but that the infrastructure of production know-how has weakened. A change in relative prices achieved through changes in exchange rates will not quickly reverse this erosion.

In the late 1960s and early 1970s, American firms faced with foreign competition often concluded that their rivals used low-cost labor to achieve competitive advantage. Few firms realized that innovations in production, usually achieved with limited technological advance and considerable organizational imagination, were occurring. The flight of American firms offshore to low-cost production sites represented, finally, a means to defend existing production structures. It sheltered firms from the need to rethink their own production strategies.

If our argument is correct that American industry is not effectively implementing the potentials of production innovation, what additional forms of evidence should we expect to find? First, the ways America uses advanced technologies would differ from ways our best competitors use them. American firms would not capture the full potential of new technologies: rather than creating flexible systems, they would implement new technologies in traditional ways. Second, advanced technologies for innovative production would not diffuse as widely in the United States. Standard data sets for measuring economic activity do not address the question of production organization. Large-scale comparative studies that would directly test our notion do not exist. Yet there are narrower, more limited studies that support the argument. Let us consider two such studies.

USE OF NEW TECHNOLOGIES

The first question is how new technologies are used. Jaikumar's study compares the use of flexible manufacturing systems (FMS) for the production of comparable products in Japan and the United States. The average number of machines in the Japanese FMS was six, and in the American system seven.[21] However, "the number of parts made by an FMS in the United States was 10; in Japan, the average was 93, almost ten times greater. . . . The annual volume per part in the United States was 1,727; in Japan only 258."[22] The Americans used the tools as instruments of an old-style approach to manufacturing. They also failed to exploit them for introducing new products. The rate of new product introduction was twenty-two times as great in Japan as in the United States. Jaikumar concluded that, with few exceptions, the flexible manufacturing systems installed in the United States show an astonishing lack of flexibility in use, in many cases performing worse than the conventional technology they replaced. "The technology itself is not to blame. It is the management that makes the difference."[23]

The risk is that the social inertia of existing arrangements locks American producers into reinforcing rather than replacing existing production systems. A few examples give a sense of the situation. General Motors invested $50 billion in production during several years only to discover that its margins were the lowest in the industry, its break-even volume point was the highest, and that no clear production strategy had emerged.[24] The purposes of automation and the organization suited to capture the advantages of new technologies have not been worked out in many American firms; thus new technologies are not introduced or have limited impact when they are.

The second dimension is the diffusion of advanced technology. Arcangeli, Dosi, and Moggi examined the introduction of advanced automation technology into factories in advanced countries.[25] Their techniques and data sought to separate advanced from traditional manufacturing investment. Two conclusions are suggested. First, the United States leads the way in office automation, but trails in factory automation. Second, America invests more in traditional automation and less in flexible manufacturing than do other advanced industrial nations. The pace at which advanced technologies are introduced is slow—that is, only a small percentage of firms use such things as flexible manufacturing systems. Yet those American firms that use them tend to be leaders in their sectors. This data is consistent with studies of specific technologies, such as robots. Numerically controlled machine tools and the advanced languages to implement them emerged early in the United States, as did the technology and use of robots. However, as is widely known, they are used much more extensively in Japan than in the United States; diffusion is several times broader, with some 40 percent of the machines in smaller firms.[26]

The evidence is powerful. Aggregate trends reinforce factory and sector studies. The argument that there is a problem in the evolution of American manufacturing is now strong enough to require refutation rather than demonstration.

Despite the disturbing past, there is no reason that these trends must continue. The picture is complex and changing. Many American firms have begun to innovate in production organization. Allen Bradley, Black and Decker, Cypress Semiconductor, Texas Instruments, and IBM all provide examples. It is not yet possible to judge whether there is new life in American industry or whether the successes are "valiant but isolated." The future is being created, and the outcomes are inherently not knowable.[27] The more systematic data, however, suggest that the difficulties outbalance the advances. Jaikumar summarized the problem well: "The battle is on and the United States is losing badly. It may even lose the war if it doesn't soon figure out how better to use the new technology of automation for competitive advantage. This does not mean investing in more equipment; in today's environment, it is how the equipment is used that is important."[28] A "manufacturing gap," the counterpart of the technology gap of earlier years, has emerged, and this time it is the United States that lags behind.

CONCLUSION

We have tried to show that weakness in production innovation is central to America's competitiveness and trade problem. For a firm, production capability is a decisive competitive tool. It is not just a question of marginal cost advantages; a firm cannot control what it cannot produce competitively. There is little chance of compensating for production weakness by seeking enduring technological advantage.[29] A production disadvantage can quickly erode a firm's technological advantage. Only by capturing the "rent" on an innovation through volume sales of a product can a company amortize its R&D costs and invest in R&D for the next-generation product. The feeble American presence in next-generation consumer electronics indicates the cost of failure to produce competitively in the previous generation. Finally, if a firm simply tries to sell a laboratory product to someone else to produce, the value of the design is lower than that of a prototype, and prototypes are valued lower than products having established markets, as each step toward the market decreases uncertainty. A producer with a strong market position often can buy a portfolio of technologies at a low price and capture the technology rents through volume sales. For the firm, manufacturing matters.

Mastery and control of manufacturing is equally critical to the nation. This fact, so central to policymaking, has been obscured by a popular myth that sees economic development as a process of sectoral succession. Economies develop as they shift out of sunset industries into sunrise sectors. Agriculture is followed by industry, which in turn is sloughed off to less developed places as the economy moves on to services and high technology. Simply put, this is incorrect. It is incorrect as history and it is incorrect as policy prescription. America did not shift out of agriculture or move it offshore. We automated it; we shifted labor out and substituted massive amounts of capital, technology, and education to increase output. Critically, many of the high-value-added service jobs we are told will substitute for industrial activity are not substitutes, they are complements. Lose industry and you will lose, not develop, those service activities. These service activities are tightly linked to production just as the crop duster (in employment statistics a service worker) is tightly linked to agriculture. If the farm moves offshore, the crop duster does too, as does the large-animal veterinarian. Similar sets of tight linkages, but at vastly greater scale, tie "service" jobs to mastery and control of production. Many high-value-added service activities are functional extensions of an ever more elaborate division of labor in production. The shift we are experiencing is not from an industrial economy to a postindustrial economy, but rather to a new kind of industrial economy. The challenge for the United States will be to respond to the pressures of a paradigm of production and technology that it did not create and whose development it can only struggle to follow.

If, then, a distinct new paradigm of production has emerged from Japan, if a separate and significant technology trajectory is in place, how did it happen? That is our concern in the next chapter.

NOTES

1. This chapter by Stephen Cohen and John Zysman first appeared as "Manufacturing Innovation and American Industrial Competitiveness," *Science* 239 (March 4, 1988): 1110-5. Copyright © 1988 by the American Association for the Advancement of Science. Reprinted with permission.

2. See, for example, Stephen Cohen and John Zysman, *Manufacturing Matters: The Myth of the Post-Industrial Economy* (New York: Basic Books, 1987); Stephen Cohen, David Teece, Laura Tyson, and John Zysman, "Competitiveness," vol. 3, President's Commission on Industrial Competitiveness, Working Paper 8, Berkeley Roundtable on the International Economy, University of California, Berkeley, November 1984, Paul Krugman and G. Hatsopoulos, "The Problem of U.S. Competitiveness in Manufacturing," *New England Economic Review* (January/February 1987); B. R. Scott and G. Lodge, eds., *U.S. Competitiveness in the World Economy* (Boston: Harvard Business School Press, 1985).

3. Elizabeth Kremp and Jacques Mistral, "Commerce Exterieur Americain: d'ou vient, ou va le deficit?" *Economie Prospective Internationale* 22 (Paris: Centre d'Etudes Prospectives et d'Informations Internationales, 1985).

4. Stephen Cohen and John Zysman, *Manufacturing Matters: The Myth of the Post-Industrial Economy* (New York: Basic Books, 1987).

5. Cohen and Zysman, *Manufacturing Matters*, tables 8.1-8.3.

6. Kemp and Mistral, "Commerce Exterieur Americain."

7. See, for example, Giovanni Dosi, "Institutions and Markets in a Dynamic World," *The Manchester School* (in press); K. Pavitt, "Sectoral Patterns of Technical Change: Towards a Taxonomy and a Theory," *Research Policy* 13 (December 1984): 343; Nathan Rosenberg, *Inside the Black Box* (New York: Cambridge University Press, 1982).

8. "Honda Prepares to Survive Yen Rise up to 120 to U.S. Dollar," *Japan Economic Journal* 24, no. 1 (December 27, 1986).

9. I. B. Kravis and R. E. Lipsey, "Productivity and Trade Shares," National Bureau of Economic Research, Washington, D.C., March 1984; R. E. Lipsey and I. B. Kravis, *Banco Nazionale Lavoro Quarterly Review* 153 (June 1985): 127. For an extended critique, see Cohen and Zysman, *Manufacturing Matters*.

10. Cohen and Zysman, *Manufacturing Matters*.

11. See Alfred D. Chandler, *Strategy and Structure: Chapters in the History of the Industrial Enterprise* (Cambridge, Mass.: MIT Press, 1962), *The Visible Hand: The Managerial Revolution in American Business* (Cambridge, Mass.: Belknap Press, 1977); *Managerial Hierarchies: Comparative Perspectives on*

the Rise of the Modern Industrial Enterprise (Cambridge, Mass.: Harvard University Press, 1980).

12. Chandler, Strategy and Structure.

13. James C. Abbeglen and George Stalk, Jr., Kaisha: The Japanese Corporation (New York: Basic Books, 1985), p. 80.

14. S. Wheelright and R.M. Hayes, Restoring Our Competitive Edge: Competing Through Manufactures (New York: Wiley, 1984).

15. This is emphasized by Wheelright and Hayes, ibid. Often the introduction of new technology leads to a drop in productivity levels. Only when the reorganization is effective are the potentials of new equipment captured. Our view is that when equipment is crafted in-house to fit the needs of organization developed on the shop floor, the disruption is limited or nonexistent.

16. Yasusuke Murakami and Kozo Yamamura, in Policy and Trade Issues: American and Japanese Perspectives, Kozo Yamamura, ed. (Seattle: University of Washington, 1982), pp. 115–16.

17. Michael Piore and Charles F. Sabel, The Second Industrial Divide: Possibilities for Prosperity (New York: Basic Books, 1984) is a major contribution focusing American attention on flexible specialization. See also, Benjamin Coriat, Automatisation Programmable et Produits Differencies GERTTD Conference (Paris: GERTTD, 1986); "Information, Technologies, Productivity, and New Job Content" (Paper presented at a BRIE conference, Production Reorganization in a Changing World, Berkeley, California, September 10–12, 1987); Benjamin Coriat and Robert Boyer, "Technical Flexibility and Macro-Stabilization" (Paper presented at The Venice Conference on Innovation Diffusion, Venice, April 2–4, 1986); A. Sayer, "New Developments in Manufacturing and Their Spatial Implications," Working Paper 49, University of Sussex, Urban and Regional Studies, October 1985.

18. Joel D. Goldhar and Mariann Jelinek, "Plan For Economies of Scope," Harvard Business Review 61 (November/December 1983): 141.

19. Burton Klein, "Dynamic Competition and Productivity Advances," in R. Landau and N. Rosenberg, eds., Positive Sum Strategy: Harnessing Technology for Economic Growth Washington D.C.: National Academy Press, 1986).

20. R. Jaikumar, "Postindustrial Manufacturing," Harvard Business Review 64 (1986): 69.

21. Ibid., p. 69.

22. Ibid., p. 10.

23. Ibid., p. 69.

24. See, for example, "Fiddling with Figures while Sales Drop," Forbes, August 24, 1987, pp. 32–34; D.Quinn, "Dynamic Markets and Mutating

Firms," Working Paper 26, Berkeley Roundtable on the International Economy, University of California, Berkeley, August 1987.

25. F. Arcangeli, G. Dosi, and M. Moggi, "Patterns of Diffusion of Electronics Technologies" (Paper prepared for the Conference on Programmable Automation and New Work Models, Paris, April 2–4, 1987).

26. Klein, "Dynamic Competition and Productivity Advances."

27. See, for example, "The Manufacturing Zeal of Tracy O'Rourke," *Electronic Business*, September 15, 1986.

28. Jaikumar, "Postindustrial Manufacturing," p. 70.

29. Cohen and Zysman, *Manufacturing Matters.*

POLITICS AND PRODUCTIVITY

3 DEVELOPMENTAL STRATEGY AND PRODUCTION INNOVATION IN JAPAN

Laura D'Andrea Tyson
John Zysman

In the late 1970s America discovered Japan. We discovered that the Japanese made more than textiles and cheap televisions. As robots captured the attention of the press, we had to recognize that American preeminence in industrial manufacturing was being challenged by fundamental production innovations that permitted the Japanese to gain advantage in a range of sectors from consumer electronics to machine tools and automobiles. Suddenly we began to try to understand the Japanese miracle and find policies to respond. A stream of books sought the source of Japanese success variously in management styles, worker attitudes, government subsidy, and business-state relationships. A small industry grew up to explain the success of the Japanese economy. There have been several alternative categories of explanation: cultural arguments that concentrate on features of Japanese management style and the attitudes of Japanese workers; institutional arguments that focus on production cartels, lax or relaxed rules for antitrust, and Japan's Ministry of International Trade and Industry (MITI); economic arguments that consider such things as high savings rates and the convoluted workings of the distribution system; and political arguments that point to the concerted political will required to mobilize the state policy supporting and promoting growth. No one of these elements in and of itself was critical to the success of Japanese policy. Rather, it is the mix of policies and market structure and the purposes to which the elements of policy are put that we must understand.

Too often cartoonlike images dominate debates about the roots of Japanese economic success. Many of these images are incompatible. Each emphasizes to the point of exaggeration one aspect or element of Japanese experience. Policy analysts and academics alike have often selected and emphasized material to force the Japanese case to fit their preferences for the United States. A few years ago, the cartoon image of Japan Inc. claimed that the government dictated and shaped the course of development with a limited role for the private sector. Another cartoon image highlights the role of market forces and of private management, seeking to underplay or discount the role of government. Similarly, in attempting to suggest the extent of recent change in Japan, some analysts seem to claim that the Japanese market has never really been closed to outsiders or that closure has not been critical. Others contend that closure has been decisive in international competition. One image highlights giant corporations, another small, flexible manufacturing. The result of selecting facts to fit preexisting explanations has been a series of caricatures. Certainly some of the arguments are simply contradictory; that is, we have to choose between them. For the most part, however, the task is not to select between competing explanations but to understand how elements of the Japanese system fit together.

The stream of caricatures flows on perhaps because it has been most difficult for America to recognize that there are different national economic strategies, each representing a different way of organizing a capitalist marketplace. It has been difficult to acknowledge that there is more than one form of capitalism, more than one way of structuring business state relations in a democratic society with a marketplace economy.

POLICY, MARKETS, AND PRODUCTIVITY: THE THREE TIERS

The view presented here is that the Japanese government has pursued a conscious strategy of industrial development that has influenced the nation's patterns of domestic growth and international trade. The argument demonstrates how the government influenced and shaped the dynamics of a highly competitive market system. Further, this argument details the way in which controlled competition, and the business pacts on which it rests, shaped the outcomes of policies. Competitive markets induced the investment that underlay rapid growth and manufacturing innovation. The character of the interplay between policy, markets, and corporate strategy created and continue to sustain the logic of the pattern of Japanese development and foreign trade. A new paradigm of technology and development was established.

Government, markets, and interest groups cannot be disentangled in the story or unbundled in the analysis. Economists assume that a market consisting of a few large firms will behave differently than a market composed of many small ones. Indeed, an entire subfield of industrial organization exists to examine the link between different market structures and industrial behavior. Yet there is little analysis of the way the institutional structure of the economy shapes industrial behavior, and the absence of such analysis limits our understanding of how modern economies work.[1]

Markets do not exist apart from the rules and the institutional settings in which they operate. There are rules that structure how buying and selling take place. The institutions of finance and the organization of labor alter the way firms can operate in capital and labor markets. The relations between governments and business and among businesses are organized differently in each nation, and consequently the dynamics of markets are different. Political scientists now debate how to characterize these relationships, using notions such as the strong or weak state, "policy compacts," state-led growth, and corporatism.[2] However, they rarely try to establish that these institutional relationships, however characterized, shape market behavior. Economists, by contrast, generally ignore or caricature the role of institutions and proceed with their analysis as if institutions did not exist and as if history did not matter. In this chapter we try to avoid some of the pitfalls of standard political science and standard economics by integrating an analysis of policy and institutional relations with an analysis of market behavior.

The argument is built in tiers. The argument in the first tier is not controversial or new. The Japanese government, dominated in the years after World War II by a conservative coalition, used the institutions of a centralized state to create a developmental policy. Crucial elements of market arrangements that facilitated rapid adjustment and growth were the product of conscious choice in the postwar years and were not embedded in Japanese cultural traditions. The system constructed by a policy elite with its stronghold in the state bureaucracy was meant to rebuild Japan's economic position. Policy choices profoundly affected the dynamics of domestic markets in Japan.

The second tier of our argument contends that the policy of domestic promotion and external protection in an industry structure composed at once of large firms and large integrated groups and layers of small firms generated an intense investment-driven competition for market share. As a result of competing for market share while borrowing technology from abroad, Japanese firms developed a pattern of continuous production innovation. A new paradigm of technology development and market strategy was created.

The third tier proposes that the system of domestic development, with its market dynamics created and reinforced by policy, produced particular features of Japan's pattern of international trade. The hypothesis is that the pattern of policy generated specific trade outcomes, that it gave a distinct character to Japanese trade in manufactures, because it made access to Japan's market uniquely difficult.

This three-tier analysis permits us to consider the nature of the present opening of the Japanese economy. Since the midseventies the Japanese government has sought to liberalize the economy and to dismantle the structure of protection. Indeed, it has removed quotas and lowered tariffs, and these measures have left Japan with low levels of overt trade restriction. Yet claims of market closure and domestic promotion persist.

The question is not whether the economy is opening or becoming more entangled in international markets. It is. The critical questions are how much of the developmental structure remains in place and how much needs to stay in place for Japan to sustain its international market position, or more precisely to sustain its trajectory of advance. Real openness has been established where it least matters, in sectors where Japanese producers already have a dominant domestic position. In sectors where Japanese policymakers and industrialisms may wish to establish or reestablish advantage, real protection remains.

Any discussion of Japan's postwar success must be put in the perspective of longer term industrial growth that began in the nineteenth century.[3] Industrialization was initially built on textiles, as has been the case in so many places. Beginning in the 1930s there was a long upward swing that rested on borrowed technology and cheap labor, which rooted Japan firmly in heavier industries. In a sense that phase of Japan's development was simply interrupted by World War II.[4] The prewar and postwar period, moreover, shared a focus on self-reliant domestic development. In the 1930s that took the form of an imperium and Japanese partial withdrawal from the world economic system. The postwar neomercantilism that is emphasized here preserved the combination of insulated domestic markets and borrowed foreign technology. What has been most distinctive though is the new paradigm of production that has been created.

THE FIRST TIER: THE BASIS OF A DEVELOPMENTAL STRATEGY

Japanese government policy for development created an intense but controlled competition in a protected market. The logic of that competition provoked manufacturing innovation that established internationally competitive firms in a variety of industries. A conservative coalition used the institutions of a centralized state to create a developmental policy whose primary objective was the restoration of national wealth and economic power.

Our purpose in this first tier of argument is to establish the parameters of the policy and to show that the policy was the product of a clear political choice. The next section demonstrates that market dynamics in Japan are not the product of some universal set of economic rules, but rather the result of the structure of national institutional arrangements that reflect political choices. To show that market dynamics can only be understood within a specified institutional and political context, this discussion focuses on the promotional and protective policies of the state. We could reach the same conclusion in the Japanese case by focusing on the labor market or on the history and development of specific industrial sectors. For example, much has been made of the fluidity and flexibility of management and labor arrangements within Japanese companies. It is less often recognized that such arrangements were responses to real political and economic conditions, not predictable consequences of some inherent cultural bent. The Japanese pattern of giant companies offering lifetime employment, albeit to one segment of the work force, has unquestionably allowed closer working ties between management and shop floor employees and great adaptability on the shop floor. Lifetime employment, however, was not some element of the traditional world carried over to the present, but rather a corporate and political response to the emergence of a radical trade union movement in the 1950s.[5] More powerfully, the Japanese labor market is segmented; that is, workers are divided institutionally into largely separated parts of the labor market. That institutionalized segmentation provides some workers long-term employment guarantees and leaves others to absorb both the shocks of economic cycles and longer term economic evolutions. This combination of rigidities and flexibilities not only produces unique dynamics on the shop floor, but makes it difficult to mobilize a broad-based labor movement as a political challenge to the direction of development.

The Emergence of the Policy:
The Case of Chemicals and Steel[6]

The postwar pattern of developmental policy was first evident in the 1950s when Japan's government decided to give priority to the heavy and chemical industries as a means to lead the nation's development. In a basic sense the policy was not new. Modern Japanese politics began with the Meiji restoration, which had as its core purpose the preservation through economic development of the Japanese community against the intrusion of the West. The centralized and insulated character of the state bureaucracy that was a creation and descendant of that restoration gave great influence in formulating and shaping policy, not just implementing it, to a caste of senior civil servants.[7] State administration did not replace politics. Rather, bureaucrats became an important part of the policy alliance, and the state bureaucracy provided a political stronghold for a developmental coalition.[8]

In a moment we will characterize the overall pattern of policy, but let us examine it here in the initial case of heavy and chemical industries. These industries were protected against imports and foreign direct investment. Imports were controlled by tariffs and the Foreign Currency Allocation System. The fund allocation system required importers to ask MITI to allocate foreign currency to import goods and permitted MITI to decide who imported what. Development or promotional measures gave tax privileges in the form of special and accelerated depreciation of investment and priority financing through government-owned banks and major city banks dominated by policy. In the late forties and early fifties, the Japanese government sought to create an infrastructure for sustained development by investing in energy, including electrical generators as well as mining equipment, supporting road and port construction, developing transportation through investment in shipbuilding and trains, and establishing communications networks. In the midfifties the government moved beyond basic infrastructural activities to support a broader range of heavy investment sectors.

The decision to support the heavy and chemical industries grew into a choice to pursue a strategy of creating advantage and then into a conscious challenge to traditional economic theory. In the late 1940s the debate was between a strategy of "developmentalism" or autonomous state-directed development and one of "tradeism" or integration into world markets.[9] The debate in journals and in the government was settled with the creation in May 1949 of the Ministry of International Trade and Industry to "establish Japan's participation in the international economic system and in order to let export industries drastically develop."[10] The advocates of both positions were members of the Economic Reconstruction Committee, leading one observer to remark that "MITI selected Tradeism [to solve problems through expansion of world trade] in the Developmentalist way [through government planning]."[11]

In late 1955 a five-year plan for economic independence called for strengthening Japan's industrial structure through developing secondary industries, particularly heavy and chemical industries. As the Japanese took back control of their economy from the occupying forces, basic industries such as steel, coal, energy, and transportation required for economic redevelopment were favored. At the same time in the late forties and early fifties, a strategy of developing heavy industry as a means of expanding exports had been emerging. Such a strategy, though, contradicted economic traditional theory, which argued that successful exports required industries in which Japan had a comparative advantage. At the time that meant light industries where little capital was needed and cheap labor could provide advantage in international markets. Yoshida Shigeru, the Prime Minister, and Ichimada Naoto, president of the Bank of Japan, believed in this traditional theory. As long as Yoshida controlled the cabinet, the heavy and chemical industrialization strategy was not possible.[12]

The decision to pursue development and trade through heavy industry required planners to confront traditional theory. The decision was not made because of new theory, but rather new theory emerged as part of the debate surrounding an evolving policy. The concrete decision was whether to invest in heavy industry or in sectors of light industry where traditional theory suggested that Japan had an advantage. Shinohara Miyohei argued that a static economic theory cannot assess the different development possibilities of light and heavy industries. For instance, as national income increases, the demand for the products of heavy industries will grow more rapidly than those of light industries. Miyohei contended that while dependence on light industries might have been more advantageous and profitable for Japan at the time, it was likely that heavy industry would make a bigger contribution in the future.[13] MITI used this perspective to develop and justify its industrial policies. A cabinet report laying out this theory became official policy and represented MITI's challenge to traditional economic theory while formalizing its own strategy for Japan's development.[14]

MITI's case was made as follows:

> There are some cases when the internal market mechanism does not work completely. International division of labor based on comparative advantages does not necessarily give us an advantageous industrial development in terms of long-term income elasticity of demand.
>
> Industrial Structure Policy, while it removes those market failures, has significance in the sense that it develops industries in which increase of productivity can be expected.
>
> In order to heighten the industrial structure, we plan to develop those industries in which we can expect growth. Particularly, autos, large machine tools, industrial machines, large computers, specialty steel, petrochemical industries etc. are still on the way to development. They do not have enough international competitiveness. But because they have high income elasticity of demand and have a big possibility of productivity increase, we can expect them to perform a leading role in heightening the industrial structure. We have to rely on them to get foreign currencies in the process of achieving an advanced country's type of industrial structure.[15]

One observer put it this way:

> In short according to the Japanese government's economic plan, the country first tried to reconstruct basic industries such as steel, coal, electricity, and transportation from the late 1940s to the early 1950s. From 1950 to 1955, the government plan shows it was gradually favoring the idea of heavy and

chemical industries for the development of the industrial structure. In 1955, the government clearly moved toward heavy and chemical industrialization, but at that time, they lacked a supporting economic theory.[16]

The theory was proposed and published in 1965 when Japan had already begun to realize the development of its heavy and chemical industries, and indeed had begun to develop in other directions.

Practice, it seems, preceded theory. We can only speculate on, but not detail, the political fight that preceded the victory on which the new theory rested. In a sense modern Japan has always chosen the image of the economy it wished to have and then pursued it. The Meiji restoration was a revolution undertaken to permit Japan to develop an advanced society and economy. It would appear that Japanese officials in the postwar period sought to recreate the course of development underway before and during the war.

The Developmental Years: An Interpretive Sketch of the Interplay of Government and Market

There is a debate not so much about what the Japanese government attempted to do, but about whether the stated policy was implemented and whether the policy worked. What does it mean to say that the policy "worked"? Considering whether the government could directly and systematically impose its will on particular companies or on the market misstates the question. Firms in Japan must consider government purposes in their strategies and must still inform and often negotiate with government about the direction of corporate strategy. It is the character of the interaction between government and firm, and state and market, not the domination of one by the other, that is the issue. Market outcomes cannot be understood without evaluating the influence of policy on the dynamics of competition.

During the period of orchestrated development from the mid-1950s to the late 1960s, the Japanese government's primary commitment was to economic growth and the transformation of the economic base from agriculture and light industry to heavy industry. To pursue this goal, the government sought to establish the infrastructure necessary for private firms to expand, develop, and compete. Infrastructure was very broadly defined; it included entire industrial sectors, such as steel and shipping, that reduced the cost of imported materials and were critical to the entire economy. The government assured critical sectors the financial resources they needed to expand competitively, both by providing budgeted funds and by manipulating the financial system to do this. Similarly, it encouraged the importation and domestic development of basic technologies. In this sense, in the parlance of the trade debate, Japan targeted certain industries. But that metaphor misleads, and it understates the complex web of arrangements that underlay the competitive drive for success within Japan.

The Japanese government exerted influence on the industrial economy during the boom years; that is, it set the market rules and determined the logic of the incentives firms faced in two principal ways.[17] First, the government was a gatekeeper, controlling external access to the domestic economy; perhaps more accurately, it patrolled the channels that tied the national to the international market. The discretion to decide what to let into Japan permitted the government to break up the packages of technology, capital, and control represented by foreign multinational corporations. MITI was the primary functionary in these gatekeeper activities. As Chalmers Johnson explains:

> Before the capital liberalization of the late 1960s and 1970s, no technology entered the country without MITI's approval; no joint venture was ever agreed to without MITI's scrutiny and frequent alteration of terms; no patent rights were ever bought without MITI's pressuring the seller to lower the royalties or to make other changes advantageous to Japanese industry as a whole; and no program for the importation of foreign technology was ever approved until MITI and its various advisory committees had agreed that the time was right and that industry involved was scheduled for "nurturing."[18]

There is little doubt that policy had the effect of reducing the cost of adopting foreign technology. The government, using the Foreign Capital and Foreign Exchange Control Law, could restrain interfirm competition for the acquisition of foreign technology by narrowing the number of firms eligible for foreign capital. It is reported that in the case of the steel industry, the first industry promoted, the royalty for the oxygen-furnace process technology for steel (which was originally purchased from Austria) was 1 cent per ton of steel, while the same technology was bought at the price of 35 cents per ton in the United States, where severe interfirm competition occurred.[19]

The closed market gave Japanese firms a protected base of demand that facilitated the rapid expansion of production and innovation in manufacturing. This served to negate the product or production advantages foreign firms would have used to enter the Japanese market in a range of products including automobiles. The Japanese automobile market was quite closed to foreign firms. Indeed, a reciprocal agreement limited Fiat, a firm quite capable of producing small cars that were in demand in Japan, to selling 3,000 cars a year. By the mid-1970s, such restrictions on imports did not matter. By that time, Japanese firms had achieved a competitive position. But the restrictions played a role in creating advantage during the earlier period.

Second, agencies of the Japanese government, notably MITI, sought to influence the development of the domestic economy. Seen from the perspective of the firm, government policy helped provide cash for investment, tax breaks to sustain liquidity, support for research and development, and aid to promote exports. We shall examine these policies in a number of cases as we proceed. This web of public policies changed the options of companies. Without inexpensive debt finance, the funds to expand production rapidly would not have been available. With a protected market the availability of inexpensive capital and imported technology was bound to attract entrants to favored sectors. Protection and promotion in Japan served to produce real domestic competition. Policy changed the structure and pattern of choices made by market actors.

MITI was not so much a director of this competition as a marketplace player, with its own purposes and its own means of intervening in the market to achieve them. The balance of initiative between business and government varied across sectors. In some cases policy reflected objectives conceived by government and pursued with industry, in other cases it appears policy directions emerged from industry and were supported by government. While the details of policy varied across industries, the combination of protection from imports and foreign investment and promotion through investment and research and development was essential.

The theory underlying industrial structure policy was to place underdeveloped domestic industries with little competitive power under the government's active interference and to build up large scale production system, while limiting entry into the domestic market of foreign enterprises with already established mass production systems and restricting the competition of foreign manufacturers in the domestic market."[20]

The constant purpose of policy was to shape comparative advantage, to use sectoral policy to restructure the entire economy. Policies favored sectors considered to be critical to Japan's long-run development. In the years after the war this meant favoring capital-intensive industries rather than the labor-intensive industries that might seem appropriate to an economy with a scarcity of raw materials and capital. Priority industries were those industries that (1) were likely to expand with increases in national income, (2) offered the possibilities of economies of scale from concentrated investment, (3) would tow the rest of the economy along in their wake, and (4) could become export industries.[21]

A Pattern of Controlled Competition

The Japanese government's industrial strategy assumed that the market pressures of domestic competition would serve as an instrument of policy. It is not simply that the government made use of competitive forces, but rather that it often induced the very competition it sought to direct. There was (in the phrase used by Professor Murakami of Tokyo University) intense but controlled competition.[22] Richard Samuels calls it the politics of oligopoly. What was unusual was that the politics intensified rather than muted competition. Domestic competition substituted for the pressures of the international market to promote development and efficiency. Promotional policy attracted market entrants, and the stampede for entry and the resulting battle for market share were then termed by MITI as excessive competition that had to be controlled.[23] Under these circumstances, the government and private sector worked together to avoid "disruptive" or "excessive" competition. There were a variety of mechanisms to control competition; they included expansion plans agreed to jointly by government and industry, routine exemptions from antitrust laws, debt financing of rapid expansion that made the bankruptcy of major firms a threat to the entire economy and hence unthinkable, and somewhat later the oft-cited recession cartels. Equally important, joint research and development programs initially funded in part by MITI for the development of generic technologies assured wider diffusion of a technology base than might have occurred from purely private programs, whether government-subsidized or not. Similarly, technical standard setting served to channel competition into applications and manufacturing. Although corporate arrangements to manage the market sometimes broke down, this should not be taken as evidence that they did not operate or do not matter. In semiconductors today, as in steel a generation ago, such arrangements have been central to the international success of Japanese producers.

Finally, it is important to note that the complex of policies that encouraged rapid entry and a scramble for market share rather than short-term profits, also encouraged surges of exports as aggressive firms competing for domestic market share reached the international market together. These surges, in fact, began to lead to criticisms of Japanese economic policy by Japan's major trading partners.[24]

The Basis of the Developmental System: Politics and Market Structure

The developmental system and the interaction of market and state in Japan rest on a special set of institutional arrangements and bargains in politics and business. Of importance are the political priority accorded development, the political capacity to pursue that priority, and the market arrangements that make controlled competition or cooperation amid competition possible. The brief remarks that follow cannot fully characterize national policy and the business system. The intent is only to suggest how a developmental policy could be built and to identify the mechanisms that permitted it to be implemented and to produce an outcome of controlled competition. Our approach is systematic and builds on two key notions: governing coalitions[25] and the institutional structure of the economy.[26]

Structural arguments are commonplace in politics and the subfields of economics known as industrial organization and comparative systems. Here we are concerned with how institutional arrangements and market structures, the institutional structure of a nation's political economy, act as constraints on politics and policy. The structural approach holds that a structure creates an enduring set of penalties and rewards that mold actions independent of the motivations or purposes of the actors.[27]

According to the structural approach, there will be regularity in the form of policy, in how policy is formulated and implemented, whatever its objectives, because of institutional constraints. Institutional structure defines the range of policy instruments realistically available and the processes by which they are used.[28]

Thus, for example, in the case of France the Left and Right put the instruments of the centralized state to quite different ends, but there are common elements in their approaches to policy simply because they faced the same institutional constraints and options. A government is apt to find some problems more intractable than others. In France, again, very similar policies succeeded in some French industries, but not in others. Although the policies looked very much alike, the outcomes were different because effective solutions required to the problem at hand depended on the institutional characteristics of the industry in question. Structural arguments suggest that particular institutional structures that create or circumscribe capacities for state action will establish patterns of distinctive national competence and weakness. If the tasks that face a nation require capacities that exceed or are different from the capacities that the structure creates, then new capacities are required. When new tasks require new capacities, then pressure to alter or develop the structure can be powerful.

The second contention of a structural position is that institutional structure—both of politics and the market—shapes political processes. On the one hand, structure creates channels through which influence can be developed and exercised and in so doing makes some coalitions easier and some policies simpler. On the other, new strategies or new problems may require changes in the institutional structure. Institutional reforms involve much more than redesigning organizations to achieve greater effectiveness. Since the arrangements between and within organizations establish position of privilege, reform means dislodging incumbents from their strongholds. When these incumbents represent specific groups in the society, institutional reforms entail political change in the social balance of power. If new tasks create a need for new state or social capacities, there can be real challenges to existing social and political structures. Surviving the challenge may require substantial reform; failure to achieve reform may bring decline or collapse.

Structure will not simply set down regularities in policy but will create predictable kinds of political battles. The how of policy and politics will affect who will be allies and enemies as well as the tactics used in their fights. The institutional structure of the economy does not create politics, but by delimiting some of the possible issues and alliances, it can establish channels through which political fights are fought. Simply stated, what is attempted and achieved is affected by how it must be done.

At the same time, politicians and political groups reflect the economic and social composition of the economy. Those who govern devise the policies and purposes of government and their choices reflect their origins. The governing coalition is a notion of the social composition of the ruling groups and how they are organized. Consequently, we can imagine that the economic objectives espoused by the ruling groups reflect the economic interests of their supporters and the political processes by which they take power. From this perspective, to make sense of the objectives and policies pursued in Japan we must consider both its institutional structure and its governing coalition.[29]

The policy base in Japan has two crucial components: a conservative coalition that underpins and gives movement to the whole, and an administrative apparatus and financial system that permits implementation of the coalitions objectives. The political underpinning of the system has been a conservative coalition of organized agriculture and business interests that has insulated the bureaucracy from radical political shifts. The Liberal Democratic party (LDP), the embodiment of this coalition, was initially based on rural and small town votes and big business finance. It has been in power for more than three decades.[30] Power shifts between factions within the party, but the party itself has been the government. The factions themselves have been the focus of political negotiation within the party and of electoral mobilization.[31] The faction system has managed popular participation while limiting the scope of mass mobilization.

As significant as the strength and cohesion of the governing coalition has been the fragmentation and weakness of the opposition. While there has been a substantial socialist party, the Left has not posed a challenge as an alternative governing party for years. Nor, despite the radical public sector trade unions and the annual orchestrated spring wage offensives, have the unions been the basis of a challenge to corporate authority.[32]

The political trick has been to create a mass political base for a developmental policy conceived by an elite but to insulate the bargains struck within that elite from sharp electoral change. The conservative coalition has not just sponsored the market process but has assured it would continue in the face of potential political disturbances produced by market dislocation. Economic development is not a bloodless and smooth process. It involves real disruptions and dislocations. Peasants are moved off the land; a working class emerges; the relative position of individuals, social groups, and communities in the society and economy changes sharply.[33] The notion that national income and wealth is expanding is never reassuring to those who are being displaced. Unless the political problem of allocating the gains and costs of change is resolved, the resulting conflicts and struggles can paralyze the market.[34]

The LDP helps provide a Japanese solution to this problem. Despite the fundamental social transformation that saw a rural society finally and definitively transformed into an industrial one, the conservatives (and more precisely the Liberal Democratic party) have held on to power.

A contract with France is instructive. In France, where a very similar process was at work, a conservative coalition sponsored growth only to be overturned and then altered by the results of its handiwork. During the period of rapid growth, the modernizing party in France, fundamentally the Gaullist party in its many names, rested its appeal on personal and institutionalized charisma, the appeal of the great man and then the party that claimed his mantle. Later Giscard made an appeal on the basis of technical skills in managing the economy. The conservatives also campaigned against the communist menace. When with the emergence of a coherent anti-Soviet Socialist party the Communists no longer seemed a foreign menace, and when the economy turned down with no politically meaningful explanation provided by the ruling conservatives and no hope of relief, the French Left found an opening to win. The ties of the French conservatives to the populace could not withstand the social transformation of France.[35]

In Japan, the LDP with its local roots and faction system has adapted and adjusted without allowing political interference in the core elements of its developmental policy. While business has provided massive support for the LDP, for the most part this has bought protection against a basic transformation of policy. Industries crucial to development have generally been under the tutelage of ministries such as MITI that have been relatively insulated from the patronage system. There has been extensive corruption in the form of patronage and payoffs, but it has remained situated in ministries such as the Ministry of Posts and Telecommunications (MPT) and Ministry of Transportation. The transformation of telecommunications policy has been significant precisely because the MPT has been an instrument of patronage. Construction, as in so many societies, has been entangled with local and national politics.[36] Appointments in the postal system and educational ministry have also been important elements of patronage.

The administrative apparatus is structured in a fashion that permits a group of elite bureaucrats—most prominently those at MITI and the Ministry of Finance to formulate conscious strategy for industry and provides them with instruments to implement it.[37] The elite bureaucrats themselves form something best thought of a caste, recruited from the most prestigious national university schools and rising within the system together. The senior administrative positions, beginning with the deputy minister, are assigned to members of the senior administrative elite, not filled with political appointments. In the United States, in contrast, political appointments reach five or six layers down into the administrative system. The Japanese administration is centralized, which makes the national bureaucracy the crucial locus of government policy.

The bureaucracy has tended to dominate the processes of policymaking and legislation. Legislation is very much a creation of the bureaucracy; that is, legislation for the most part emerges from bureaucratic rather than legislative initiatives. The administration has extensive discretion in determining and applying rules, which gives it extensive power in bargaining with the private sector. The result is a system colorfully described by Johnson as one in which "Politicians reign and bureaucrats rule."

The bureaucracy is by no means coherent. There are real and intense rivalries among ministries, and different bureaus within ministries quarrel as well. The location of a policy decision—which ministry it falls in—powerfully influences how it is made. Battles over the boundaries of policy are normal. An instance of this fight between political and developmental ministries is told in Chapter 5, on telecommunications. Overall, however, despite such rivalries, bureaucracies, and bureaucrats are significant and somewhat autonomous players in the economy.

In a sense it could not be otherwise in Japan, where the state has traditionally been both a marketplace and political player. The Meiji restoration displaced the Shogun with a group composed of the traditional equivalents of modern bureaucrats. A small elite ruled in the name of the emperor without a constitution or roots in mass politics. After the Second World War, when the prewar ruling cliques and the military were discredited, the economic bureaucracy emerged as the central element of policymaking. The capacity of this bureaucracy to implement policy directions in economic affairs rests then in substantial ways on its influence in developing legislation and its administrative discretion in implementing it. It also rests on a web of consultative groups or councils organized by each ministry. These groups are a source of advice, legitimation, and assistance in conducting policy and implementing policy. In this way interest groups are themselves shaped by state action and tied to the bureaucracy even more than to the legislature.

Equally important, the structure of the financial system gives the bureaucracy instruments to intervene selectively as a player in the industrial economy or to assemble policy compacts that join public and private purposes. As Ueno has argued, at least through the early 1970s the financial system was a crucial instrument in the government's repertoire of domestic policies.[38] It permitted the government to direct not just budget funds but the flow of savings and investment in the economy.

As Ueno summarized the situation:

Broadly speaking, the total supply of funds in Japan was controlled by the Bank of Japan, the level and structure of interest rates were artificially regulated by the Ministry of Finance, and private funds were allocated, under the guidance of public financial institutions, by city banks which competed for market shares. In this process, the Bank of Japan followed the guidelines of the Economic Planning Agency and the MITI and determined the total amount of funds so as to satisfy the demands to growth industries. At the same time, the Ministry of Finance maintained the low interest policy inasmuch as the policy did not lead to large deficits in the balance of payments or to sharp price rises.[39]

Zysman has summarized the importance of the financial instrument in the following way:

The credit-based financial system served the government as a powerful instrument of policy. The political and policy strategies of the Japanese government would have been difficult to accomplish within the constraints of a capital market-based financial system with freely moving prices and an elaborate securities market. The financial instrument in Japan served several purposes. Most generally, it helped force the household sector to bear the costs of expansion in the form of artificially low interest rates. At the same time, the system socialized those costs by diffusing or absorbing the risks of investment and corporate failure. It also reduced the price of expanding and stockpiling goods in anticipation of market development, which has been a constant Japanese market tactic. Access to credit was selectively manipulated to provide preference to favored sectors and to push the economy slowly toward capital-intensive and knowledge-intensive production.[40]

The Institutional Structure of the Japanese Economy: The Organization of Industry

The market dynamics so critical to the success of the developmental strategy turned on market structure not just government policy. Of course, we hasten to repeat, market structure itself embodies and expresses past policies. Our task here is limited. We want to identify elements of the industrial structure that give character to the logic of market dynamics in Japan and make plausible our account of Japanese development. We are interested in both "controlled competition" and the mix of flexibility and strength in industrial sectors.

Japan is characterized at once by very intense domestic competition and by a range of mechanisms for cooperation or collusion. Whether it is joint planning of expansion in capital-intensive industries to avoid excess capacity and to assure the introduction of plants of sufficient size to capture scale economies, or joint research on generic technologies, or reallocation of domestic market share in the aluminum industry to firms that move production offshore, or efforts to allocate domestic market to foreign firms—the evidence is overwhelming that competition is bounded and orchestrated. The deals may or may not be stable; that is, the market divisions may or may not be fixed. However, market outcomes are certainly different because such mechanisms for collaboration, collusion, and bargains exist.

Elaborating how this system works requires specifying the rules of controlled competition, in other words the circumstances or terms of competition and the circumstances or terms of collaboration. In steel in the 1950s, competition was structured by setting the order and scale of new plants. In numerically controlled machine tools the emergence of a dominant supplier of controllers channeled competition into applications. The debate is whether these arrangements were created or confirmed by MITI.

Bounded competition is certainly not unique to Japan. American automobile companies in the 1950s and 1960s eschewed radical product change or fundamental innovation in production. They choose instead to compete on marketing and superficial product change. European steel makers have historically arranged matters in both national and regional cartels, the cartels arranged privately, with collaboration of governments, and now with the collaboration of the European Economic Community. The National Football League is in fact a formal and structured system of bounded competition. Teams collaborate to sustain the league and its rules, and compete to gain position within it.

What is distinctive in the Japanese case are the mechanisms for controlling competition through collaboration. This is not so much because Japan is an economy of giant firms, although levels of concentration in the economy as a whole and in specific markets are as high as or higher than in the United States. Rather, a number of mechanisms draw large firms together in common institutions. The trading companies, an early link between the insulated domestic economy and its external sources of supply, represent one such mechanism.[41] A second mechanism, the zaibatsu groupings of companies, were dissolved in the American occupation. However, *keiretsu*, groupings of firms around large banks, based on the zaibatsu tie firms together in a variety of ways. There are several forms of *keiretsu*, ranging from groups with close intercompany ties to loose, basically financial arrangements. While there is a debate on the precise form or degree of operating cohesion in these groups, the fact is that a majority of company stock in Japan is held by other companies or banks.[42] Third, the world of small firms is not the anarchic site of perfect competition either, because many of the small firms are linked as suppliers to larger companies. Small firms are not inevitably relegated to subordinate supplier status; some independent small firms have grown to compete directly with the giants. But the well-known and much publicized examples, Sony and Honda, are rather exceptional.[43] Last, while cartels are nominally illegal, an enormous number are in fact exempt from the general prohibition. These several forms of intercompany linkage provide the organizational infrastructure for controlled competition.

There are a range of government mechanisms to facilitate coordination among firms; that provide what Dan Okimoto calls "handles."

As he notes:

> In Japan, MITI's capacity to administer industrial policy is greatly facilitated
> by the vast and amorphous network of formal and informal intermediate
> organizations that lie in what I call the "intermediate zone" between state
> and private enterprise.[44]

Some of these handles are evident. Much has been made of MITI's
structure councils, where private business leaders, government officials, academics, and even press leaders meet to formulate policy
directions. Equal attention has been focused on the MITI research
consortia intended to develop next-generation technologies. Projects organized by Nippon Telephone and Telegraph (NTT), now a
nominally independent but state-owned company, translates into
purchases from "family" firms that permits NTT to influence company strategies. A range of cartels for a variety of purposes have been
and still are normal practice. It is not a matter of government dictat-
ing outcomes, as we have been emphasizing, but its role in balancing
and facilitating. Again, Okimoto argues this well:

> The state is thus a linchpin. Its power is not based on the concentration of
> legal authority sufficient to overwhelm recalcitrant groups. Rather it is de-
> rived from the state's strategic role as the indispensable linchpin that holds
> the functioning units of society together and permits it to act in ways that
> advance collective interests. Perhaps it can be called a "network" or "rela-
> tional" state in the sense that its power is largely derived from the nature
> of its relationship as central coordinator of strong constituent groups in
> society.[45]

Such cooperative arrangements do not determine the behavior of
markets. The arrangements are not always stable and firms clearly
violate them. Indeed, the Japanese government's defense against U.S.
legal charges that television firms conspired to penetrate the American market was that the government had ordered cooperation but
the competitive instincts of Japanese firms had made cooperation
impossible.[46] Struggles have even occurred within the government.
When MITI excluded Oki from next-generation technology semiconductor development, NTT helped it rebuild its technology position.[47] Despite such exceptions, collaborative agreements among
firms exist and matter. The market functions differently because
they are present; they create the conditions for "controlled competition" as an instrument of developmental policy.

The second major feature of the economy important to our analysis is that Japanese industry combines in an innovative manner the strengths of large firms that are able to mobilize substantial resources in pursuit of long-term objectives and the flexibility and mobility of small firms. The advantages of large Japanese firms have been the subject of much discussion, but in many countries, not least the United States, many giant corporations have been lumbering giants. Less has been said about the flexibility that has made large Japanese firms agile, not lumbering, giants.

Small firms play a decisive role in this. Despite American rhetoric about entrepreneurship and our fascination with large, integrated Japanese firms, small manufacturing companies have a much larger place in the Japanese economy than in the American one. Manufacturing firms with under 500 employees represent a much larger percentage of both employment and output in Japan than in the United States.[48] The relative importance of very small firms, those with fewer than fifty employees, is even greater in Japan.[49] Moreover, the importance of small firms grew in many industries during the 1970s.[50] Small firms have survived in Japan because of its late start in development and because of the political necessity of preserving what were once not only small but also traditional firms. Many such firms have been protected by law and have been sources of inefficiency. But it also appears that many have been a part of the pattern of Japanese dynamism.

Small firms help provide flexibility in two ways. First, they have permitted large Japanese firms to establish production systems that captured economies of scale without relinquishing flexibility. Small firms that are suppliers and contractors to larger firms play a vital role in this. In the American system many of the tasks these small firms play are integrated in the parent company. In Japan, subcontracting links component suppliers to the parent assembler by market ties rather than by hierarchy inside a firm. The small firm must scramble to adjust to changes in the market demands of the large parent firm. Subcontracting ties fluctuate radically as new technologies are introduced. This represents an important mechanism for accelerated adjustment in the face of changing market or technological conditions.[51]

We must not be lost in the Anglo-American dichotomy between market and administration. The Japanese system combines both along lines different from those with which we are familiar. Inside the company we find market ties among nominally independent firms to permit coordination but maintain market discipline where in the U.S. firms we often find administrative control linking similar activities. By contrast, we find agreement and the mechanisms of collaboration in the midst of market competition.[52]

Second, many Japanese companies begin as spinoffs from larger firms. Elsewhere they might be structured as divisions or tightly controlled subsidiaries. In Japan firms such as Fujitsu Fanuc are organized as quite independent operations.

There is substantial variation across sectors, however, in the types of relations linking small and large firms. In the textile and apparel complex Nakamura shows us that small firms transformed materials provided by large producers and sold by large distributors into final products.[53] In the automobile industry the pattern has been a more vertical one, with tiers of contractors supplying final assemblers. A third, more complex pattern of relations appears to exist between large and small firms in the consumer electronics industry.

THE SECOND TIER: THE LOGIC OF MARKET DYNAMICS THAT GENERATED INVESTMENT AND PRODUCTION INNOVATION

Although government policies were critical, the direct engine behind growth was domestic competition. Structured competition in a rapidly growing domestic market, closed to outsiders, generated the product and production strengths that the Japanese have taken into world markets. Elements of Japanese culture and of the Japanese business structure may have facilitated these market innovations, but the driving force was marketplace incentives. Many supposedly Japanese characteristics, including the pursuit of market share and the tactics of internal organization, follow logically from the nature of the market situation, a situation that is itself shaped by policy.

The second tier of our argument focuses on how the policy of promotion and protection in an industry structure composed at once of large groups and layers of small firms generated an intense investment-driven competition for market share. Competing for domestic market share while borrowing technology drove a pattern of continuous production innovation that now characterizes Japanese companies and has helped them create real enduring advantage on world markets.

Market Dynamics and Corporate Strategy[54]

Market dynamics in Japan drove firms to pursue market share aggressively as a means of maximizing profits, goals traditionally assumed to be contradictory. As all firms sought to maximize market share, excess capacity and "excessive competition" resulted. This in turn led to efforts to regulate or bound competition. Equally important, constant efforts to import and develop foreign technologies created a basis for government-organized consortia for technology development, which also structured and bounded competition. The argument we build rests on three premises:

1. The Japanese market was relatively closed to the implantation of foreign firms.
2. Financial resources could be channeled to expanding sectors.
3. Foreign technology could be readily borrowed and implemented.

For the Japanese firm the primacy of the pursuit of market share is a product of the logic of market conditions in postwar Japan, not the particularities of Japanese culture. Intense domestic competition in a protected and rapidly growing internal market among firms that had access to international product and production technologies had predictable results. As long as the Japanese were aggressive and systematic technology borrowers in a rapidly expanding domestic market, they faced a fundamentally different economic situation from that of foreign companies. The differences in the situation produced the emphasis on market share and production innovation so often remarked on. Yasusuke Murakami and Kozo Yamamura have developed an intriguing analysis of the consequences, more precisely the advantages, of Japanese efforts to overcome technological backwardness.[55] Japanese firms faced long-run declining cost curves, rather than the usual U-shaped concave cost curves.[56] Assuming a concave cost curve, a firm will eventually face rising production costs as volume rises. To avoid rising costs it must innovate and jump to another production cost curve. That new production cost curve represents a new technology. (See Figure 3–1.) A firm will make the

Figure 3-1. Production Innovation, the Evolution of Costs, and Corporate Choice: (a) Continuous Production Innovation, (b) Discontinuous Production Innovation.

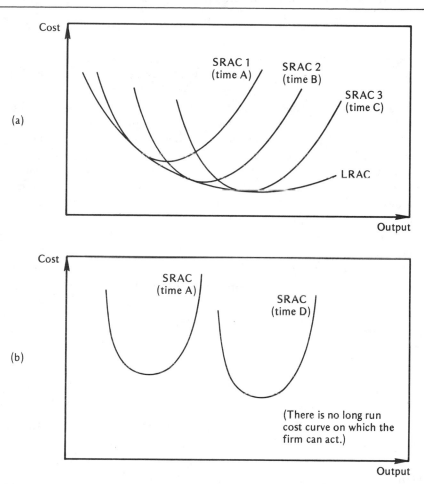

jump if it can anticipate that an increase in demand will justify the investment, if rivals are making or are likely to make the jump imposing competitive pressure to do so, and if the cost of innovation is low and the predictability of its success is high.[57]

In the Japanese case, firms faced rapidly expanding domestic demand and a stream of replacement technologies available abroad. The jump to new technologies was very attractive. It is easy to demonstrate that firms following a market-share-maximization (MSM) strategy, as the Japanese firms were doing, would behave in the same manner as firms pursuing a profit-maximization strategy. Murakami and Yamamura explain the situation the following way:

> when firms are operating on their decreasing long-run average cost curve (i.e., decreasing long-run AC, thus also decreasing long-run minimum average cost), we can also show that aggregate industry supply consists of long-run MAC curves of individual firms pursuing the MSM strategy. However, a crucial fact to be noted is that an equilibrium reached can be an unstable one.
>
> Furthermore, it is not difficult to see that if this is the case, both the firms following an MSM strategy and those pursuing a profit maximization strategy will behave in the same manner. This is so simply because, when average cost is falling and the market price of output is given, an individual firm can increase its profit by increasing output. A result is that all firms are anxious to supply output that is greater than the quantity they are now producing, provided that an increase in output can be obtained anywhere above the AC curve. This is to say, when AC curves are "added" up, we obtain the amount that all the firms in the industry wish to produce collectively. This simply means that when faced with decreasing long-run average cost, both the profit-maximizer and the MSM firms behave in virtually identical fashion, and there is no need to distinguish the difference in their respective motivations. In both cases, the equilibrium reached will be unstable, as expected of any decreasing cost industries. The point we wish to emphasize here is that profit-maximizing firm behavior is indistinguishable from MSM behavior.[58] [Italics in original.]

Under the cost conditions described here, additional market share pushes a firm down its cost curve, setting off a continuing cycle. As the firm increases volume, it takes additional market share, which lowers its costs, making it able to increase sales, thus starting the cycle over. In sum, firms are motivated to move down their cost curves faster than their competitors or to force a sharper reduction in their costs for each increment in production volume.

We can predict much of the behavior of Japanese firms with this analysis. We do not need to resort to arguments about the art of Japanese management or the character of the Japanese work force. In the United States, a similar analysis is often applied to high-technology industries where new products are being introduced. Because of well-documented learning curve effects in such industries, each doubling of total output will generate a predictable decline in average production cost. As new products are introduced in low volume their costs are high, but as output increases, production costs drop. Therefore firms must move to establish market position and defend market share by steadily lowering costs. When applied to industries such as semiconductors, this analysis suggests that firms will be encouraged to price below existing costs to capture market share. The resulting volumes will lower costs below existing prices. Indeed, management practice books often identify some American firms operating or organized in the Japanese style, and these firms are generally ones in high-technology sectors where the learning curve logic that generates long-run declining costs is at work.

What is distinctive in the Japanese case is the ability to apply the logic to traditional industries, such as automobiles. Such sectors, which in the United States were mature, were in their infancy in Japan. Given the same market conditions, producers of many nations would likely have responded in similar ways. Automobile production in Japan jumped from 160,000 cars in 1960 to some 10 million by the end of the 1970s. Each new assembly line was an experiment station for production, and Japanese companies could innovate and learn production. In essence, the Japanese imported the best available production technology and then improved on it. The marginal improvements accumulated into a fundamental manufacturing innovation. Rapidly expanding markets meant that firms faced powerful incentives to learn how to improve on imported practices.

What are the consequences for an industry if all firms in it face declining cost curves and consequently seek to maximize market share? The firm with the largest market share is in the best position to drive costs down and continue in a dominant position. Consequently firms are induced to establish capacity to capture the market share they require to be successful. However, if all firms build production capacity to fit the long-term strategic objective of holding dominant market share, then excess capacity inevitably results. The more aggressively firms believe their competitors will pursue market share by building capacity in anticipation of demand, the more aggressively they must respond. The only alternative is to withdraw from the game. The outcome of such aggressive competition will be periodic bouts of excess capacity.

How, then, to manage the excess capacity? One mechanism is to export the excess output. Yamamura contends that in the 1970s there were surges of exports from Japan, a downpouring of exports, as the domestic Japanese market was saturated.[59] This sale of excess product encouraged firms to sell at marginal cost, leading to very low prices in foreign markets. As a result, Japanese firms were frequently accused of dumping. These trends have continued to the present. In some sectors, such as semiconductors, and for some products such as random access memory chips, Japanese firms have begun to define the market to include U.S. as well as Japanese demand. The result is that each product generation now sees sudden saturation of the U.S. market. Consequently, prices in both the Japanese and U.S. market are driven down almost as each product introduction occurs, leading to an intensification of charges of dumping.

A second mechanism of managing excess capacity has been cartels or production controls negotiated among firms often with the assistance of the government. Here the mechanisms of controlled competition come into play. As Yamamura notes, these agreements are often not very stable, because the imperatives of pushing down the cost curve further and faster will induce firms to break agreements.[60] Nonetheless these arrangements have often served to bound or regulate the consequences of excess capacity.

Corporate Strategy and Production Organization

With large protected domestic markets and access to borrowed technology, Japanese firms were encouraged to grow rapidly, to pursue market share, and to exploit increasing returns. The corporate practices fashioned in the era of rapid growth significantly affected the tactics of production organization in the factory. The key to organization became flexibility. Those Japanese firms that could organize themselves flexibly to capture the gains of introducing successive waves of borrowed technology had as advantage.[61] The managerial and organizational styles developed during the earlier years of technology borrowing continued to be successful even after Japanese firms began their own independent production innovation. The history of Honda Motors, for example, shows this story clearly. Honda borrowed and improved upon technology after technology as it moved from a marginal position in the motorcycle industry to an established player in the motorcycle and automobile industries.[62]

Competition among Japanese firms turned in no small part on manufacturing innovation and the introduction of new product. Consequently, firms were organized to sustain constant evolution in their production processes to improve productivity and sustain the flow of new product. They evolved a practice that "can be described as dynamic flexibility . . . concerned with designing production lines in a way that they can quickly evolve in response to changes in either the product or production technology . . . the central preoccupation is to get ideas into action quickly."[63]

The commitment to flexibility in Japanese firms is reflected in the structure of the market for computer-controlled manufacturing equipment. In Japan many firms develop their own production equipment internally. "Almost every large Japanese auto company has a large machine tool operation in which 200 to 400 people do nothing but create new tools, which are quickly introduced into the production process."[64] When successful, these machines are then sold on the market. As a consequence, the Japanese machine tool market is highly fragmented, shared among many producers who develop equipment for their own internal purposes and then sell it on the open market. In the United States, where less production equipment development occurs internally, the market for programmable machine tools is highly concentrated. In contrast to the United States, where production innovation tends to occur in discontinuous jumps from one prototype to another, in Japan production innovation tends to be more continuous and more iterative. This finding is consistent with the incentives for flexibility that our analysis suggests.

The process of absorbing foreign technologies while aggressively pursuing market share produced substantial production innovation. Something very real did happen on the shopfloor. Andrew Sayer summarizes it well.

> the Just in Time (JIT) system is a learning system which generates economies by making fabrication and assembly more closely approximate a continuous flow line, by reducing the amounts of machinery, materials or labor power which are at any time inactive or not contributing to the production of saleable output. . . . Economies do not follow simply from major technological developments, though that is likely to occur too, but from a different way of organizing the labor process coupled with piecemeal changes to the machinery.[65]

The revolution on the Japanese shop floor is at the heart of continued rapid increases in industrial productivity.

This system did not emerge from the mists of Japanese history, nor was it adopted full blown. It was a logical extension of corporate responses to the market dynamics of Japanese economic growth and the emergence of internationally competitive firms. As with the American system, which became known as Fordist, the production revolution is thought to have begun in the automobile sector with Toyota. The first phase in the postwar development of Japan was based on labor-intensive industry. Low-cost labor gave Japanese firms advantage in world markets in sectors such as textiles.

In the second phase heavy investment in equipment allowed Japan to enter capital-intensive industries such as steel and shipbuilding. New world-scale facilities based on advanced technologies created economies of scale. Labor productivity jumped, giving the Japanese higher output per manhour and increasing cost advantage over their American competitors in these sectors. Indeed, the disadvantages of a lack of raw materials and a steel industry destroyed by war were turned into substantial advantages.

The third phase of development, in the late 1960s and 1970s, could be described as one of focused manufacturing. Although Japanese groups are known for their size and financial muscle and although some capital-intensive industries have world-scale facilities, many Japanese firms in these years were smaller than their foreign competitors. When attempting to compete with much larger European and American companies, the Japanese found they could not efficiently produce as wide a range of products. This disadvantage was turned into a virtue. The Japanese focused "all their available resources on those portions of the product line where market demand was the greatest and access to the customers was the easiest."[66] This focus created substantial cost advantages. It also is thought to have begun the process of shop floor reorganization that culminated in the full just-in-time system. Producing a wide variety of products adds enormous complexity to the production process. That complexity generates substantial overhead costs to manage the physical flow of materials and to maintain control of the process. Having first reduced cost by limiting complexity, the Japanese then learned to manage complexity more effectively, with the result that they could increase product variety and the rate of product introduction while continuing to reduce overheads and increase labor productivity.

Product variety means complexity in production, which adds costs in two important ways: the time it takes to shift from one task to another is the cost, while handling and storing the multitude of parts required to make a diversity of products is a second.

Innovative Japanese producers were determined to reduce change-over times. They did so by designing machines and locating them to accomplish this.

In the 1950s the production engineers at Toyota concentrated on significantly reducing changeover times and run lengths in Toyota's factories. Toyota set one minute as a goal for the changeover of a machine from one part to any other part the machine was intended to produce. For machining operations, changeover times were reduced by investing in extra tooling and related equipment rather than in inventories. Extra machine components were purchased so that tools could be left set up to make specific parts. Jigs were fabricated so that the tools could be placed in or removed from machines quickly. The extra tools and jigs were moved . . . to locations beside the machines.[67]

The success was staggering. James Abegglen and George Stalk report drops in turnaround times from eight hours to one minute in some cases.[68]

Machines were arranged so that workers could move between them. Because many machines or a variety of tools for a specific machine would be employed at any work station, the machine tools were made lighter and less expensive. Consciously, scale economies were sacrificed for the economies of flexibility. As we well know, the Japanese did not raise costs to gain flexibility, they simply went about lowering costs in a different way than American producers.

A reduction in turnaround time is the first step in an interconnected set of steps, each producing pressure to adopt the others. It permits the most efficient production runs to be reduced in length. That is, it becomes efficient to produce any given component in smaller quantities because the machines can immediately be put to use making something else. However, reducing production runs puts pressure on material handling. The right materials must arrive at the right spot exactly at the right moment. Otherwise, the advantages of small batch production, manufacturing in small quantities, are lost because the machines sit idle. Production lines that permitted a simpler flow of parts from one step to the next without need for intermediate storage were created. "Departments based on manufacturing technologies were dismantled and their machines were moved to newly created product departments."[69] Assembly and fabrication were tied together. This permitted the entire production process, the mechanisms by which flows through the factory are regulated and in which production schedules are set, to be controlled differently than in Western factories. The elaborate *kanban* or just-in-time system thought to have begun with Toyota was the result.

The advantages of the full-blown system are substantial, from the ability to produce a greater variety of products to the ability to introduce new products more quickly without cost disadvantages. Having begun to reform the production system to gain cost advantage by focused product strategies that limited variety, many Japanese firms ended up by being able to create even greater variety at ever lower costs. The result was nothing short of a production revolution.

Conclusions

We want to emphasize four things about the Japanese experience. First, the system is based on concrete choices about how to organize production. The structure of the labor market and labor management relations are crucial elements in shop floor decisions and organization. These distinctive features rest more on the postwar politics of Japan than on Japanese culture.[70] Indeed, woven in the pattern of increased worker responsibility is diminished protection for many workers and what some consider an outright increase in the pace of work.[71]

Second, much of the production innovation has rested on the reorganization of skilled workers, *not* on heavy capital investment or on technological innovation. Indeed, the reorganization of skilled workers has created the possibility for technological development.

Third, the system has not resulted in a pattern of extended flexibility in all directions. For example, there is evidence that the number of basic product types in the Japanese automobile industry, measured by chassis and motor sizes, is greater than in the United States.[72] This makes sense because there are more firms. There is also evidence that the Japanese have more flexible production lines, producing several types of cars or cars and light trucks on the same line. This may have been needed to compensate for the lost economies of scale from market fragmentation. However, Japanese producers are (by other evidence) able to tolerate fewer changes in design than American producers. As anyone who has bought a Japanese car knows, they come in tightly defined packages of options that clearly reduce the number of model types on the assembly line. Others suggest that the elaborate network of suppliers and a stratified work force tightly tuned to just-in-time delivery are less able to absorb radical fluctuations in demand than the American system.[73] According to this view, the inability to withstand such fluctuations translates into a downpour of exports and radical price-cutting when domestic demand is insufficient.

Fourth, the presence of an exceptionally large and innovative small business sector has facilitated the dynamic flexibility that characterize Japanese development. The fluid semimarket arrangements tying suppliers to final assemblers has permitted the rapid internal reorganization that flexibility require. Equally the possibility of replacing existing suppliers represents a constant pressure for the smaller firms to sustain their own technological development, both absorbing advanced practice emerging in larger firms and producing their own innovations. Thus, the introduction of new technologies has been facilitated by the flexibility provided by the small firm sector, which has never been displaced by traditional modernization. At the same time, we suspect that during the postwar period of very rapid development, relations between small and large firms changed sharply. Earlier, large firms and the zaibatsu operated somewhat independently, in different sectors and different products. In essence, the small firms facilitated and were transformed during the postwar period of rapid growth.

Japan established an advantage on the one hand in industries in which high-volume standardized production gives quality and cost advantages, and on the other in many dynamic equipment sectors that provide the tools for this production. Competitive advantage in modern volume production sectors hinges not simply on wage rates, but on the operational control of complex systems that reduce per-unit labor costs substantially. According to the arguments presented here, the Japanese development strategy of controlled competition and rapid growth behind a wall of market closure provided firms the incentives to achieve such competitive advantage. That competitive advantage has now consolidated in a distinctive technology paradigm.

THE THIRD TIER: DEVELOPMENTAL STRATEGIES AND INTERNATIONAL TRADE

The third tier of our argument is that the logic of developmental policy and the market dynamics it induces generate troublesome features of Japan's pattern of international trade. Our model has implications for both the pattern of trade and the evolution of policy.

Policy drives import substitution in targeted sectors. The domestic market serves as an instrument of promoting the development of advantage for Japanese industry in global markets. In the developmental years, the policy was clearer and more fully developed. But there is substantial evidence that the processes are still at work and their effects just as important.

Where foreign products or technologies are critical to present needs they are imported, but foreign firms are prevented from establishing an entrenched market position. Obviously, there is a tension between firms that produce intermediate goods primarily for the domestic market and those that need world-class inputs to produce internationally competitive final goods. Our hypothesis is that the bulk of such conflicts are resolved by permitting imports, but not the entrenchment of foreign firms. Consequently, as Japanese firms develop the technological capacity to produce the necessary intermediate goods, they first substitute for imports in the domestic market and then build from their domestic positions into world markets. Our hypothesis is that an aggressive developmental strategy based on protection of the domestic market and promotion produces a distinctive pattern of trade.

Our argument also suggests a distinctive pattern of policy development. There is a tension between the Japanese desire to continue to make its developmental system work and international demands that it reconcile its practices to international expectations. The hypothesis here is that as firms establish international competitiveness, formal and informal restrictions on entry may be reduced, but in sectors where Japan wishes to create advantage, developmental policies are maintained in one guise or another. A distinctive paradigm of production and technology helps explain Japan's pattern of trade, but substantive policies of import substitution both contributed to and permitted exploitation of those innovations. Let us first consider the argument, and then the evidence for it.

Trade in Manufactured Goods: The Argument

Trade in manufactured goods is the most important test of the overall argument because Japan's developmental policy has concentrated on manufacturing, with the expressed intention of moving the manufacturing base from light industry, to capital-intensive and volume-intensive industry, to high-technology sectors. The thrust of developmental policy has been to prevent foreign manufacturing firms from entrenching their position in the Japanese market as a means of assuring the development and international competitiveness of Japanese producers. The size of the domestic market makes a strategy of international competitiveness built around import substitution feasible. One would expect such a policy to produce a reduction in manufactured imports and an expansion in manufactured exports in those products that have been the target of the import-substitution strategy.

These effects have been realized in two ways. First, policy has directly reduced imports by restriction and promoted exports by subsidy. Second, more importantly and more controversially, because of the size of the Japanese market, temporary policies favoring import substitution have generated enduring marketplace advantage in global markets for Japanese firms. In the conditions of the Japanese market, a standard import-industry argument for temporary protection makes sense. Under these conditions, the market is not like a rubber band that when pulled out of shape by policy will snap back into shape when the offending policy is removed. The better analogy is clay: once modeled it holds its shape. Policies that promote import substitution and global advantage today permanently change the terms of global competition and put the Japanese industry on a new trajectory. Even if promotional policies are abandoned or changed, the industry is permanently altered.

The effects of past policy on current trade can be seen by imagining a three-phase process that in our view represents Japan's postwar development in a range of sectors. In the first phase, Japanese firms are at a disadvantage in both product development and production cost. Consequently foreign firms can dominate the markets, building up their own distribution and service systems. If this occurs, displacing foreign firms will be difficult. Tariffs or quantitative restrictions on imports will encourage foreign firms to open production in Japan to defend their markets. Only outright discrimination preventing foreign firms from establishing distribution, service, and production in Japan can preserve the domestic market for domestic producers. In this first phase, only outright discrimination forcing foreign firms to transfer technology and distribute through Japanese channels will be effective.

In the second phase Japanese firms, by borrowing technology, close much of their product and production disadvantage. They build up distribution and service channels. Foreign firms, having lost all or most of their product and production advantage, no longer have a base for easily entering the Japanese market. Moreover, because they are largely excluded from direct contact with the Japanese market and sell mainly through distributors, foreign firms will not design products for Japanese consumers or evolve production processes needed to remain competitive in the rapidly expanding Japanese market.

There appear to be three reasons for this phenomenon. First, distributors are not dependent on foreign producers to increase sales. They can often shift to alternate sources as products are initiated. Second, foreign firms do not have the market information required to effectively address the market. Because current sales are low and future sales uncertain, particularly without contact with the market, the risk of investment in designing products specifically for Japan is very high. In addition, foreign firms not entrenched in the Japanese market will overlook signs of real product and production innovation by Japanese firms. Consider by contrast the development of American auto producers in Europe where Ford and General Motors have developed distinctive products for European markets and competitive production processes. By the end of this second phase, direct protectionist policy is no longer crucial. When the policy is relaxed, foreign firms will not flood into the market as they once might have. Indeed, it will become very difficult for foreign firms to establish the corporate infrastructure in the form of personnel and distribution networks required to build enduring market positions for those products where they still retain real advantage.

In the third phase Japanese producers begin to build world market position. They develop distinctive products for the Japanese market that provide the basis for market entry abroad. This was certainly the case in automobiles, for example. Now the ordinary market logic of the product cycle will be at work. On the basis of distinctive products, often developed by Japanese firms originally for Japanese markets, exports can begin and distribution networks abroad can be built. Just as important, the production innovations generated by the logic of declining cost curves will give Japanese producers real cost advantage as well. The presence of foreign producers holding substantial market positions would have precluded Japanese producers from driving down those cost curves in the same way. Having done so, local firms can produce internationally competitive goods that are then pumped into the domestic market through the channels established in the second phase. There are exceptions of course, where the Japanese have not played catch-up but have surged ahead. Often, though, where Japanese firms have pushed ahead they have done so in the components, such as linear microcircuits and semiconductor memory devices, where they dominate the final product market at home and abroad or are able to control access to the Japanese market.

Trade in Manufactured Goods: The Evidence

Japan's trade in manufactured goods clearly fits the predictions suggested by our model. The evidence comes both from an analysis of trade data and from sectoral cases. The evidence presented here draws heavily on the recent work of Stephen Krasner and Bela Balassa and the case study work done by researchers at the Berkeley Roundtable on the International Economy (BRIE).[74]

Japan's trade in manufactured goods is very different from that of the other advanced countries. The others exchange large quantities of very similar products. Such trade does not rest, in theory, on radically different factor inputs or production costs, but on firm- and product-specific advantages that mean some products are exported and other, similar ones are imported. Market imperfections and product characteristics shape the levels and direction of such trade. The French sell Renaults to the Germans and the Germans sell BMWs to the French. Such trade differs from each country's trade with the developing countries, in which manufactured goods are exchanged for imports of raw materials and semimanufactures.

Japan, by contrast, tends not to import in those sectors in which it exports. In other words, in manufactured goods where Japanese firms have established a position in world markets, foreign firms are unable to maintain or establish position in Japanese markets. Krasner summarizes it well. "Japan has the most sectorally skewed distribution of imports and exports of any major industrialized country. It has relatively little intrasectoral trade and imports relatively few

Table 3-1. Import Penetration Ratios in Manufacturing (*Imports as a percent of Apparent Consumption*).[a]

	United States	Canada	Belgium	Finland	France	Germany
World						
1975	7.01	29.75	64.56	29.40	17.91	24.25
1983	10.28	28.17	100.30	30.12	26.21	35.11
1983/1975	146.6	94.7	155.4	102.4	146.3	144.8
OECD						
1975	4.85	27.97	59.53	24.48	15.86	20.51
1983	6.65	25.19	90.52	24.39	22.27	28.86
1983/1975	137.1	92.6	152.1	99.6	140.4	140.7
Developing Countries						
1975	2.09	1.53	3.75	1.36	1.52	2.61
1983	3.57	2.15	6.87	1.78	2.95	4.31
1983/1975	170.8	138.7	183.2	130.9	194.1	165.1
Japan						
1975	1.16	1.25	1.15	0.86	0.47	0.78
1983	2.16	1.88	2.75	2.24	0.92	1.74
1983/1975	186.2	150.4	239.1	260.5	195.7	223.1
Imports into Japan						
1975	1.39	0.18	0.03	0.01	0.11	0.28
1983	1.70	0.21	0.03	0.02	0.13	0.25
1983/1975	122.3	116.7	100.0	200.0	118.2	0.89

a. Apparent consumption is derived as domestic production plus imports minus exports.
Source: Anders Brokin and Derek Blades, "The OECD Compatible Trade and Production Data Base, 1970–1983," Working Paper 31, OECD Department of Economics and Statistics, Paris, OECD, May 1986.

manufactured goods in comparison with other major states."[75] Balassa reaches the same conclusions. One can see from Tables 3–1 through 3–3 the distinctive pattern of trade. Japan's pattern of manufactured imports contrasts with that of the other major industrial countries. Between 1975 and 1983 the average import penetration ratio for manufactured goods rose from 7.0 to 10.3 percent in the United States, from 17.9 to 26.2 percent in France, from 24.3 to 35.1 percent in Italy. In Japan it rose from 4.9 to 5.3 percent, as shown in Table 3–1. The import penetration ratio in manufactured

Table 3-1. continued

Italy	Netherlands	Norway	Sweden	United Kingdom	Australia	Japan
21.92	55.37	43.84	35.12	21.95	22.78	4.94
31.19	67.10	44.29	44.92	29.32	23.45	5.26
142.3	121.2	101.0	127.9	133.6	102.9	106.5
18.68	48.79	40.25	30.90	17.58	19.03	2.92
24.90	56.19	39.89	28.58	24.58	18.50	3.16
133.3	115.2	99.1	92.5	139.8	97.2	108.2
2.23	4.20	2.24	2.09	2.98	3.43	1.82
4.98	6.73	2.86	2.89	3.47	4.56	2.01
223.1	160.2	127.7	138.3	116.4	132.9	110.4
0.41	1.06	3.06	1.12	0.85	4.42	n.d.
0.65	1.96	2.68	2.06	1.78	5.25	n.d.
158.5	185.5	87.6	183.9	209.4	118.8	n.d.
0.09	0.05	0.02	0.05	0.20	0.25	n.d.
0.10	0.04	0.02	0.05	0.16	0.17	n.d.
111.1	0.80	100.0	100.0	0.75	0.68	n.d.

products from advanced countries rose in Japan from 2.9 to 3.2 percent while the ratio for the United States grew from 4.9 to 6.7 percent, in Germany from 20.5 to 28.9 percent, for France from 15.9 to 22.9 percent.[76]

Engineering products are virtually the prototype of trade among advanced countries and are a critical test of our argument. These products include machinery for specialized industries, office and telecommunications equipment, motor vehicles, as well as other machinery and household equipment. Many are inputs into further production, so differences in quality and price affect the quality and price of the goods they produce, and many of the buyers are sophisticated. Moreover, specialized firms develop specific product advan-

Table 3–2. Manufactured Imports as a Percentage of GDP.

Country	1970	1980	Percentage Increase 1970–80
Japan	2.41	2.87	19
United Kingdom	10.76	16.03	57
Italy	7.96	12.70	59
France	9.23	13.09	42
Germany	10.41	15.03	44
United States	3.48	5.73	64
Canada	16.40	20.20	23

Source: From Stephen D. Krasner, *Asymmetries in Japanese-American Trade: The Case for Specific Reciprocity* (Berkeley, Calif.: Institute of International Studies, University of California, 1987), p. 23. Derived from figures in World bank, *World Tables*, 3rd Edition: Comparative Economic Data, Table 6 and Country pages, Economic Data, Sheet 1, using current prices to determine imports as a percentage of gross domestic product.

Table 3–3. Manufactured Imports as a Percentage of Total Imports, 1972–84.

	1972	1974	1976	1978	1980	1982	1984
Japan	29	23	20	22	18	20	24
United States	68	55	54	54	49	58	66
EEC	60	55	56	58	53	58	66
EEC, excluding intra-EEC	40	38	40	43	40	41	45

Source: Taken from Stephen D. Krasner, *Asymmetries in Japanese-American Trade: The Case for Specific Reciprocity* (Berkeley, Calif.: Institute of International Studies, University of California, 1987), Table II.

tages that make their goods attractive abroad, but specific development in foreign firms generates products attractive to domestic buyers. Engineering goods, moreover, are "at the core of Japan's industrial policy."[77]

Krasner's evidence shows the distinctive character of Japan's trade in these sectors. He notes that in the 1972–1984 period, engineering products accounted for an average of 8 percent of Japan's imports,

Table 3-4. Engineering Products as a Percentage of Total Imports, 1972-84.

	1972	1974	1976	1978	1980	1982	1984
Japan	11	8	7	9	7	7	9
United States	35	29	28	31	29	34	40
EEC[a]	26	22	24	27	24	26	27
EEC[b]	17	14	16	20	18	20	23

Source: Taken from Stephen D. Krasner, *Asymmetries in Japanese-American Trade: The Case for Specific Reciprocity* (Berkeley, Calif.: Institute of International Studies, University of California, 1987), Table III. Derived from figures in General Agreement on Tariffs and Trade, *International Trade*, 1976-77, 1980-81, 1984-85, appendix tables for Japan, the United States, and the European Community.

a. The membership of the European Community increased during this period.

b. Excluding intra-EEC trade.

32 percent of U.S. imports, and 18 percent of EEC imports (even if we exclude intra-EEC trade, although that improperly lowers the willingness of European countries to import in these sectors.[78] (See Table 3-4.) He argues that "while Japan is a major exporter of many kinds of machinery it is not a major importer of any. The highest percentage of imports accounted for by Japan in any category is 5.5 percent. . . . In most cases Japanese exports were more than ten times greater than its imports."[79]

The distinctive Japanese pattern in engineering is evident in its overall trade performance in manufactured products. Using a variety of different measures and even allowing for Japan's distance from other major markets and its considerable dependence on raw material imports, Balassa finds that Japan imports less relative to its GNP than its size and level of development predict. His results indicate that Japan is an outlier compared to all of the other advanced industrial countries—irrespective of whether one considers imports from all sources, from the industrial countries or from the developing countries and irrespective of whether one considers total imports or just imports of manufactured goods.[80] As far as trade with developing countries is concerned, Japan's imports from such countries have grown much less rapidly than have the imports of the other advanced industrial countries despite the fact that Japan began at a lower initial level.[81] In other words Japan, whether by policy or competitive will, has resisted the restructuring and shifting of comparative advantage that has occurred in the other advanced countries.

Are there explanations other than present or past discrimination that might account for such outcomes? Exchange rates cannot account for Japan's distinctive pattern of trade, in particular for its tendency relative to other advanced countries not to import in sectors in which it exports, that is not to engage in intrasectoral trade. But can exchange rates explain differences in overall import penetration in Japan and the other advanced industrial countries? In the decade through 1985 the Japanese yen depreciated in real terms vis-à-vis the U.S. dollar, but it changed little vis-à-vis the European currencies. As Balassa notes, the European countries experienced similar trends in import ratios as the United States. They, like Japan, had sharp increases in their oil bill. Moreover, "Japanese import penetration in Western Europe increased much more rapidly than mutual ratios of import penetration among European countries. And increased Japanese import penetration in the major European countries was not accompanied by increased European import penetration in Japan. In fact the share of Germany and the United Kingdom in the Japanese market declined between 1975 and 1983."[82]

Perhaps, then, Japanese producers are simply so competitive that their trade pattern reflects existing Japanese advantage. Consider for instance, U.S.-Japanese competition. Any real Japanese advantage should be reflected by Japanese penetration of third markets, that is, markets other than the U.S. and the Japanese. Krasner presents some compelling evidence on Japanese–U.S. competition in third markets. He examines all three-digit SITC numbers under the general designation of machinery for all products in which the United States and Japan are among the ten largest exporters in 1982 and either the United States or Japan was among the twenty largest importers. He finds that Japanese exports of such products exceeded American exports of such products in third country markets only in five of twenty-three product categories for which data were available. Using sales in third country markets as a predictor of sales for American and Japanese products in each other's market, he finds that there is not one product in which the United States is selling more in Japan than would be predicted on the basis of sales in third-country markets; in most products it is selling less than one-fifth, and in many products less than one-tenth of the predicted value.[83]

Despite the reduction of formal barriers to entry to the Japanese market over the last decade, the basic patterns of Japanese trade have not altered. This suggests either the current patterns of trade reflect past discrimination or that informal mechanisms of protection through policy or business practice continue.[84] A review of a series of sectoral cases suggest both are true.

In automobiles and commodity semiconductor products, the Japanese position in its home market and world markets cannot be understood without reference to past market closure.[85] In advanced computers and telecommunication switching equipment, present discrimination clearly exists.[86] Indeed, in advanced technologies a pattern of continuing and seemingly orchestrated import substitution appears to be at work.

Stories of individual companies are instructive, although they do not permit the same generalizations as aggregate or sectoral data. Consider the experiences of IBM and Texas Instruments. IBM was compelled to license its technology in order to survive in the Japanese market. One senior MITI official stated that "We will take every measure possible to obstruct the success of your business unless you license IBM patents to Japanese firms and charge them no more than a 5 percent royalty."[87] As Krasner notes,

> IBM capitulated, sold the patents and accepted MITI administrative guidance on the number of computers it could market domestically in exchange for the right to manufacture in Japan. The company hired former MITI officials whose loyalty may have been stronger to the Ministry than to IBM. Approval to produce new models was held up if they could compete with products being developed Japanese firms. Despite being a Japanese company with an almost entirely Japanese staff IBM Japan was kept out of policymaking, indeed it was the target of the policymaking.[88]

In recent years IBM has radically changed both its approach to Japanese firms, treating them as its central competitive challenge, and the organization of its Japan operations. We believe it was in response to these strategies and approaches by the Japanese.

Texas Instruments' experience was similar to IBM's. It could not form a subsidiary in the 1960s unless it transferred technology to the Japanese. Despite formal "liberalization," its applications to establish a Japanese operation were ignored. Eventually it was permitted to form a joint venture with Sony in exchange for a general licensing of its critical semiconductor patents.[89]

More formal data confirms the forced transfer of technology. A comparison between the experience of American firms in Japan and in Europe is significant. Krasner's data are again revealing. In Japan the fees and royalties paid by unaffiliated Japanese firms to the United States *exceeded* the earnings from U.S. direct foreign investment in manufacturing. Such fees from unaffiliated European firms were only 10 percent of earnings from U.S. direct foreign investment in manufacturing in Europe. In Japan, such fees and royalties by unaffiliated Japanese firms were twice as high as the fees and royalties paid by American firms operating in Japan. In Europe such fees were 38 percent of fees paid by American firms to themselves for the use of their own technology.[90] Overall, in the Japanese case American firms could only earn by selling their technology, not by exploiting it as a producer.

This analysis of trade in manufactures is consistent with the predictions of our three-phase model showing how developmental policy structures trade outcomes. Moreover, the three-phase model is consistent with the history of competition in a range of sectors. Business complaints of discrimination cannot be dismissed as purely special pleading or anecdotes. BRIE analyses of U.S.–Japanese competition in semiconductors and telecommunications indicating persistent market closure in Japan cannot be dismissed as isolated cases. In industry after industry and in country after country, there is a wealth of anecdotal information suggesting a persistent pattern of discrimination against foreign producers in Japanese markets. This information is consistent with the more formal aggregate analyses of Balassa and Krasner revealing significant barriers to import penetration in Japan, even after the formal liberalization of Japanese markets in the late 1960s and early 1970s.

THE OVERALL PATTERN OF TRADE

Japan is a rich industrial country that lacks natural resources, and its general trade pattern reflects that. Like other countries in a similar situation, Japan imports raw materials and exports manufactures to pay for them. Indeed, its ability to sustain increasing national wealth depends on this pattern. As far as the overall structure of trade is concerned, the Japanese pattern is not distinctive. This observation has led some observers to conclude that market forces rather than government policies are the determinants of Japanese trade.[91]

Gary Saxonhouse sought to test the notion that Japanese trade patterns are a product of open trade and market processes. He sought to build a model that would allow us to judge whether government policy had influenced Japanese trade patterns. He uses a modified version of the Hecksher-Ohlin-Samuelson theory of comparative advantage, which analyzes trade flows in terms of the global distribution of input and production factors. He argues that Japan's manufactured imports as a percentage of its total imports is very low (21.5 percent in 1981 compared to 55 percent in the United States and 63.4 percent in Britain). However, he contends that this pattern falls within the normal range of trade outcomes predicted by his model. As Balassa notes, this conclusion is only true if developing countries are included in the standard of comparison. Correctly compared to developed countries alone, Japan is an outlier.

Saxonhouse argues that the aggregate pattern is one in which a resource poor country has built a stock of capital and skilled labor, imports its raw materials, and exports manufactures. This is certainly true; indeed, it is tautological and hardly surprising. But as Balassa demonstrates, even allowing for Japan's excessive dependence on raw material imports, the level of import penetration for manufactured goods is very low compared to that of the other industrial economies.

In Saxonhouse's view, Japan's trading patterns are driven by its high national literacy and national savings, both of which tend to encourage a comparative advantage in trade in capital intensive and knowledge intensive manufactures. The literacy rate is quite remarkable. This can only facilitate the move toward an electronics economy, and indeed many who know Japan well speak of a love affair with electronics that is the equivalent of the American affair with the automobile a generation ago. It would seem clear that high Japanese saving rates, which make capital relatively available, give the Japanese an advantage in industries in which the price or availability of capital resources affects the competitive position of firms. The pool of educated labor and capital mean that we might well expect Japan's exports to be concentrated in sectors in which capital resources and an educated work force matter. According to this argument, Japan should increasingly export capital-intensive and knowledge-intensive manufactures. This hypothesis is consistent with empirical evidence on the changing composition of Japanese exports and imports over time. For example, Balassa and Marcus Noland find that between 1967 and 1985, Japanese trade shows increasing specialization in human-capital-intensive and R&D-intensive manufactured products at the expense of physical-capital-intensive and in particular unskilled-labor-intensive and natural resource products.[92]

This argument, although correct, cannot account for Japanese domination of its domestic markets or for the seeming tendency of Japan to import those goods it does not make but not those that it does. The Saxonhouse model by its assumptions and construction cannot explain the distinctive lack of intrasectoral trade in manufactured goods in Japan. Yet intrasectoral trade flows are the key to understanding Japanese trading patterns. How in this model, for example, do we account for the enormous stability in American market share in very rapidly growing Japanese markets? As an illustration, in semiconductors the American firms have held roughly 10 percent of the Japanese market while they have captured 70 percent of the market outside Japan. At the beginning of the 1970s Japanese producers were not cutting-edge competitors on world markets. Between that time and the mid-1980s, the Japanese market for semiconductors grew to match the scale of the American market.[93] The industry underwent three virtual product revolutions. The market positions of firms throughout the world were reshuffled. Japan's share of the American and European markets went up. Yet, the American share of the Japanese market remained constant throughout these changes, it neither rose nor fell. Literacy and savings rates cannot account for intrasectoral patterns of trade such as this one.

Perhaps, some might argue, Japanese design, development, and manufacturing are so inherently superior and have established a dominance so complete that once Japanese producers enter foreign markets, their domestic market is secure. BRIE analyses of the semiconductor industry indicate that the three-phase policy-supported import substitution described here lies behind the disclosing advantage of Japanese producers in this and other markets.[94] This model, based firmly on the notion of the developmental state, rather that the Hecksher–Ohlin model developed by Saxonhouse and based firmly of the notion of the market, is required to understand important features of Japan's trade.

In sum, the pattern of Japanese trade with the rest of the world is different from the pattern exhibited by any of the other advanced industrial countries. The critical difference is its trade in manufactures. Japan, relative to the other advanced industrial economies, tends not to import manufactures in sectors in which it exports. This is consistent with a particular pattern of import substitution. Japanese domestic policies for industrial development, adjustment, and managed decline that are intended to affect the production profile of the nation have affected Japan's pattern of foreign trade as well. That pattern reflects outright discrimination and the legacy of past discrimination.

The importance of past discrimination is sometimes underestimated. Past discrimination lives on in the institutions of the economy and the attitudes of the community. Arrangements of suppliers and of distribution have been established in a closed market. They are now remarkably difficult for foreigners to penetrate. Japan for many years was a marginal market for most foreign producers. Being present in Japan was not important to their basic well-being. That is no longer true. Japan's emergence as a strategic market, one in which the fate of companies is settled, is an important part of present trade tensions. In many product lines, especially electronic goods and R&D-intensive products, entry to the Japanese market now matters, and matters a great deal. Since investments in a Japanese presence was not made earlier, the skills and experience needed to succeed now are not there. There is a serious asymmetry that must now be overcome.

Remarkable views in Japan of the impenetrability of the Japances market serve to make market entry for foreigners more difficult, sustaining the present pattern of trade. The American Chamber of Commerce in Tokyo jointly sponsored with a Japanese counterpart a now widely publicized study of U.S.-Japanese trade and the possibility of American success in Japan.[95] The study was conducted by McKinsey and Company. Both the conclusions and the way they were arrived at are instructive. Academics often worry about methodology; that is, the way you go about reaching a conclusion and the assumptions you begin with determine the results of an analysis. Given the assumptions, the conclusions of the book are not surprising. The sectors in Japan identified as open for U.S. penetration are service sectors, not manufacturing. What assumptions lead to this conclusion? The self-proclaimed methodology of the U.S.-Japan study group rested on the assumption that in those sectors in which the Japanese were exporters there would be no market for imports in Japan. This is an astounding statement. It means that in any sector in which the Japanese are present as exporters in world markets we should assume as normal the absence of imports. To make the analysis concrete, the position implies that since the Japanese export semiconductors the Americans should abandon their efforts to penetrate the Japanese market. If the Germans or the French were to follow a similar logic, it would then mean that since both are substantial exporters of autos there would be no place for Japanese cars in Europe.

In our argument, the particular Japanese pattern of trade is in important ways the result of policy at a sectoral level. The formal logic we develop is that a closed market in a large country and a pattern of rapid import substitution prevents foreign firms from establishing an enduring position in the domestic market. That is, as a general rule, foreign firms are prevented from using a temporary competitive advantage as a means of building a longer term position. Intense domestic competition then builds a product and production base that sustain strong entry into international markets by domestic firms. Entry into the home market by outsiders is initially forbidden, and later made difficult by the entrenched position of domestic producers. The result is a pattern of exports without imports. In some sectors these processes are important; in others they are of much less significance. What matters for this discussion is that a domestic pattern of policy intended to achieve goals of creating advantage, promoting structural adjustment, and managing transition and decline can shape the pattern of trade in a sector and in the country as a whole.

Emphasizing the importance of policy produces the same aggregate predictions as a model resting on traditional factor proportions. Indeed it must because the overall pattern of Japan's trade is not unusual, it must be competitive in manufactures if it is rich as a nation but poor in raw materials. Its competitive position in manufactures must rest on such things as education. Moreover, the general form of trade would be a product of any conscious government policy of development. A decision to promote rapid industrial development in Japan requires that a trade pattern of imported raw materials and exported manufactures be created.

The advantage of our approach is that it does a much better job of accounting for the pattern of trade in manufactures and for low import penetration in most manufactured goods in Japan. These characteristics can be explained as a product of the form of conscious domestic development adopted by the Japanese.

Macroeconomic forces, in particular the balance between domestic saving and domestic investment, have been important in the generation of huge current account surpluses in Japan during the 1980s. But the macroeconomic explanation is incomplete for two reasons. First, it assumes that saving and investment are exogenous forces that drive the overall levels of Japan's trade surplus and its current account surplus. In reality, of course, both saving and investment depend upon current levels of economic activity and these in turn are affected by trade. Without growing exports to the United States during the 1981–86 period, for example, Japanese economic growth would have been slower, with negative repercussions for domestic saving and perhaps domestic investment as well. Over the longer run, developmental policies that promoted exports and discouraged imports in Japan contributed to domestic expansion that fueled both investment and saving. In short, there is no simple unidirectional causality between domestic macroeconomic conditions and a country's trade balance or current account balance. Causality runs in both directions. Thus it is erroneous to conclude that the emergence of the huge Japanese trade surpluses of the 1980s had nothing to do with its developmental strategies of promotion and protection, since the cumulative effects of such strategies undoubtedly affected its macroeconomic performance over time.

Second, even accepting the exogeneity of macroeconomic factors, a gap between domestic saving and domestic investment predicts only that a country will experience a current account gap of roughly similar magnitude. Nothing is implied about the level of exports or the level of imports associated with such a gap. In this respect, the contrast between Germany and Japan in recent years is revealing. Germany has run a large current account surplus with high levels of both exports and imports. In contrast, Japan has run a current account surplus with sharply rising exports and imports that remain low by the standards of the other advanced industrial countries. Japan's performance is consistent with the cumulative effects of the import-substitution strategy described here.

DOES THE DEVELOPMENTAL POLICY CONTINUE?[96]

Does Japan's developmental policy continue? The critical mechanisms of that policy have been protection of the home market and promotion of domestic producers through a variety of means. If these mechanisms continue to operate, they will continue to influence market outcomes. One would expect the same logic of policy and market producing one-way trade described earlier to be at work.

Japan is no longer a relatively backward industrial country trying to rebuild and to close technology gaps. It is the second largest national economy in the noncommunist world. And its developmental policy, if it persists, no longer affects only traditional sectors such as steel, automobiles, and consumer electronics, but economically and strategically critical sectors such as advanced electronics, biotechnology, and new materials. Will foreign firms in these advancing industries be able to use their advantages to establish enduring positions in the Japanese market? Will a mix of effective protection and domestic promotion recreate the same dynamic and the same pattern of trade in these new sectors as it created in more traditional sectors at an earlier time? Equally, in many traditional sectors, firms from other Asian nations are emerging, building on their advantage of dramatically lower wages. Will firms in such sectors have access to the Japanese market, or will Japanese producers continue to be protected?

Real changes have occurred in Japan in the last several years, both in the internal workings of the economy and in its relation to its trading partners. Formal barriers to entry have been reduced. The government role in industrial affairs has been cut back in a large number of sectors. Apparent "liberalization" within and without is thought to be a logical outgrowth of the development of the economy. For example, firms that are richer and technologically more independent are less subject to government influence. Growing wealth and influence reduce the need for government to promote development. Has success made the old role of government obsolete?

In many sectors American and European companies complain that Japanese markets remain closed to outsiders, and that promotional strategies by the government continue to give Japanese companies advantages in international markets. Every country has its arrangements and practices that make business difficult for outsiders. Such practices take many forms in Japan. Perhaps uniquely Japanese are methods of administrative guidance in which MITI or other government agencies give suggestions or advice to private companies, advice that is not binding but not originates with officials "who may have the power to provide or withhold loans, grants, subsidies, licenses, tax concessions and the like."[97] Other restrictive practices include customs procedures; standards, testing, and certification requirements; public procurement; policies to rationalize declining industries; policies to promote high-technology industries; and limited access of foreign suppliers to domestic distribution channels.[98] Business practice as much as policy keeps the markets insulated. The mix of policy and business practice combine to sustain the powerful processes of manufacturing innovation and import substitution.

Loosening or Liberalizing: Posing the Problem

The American policy debate about Japan has all too often focused on the wrong questions. It has asked, "Is the Japanese market open or closed?" or differently, "How far has liberalization gone?". Posed this way, there is not a useful answer. Anecdotes and measures of closure are set against anecdotes and measures of improved access. We are pressed to assess whether to characterize the system as "opening" or "remaining closed" by weighing up these anecdotes and measures. Having said it is one or the other, open or closed, evidence of the opposite is dismissed as either anecdotal or insignificant.

The proper concern is the *pattern* of change that has occurred. Japan can perfectly well be open in some sectors or types of sectors and closed in others. More properly, the developmental strategy can have become irrelevant or have been abandoned in some areas and continue unabated in others. The proper question is whether the developmental strategy continues, and how it has evolved if it does. Or better still, in which sectors and under what circumstances is the developmental policy mix currently in operation?

If the developmental model has been scrapped, then we would expect a broad and even reduction in restrictions on trade. If the model is retained in one form or another, then we would expect to see a selective pattern of protection aimed again at retaining the domestic market for the development of Japanese firms in sectors intended to promote the continuing structural evolution of the Japanese economy as a whole.

What does the evidence show? A prima facie case for broad liberalization can be made. Under pressure from trading partners abroad, most formal restrictions on entry into the Japanese market have been lifted. There have been genuine efforts at removing formal tariff barriers and other forms of direct discrimination against foreign imports. The Japanese have reduced formal barriers to trade to a greater extent than many of their trade partners. Quota restrictions were reduced from 466 in 1962 to 27 by 1983. The bulk of those remaining (22) are in agriculture, where everyone acknowledges that real protection continues. Japan also lowered its tariff rates to a significant extent in the 1960s and 1970s. On average, tariff rates on non-agricultural products in Japan now approximate those in the European Common Market and in the United States.[99]

Formal barriers, however, are only a part of the story of how the developmental system operates. As the system has evolved, its domain of action has been restricted. Government-led policy no longer seems to try to control the evolution of the whole economy. Not only is it unnecessary but in most sectors firms are too rich, too technologically sophisticated, and too well entrenched in world markets to be easily influenced by the preferences of bureaucrats. However, the instruments of policy and the capacity to resist foreign competitors by protection and promotion remains. Is that capacity used, and if so where?

The developmental policy continues for two objectives: to ease the transition of declining sectors and to promote the expansion of new industries. In other words an active interventionist strategy continues in sectors in which the Japanese government would like to create advantage or those in which industry has lost advantage in world markets. In these sectors arrangements that give structural advantages to the Japanese in their home markets, and often in international markets, endure. The capacity to resist foreign competitors in crucial sectors remains, even though there is a marked reduction in the government's ability to control the domestic economy. The high-technology sectors (microelectronics, machine tools, computers, and telecommunications are examples of currently contested industries) are not, in our view and that of many others, open to full foreign competition.

Indeed, the policies, public remarks, and private statements do suggest a pattern. We propose that *restrictions on the ability of foreign firms to develop a permanent presence in the Japanese market have been removed only where Japanese firms have already achieved a dominant position at home and a strong often dominant position abroad. In other words restrictions have been removed when they don't matter any more.* In sectors in which Japanese firms are strong, foreign competitors are unlikely to gain a strong and enduring presence in the Japanese market. Even for such products, the patterns of Japanese trade are different from elsewhere in the advanced world. The inability of strong foreign firms to find products and mechanisms to establish an enduring presence in the Japanese market despite considerable efforts to do so suggests mechanisms of continued closure be they formal or informal. Markets are open to imports from abroad where Japanese firms continue to need foreign technology, particularly in capital goods. In this case there is often very rapid import substitution of domestic for foreign products as Japanese producers enter the market. In part such import substitution reflects market conditions and the domestic strengths of Japanese firms. In part it appears to be a product of collective choice, both governmental and private.

Our hypothesis is that a moving band of protectionism and developmental policy continues. Or differently, there is a moving band of openness. Restrictions in sectors in which Japanese firms are established at home and abroad are loosened. They are maintained and combined with selective promotion policies in emerging and declining sectors. It is not, moreover, a simple matter of sunrise or sunset industries; rather it is as much an issue of the reorganization of traditional sectors and the use of the advanced transformative technologies in the reorganization of these sectors.

Protection no longer lies in formal external barriers such as tariffs or quotas. If closure exists, it now rests in a pattern of policy and business practices. Precisely because formal barriers have been removed, evidence on closure is indirect and fragmented. One body of evidence lies in the trade patterns considered above. These patterns are consistent with but do not directly demonstrate closure. A second body of evidence lies in a series of cases where foreign products have been denied entry to the market and Japanese competitive products have developed in the vacuum. In some cases such as semiconductors and computers, satellites and satellite launchers, optical fiber and switching equipment, there appears to be an explicit intention of closure to create conditions for Japanese development. The instances are too numerous and form too clear a pattern to be dismissed as anecdotes. In sectors where Japanese policy point to the need for long-term development, entry is difficult and foreign market share limited.[100]

The mechanisms of closure are mixed and do not always rest explicitly in policy. Closure continues in business practices in which quality control engineers, in a seemingly hyperbolic case, reject all foreign products regardless of price.[101] It lies in the importance of long-term customer and supplier relationships and the diminished importance of entirely open markets. As Ronald Dore in discussing the textile industry notes, because "imports penetrate into markets, where there are no markets, only a network of established customer relationships, it is hard to make headway."[102] It continues in the wish of bureaucracies, such as NTT, to continue established relationships and practices even when principles are changed at the top. The government's failure to act on Corning Glass's applications for optical fiber patents while Sumitomo with support from NTT developed a competing product is one in a series of instances.[103]

When policy gives direction, it becomes easier for informal mechanisms that make markets impenetrable to function. Sometimes the intent of policy is very explicit: the software development law that MITI proposed but finally withdrew, the new satellite development policies, and the deregulation of NTT without permitting real access to foreign producers are obvious examples. There are market "openings," sometimes autonomously and sometimes under intense international pressure, but they often have the feel to outsiders of tactical repositionings, not a restructuring of the system itself to permit access.

It is difficult to judge the nature of the changes. Consider capital market liberalization. There was a fear that capital market liberalization would open the Japanese market to foreign access through takeovers which would most likely be hostile. As liberalizarion proceeded, a complex network of cross ownership arrangements were constructed, with the encouragement of the government. Thus the notion that some "natural features" of the market impede access and are therefore not elements of government policy clouds the reality that the structure itself is often a choice made by or facilitated by government. Okimoto's work reveals this.[104]

Our conclusion is that real and effective protection continues both through business practice and government policy. The two are often intertangled. As we have already noted, as liberalization proceeded in the capital market, ownership holdings were reshuffled to limit the possibility of disruption through foreign takeover.

In microelectronics the absolutely steady level of foreign sales from eras in which American firms held absolute advantages through periods in which Japanese firms had surged into the lead in many products and technologies makes the observer doubt that purely market forces are at work. Of course the president of NEC has now argued that the market is wide open and that closure is the result of American inabilities to work hard to make sales. Such public remarks have to be balanced against private comments from Japanese business and government sources that the markets are essentially closed and insistence that in the case of supercomputers Japan will not buy any from the United States.

The sense of chosen closure reasserts itself in other advanced sectors such as biotechnology. Here, government policy choice stands out clearly. One Japanese observer concluded that "Japanese bureaucrats and scientists intend to use Japanese hardware for Japanese sequencing efforts, even if U.S. machines are currently available."[105] Indeed, substantial government investments are being made to support the development of Japanese equipment that will compete with American products that are currently doing well in the Japanese market. Even more important in the biotechnology sector than the effort to develop Japanese hardware to displace foreign product are practices concerning repository and data banks for gene and culture information. Internationally open nonprofit institutions are presently developing to assure genetic collections and genetic data. In Japan joint programs, as always involving a set of dominant firms in the sector, are emerging. Critically there is every impression that unique national repositories and data banks are meant to be alternatives to international ones. If these data banks are supported heavily by corporate funds, will they be open to smaller Japanese firms, let alone foreign companies? One key here will be whether Japan attempts to develop unique and closed depositories and data bases. A second is where Japanese efforts to commercialize products are situated.[106]

To judge the pattern of liberalization we must consider whether the bands of developmental policy predicted exist. To do so we consider two sets of policies: those intended to promote "sunrise" industries and those for "sunset" industries. To assess whether a broader opening in the Japanese market is at work or whether in the loosening of control there is a continued developmental bias, we also examine recent policies to alter the dynamics of the financial system. It is these policies, both in general and in their constituent elements, that have created the most intense trade controversy.

Political forces have affected and will continue to affect the evolution of Japan's liberalization over time. The process of adjusting the developmental strategy or of opening domestic markets cannot be simple or straightforward in Japan, because international liberalization directly affects Japanese politics, not least in the form of interministerial struggles over policy direction and responsibility. International liberalization inevitably means a change in traditional internal policy practices. Such changes are simultaneously promoted and resisted by different interests in Japan. Conflict among interest groups affects the extent, pace and pattern of liberalization in the economy.

Policies for "Sunrise" Industries

Japanese policy is committed to developing the industries of the future, the sunrise industries. It has avowed a determination to shift the country's industrial structure away from the base of heavy and chemical industries and complex manufacturing toward knowledge-intensive industries.[107] The issue is whether the pattern of protection and promotion that characterized the whole economy at an earlier date continues in the sunrise industries. We are not going to review the entire pattern of policy in the range of high-technology sectors. Rather we want simply to show enough evidence of continued promotion and protection to make convincing our assertion that the dynamics of expansion and import substitution are still at work and are still sought through policy.

Government efforts to develop each of the important new technology areas—electronics, new materials, and biotechnology—are solidly in place in Japan. The range of policies used to promote emerging activities includes formal government legislation and pronouncements, measures to capitalize on certain features of the domestic market structure for competitive gain, collaborative R&D

measures, subsidies, and tax incentives, and finally, measures to foster industry rationalization, and the creation of cartels in designated
sectors.

Policy development often begins with a vision. Those formulated
by MITI are most publicized in the West, but other agencies are involved as well. MITI's visions (*bijon*) are merely government-sponsored studies that present a coherent but purposely sketchy outline
of likely future trends. These have served not only as public relations ventures intended to draw attention to concerns the government deems significant but also as tools for building a genuine consensus of expectations among groups most directly concerned with
the problem at hand.[108] Once a political consensus has been reached,
the formal legislation enacted to give teeth to those visions and policy statements follows. The case of Japan's computer industries
demonstrates that these visions do not remain mere pronouncements
once a broad consensus has been reached. In a series of three laws—
the Law on Extraordinary Measures for the Promotion of Electronic
Industries and the Machinery Industry (June 1957), the Law on
Extraordinary Measures for the Promotion of Electronics and the
Machinery Industry (April 1971), and the Law on Extraordinary
Measures for the Promotion of Specific Machinery and Information
Industry (June 1978)—the computer industry received the benefits
of being named a "strategic industry" in Japan's policy scheme.[109]

The policy instruments accomplish several purposes. Public and
private collaborative R&D measures encourage the diffusion as well
as the development of technology among domestic producers.[110]
There are a variety of private as well as public joint R&D programs
in Japan. A number are organized within particular industrial groups
and involve vertical links, applications of a technology developed by
one producer to the products of another. Samuels estimates these
joint efforts to be four-fifths of the total.[111] Others are in fact horizontal, linking competing producers in research efforts required to
reach the product stage. Joint efforts are rarely stable, reflecting
shifting needs, market, and technological positions of the firms.
Equally, they are simply a fraction of research done in Japan, the
bulk being proprietary single-firm undertakings. They are no less
effective for that.

Government-sponsored programs are often developed through
trade associations and in careful collaboration with potential part-

ners. One mechanism for such efforts is the Engineering Research Association established by the government; another is the action of public/private firms such as NTT. The relations between government agencies in these efforts is as often competitive as collaborative.

Government R&D funds for selected technologies serve to reduce risk, initiate competition, and signal enduring government interest. While the pool of government funds is not in itself large enough to support corporate programs, it can serve to induce other investments, and corporate commitments. Samuels argues that it merely reconfirms industry commitments; but in our judgment while the projects conform to industry's conception of their needs, the boldest of the efforts would not be undertaken without government action. Solving the problems of collective action without a leader would be difficult. Collaborative public and private R&D efforts have borne fruit for the Japanese. A noteworthy instance of this was the research programs of the very-large-scale integrated circuit (VLSI) Technology Research Association created by MITI and NTT in 1976. Under the direction of MITI and NTT (the government telecommunications monopoly), and with the cooperation of Japan's largest private producers, the VLSI projects assisted Japanese firms in besting their U.S. merchant competitors to move quickly to introduce 64K random access memory for computers and to move into volume production.[112] Samuels nicely summarizes MITI's role, referring to its three functions: first, as cheerleader vis-à-vis the Ministry of Finance to raise funds; second, as champion with the Fair Trade Commission to avoid interference in joint undertakings; and third, as coordinator playing a role of neutral, credible, and authoritative broker to encourage cooperation.[113]

Bold new joint development efforts in cutting-edge technologies could not emerge and mature quickly and frequently without government creating a mechanism for collective action. It also seems credible that the path of private research and technological development would be different in the absence of these collaborative programs. Several new collaborative technology development programs have been initiated in the last few years. The program objectives are startlingly, ambitious, and the funds involved are staggering in their magnitude. They represent an important shift. The shift is away from programs intended to absorb and diffuse foreign technologies to those intended to create new technological advance.[114] These programs may prove critical in areas as diverse as human genetyping, where funds are being spent to create a biotechnology breakthrough, and microelectronics.[115] In microelectronics, for example, the limit of optical lithography has probably been revealed. MITI is now financing a new collaborative investment in x-ray lithography. The long-term costs of this one investment are beyond the capacities of even the largest American companies such as AT&T. IBM's active support for the joint semiconductor manufacturing effort, Sematech, grows from its genuine concern with the industrial infrastructure of the electronics industries.[116] Okimoto draws some clear conclusions about the continuing and important effects of these Japanese programs.[117] His work emphasizes the information technology sectors, but significant programs in biotechnology and new materials continue as well. Crucial in each of these cases, we might add, will be the question of foreign research and commercial access to the results and activities.

Government procurement has also served to develop and to diffuse technology. In this regard, the role of NTT as "creative first user," much as the U.S. Department of Defense was in the early history of the microelectronics industry in the United States is illustrative of the significance of government procurement in Japanese industrial policy. In addition to controlling the country's telephone and telegraph networks, NTT monopolized all common carrier network transmission in Japan (including data transmission), offers data processing time-sharing services, licenses all communications, and runs very advanced R&D and systems-engineering laboratories in all of these areas.[118]

> Importantly, NTT is a procurer of systems in these areas from Japan's major electronics companies. NTT's policies, like the policies of some Western-European countries, encourage domestic suppliers and severely restrict the purchase of imported telephone equipment. In the words of one observer: "Technical specifications are based on design rather than performance and are written to favor the specific products of a small group of local suppliers known as the "NTT Family." Because NTT does not have a manufacturing subsidiary (such as Western Electric), it obtains virtually all of its equipment for the exchange and transmission markets from members of this family of suppliers. NTT has never permitted foreign firms to join this family. NTT's practices of procuring equipment from a relatively small group of trusted suppliers is not unusual, because most Western European phone systems are supplied in the same way. However, the practice of excluding foreign firms, even foreign firms with local subsidiaries, is unusual.[119]

The fact that even such long-established and locally based but foreign-owned firms as IBM Japan were excluded catapulted the issue of government procurement in Japan into the trade debate arena. Moreover, as was the case with the VLSI program, the practice of distributing patents, at least initially, only to participating companies (all of which were, of course, in the "family") through a research association, is an irritant to Japan's trading partners. Since the signing of the U.S.-Japan Agreement on NTT procurement, there has been a steady increase in NTT's procurement from American firms. However, it should be noted that there is a wide gap between the performance of foreign firms in the private market (sales to nongovernmental sectors) and their performance in the governmental market (sales to various government agencies, including NTT).

The question should be posed differently. There are three distinct national strategies for managing the emergence of new telecommunications infrastructure. The United States has deregulated—that is, left market competition to shape the basics of the public infrastructure. The European countries with the debatable exception of Britain have retained a traditional utility structure of regulation. Japan has "reregulated" with a developmental objective—that is, it is changing the terms of regulation both to provoke competition as a means of assuring rapid diffusion and product development and to retain public control over the nature of the system as a whole.[120] Telecommunications policy is still evolving, and the regulatory strategy is an issue of intense political conflict (see Chapter 5).[121] But NTT will remain the centerpiece of the telecommunications system for two reasons. First, its existing networks and technology provide massive advantages. Second, the acknowledged responsibility of providing universal service will limit the extent of competition the Ministry of Posts and Telecommunications can permit.[122] In any case there is little doubt that the regulation of services will serve as a means to drive the continued evolution of the equipment sector.

The use of standards to structure and channel competition is a third crucial but little explored instrument of developmental policy. Common operating standards, such as those adopted in personal computers and established in machine tools by Fujitsu Fanuc's domination of the controller market. Where such standards exist, competition is channeled away from a struggle about basic operating parameters and into products with different applications. Indeed, if the government's encouragement of standards is intentional promotion (and we cannot judge clearly whether it is), it is an extremely clever use of market forces. The fact that standards shape competition is of international concern. The international issue is how the standards are set. Product standards, often developed within MITI structure councils, serve to define the lines of an industry's evolution. American firms note that shortly after the formal promulgation of standards, products flood the market so quickly that they would seem to have been in development during the processes of adopting standards. Samuels has termed this "preemptive collaboration." Thus the Japanese decision to include foreigners in structure-council deliberations is quite important.

The standard setting mechanisms raise a more general problem troubling U.S.-Japanese relations. The "transparency" issue has come to represent a thorn in the side of U.S.-Japanese trade relations. Trade negotiators from the United States have repeatedly charged that the American policymaking system is much more transparent than the Japanese system and that it is far easier for Japanese officials to know what is going on in Washington and to influence the course of events than it is for any foreigner to have an impact on Japan's highly private, "opaque" processes of decisionmaking. For this reason, during January 1984, the then U.S. Undersecretary of Commerce for International Trade, Lionel Olmer, succeeded in extracting concessions from the Japanese allowing U.S. representatives access to and permission to address meetings of MITI's Industrial Structure Council. It was, he suggested, merely a matter of reciprocity, no different from the ease with which Japanese and other foreigners can lobby the U.S. government. While there was optimism expressed at the time over Olmer's achievement, there is substantial concern that the concessions have produced no worthwhile results. For instance, even if U.S. representatives are allowed to sit in on the Council's deliberation sessions, they do not have means to influence the decisions of its sponsoring ministry, not to mention other ministries concerned with a particular issue, or the trade associations of an industry affected by a council recommendation. Thus, although the transparency issue lies submerged, it may not be long forgotten.[123] Some believe that the "Japanese have simply called our bluff, that we do not have Japanese language speakers with policy expertise who can make the most of opportunities or force new ones."[124]

Subsidies and tax incentives are a fourth category of promotional policies. Actually, the term *subsidy*, as applied to Japanese industrial policy is something of a misnomer. More precisely, subsidies are usually either grants that take the form of conditional loans (*hojokin*) or government-contracted work, that takes the form of consignment payments (*itakuhi*).[125] Here the case of government subsidies to Japan's machine tool industry, a case that gained notoriety in this country because of the petition for relief filed by Houdaille Industries, provides an interesting example.[126] In this case the U.S. industry contends that subsidies gave an unfair advantage to Japanese producers. The evidence suggests that the subsidies were designed to support the diffusion of machine tools to Japanese users. The funds serve, in one sense, to create a market for automated production equipment by encouraging use, but equally it encourages the transformation of traditional small and medium-sized firms.

Also, certain measures within Japan's corporate tax system are used to target specific industrial policy objectives. For example, the pattern of special depreciation measures tends to be biased toward manufacturing in general, and the measures are purposely geared to stimulate markets for types of goods for which the government would like to see greater domestic production.[127] Aircraft is the most recent instance. The market failure of Japan's first entry into the commercial aircraft business saw the government writing off nearly $100 million in loans. Its second entry will be jointly financed by the government and a group of firms in a venture with Boeing. These loans lower and diffuse the risk of new ventures.[128]

Fifth, control of the domestic market is still managed. The mechanism are often less overt, but nonetheless the Japanese government is able to exert significant influence over foreign participation in Japan. Take the case of joint ventures. The government divides them into three types: those that can receive automatic authorization, those requiring only limited examination, and those which require formal approval. The distinction depends on how critical the industry is in the opinion of the government. "Automatic approval may be denied if the Japanese partner lacks experience in the business, if the Japanese investor is required to transfer capital assets to the joint venture, or if the joint venture involves foreign capital participation in the Japanese firm. Even where authorization is automatic, foreign firms are often subjected to long delays and have no recourse if a joint venture application is denied."[129] Export licenses are required, which limits the amount of technology a U.S. licensor can obtain in the deal. How often these controls are used is not clear, but they remain in place and express intent of policy.

Finally, policies to promote industry rationalization and to create cartels in designated industries represent a sixth broad category of measures designed to nurture promising new industries. In a 1973 policy statement issued by the Japan Economic Planning Agency, the importance of industry rationalization in Japan's future growth industries is clearly articulated:

> At the same time as all industries should be induced to become knowledge-intensive through (1) promoting a higher degree of processing and higher product quality, (2) even when the finished product remains the same, attempting to make the processes of its production and distribution information-intensive, labor-saving, and pollution-free, and (3) trying to systematize vertically several industries from material procurement to processing and distribution or to establish horizontal systems unifying diverse functions.[130]

The Japanese government has encouraged the creation of cartels in designated industries, such as machine tools, in order to avoid the pitfalls of excess competition. It is believed by many that the Japanese government aids its chosen cartels by its lax enforcement of Japan's Law Concerning Prohibition of Private Monopoly and Maintenace of Fair Trade (the Anti-Monopoly law).[131]

The intent of the policies, to create advantage in advanced technology sectors, is clear. These cartels may be more interesting for what they say about the intent of policy than about its direct effects. Whatever the intent of the policies to rationalize industries, they have not always achieved their stated purpose.[132] In the automobile sector, efforts at rationalization were blocked by the stubborn refusal of the smaller companies to follow government plans. In the machine tool industry, a series of plans to force concentration and product controls collapsed.[133] More may be at issue than simply intent, even when the policies do not achieve their state effects. For the most part, the issue is simply posed as whether the policy achieved its stated goals. Whether, and how, policies altered market structure or behavior is seldom examined.

In sum, observing a range of advanced technological areas in information technologies and biotechnologies leads to the conclusion that the mechanisms of market closure that were critical in earlier phases of Japanese growth will operate in this new era. In sunrise sectors the mechanisms of a developmental strategy clearly exist and the will to use them is continually restated.

Policy for Sunset Industries: Measures to Ease the Transition

The rapid growth of the Japanese economy before 1973 was due in part to a massive shift of resources from less efficient sectors into new and more efficient sectors.[134] After the oil crisis and the worldwide recession that ensued, Japan had to begin to resist the encroachment of new competitors into its markets, countries trying to follow Japan up the development ladder. Are industrial adjustment efforts in Japan moving in the direction of international economic equilibrium and the redistribution of comparative advantage? After "structural adjustment" the shares of the export market and the domestic market of firms in Japan's declining industries are not likely to decrease appreciably and, thus, foreign competitors in the relevant Japanese markets may not increase their market share to any great degree. For example, South Korea's shipbuilding orders tend to increase, not at the expense of Japan's market share, but of the Europeans' share! With the exception of a relatively few items (such as polyvinyl chloride and polyethylene), competing products from foreign producers (such as aluminum ingots, urea, cardboard and napthon) are not making great headway in the Japanese market.[135]

Indeed, it appears that the intent in declining industries (whether export or import oriented) is often to recapture competitive position, not simply to scale down capacity. Policy combines domestic and trade policy in ways reminiscent of traditional developmental policies. The domestic market, the evidence suggests, is effectively quite closed in many sunset industries. The intent seems to be to create time and market space so that domestic firms have the opportunity to adjust.[136] Often in sectors where there is worldwide overcapacity, or where the advanced countries have all lost advantage to the next tier of competitors, the Japanese market has not been successfully penetrated. Import penetration ratios have changed little even in the depressed industries in Japan while they have increased to a significant extent in the other major industrial countries, and production in many industries with worldwide overcapacity such as chemicals, iron and steel, nonferrous metals, and textiles has grown more rapidly in Japan than in most of these countries. Significantly, in the aluminum industry, where the import penetration ratio has increased, offshore subsidiaries of Japanese firms have been the source of growing imports.[137]

The issue of structural adjustment in Japan became significant only in the 1970s, and its rise to salience was the result of four factors: higher costs of energy and raw materials; slower world growth and hence stagnant demand for some traditional Japanese exports; competition from the newly industrializing countries (NICs); and the higher value of the yen. Higher costs of energy and raw materials had a tremendous impact on import-competing industries such as petrochemicals. Slower growth and stagnant demand sent negative reverberations throughout Japan's shipbuilding industry, and the rise of the NICs contributed to the relative decline of low-value-added industries, such as textiles, which for the most part had been in the shadow of technology-intensive and capital-intensive industries since the 1960s. Meanwhile, a higher priced yen had the effect of drastically altering the terms of trade by exerting pressure on all of Japan's export-oriented industries.

According to MITI, Japan has some eleven structurally depressed industries—industries that are depressed not in terms of profit rates but in terms of their viability as demonstrated in their production and market conditions. Some characteristics of these troubled industries include uncontrollable costs of production, dependence on government aid, lack of product diversification, price inelasticity, export dependence, a marked gap between supply and demand, a high degree of competition, and importance for national security. The eleven industries classified as structurally depressed are textiles, sugar refining, corrugated cardboard, chemical fertilizers, vinyl chloride, open-hearth and electric-furnace steel, aluminum refining, shipbuilding, plywood, and shipping.[138] A common denominator among these industries is a high rate of capacity and little possibility of upturn even in times of economic recovery.

Japan's policy for structural adjustment in these industries was embodied primarily in a 1978 law that was granted a five-year extension in 1983.[139] Prior to the enactment of this law, titled the Temporary Law for Structural Improvement of Specific Industries, several temporary measures were undertaken to confront the problems caused by the severe recession of 1973–76, which had a chilling effect on those eleven declining industries. For example, between

1973 and 1977, while the overall rate of capacity use was lower in Japan than in America, the rates of the eleven declining industries were even lower than the average for Japanese industries. The bankruptcy rate was, of course, much higher than average. During those years, a series of recession cartels were installed to cut production and raise prices. In addition, for industries dominated by small enterprises, such as textiles and plywoods, other ameliorative programs were implemented under the rubric of the Small Industry Switchover Act (1976–80), which, for example, created a special fund for low-interest loans.

The 1978 law was basically a device to provide some public assistance in exchange for an industry's commitment to reduce capacity (the 1983 law had an additional function, namely to promote cooperation in business operation). To qualify for this assistance, an industry has to apply for the designation "structurally depressed industry" by demonstrating that most firms in the industry are in dire financial condition, with severe surplus capacity, and agreement must be reached that some capacity scrapping is necessary. After consultation with labor and management, the ministry concerned will then draft a stabilization plan. The main purpose of the operation, of course, is to cut capacity. The major incentive is provided by the Credit Fund (a fund with an ¥8 billion contribution from the government, specifically the Japan Development Bank, and ¥2 billion from private companies to be used to guarantee the part of the loan that holds scrapped equipment as collateral). Although there are variations among industries, in most cases the reduction in capacity follows the principle of "proportional cuts"; in other words all enterprises in an industry cut the same or a similar percentage of production capacity.

Coordinated capacity reduction is not the whole story, for the government has introduced an array of additional industry-specific measures to facilitate structural transformation. In the textile industry, for example, arrangements for the direct purchase of excess capacity have long existed, and in two cases (silk and silk products from China and South Korea) import quotas have actually been set. (It is widely assumed by exporters to Japan that some sort of tacit agreement among Japanese importers serves to erect "informal" import quotas for other categories of foreign textiles.)

In the aluminum refining industry, to give another example, the policy package includes a dual tariff structure (a small quantity of imports almost or entirely duty free, and additional quantities of imports at a higher tariff rate) imposed on the importers of aluminum ingots, the transfer of almost half of the import duty revenue to an industry fund for aluminum smelters, and a variety of subsidies (for R&D in aluminum smelting, for energy-conserving electric power rates, and for lower tax rates for firms converting their energy base). Also note that the basic quantity of free or almost tariff-free imports is, incidentally, equivalent to the amount of domestic capacity reduction in the stabilization plan! Moreover, aluminum ingots produced by Japanese-owned smelters overseas are exempt from the limitations of the tariff system.[140] In the shipbuilding industry, the Japanese government scrapped its ships ahead of schedule, purchased excess ships from the domestic industry, and used them as foreign aid items, and converted some ships into floating storage facilities for certain strategic materials (chiefly crude petroleum). In short, the government increased its demand to offset declining demand for ships from commercial users.[141]

It should be noted that the government has also introduced several important horizontal policies, policies that are not clearly industry-specific, intended to address the problems caused by declining industries. These include special funds, programs for small and medium-sized enterprises, and measures tailored to aid depressed communities. Employment assistance is designed to encourage the retraining of workers at the factory level and to shore up assistance with the commitment to retraining. Assistance to small and medium enterprises is geared to promoting mergers and switchovers. Community assistance measures are twofold: incentives are provided to any new industries that are willing to invest in depressed areas, and government investment in the infrastructure of these areas also serves to attract new industries.

Cartel action and a mix of sector specific and general support policies are nothing new in the Japanese system. However, the objective of their policy mix is different in sunset industries than in the sunrise ones. In the former, policy is intended to provide a breathing space during and after which the inefficient firms within a structurally depressed industry will be eased out, while those that are more efficient will be preserved and strengthened. The question that concerns us here is not whether Japan's policies toward its declining industries have realized these objectives, although there is ample reason and evidence to think that in any simple sense they have not.[142] Indeed, there is evidence that capacity reduction has not been more rapid in the designated declining sectors than in others. The cartels appear to be mechanisms for managed reduction in oligopolistic sectors.[143]

Our concern is the effect on foreign access to the Japanese market of the adjustment programs, whether they have served to protect domestic producers in these industries, shifting more of the burden of adjustment to Japan's trading partners.

The Japanese market, we have already seen, is less permeable to exports from developing countries than the markets of the other advanced industrial countries. Even in the United States, where orderly marketing agreements restrict access to the U.S. market in many sectors, import penetration is still substantial. In steel, autos, and textiles, for example, imports account for more than 20 percent of the market. Overall, the penetration by the NICs in the American market is several times that in the Japanese market. The penetration by the NICs in manufactured goods into the United States is 1.8 times as large in the United States as in Japan (see Table 3–1).[144] The penetration in sectors where American firms have lost advantage in world markets compared with those where Japanese firms have lost advantage in world markets is even higher.[145] Similarly, the United States has in recent years absorbed roughly two-thirds of manufactured exports from the newly industrializing countries, while Japan has absorbed 7 percent of such exports.[146]

The real difference between Japan and the other advanced industrial countries is at what level of import penetration the domestic market is sealed or protected. Here the figures show the Japanese market to be closed off at very low levels of import penetration. One set of market sealants lies in business practices. Long-term business relationships, what Ronald Dore calls "relational contracting," serve to slow or impede shifts provoked by price changes in the market.[147] Purchasing relations do not change immediately in response to changes in market prices. Consequently suppliers have time to adjust. Thus, for example, in the textile industry adjustments in both production costs and product quality were provoked by pressure from importers. Moreover, given the role of trading and distribution companies in Japan, buyers can maintain long-term control of the market by helping their traditional suppliers adjust. As Dore puts it, there is a "'natural immunity', making official protection unnecessary, of industries formed by a dense web of 'relational contracting' between firms specializing in different parts of the production process, or between manufacturers and trading companies, between trading companies and retailers."[148] Dore carefully notes that this 'natural immunity' does not last for ever, but that there is a substantial lag and the lag accounts for the slow response of the Japanese economy to import price differential.

Official restrictions, including the adjustment cartels, do exist and do matter. Recall that in the aluminum industry real adjustments did occur in the face of the increases in energy costs that put the domestic producers at an absolute cost disadvantage. Domestic production fell, and quickly, from a high of 1,188,197 metric tons in 1977 to 255,900 metric tons in 1983.[149] The adjustment, however, did not result in a radical increase in imports. The domestic industry used breathing space to retreat to offshore production. The move offshore was facilitated both by sharing revenues collected from the special tariff with the industry and by permitting Japanese firms to import duty free. Imports rose but non-Japanese firms continued to have trouble entering the market. Here continued national control of supply proved both an objective and outcome of policy. Where official policy aims at restructuring to retard imports and finance adjustment, then longer term business relationships are likely to prove more enduring. We cannot, once again, unbundle policy and business practice.

TRADE AND DEVELOPMENT IN JAPAN: A SUMMARY

Developmental policy has affected the pattern of Japanese trade in two interconnected ways: import substitution and production innovation. Import substitution created circumstances in which innovation took place and allowed maximum advantage to be harvested from such innovations.

The developmental policy itself was a clear political choice. It affected the dynamics of the market and generated a new production paradigm. During the process of industrial catch-up, the rapid expansion of demand and the continuous borrowing of technology from foreign companies that could not implant themselves in the Japanese market created learning-curve effects in the Japanese firms that were expanding behind protected walls. The sectors, moreover, had reached maturity elsewhere and consequently the learning could not be easily replicated let alone captured outside Japan. Firms were pressed to capture market share because they faced conditions of declining cost curves. In doing so they generated production innovations that accumulated into distinctive strategies, into virtually a new production paradigm.

The pattern of import substitution in the manufacturing sector does not have a purely economic explanation. It cannot be explained by exchange rates or attributed solely to the competitive advantages of Japanese firms and their distinctive geographic location. Policies of discrimination against foreign producers and promotion of domestic ones played a critical role. The purpose of policy was domestic development, and it grew out of a conviction that comparative advantage can be created by intentional government policy.

The system of controlled competition permitted the government to pursue a strategy of creating enduring advantage for national producers in international markets. Production technologies and factor availabilities, unlike mountains, are not immutable features of a nation's economic topography. There are only a few industrial sectors such as coal or oil in which comparative advantage is given in the form of fixed natural resource availability, and even here production and transportation facilities may alter a seemingly self-evident calculus. Japanese transportation policy gave its basic industries a cost advantage in importing raw materials. In most sectors, particularly the manufacturing sectors that dominate the production and trade of advanced industrial countries, comparative advantage is partly the product of national economic policies. Such policies in Japan, for example, have influenced the accumulation of physical capital, the pace of research and development, and the development of labor skills and education, all of which underlie the "exogenous" factor "endowments" and production technologies dear to classical theory.

For twenty-five years after World War II, Japanese markets were selectively closed to foreigners while the government actively promoted the expansion of sectors considered critical to its economy. There has been a real asymmetry in trade relations between Japan and the United States, and this in turn affected the international strategies of corporations in both countries. For Japanese firms the American market, which was easily accessible, was the single most important export market and in many sectors a strategically critical market. By contrast, American firms found the Japanese market closed. Moreover, the closed Japanese market was not viewed by American producers as a strategically important or vital export market through the mid-1970s. At most the Japanese market was important for tactical gains and marginal increases in profit. Struggling against trade and direct investment barriers was not worthwhile for most companies. Of course, as Japan emerged as a powerful industrial rival, many American firms found themselves without the experience and infrastructure required to compete in Japan. Consequently, they were cut off from a growing market, evolving technologies, and an understanding of the strategies of their now powerful rivals. While Japanese firms entrenched themselves in the American market and developed expertise in doing business here, American firms were not allowed to build a position or expertise in the Japanese market. Now that firms from the two nations are meeting in international competition, this legacy matters. American firms must now learn in a hurry to compete in Japan against very strong competitors. Past discrimination remains an element in today's competition. Without Japan's developmental policies, including protection of its domestic market, the shape of industries from automobiles through electronics would be very different.

Developmental policy continues to ease the transition of declining sectors and to promote the expansion of new industries. In other words, an active interventionist developmental strategy continues in sectors in which the Japanese government would like to create advantage or those in which industry has lost advantage in world markets. In these sectors arrangements that have given structural advantages to the Japanese in their home markets, and often in international markets, have endured. The capacity to resist foreign competitors in crucial sectors remains, even though there is a marked reduction in the government's ability to control the domestic economy. The high-technology sectors (microelectronics, machine tools, computers, and telecommunications) are not open to full foreign competition. Indeed, the pattern of policies, public remarks, and private statements suggests that restrictions on the ability of foreign firms to develop a permanent presence in the Japanese market have been removed where Japanese firms have already achieved a dominant position at home and a strong often dominant position abroad or where the Japanese government does not have explicit developmental objectives, as in some services. In other words restrictions have been removed when they have not mattered.

The difficulty of strong foreign firms to find products and mechanisms to establish an enduring presence in the Japanese market despite their growing efforts and attention suggests mechanisms of continuing closure be they formal or informal. Markets are open to exports from abroad where Japanese firms continue to need foreign technology. However, there is often very rapid import substitution of domestic for foreign products as Japanese producers enter the market. Part of that import substitution reflects market conditions and the domestic strengths of Japanese firms. Part of the process of import substitution appears to be a product of collective choice, both governmental and private.

Overall, the evidence presented here supports our hypothesis that a moving band of protectionism exists and developmental policy continues. Restrictions in sectors in which Japanese firms are established at home and abroad have been loosened. But they are effectively maintained and combined with selective promotion policies in important emerging and declining sectors.

NOTES

1. There are of course exceptions. Both Zysman and Tyson have in different national contexts addressed these issues. See, for example, John Zysman, *Governments, Markets, and Growth* (Ithaca, N.Y.: Cornell University Press, 1983); and Laura Tyson, *The Yugoslav Economy and Its Performance in the 1970's* (Berkeley, Calif.: Institute of International Studies, 1980).

2. The notion of strong/weak state is widely used in political science. In political economy, it is best defined in Stephen Krasner, "U.S. Commercial and Monetary Policy: Unraveling the Paradox of External Strength and Internal Weakness," in Peter Katzenstein, ed., *Between Power and Plenty: Foreign Economic Policies of Advanced Industrial States* (Madison: University of Wisconsin Press, 1978). State-led growth and the developmental state are found in work by Zysman, *Governments, Markets, and Growth* and Chalmers Johnson, *MITI and the Japanese Miracle* (Stanford, Calif.: Stanford University Press, 1982); the term is introduced on p. 17. The corporatism debate was reintroduced by Schmitter and best explained by Suzanne Berger in *Organizing Interests in Western Europe: Pluralism, Corporatism, and the Transformation of Politics* (New York, N.Y.: Cambridge University Press, 1981). Policy compacts is a notion developed by Richard Samuels in his recent book, *The Business of the Japanese: Energy Markets in Comparative and Historical Perspective* (Ithaca, N.Y.: Cornell University Press, 1987).

3. See, for example, Thomas C. Smith, *Political Change and Industrial Development in Japan: Government Enterprise, 1868-1880* (Stanford, Calif.: Stanford University Press, 1954); William W. Lockwood, *The Economic Development of Japan: Growth and Structural Change, 1868-1938* (Princeton, N.J.: Princeton University Press, 1965); Kazuki Ohkawa and Henry Rosovsky, *Japanese Economic Growth: Trend Acceleration in the Twentieth Century* (Stanford, Calif.: Stanford University Press, 1973).

4. Bruce Cumings makes this argument in "The Origins and Development of the Northeast Asian Political Economy: Industrial Sectors, Product Cycles, and Political Consequences," in Frederick Deyo, ed., *The Political Economy of New Asian Industrialism* (Ithaca, N.Y.: Cornell University Press, 1987).

5. See, for example, T. J. Pempel, *Policy and Politics in Japan: Creative Conservatism* (Philadelphia: Temple University Press, 1982), p. 96; Johnson, *MITI and the Japanese Miracle*, pp. 11-14; R. P. Dore, "Industrial Relations in Japan and Elsewhere," in Albert M. Craig, ed., *Japan: A Comparative View* (Princeton, N.J.: Princeton University Press, 1979), p. 327. Soloman Levine and Taira Doji, "Interpreting Industrial Conflict: The Case of Japan," in Benjamin Martin and Everett M. Kassolow, eds., *Labor Relations in Advanced Industrialized Societies: Issues and Problems* (Washington, D.C.: Carnegie Endowment for International Peace, 1980).

6. Much of this discussion is drawn from the paper by Sasaki Nobuhiko in a seminar for Zysman in the spring of 1986.

7. The best study of the Japanese bureaucracy in development policy is Johnson, *MITI and the Japanese Miracle*.

8. The parallel of course is to France. See, for example, Zysman, *Governments, Markets, and Growth*.

9. Tsuruta Toshimasa, *Sengo Nihon no Sangyo Seisaku* (Japanese Industrial Policies in the Post War Period), (Tokyo: Nihon Keizai: Shimbunsha, 1987), pp. 24-30. Professor Arisawa Hiromi at the University of Tokyo defended the "developmentalism" position, and Professor Nakayama Ichiro at Hitosubashi University defended tradeism.

10. Ibid., p. 31, n. 16.

11. Sasaki, cited in note 6 above.

12. Ibid.; Tsuruta, *Sengo Nihon no Sangyo Seisaku*, pp. 39-40, and Johnson, *MITI and the Japanese Miracle*, p. 201.

13. Shinohara Miyohei, ed., *Sangyo Kozo* (Industrial Structure) (Tokyo: Shunju-sha, 1959), pp. 77-80; and Shinohara Miyohei, *Nihon Kezai no Jukogyo-ka* (Heavy Industrialization of Japanese Economy) (Tokyo: Shunju-sha, 1964), pp. 209-25.

14. Murukami Yasusuki, "Shin Chukan Taishu no Jidai" (The Age of the New Middle Mass), 1984, pp. 115-16.

15. Ibid.

16. Sasaki, cited in note 6 above.

17. T. J. Pempel, "Japanese Foreign Economic Policy: The Domestic Bases for International Behavior," in Katzenstein, ed., *Between Power and Plenty*, p. 139. Pempel's formulation remains the best available.

18. Johnson, *MITI and the Japanese Miracle.*

19. Goto Akira and Wakasugi Ryohei, "Gisyuto Seisaku" (Technology Policy) in Komiya Ryutaro, Okuno Masanori, Suzumura Kotaro, *Japan's Industrial Policy* (Tokyo: Tokyo University Press, 1984), pp. 159–80. Thanks to Yamada Taka for finding these data.

20. Pempel, "Japanese Foreign Economic Policy."

21. Zysman, *Governments, Markets, and Growth*, p. 240.

22. Murakami Yasusuke, "Toward a Sociocultural Explanation of Japan's Economic Performance," in Yamamura Kozo, ed., *Policy and Trade Issues of the Japanese Economy: American and Japanese Perspectives* (Seattle: University of Washington Press, 1982), pp. 3–46.

23. Ibid.

24. Ibid.

25. This notion has emerged into contemporary social science parlance through Barrington Moore's *Social Origins of Democracy and Dictatorship*. The best recent use of the concept to understand the political and policy dynamics of the advanced countries in Peter Gourevitch's *Politics in Hard Times*. His argument suggests that the increasing entrenchment of political and market institutions has increased the importance of institutional structures in shaping political dynamics. See also Richard Samuels, *The Business of the Japanese.*

26. This notion is a core of Zysman's *Governments, Markets, and Growth*; the idea is developed in Chapter 2. The case this notion is applied to is one of financial systems, but the argument is more general. The more general notion is suggested in Zysman, "The French State in the International Economy," in Peter Katzenstein, ed., *Between Power and Plenty*.

27. Zysman, *Governments, Markets, and Growth*. Much of the language here is taken from pp. 78–79 of that book.

28. Okimoto develops this notion in Daniel Okimoto, "Regime Characteristics of Japanese Industrial Policy," in Hugh Patrick, ed., *Japanese High Technology Industry* (Seattle: Washington University Press, 1986).

29. The tactics of coalition building depend on the position of the various groups, partly determined by their positions in the structure of the system and the strategies they have adopted earlier. Gregg Luebbert's work is sensitive to these issues. See, for example, "Social Foundations of Political Order in Interwar Europe," *World Politics* 39 (July 1987): 449–78.

30. James Arthur Ainsco Stockwin, *Japan: Divided Politics in a Growth Economy* (London: Weidenfeld and Nicolson, 1982), p. 67.

31. Ibid.

32.   T. J. Pempel, *Policy and Politics in Japan: Creative Conservatism* (Phila-
      delphia: Temple University Press, 1982), pp. 100–109.
33.   This process is very similar to the French process. Analyses of the French
      case in fact bring insight to the Japanese story. See, for example, Zysman,
      Governments, Markets, and Growth, ch. 3; Stephen Cohen, *Modern Capi-
      talist Planning: the French Model* (Berkeley: University of California Press,
      1977).
34.   Zysman, *Government, Markets, and Growth*.
35.   Ibid.; Cohen, *Modern Capitalist Planning*.
36.   Daniel Okimoto, *Between MITI and the Market: Japanese Industrial Policy
      for High Technology* (Stanford, Calif.: Stanford University Press, forth-
      coming 1989).
37.   Johnson, *MITI and the Japanese Economic Miracle*.
38.   Ueno Hiroya, "The Conception and Evaluation of Japanese Industrial Pol-
      icy in Kasuo Sato, ed., *Industry and Business in Japan* (White Plains, N.Y.:
      Sharpe, 1980), pp. 400–407.
39.   Ibid., p. 403.
40.   Zysman, *Governments, Markets, and Growth*.
41   Yamamura Kozo, "General Trading Companies in Japan," in Hugh Patrick,
      ed., *Japanese Industrialization and Its Social Consequences* (Berkeley: Uni-
      versity of California Press, 1976).
42.   Miyasaki S., "Japanese Structure of Big Business," and Futatsugi Yusaku,
      "The Measurement of Interfirm Relationships," in Kazuo Sato, ed., *Indus-
      try and Business in Japan*, ed. (White Plains, N.Y.: Sharpe, 1980).
43.   Good studies of the role of small business include that of Yoshikawa Aki-
      hiro, "Dynamism of Japanese Entrepreneurs: Turbulence Productivity and
      Innovation" (Ph.D. dissertation, University of California, Berkeley, 1987);
      and Kodama Fumio, Yakushuji Taizo, and Hanaeda Mieko, "Structural
      Characteristics of the Japanese Automotive Supplier Relationship," work
      in progress.
44.   Okimoto, "Regime Characteristics of Japanese Industrial Policy," p. 41.
45.   Ibid., p. 45.
46.   A reading of the Japanese defense of the lawsuit brought by Zenith is a
      rich load of information.
47.   Hitachi Hiromatsu, *Denwa no Muko wa Konna Kao: Denden Kosha KDD
      no Uchimaku* (1980), as cited in *An Assessment of International Competi-
      tion in Microelectronics: The Role of Government Policy in Enhancing
      Competitiveness* (Cupertino, Calif.: Semiconductor Industry Association,
      1987).
48.   Yoshikawa Akihiro, "Turbulence in the Japanese Economy: A Schumpe-
      terian Perspective" (Paper presented at the 57th Annual Southern Eco-
      nomic Association Conference, November 22–24, 1987, Washington, D.C.).

49. Ibid.
50. Ibid.; and also see David Bennet Friedman, *The Misunderstood Miracle: Industrial Development and Political Change In Japan* (Ithaca, N.Y.: Cornell University Press, 1988).
51. Kodama et al., "Structural Characteristics of the Japanese Automotive Supplier Relationship."
52. Imai Kenichi, "Japan's Industrial Policy for High Technology Industries" (Paper presented at the conference on Japan's Industrial Policy in Comparative Perspective, March 17–19, 1984, New York).
53. Nakamura Takafusa, *The Postwar Japanese Economy* (Tokyo: University of Tokyo Press, 1981).
54. This section is adapted from Stephen Cohen and John Zysman, *Manufacturing Matters: The Myth of the Post Industrial Economy* (New York: Basic Books, 1987), and from Zysman, *Governments, Markets, and Growth.*
55. For an interesting perspective, see Murakami Yasusuke, "Toward a Sociocultural Explanation of Japan's Economic Performance," in Yamamura, ed., *Policy and Trade Issues of the Japanese Economy.*
56. Or to use Burton Klein's analysis, the Japanese have a style of continuous production innovation that compels firms to maximize dynamic flexibility. Klein, "Dynamic Competition and Productivity Advances," in R. Landau and N. Rosenberg, eds., *Positive Sum Strategy: Harnessing Technology for Economic Growth* (Washington, D.C.: National Academy Press, 1986).
57. This figure suggests the difference between a firm with fixed production technology and one in which the production technology is constantly being revised. In the first case, the firm has a concave production curve, which may change from time to time. However for extended periods the production technology and consequently the cost curve are fixed. In the second case, the technology is constantly evolving. At any moment there is a concave cost curve, but the real choices facing the firm, and the options on which the firm acts, are expressed by the long-term curve connecting several static curves. This dynamic curve is downward sloping, fundamentally altering the logic of the market dynamic.
58. Murakami and Yamamura, "A Technical Note," in Yamamura, *Policy and Trade Issues of the Japanese Economy*, pp. 115–116.
59. Yamamura Kozo, "Success That Soured: Administrative Guidance and Cartels in Japan," in Yamamura, ed., *Policy and Trade Issues of the Japanese Economy*, pp. 77–112.
60. Ibid.
61. Private conservation.
62. Two sources for the development of the Honda Corporation are Tetsuo Sakiya, *Honda Motor: The Men, The Management, The Machines* (New York: Harper & Row, 1982), and Sol Sanders, *Honda: The Man and His Machines* (Boston: Little, Brown, 1975).

63. See Klein, "Dynamic Competition," p. 85; and Friedman, *The Misunderstood Miracle.*

64. Klein, "Dynamic Competition," p. 86.

65. Andrew Sayer, "New Developments in Manufacturing," Working Paper 49, University of Sussex, Urban and Regional Studies, 1985, p. 19.

66. James C. Abegglen and George Stalk, Jr., *Kaisha: The Japanese Corporation* (New York: Basic Books, 1985), p. 80.

67. Ibid., p. 96.

68. Ibid.

69. Ibid., p. 98.

70. Johnson, *MITI and the Japanese Miracle* is the best available history of the politics of postwar Japanese development.

71. Sayer, "New Developments in Manufacturing," p. 20.

72. David B. Friedman, "Beyond the Age of Ford: The Strategic Basis of Japanese Success in Automobiles," in John Zysman and Laura Tyson, eds., *American Industry in International Competition: Government Policies and Corporate Strategies* (Ithaca, N.Y.: Cornell University Press, 1983), ch. 7. See also Abegglen and Stalk, *Kaisha.*

73. Sayer, "New Developments in Manufacturing."

74. Bella Balassa, "Japanese Trade Policies," unpublished paper prepared for the Institute for International Economics; and Stephen Krasner, *Asymmetries in Japanese-American Trade: The Case for Specific Reciprocity* (Berkeley, Calif.: Institute for International Studies, 1987).

75. Ibid.

76. Balassa, "Japanese Trade Policies," p. 12.

77. Krasner, *Asymmetries in Japanese-American Trade*, p. 22.

78. Ibid., p. 24.

79. Ibid., pp. 26-27.

80. Balassa, "Japanese Trade Policies," pp. 8-11.

81. Balassa, "Japanese Trade Policies," p. 13. The share of the developing countries in the consumption of manufactured goods in Japan increased to a much lesser extent than in the other major industrial countries. The relevant ratios for 1975 and 1983 are 1.8 and 2.0 percent for Japan, 2.1 and 3.6 percent for the United States, 1.5 and 3.0 percent for France, 2.6 and 4.3 percent in Germany, 2.2 and 5.0 percent in Italy, and 3.0 and 3.5 percent in the United Kingdom.

82. Ibid., pp. 12-13. Balassa last tested directly for the effects of changes in real exchange rates on national import penetration ratios but failed to find a statistically significant relationship.

83. Krasner, *Institutional Asymmetries and Japanese Economic Conflict*, table 4 and pp. 33-35.

84. That such informal mechanisms continue to exist is suggested by a wealth of anecdotal evidence. For example, one Japan businessman described his

purchasing strategy as follows: First, we buy from ourselves, then we buy from other Japanese producers, and only then, if we still have unsatisfied demand, do we buy from foreign suppliers.

85.   Our sectoral studies and work in this area include textiles, apparel, steel, automobiles, semiconductors, and computers.

86.   See Michael Borrus, François Bar, Patrick Cogez, Anne Brit Thoresen, Ibra-Him Warde, and Aki Yoshikawa, "Telecommunications Development in Comparative Perspective: The New Telecommunications in Europe, Japan and the U.S.," Working Paper 14, Berkeley Round Table on the International Economy, University of California, Berkeley, May 1985; and Michael Borrus, *Competing for Control: America's Stake in Microelectronics* (Cambridge, Mass.: Ballinger, 1988).

87.   Krasner, *Institutional Asymmetries and Japanese Economic Conflict*, p. 43.

88.   Ibid.

89.   The TI story is widely told. More detailed accounts can be found in Borrus, *Competing for Control*; and Krasner, *Institutional Asymmetries and Japanese Economic Conflict*, p. 44.

90.   Krasner, *Institutional Asymmetries and Japanese Economic Conflict*, table IX.

91.   See, for example, Fred Bergsten and William Cline, *The United States-Japan Economic Problem* (Washington, D.C.: Institute for International Economics, 1986); and Gary Saxonhouse and Kozo Yamamura, *Law and Trade Issues of the Japanese: The American and Japanese Perspectives* (Seattle: University of Washington Press, 1986).

92.   Bela Balassa and Marcus Noland, "The Changing Comparative Advantage of Japan and the United States," in Balassa and Noland, eds., *Japan in the World Economy* (Washington, D.C.: Institute for International Economics, forthcoming 1988).

93.   Borrus, *Competing For Control.*

94.   Baldwin and Krugman (1987) also found that market closure in Japan in the 1970s was critical to the development of an internationally competitive semiconductor industry in Japan. Without protection, Japanese producers could not have competed with U.S. producers in the mid- to late 1970s.

95.   McKinsey & Company, Inc., and the U.S.-Japan Trade Study Group, *Japan: Business Obstacles & Opportunities* (Tokyo: President Inc., 1983).

96.   This section of the chapter draws on work at BRIE for the U.S.-Japan Trade Advisory Commission. Much of the work was done by Brian Woodall and Akihiro Yoshikawa.

97.   Balassa, "Japanese Trade Policies," p. 29.

98.   Ibid.

99.   Gary Saxonhouse, "Evolving Comparative Advantage of United States-Japan Trade in Steel," in Yamamura, ed., *Policy and Trade Issues of the Japanese Economy*, p. 197.

100. In the last generation of products, Cray sold only a handful in Japan and no other products were purchased. However, the year that Hitachi announced its rival product to Cray, it sold several dozen machines. Perhaps demand only matured at that moment, but it seems more likely that it was suppressed for the arrival of the Hitachi product.

101. *Japan Economic Journal* (August 30, 1986).

102. Ronald Dore, *Flexible Rigidities* (Stanford, Calif.: Stanford University Press, 1986), p. 248.

103. Borrus et al., "Telecommunications Development in Comparative Perspective."

104. Okimoto, *Between MITI and the Market*, p. 84.

105. Yoshikawa Akihiro, "Turbulence in the Japanese Economy."

106. Ibid.

107. For evidence of the Japanese government's decision to restructure the economy from a heavy and chemical industries orientation toward a knowledge-intensification of industry, see Japan Economic Planning Agency, *Basic Economic and Social Plan, 1973–1977* (Tokyo: EPA, 1973), pp. 84–85 and passim. Industrial Structure Council, *The Vision of MITI Policies in the 1980s* (Tokyo: Industrial Bank of Japan, 1980), p. 136.

108. Wheeler et al., *Japanese Industrial Development Policies of the 1980s*, ch. 3. A related and important point is discussed by Imai, who notes: "On the software side, along with such efforts as implanting in society the concept of increasing importance of information in the economy and the idea of an information society through reports by the Industrial Structure Council (mainly the Information Industry Section) and through publicity concerning such a concept, the government also arranged for the information of an infrastructure in the information industry through the 'promotion of education and training related to information processing' and the 'expansion and improvement of information processing in government offices.'" Imai, "Japan's Industrial Policy for High Technology Industries," p. 8. For more on this notion of what has been termed "human capital investment," see Robert B. Reich, *The Next American Frontier* (New York, N.Y.: Times Books, 1983), pp. 232–82.

109. Former MITI Vice Minister Ojimi Yoshihisa listed the criteria for determining which industries are to be nurtured as including those "industries where income elasticity of demand is high, technological progress is rapid, and labor productivity rises fast." Organization for Economic Cooperation and Development, *The Industrial Policy of Japan* (Paris: OECD, 1972), p. 15. For a technical discussion of these criteria, see Shinohara Miyohei, *Industrial Growth, Trade, and Dynamic Patterns in the Japanese Economy* (Tokyo: Tokyo University Press, 1982), p. 25.

110. The details of these mechanisms can be found in a variety of places. Details of the electronics cases can be found in the Houdaille Case involv-

ing numerically controlled machine tools, see the legal brief entitled *Houdaille Industries, Inc., Petitioner: 31 July 1982, "Petition to the President of the United States through the Office of the Presidential Discretion Authorized by Section 103 of the Revenue Act of 1971*," 26 U.S.C. sect. 48(a)(7)(D). For the television case involving export promotion, see Zenith. For the semiconductor case involving development support, see Section 301 (19 U.S.C. 241), as amended by the Trade Agreement of 1979).

111. Private conversations with Richard Samuels.

112. Borrus et al., "Responses to the Japanese Challenge in High Technology," Working Paper 6, Berkeley Roundtable on the International Economy, University of California, Berkeley, July 1983, p. 68. There is little disagreement about this in other English language sources. Imai puts a different label on these same facts. Imai, "Japan's Industrial Policy For High Technology Industries."

113. See Samuels, *The Business of the Japanese: Energy Markets in Comparative and Historical Perspective*; and Richard Samuels and Reginald B. Gilmour, eds., "Japanese Scientific and Technical Information in the United States," *Workshop on Japanese Scientific and Technical Information, Massachusetts Institute of Technology, Workshop Proceedings* (Springfield, Mass.: National Technical Information Service, 1983).

114. There is an ongoing debate about the significance of the latest of the cooperative ventures in computers. Some, such as Ed Feigenbaum from Stanford, attribute great importance to the Fifth-Generation computer program. Others, such as George Lindamood (now with Burroughs), dismiss it as an exercise in the bureaucratic management of new technologies. However, in areas such as new materials and biotechnology, joint projects seem to have much greater potential and significance. By grouping together Japanese firms, it has often been a barrier to foreign market entry. See George Lindamood, "The Role of the Japanese Computer Industry," Office of Naval Research, *Scientific Bulletin* (October/December 1982).

115. Work on this at BRIE has been conducted by Yoshikawa Akihiro.

116. IBM's concern with sematech is evident in the role senior executives are now playing. That role recalls the efforts of Erich Bloch in the SRC effort. Bloch, formerly at IBM, is now director of the National Science Foundation.

117. Okimoto, "Regime Characteristics of Japanese Industrial Policy," p. 55.

118. See Johnson in this volume, but also Timothy Curran, "Politics and High Technology: The NTT Case," in I. M. Destler and Hideo Sato, eds., *Coping with U.S.-Japanese Economic Conflicts* (Lexington, Mass.: Lexington Books, 1982), p. 187.

119. Ibid.

120. See Borrus et al., "Telecommunications Development in Comparative Perspective."

121. Chalmers Johnson, "MITI, MPT, and the Telecommunications Wars," Working Paper 21, Berkeley Roundtable on the International Economy, University of California, Berkeley, June 1986.

122. Nambu Tsuruhiko, Suzuki Kazuyki, and Honda Tetsushi, "Competition and Government Policy in the Japanese Telecommunications Industry" (Paper prepared for the Conference on Technology and Government Policy in Computers and Communications, Brookings Institution, Washington, D.C., June 4–5, 1987).

123. See Robert Manning, "High Technology High Noon," *Far Eastern Economic Review* 123 (February 23, 1984): 78–79; "Japanese to Let Americans Join Councils That Advise Industries," *New York Times*, March 12, 1984; and "U.S. Role in Advisory Councils Discussed," *Japan Economic Survey* 8 (April 1984): 13–14.

124. Richard Samuels, private conversations.

125. Pempel, "Japanese Foreign Economic Policy," p. 161. For a discussion of the role of the Japanese developmental state in "unbundling" the package of control and new technology represented by multinational Corporations, see Zysman and Cohen, "Double or Nothing: Open Trade and Competitive Industry," *Foreign Affairs* (Summer 1983): 1120.

126. Johnson, *MITI and the Japanese Miracle*, p. 17. In this case the industry contends the support is an unfair support for producers. The evidence suggests the support is largely in the form of support for users, for diffusion.

127. Borrus et al., "Responses to the Japanese Challenge in High Technology," p. 82 and passim.

128. David Mowery, *Alliance Politics and Economics: Multinational Joint Ventures in Commercial Aircraft* (Cambridge, Mass.: Ballinger, 1987).

129. Duane Hall, *The International Joint Venture* (New York: Praeger, 1984), p. 131.

130. Japan Economic Planning Agency, *Basic Economic and Social Plan, 1973–1977*, pp. 88–89.

131. For a detailed discussion of Japan's Anti-Monopoly Law, see Johnson, *MITI and the Japanese Miracle*, pp. 299–303.

132. Samuels, *The Business of the Japanese State*.

133. Friedman, *The Misunderstood Miracle*.

134. For a detailed discussion of Japanese efforts to restructure the economy, see Johnson, *MITI and the Japanese Miracle*, pp. 289–91 and passim; and Ira Magaziner and Thomas Hout, *Japanese Industrial Policy* (Berkeley, Calif.: Institute for International Studies, University of California, 1981), ch. 2.

135. For a detailed discussion of Japan's policy for sunset industries, see Wheeler et al., *Japanese Industrial Development Policies in the 1980's*, ch. 7.

136. Balassa reaches a similar conclusion and provides some compelling anecdotal evidence to support it in "Japanese Trade Policies." See the section
on the defense of depressed industries, and passim.

137. Ibid., p. 41.

138. See Japan, Economic White Paper, 1977.

139. "Yaritama ni Agatta Sanhoko" (The Structurally Depressed Industries Law
Elevated to the Object of Attack), *Ekonomisuto* (February 7, 1984): 8.

140. Richard Cunningham and Susan G. Esserman, "Denial of U.S. Access
to Primary Aluminum and Aluminum Mill Products Markets in Japan,"
unpublished legal brief, Steptoe & Johnson, 1985. See also Richard Samuels, "The Industrial Destructuring of the Japanese Aluminum Industry,"
Pacific Affairs 3 (Fall 1983).

141. Ibid.; as well as field work.

142. See, for example, the evidence in Douglas Anderson, "Managing Retreat:
Disinvestment Policy in the U.S. and Japan," in Tom McCraw, ed., *America versus Japan* (Boston, Mass.: Harvard Business School Press, 1986).

143. Merton J. Peck, Richard C. Levin, and Goto Akira, "Picking the Losers:
Public Policy Toward Declining Industries," *Journal of Japanese Studies*
13 (1987).

144. Balassa, "Japanese Trade Policies," p. 13.

145. The steel industry is one example. The penetration ratio of steel imports
into the United States in 1984 was 35.5 percent, while the penetration of
steel imports into Japan was 5.7 percent. The statistics for Japan are from
Ichiro Yano, ed., *Nippon* (Tokyo: Kokuseisha, 1986), p. 189; the U.S. statistics are from *Statistical Abstract of the U.S. 1987, 107th Edition*, U.S.
Department of Commerce, Bureau of Census, 1987. See also Balassa,
"Japanese Trade Policies," p. 40.

146. Balassa, "Japanese Trade Policies."

147. Dore, *Flexible Rigidities.*

148. Ibid.

149. Anderson, "Managing Retreat."

4 KEIRETSU ORGANIZATION IN THE JAPANESE ECONOMY
Analysis and Trade Implications

Michael Gerlach

What is one to make of the persistent trade imbalances that have plagued the U.S.-Japan relationship since the 1960s? Explanation of Japan's inroads into U.S. markets seems relatively straightforward: The high value of the dollar combined with the poor performance of many American products in comparison with their Japanese counterparts led to a surge in Japan's exports in the early 1980s. More vexing, however, has been the difficulty firms from the United States and elsewhere have had in making inroads into Japan's own markets, including in many industries where U.S. products are fully competitive. Recent trade statistics show some improvements, but the bilateral imbalance remains enormous even in the late 1980s despite the near doubling in the value of the yen against the dollar since early 1985, as well as market-liberalization measures initiated by the Japanese government much earlier.

It is the peculiar imperviousness of Japanese markets that this chapter sets out to address. Both macroeconomic changes, embodied in currency realignments, and changes in government trade policies, in the form of formal tariff and nontariff barriers, have proven less powerful in explaining U.S. corporate performance in Japanese markets than orthodox trade theory would indicate. A significant reason for this is the following simple but often overlooked point: international trade is based not only on exchange rates set by capital markets and legal barriers set by governments, but also on the concrete relationships among the firms that actually make the buying and selling decisions, both in financial and in industrial (intermediate product) markets.

While this observation is true of any economy, it is particularly important in discussions of Japanese markets. Interfirm trade in Japan is dominated by long-standing networks of reciprocal ties among companies. These networks are evident when they become formalized as identifiable *keiretsu*, or industrial groupings.[1] The *keiretsu* are of two distinct, though overlapping, types. The *vertical keiretsu* organize suppliers and distribution outlets hierarchically beneath a large, industry-specific manufacturing concern. Toyota Motor's chain of upstream component suppliers is a well-known but by no means unusual example of this form of interfirm organization. Vertically organized large manufacturers are, in turn, themselves often grouped with large manufacturers from other industries, as well as with general trading companies and large banks and insurance companies. Such *intermarket keiretsu* provide for their members reliable sources of borrowed capital as well as a stable core of long-term shareholders. Moreover, like the vertical *keiretsu* they establish a partially internalized market in intermediate products, particularly in trade in raw materials and in industrial products.[2]

Within both the vertical and the intermarket *keiretsu*, trade, finance, and corporate control become closely interlinked, each set in the context of the others. Figure 4-1 is schematic of these linkages. Linkages within the intermarket *keiretsu* support the growth of the group's nucleus manufacturers, hence indirectly the growth of each core firm's own smaller satellite firms. Group financial institutions moreover are often leading suppliers of capital not only to nucleus firms but also to their satellites as well. In this way, the intermarket *keiretsu* complement rather than compete with their vertical counterparts.

Contrasting with the Japanese linkages are the functional separations inherent in interfirm relationships within the United States. The structure of the U.S. economy involves sharply delineated and often conflicting markets for investment capital. As a result of antitrust legislation, the Glass-Steagall Act, securities regulation, and other factors, banks are unrelated by equity ties to their clients or are prohibited from acting on those ties through internal "China walls," manufacturers are unrelated to each other, usually, common banking connections, and institutional investors have neither trade

Figure 4-1. Debt, Equity, and Trade Linkages in the Vertical and Intermarket *Keiretsu*.

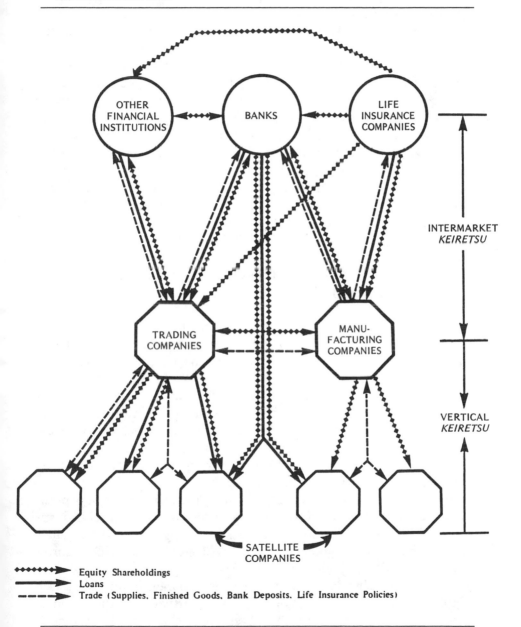

nor debt interests in the companies in which they hold shares. Interfirm organization in the United States, compared with Japan, is highly fragmented, with marked differences in the resulting openness to market newcomers.

In the analysis below, we study the nature of linkages within the *keiretsu*, focusing on the intermarket form. The basic characteristics of and membership within the six main intermarket groups are outlined. Also described are the role and operation of the group executive councils in providing a forum for representation of groupwide interests. The core of the analysis looks at *keiretsu* effects on the organization of interfirm capital and trading networks. This section demonstrates the significant extent to which each of these groups has internalized within itself the markets for debt and equity capital, as well as trade in industrial materials and products. We conclude with a discussion of the implications of the *keiretsu* for understanding structural barriers to entry into the Japanese market.

THE SIX MAIN HORIZONTAL *KEIRETSU:* AN OVERVIEW

The intermarket *keiretsu* largely comprise the firms and industries that have historically been central in the Japanese economy. Among the big six, three have direct connections to zaibatsu that dominated the Japanese economy before and during World War II; the Mitsubishi, Mitsui, and Sumitomo groups all have at their center most of the companies that were first-line subsidiaries of the zaibatsu holding company, the *honsha.* The other three, Fuji, Sanwa, and Dai-Ichi Kangyo, include firms with prewar connections, but are generally classified, because of the particularly strong role of their banks, as bank groups. The boundaries of the *keiretsu* are ambiguous. The core, however, is well defined by membership in the group presidents' council. The monthly meetings of the council serve as an institutionalized forum for communication among group firms' chief executives. This unambiguous measure of group membership correlates empirically with all major features of the group.

The membership list of the presidents' council is published (see Table 4–1 for a list from 1982). The firms affiliated with the intermarket *keiretsu* are among the largest, oldest, and most prestigious in Japan. These 182 core companies represent only slightly over 0.01 percent of the estimated 1.7 million firms in Japan, and just over 10 percent of the 1,700 firms listed on the Tokyo Stock Exchange, but their significance extends far beyond what numbers might indicate. Among the largest 100 industrial firms in Japan, 56 are council members, while 33 more are among the next 100. An additional 9 firms are not council members themselves but subsidiaries or affiliates of council member companies. In total, therefore, among Japan's 200 largest industrial firms, about one-half, 98, maintain affiliation with a group, either through direct council membership or through a parent firm that is a member.[3] The importance of group companies is striking in the financial sector. All five of Japan's largest commercial banks (Dai-Ichi Kangyo, Fuji, Sumitomo, Mitsubishi, and Sanwa) are at the center of their own groups, as are the five leading trust banks, the five leading casualty insurance companies, and four of the five leading life insurance companies.[4]

The position of the three former zaibatsu groups and of the three postwar bank groups in the Japanese economy has remained fairly stable since the 1960s. Collectively, the 182 core members in the six groups controlled 25.8 percent, or about one-quarter, of total assets in the Japanese economy 1981, up slightly from 24.4 percent in 1970. This was fairly evenly divided among the former zaibatsu groups, at 12.3 percent, and the bank groups, at 13.5 percent.[5]

The industries in which the intermarket *keiretsu* are most strongly represented are those most central to an industrial economy—capital, primary products, real estate, and construction. The final column of Table 4-1 indicates the extent of total sales in these industries held by core group firms. Natural resources (oil, coal, mining), primary metals (ferrous and nonferrous metals), cement, chemicals, and industrial machinery are all well represented, as *keiretsu* members control between 43 percent and 56 percent of total sales in these industries. Among financial institutions, group commercial and trust banks control 40 percent of total bank capital, and insurance companies 53–57 percent of total insurance capital. In real estate, 55 percent of total business is controlled by group members, while in distribution, 67 percent of sales is accounted for by formal members in one of the big-six *keiretsu*.[6]

A significant feature of the interaction between industrial and *keiretsu* dynamics is what has come to be called in Japanese business

Table 4-1. Membership in the Six Main *Keirestsu* by Industry, Presidents' Council Members Only, 1982.

Industry	Mitsui (24 companies)	Mitsubishi (28 companies) [MTB]	Sumitomo (21 companies) [SMT]
City bank	Mitsui Bank	Mitsubishi Bank	Sumitomo Bank
Trust bank	Mitsui Trust	Mitsubishi Trust	Sumitomo Trust
Life insurance	Mitsui Life	Meiji Life	Sumitomo Life
Casualty insurance	Taisho F&M	Tokio F&M	Sumitomo F&M
Trade and commerce	Mitsui Bussan Mitsukoshi	Mitsubishi Corporation	Sumitomo Corporation
Construction	Mitsui Construction Sanki Engineering	Mitsubishi Construction	Sumitomo Construction
Real estate	Mitsui Real Estate	Mitsubishi Estates	Sumitomo Real Estate
Fibers and textiles	Toray	Mitsubishi Rayon	
Chemicals	Mitsui Toatsu Mitsui Petroleum	Mitsubishi Chemical Mitsubishi Petrochemical Mitsubishi Monsanto Mitsubishi Gas Mitsubishi Plastics	Sumitomo Chemical Sumitomo Bakelite
Oil and coal	Mitsui Mining Hokkaido Collieries	Mitsubishi Oil	Sumitomo Coal Mining
Glass and cement	Onoda Cement	Asahi Glass Mitsubishi Mining and Cement	Nippon Sheet Glass Sumitomo Cement
Paper	Oji Paper	Mitsubishi Paper	
Steel	Japan Steel Works	Mitsubishi Steel	Sumitomo Metal Industries
Nonferrous metals	Mitsui M&M	Mitsubishi Metal Mitsubishi Aluminum	Sumitomo M&M Sumitomo Electric Sumitomo Light Metal Industries Sumitomo Aluminum

Table 4-1. continued

Fuyo (29 companies)	Sanwa (40 companies)	Dai-Ichi Kangyo (45 companies)	Collective Share of Industry Shares (%)
Fuji Bank	Sanwa Bank	Dai-Ichi Kango Bank	40.5
Yasuda Trust	Toyo Trust		
Yasuda Life	Nippon Life	Asahi Life Fukoku Life	56.7
Yasuda F&M		Taisei F&M Nissan F&M	52.8
Marubeni	Nissho Iwai[a] Nichimen Iwatani Takashima	C. Itoh Nissho Iwai[a] Kanematsu-Gosho Kawasho Seibu Department stores	66.7
Taisei Construction	Ohbayashi-Gumi Toyo Construction Sekisui House	Shimizu Construction	23.1
Tokyo Building			55.1
Toho Rayon Nisshin Spinning	Unitica		40.3
Showa Denko Nippon O&F Kureha	Sekisui Chemical Ube Industries Hitachi Chemical Teijin Fujisawa Kansai Paint Tokuyama Soda Tanabe Seiyaku	Denki Kagaku K. Nippon Zeon Asahi Chemical Sankyo Shiseido Lion Corporation Asahi Denka	43.3
Toa Nenryo	Maruzen Oil	Showa Oil	45.0
Nippon Cement	Osaka Cement	Chichibu Cement	48.8
Sanyo-Kokusaku		Honshu Paper	37.7
Nippon Kokan	Kobe Steel[a] Nakayama Steel Hitachi Metals Nisshin Steel	Kawasaki Steel Kobe Steel[a] Japan M&C	52.7
	Hitachi Cable	Nippon Light Metals Furukawa Furukawa Electric	56.0

(*Table 4-1. continued overleaf*)

Table 4-1. continued

Industry	Mitsui (24 companies)	Mitsubishi (28 companies) [MTB]	Sumitomo (21 companies) [SMT]
General and transportation machinery	Toyota Motors Mitsui Ship-building	Mitsubishi Heavy Industries Mitsubishi Kakoki Mitsubishi Motors	Sumitomo Heavy Industries
Electrical and precision machinery	Toshiba	Mitsubishi Electric Nippon Kogaku	Nippon Electric
Shipping	Mitsui-OSK	Nippon Yusen	
Warehousing	Mitsui Warehouse	Mitsubishi Warehouse	Sumitomo Warehouse
Other industries	Nippon Flour	Kirin Beer	Sumitomo Forestry

Sources: Membership lists are translated and reformatted from tables provided in Kosei Torihiki Iinkai (Japanese Federal Trade Commission), "Kigyo Shudan no Kittui ni Tsuite," 1983, pp. 3-4. Figures on share of industry sales come from *Nihon Kigyo Shudan Bunseki* (Analysis of Japanese Enterprise Groups), vol. 2 (Tokyo: Sangyo Doko Chosa-Kai, 1980), p. 11. These are calculated as the share of sales accounted for by *shacho-kai* members in the six groups as a percentage of total sales by all companies listed on the Tokyo Stock Exchange.

a. Membership in more than one presidents' council.

parlance the "one-set principle" (*wan setto-shugi*). This is the tendency among the intermarket *keiretsu* to have one, and only one, company representing all major industries. We see in Table 4-1 an extremely high degree of diversification in the six groups, yet with relatively little overlap between the product lines of its member companies. The one-set pattern is closely adhered to by the former zaibatsu groups. Mitsubishi and Mitsui are represented in each major industry listed here, while Sumitomo participates in all but shipping and textiles, both declining industries in Japan. In addition, there are few industrial overlaps among companies within each of these three groups.[7] The membership lists in the Sanwa and Dai-Ichi Kangyo bank groups do not follow the one-set patterns quite so clearly. While they have representation in most of these industries, there are

Table 4-1. continued

Fuyo (29 companies)	Sanwa (40 companies)	Dai-Ichi Kangyo (45 companies)	Collective Share of Indus-try Shares (%)
Kubota	NTN Toyo B.	Niigata Engineering	45.5
Nippon P.M.	Hitachi Shipbuilding	Kawasaki Heavy	
Nissan Motors	Shin Meiwa	IHI Heavy Industries	
	Daihatsu Motors	Isuzu Motors	
		Iseki	
		Ebara Corporation	
Hitachi Co.[a]	Hitachi Corporation[a]	Hitachi Corporation[a]	39.3
Oki Electric	Iwatsu Electric	Fujitsu	
Yokogawa Electric	Sharp	Fuji Electric	
Canon	Nitto Electric	Yasukawa Electric	
		Nippon Columbia	
		Asahi Optical	
Showa	Yamashita-SH	Kawasaki Kisen	58.7
		Shibusawa Warehouse	33.9
Nisshin Flour	Ito Ham	Yokohama Rubber	N.A.
Sapporo Beer	Toyo Rubber	Korakuan Stadium	
Nippon Reizo	Nittsu[a]	Nittsu[a]	
Tobu Railroad	Hankyu Railroad	Nippon K.K. Sec.	
Keihin Railroad	Oriental Lease		

internal duplications in several; trading and commerce, chemicals, steel, and electrical machinery.

Another important characteristic of membership is the extremely low overlap in participation *across* groups, as member firms are nearly all identified with just a single council. Out of 187 total memberships in 1982, there were only five multiple memberships, which involved four firms. One company, Hitachi participated in three councils, while three others, Nissho-Iwai, Nittsu, and Kobe Steel, participated in two. These reflect historical associations each of these firms has had with multiple group banks. The remaining members are all formally affiliated with only a single group, although some maintain informal ties elsewhere.

THE SYMBOLIC AND STRUCTURAL COHERENCE OF THE *KEIRETSU*

The fundamental organizational problem facing the *keiretsu* is to create a degree of coherence among its members in the absence of formal structures that define the roles and responsibilities of its participants and clear-cut purposes around which activities are to be focused. It now exists not in the legal world as a formal organization (in the classical or Weberian sense) but as a more loosely organized alliance within the social world of the business community.

The *keiretsu* has nevertheless been able to express itself as a significant organizational form through structured interaction among its members and the ongoing symbolic framework within which this interaction takes place. We consider here two processes by which *keiretsu* are collectively organized: (1) the creation of high-level executive councils that symbolically identify group members and the boundaries of social unit, as well as providing a forum for interaction among group firms; and (2) the structuring of exchange networks—specifically, debt, equity, and trade networks—that define the position of individual firms in the group and establish groupwide constraints on behavior.

Defining Membership and Representing Group Interests: The Role of the *Shacho-Kai*

Among the prominent features of the *keiretsu* are the presidents' councils or *shacho-kai*, monthly meetings that bring together the chief executive officers from the group's nucleus companies. The *shacho-kai* is a kind of informal community council, with membership limited to a set of core members.[8] Council meetings are held once a month (or, in the case of the Dai-Ichi Kangyo group, once every three months). In addition to having a chairman (a position that rotates every meeting in some groups and is fixed in others), the meetings typically also assign a secretary whose function is to record the proceedings.[9] While without legal clout, the *shacho-kai* is considerably more than a quaint business custom, for it serves both to signify membership in the group and as a common arena in which the strategic interests group firms have in each other may be expressed.

The meetings are a symbolically significant opportunity to exchange views with other chief executives and to socialize. (Even in Japan, it appears, it is lonely at the top.) Companies sometimes report on new products and technologies that they are developing or decisions to open new subsidiaries in foreign markets. Periodically, special matters of groupwide interest come up, including projects that the group is engaged in as well as various charitable activities. Infrequently group companies have financial difficulties or intra-mural conflicts.

The president's council is a forum for the representation of the coalition of shareholders, financial lenders, and trading partners defined by the group. In this sense, it is similar to an American board of directors as a representative of the interests of the external coali-tion composed of shareholders and financial lenders.[10] However, the *shacho-kai* serves these interests in a quite different way, and one that is perhaps more compatible with the structure of interorganiza-tional relationships as they have developed in Japan.[11]

First, unlike the members of the board, who retire, die, or leave for other reasons, members of the presidents' council participate in an ongoing social system that outlasts the tenure of any single mem-ber. The apparently ad-hoc manner in which board directors who exit are replaced in the United States[12] suggests that board partici-pation is a sporadic process, and perhaps one that serves to link firms not to any specific set of external constituents but to the broader community of corporate leaders. The *shacho-kai*, in contrast, con-sists of a predefined set of highly visible actors with which the firms has historically carried on a variety of lines of business.

Second, the *shacho-kai* is an informal institution. There is no de-fined or legally binding governance relationship between the council and its firms, and as a result, influence is negotiated between hori-zontally positioned firms based on internal group politics rather than on formal authority vested in law. Related to this is the fact that governance within the *shacho-kai* takes place among a known and controllable set of actors. Large Japanese corporations have been able to structure their ownership so as to avoid the dangers presented by anonymous and potentially hostile shareholders. Instead, mem-bership in the group is carefully defined, and control inside takes place among mutually positioned firms in a community-based form of governance—as both governor and governed. Where U.S. firms tend to view ownership over the firm as a discrete transaction in which ownership and control are clearly defined through 100 percent ownership and expressed in a unilateral control relationship, large Japanese corporations are more likely to view control as a mutual process, spread across a collective of similarly positioned group part-ners. Ownership becomes an influence strategy among firms rather than the prerogative of shareholders as a separate constituency.

THE STRUCTURE OF INTERFIRM
EXCHANGE NETWORKS

If the *shacho-kai* serves to define membership and express group interests, then flows of resources are the concrete manifestations of these interests in the life of each firm's interactions with other group firms. In the structure of these flows we find clear indications of the significance of the *keiretsu* in organizing interfirm exchange in Japan. Ostensibly bilateral linkages are themselves organized collectively into dense networks of ties involving other group firms. These represent structures of collective order, both by the ways in which transactions signify relationships (for example, the establishing of trading relationships through the taking of an equity position), and in the creation of exchange networks whose overall structures become important determinants of relationships within the *keiretsu.*

In this section, we look at the structures of interfirm exchange networks established through (1) borrowing from group financial institutions, (2) the mutual holding of ownership shares, and (3) trade in intermediate products. Within the group, these exchanges are closely intertwined with other ongoing relationships among group members. Each apparently discrete transaction (one firm's equity position in another) is itself embedded in a collective social construction, the group.

I have introduced in the analyses that follow two different measures of network structure to evaluate the importance of the groups in organizing linkages among their members. *Internalization* is the proportion of group members' interfirm transactions taking place with other group firms as a percentage of their total transactions. The *group bias factor* is the extent to which group firms are biased toward exchange with other companies in their own group *and* away from companies that are members of other groups. Where internalization puts the group in perspective of the entire business network, including independent and subsidiary firms that maintain no formal group affiliation, the group bias factor assesses the importance of the group only against other intermarket groups, as a measure of the strength of preferential trading patterns.

The *Keiretsu* Structure of Banking Relationships

The role of the intermarket *keiretsu* in structuring the market for capital must be put in perspective of the overall patterns of corporate finance in Japan that distinguish it from its American counterpart. Most significant is the heavy use of borrowed capital in Japan, with the resulting development of close relationships between firms and their sponsoring banks. Japanese firms have long had among the highest ratios of debt to equity of any developed country. Typical estimates have debt covering about 80 percent of total external capital as compared with only 50 percent in the United States, although these percentages have been declining recently. Banks are especially important. During the period from 1966–1978, banks provided over half of firms' external capital, double the proportion of that provided by U.S. banks. Close relationships between firms and banks are furthermore promoted by the fact that Japan has never had the equivalent of the provisions established in the U.S. Glass–Steagall Act in the United States that forbid bank ownership of companies' equity shares, and Japanese banks are typically among their client companies' main stockholders.

The bank's status as number-one lending institution, the company's "main bank," carries with it in Japan the expectation that the bank will not only provide a significant portion of the firm's capital but will also look after its interests in a wide variety of ways. The main bank acts as a signal to other banks of the financial health of the company, ensuring that the company is able to gain loans from other banks as well—a process known as pump priming (*yobi-mizu*). The Sumitomo Bank, for example, in 1971 applied for the approval of the Ministry of Finance and the Bank of Japan for a plan under which it would guarantee loans by local and mutual banks to its clients, including, prominently, other Sumitomo firms.

Bank assistance extends as well to helping its clients find business customers. A Sumitomo Bank executive explained as follows:

> Sumitomo Metal Industries does a lucrative business now selling sheet steel to the Matsushita companies, the Nissan companies, and Toyo Kogyo, among others. They enjoy this business because the bank provided a large part of the financing for these companies and acted as go-between to get this business for them. There are many, many arrangements such as this in the group.[13]

If a company does get involved in financial problems, the main bank is expected to come to its client's rescue. An example of this is Akai Electric, a major tape-deck manufacturer. During the early 1980s Akai ran into financial difficulties and underwent financial reconstruction with bank support. Significantly, it was Akai's "main bank" that took the lead in this reconstruction. This was Mitsubishi

Bank, which owned 8 percent of Akai's shares and was lender of 16 percent of its borrowed capital. As part of the assistance, Mitsubishi had sent three people to Akai—the chief secretary to the president, the department manager in charge of International Business Operations, and the department manager for International Finance—and extended additional loans to the company.

In the intermarket *keiretsu*, the main bank relationship is moved from that of a bilateral relationship to that of a larger alliance of firms, each of which employs the group bank as its main bank. These firms, moreover, are connected directly to other group companies through ownership, personnel, and trading networks. The maintenance of the central position of the group banks was ensured by the postwar economic reforms pushed by the U.S. occupation, which broke up the zaibatsu holding company but not the zaibatsu banks. As a result, and in conjunction with the Japanese government's policy of allocating scarce capital to the city banks through its own financial organs, these city banks became the leading sources of capital for group companies and were in a position to give preference to their own long-standing clients. Firms themselves were growing rapidly and had extremely high external capital requirements that could not be met by the relatively undeveloped equity market, so they turned increasingly to the banks. Groupings formed around these banks as companies were willing to forgo a degree of independence in order to gain access to scarce but needed capital, particularly during the economic resurgence in the mid-1950s. Figure 4–2 depicts schematically how these relationships now appear among the leading companies in one group, Sumitomo.

The degree to which group companies borrow from the financial institutions in their own group versus from outside institutions may be termed the internalization of capital. Internalization is the total borrowed capital divided by capital coming from financial institutions in the same group. Internalization figures for the three former zaibatsu groups and the three bank groups are shown in Table 4–2.

Overall, the core companies from these six groups borrowed in 1982 an average of 21 percent of their debt capital from group financial institutions, with internalization somewhat higher in the three former zaibatsu groups. A second measure, the group bias factor, suggests that the significance of the group is higher when considering the *source* of group versus outside capital. The group bias factor is the share of capital borrowed from own group divided by average

Figure 4-2. Intragroup Borrowing Dependency of the Leading Companies in the Sumitomo (SMT) Group.

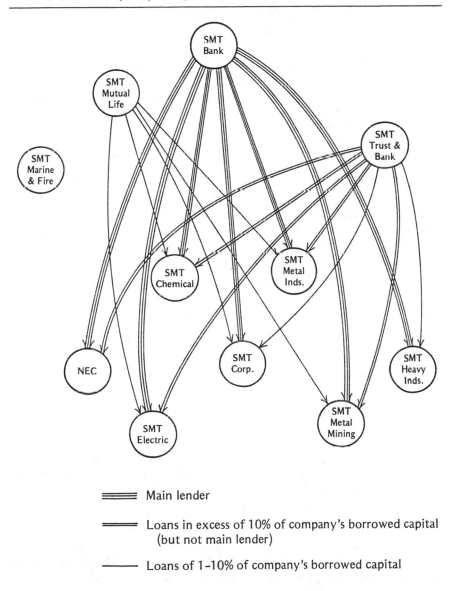

≡≡≡ Main lender

══ Loans in excess of 10% of company's borrowed capital (but not main lender)

── Loans of 1–10% of company's borrowed capital

Source: Data from *Industrial Groupings in Japan* (Tokyo: Dodwell Marketing Consultants, 1982).

Table 4–2. The Structure of Debt Capital Networks in Former Zaibatsu and Bank Groups.

	Zaibatsu Group	Bank Groups	Total
Internalization	23%	20%	21%
Group bias factor	8X	5X	6X

Source: Calculated from data provided in *Industrial Groupings in Japan* (Tokyo: Dodwell Marketing Consultants, 1982), pp. 154–329, for sixty-six group companies, eleven in each group. These are the group bank, trading company, life insurance company, and eight main manufacturing companies.

amount of capital borrowed from other groups. On average, core firms were six times more likely to borrow capital from financial institutions in their own group than from financial institutions affiliated with any of the other five groups. The group bias factor makes more explicit than the internalization measure the extent to which trading patterns are *preferential*, that is, biased toward firms within a company's own group. Complete neutrality in dealings with financial institutions would result in an even split of borrowing among group versus nongroup firms (that is, group bias = 1.0). An overall bias factor of 6 indicates clearly that relationships between *keiretsu* firms and their banks are in fact not neutral, nor even close to neutral. The implications of these and other preferential trading patterns for foreign market entrants are considered later.

The *Keiretsu* Structure of Intercorporate Shareholding

The intermarket *keiretsu* are critical as well in structuring shareholder relationships. In Japan, as in the United States, equity ownership defines in a legal sense control over the firm. However, in practical terms corporate ownership in Japan is not a neutral commodity, traded anonymously among actors who have little vested interest in the firms in which they have shares. Ownership over the firm sets the framework within which the firm's internal operations takes place, and the issue of *who* owns companies—the structure of corporate control—is a critical one.

Institutions have in Japan, as in the United States, replaced individuals as the primary controller of shareholdings. About 43 percent of shares of U.S. firms were held by institutional investors in the early 1980s, while the figure in Japan was even higher at 62 percent.[14] More important, however, is the nature of this relationship. In the United States, nearly two-thirds of institutional shareholders are representatives for pension funds and personal trust funds, investors for whom the primary incentives come in the form of portfolio returns rather than in trading relationships with the firms they hold. Institutional ownership retains an identity separate from that of management.

The interests of institutional shareholders in Japan differ dramatically, as equity shareholdings take on symbolic meaning in signifying relationships with other firms rather than as straightforward investments for capital gains. The role of shareholder becomes merged with that of business partner. In the words of one executive, "there is no sense in holding shares in a company with which business ties are slim." Equity positions become embedded in other ongoing relationships between the firms and remain highly stable over time. The symbolic role of intercorporate shareholdings to the Japanese has been pointed out by Rodney Clark:

> Unlike Western institutional shareholders, which invest largely for dividends and capital appreciation, Japanese institutional shareholders tend to be the company's business partners and associates; shareholding is the mere expression of their relationship, not the relationship itself.[15]

This relationship is evident among firms and their client banks, where the embedding of equity and loan positions transforms the nature of each. Credit, in the form of bank loans, resembles equity in allowing creditors flexibility in repayment by deferring interest and principal payments and reducing compensating balances during times of financial adversity. Loans are rolled over as a matter of practice. Furthermore, banks become active participants in the management of their client firms, especially when the company is in trouble. Common stock, in contrast, takes on many of the characteristics Westerners associate with debt. Shareholders demand relatively fixed returns on their investment (in the form of regular dividend payments), but do not ask for active influence over management.

The relationship between equity shareholder and firm remains a durable one, as shareholders are a stable constituency of well-known trading partners. An executive in Sumitomo Life Insurance, the largest holder of shares in the Sumitomo group put this as follows: "If group shares go up, we don't quickly sell them off, though naturally we're happy. If the value of a company shares goes up, that improves the financial condition of all group companies." Estimates of holdings by "stable shareholders" (*antei kabunushi*) run somewhere between 60 and 80 percent of total shares on the Tokyo Stock Exchange. Aoki estimates that banks account for only 2.9 percent of transactions on the Tokyo Stock Exchange, life insurance companies only 0.8 percent, and nonfinancial corporations 6.9 percent. In other words, while institutional investors hold two-thirds of total shares issued, they account for only 10 percent of total transactions on Japanese stock exchanges.[16]

In comparison, U.S. institutional shareholders are extremely active traders in corporate securities—and, by implication, unstable shareholders. Mintz and Schwartz report that U.S. institutional investors account for 60 percent of all transactions, while holding only 40 percent of issued shares.[17] U.S. institutional shareholders therefore hold only two-thirds the proportion of shares as do their Japanese institutional counterparts, yet they engage in six times the share of transactions. When controlling for the smaller proportion of shares held by U.S. institutional investors, this means that they engage in almost *ten times* the number of stock transactions as a proportion of shares held as Japanese institutional investors.

Institutional shareholding in Japan has furthermore developed into a pattern of interlocking ownership, or *kabushiki mochiai* ("stock joint-holdings"). The term *mochiai*, construed narrowly, means "to hold mutually." But it also carries an additional connotation from its other uses of helping one another, of shared interdependence, and of stability. Crossholdings, as Japanese businessmen point out, "keep each other warm" (*hada o atatame-au*).

Corporate ownership of business alliances is structured into internalized networks of crossholdings with other group firms. Overall, according to the Japanese Federal Trade Commission, an average of 15–30 percent of a group company's shares are held by other companies in the group.[18] This figure, however, considerably understates the significance of intragroup shareholding since it includes in this total a large number of scattered smaller shareholders. If, on the other hand, we consider only firms' *leading* shareholders (those most likely to influence corporate policymaking), the percentages of internalization of ownership within the group rise dramatically. Table 4–3 shows the extent of crossholdings among the leading share-

Table 4-3. Share Crossholdings Within and Across Groups, Top 100 Manufacturers and Top 23 Financial Institutions, 1973.

Company Issuing Shares (Number of Top Companies)	Companies Holding Shares						
	Mitsui	Mitsubishi	Sumitomo	Fuji	Dai-Ichi Kangyo	Sanwa	Independent
Mitsui (12)	55.2%	5.4	7.3	4.9	2.1	–	25.2
Mitsubishi (13)	1.7	74.2	0.8	3.8	3.8	1.0	14.8
Sumitomo (10)	1.7	0.3	68.8	3.6	1.6	0.2	23.9
Fuji (14)	3.5	6.4	6.8	49.2	5.5	4.9	23.6
Dai-Ichi (10)	4.2	9.1	4.7	6.2	42.3	2.4	31.1
Sanwa (12)	3.2	5.6	2.6	12.7	11.3	32.8	31.8
Independent (52)	11.2	13.0	9.8	9.2	9.5	7.2	40.0

Notes: Figures indicate percentage of shares held by group firms (underlined) versus other-group and independent firms. Limited to the top twenty shareholders in each company.

Source: Translated and adapted from Yuusaku Futatsugi, *Gendai Nihon no Kigyo Shudan—Dai-Kigyo Bunseki o Mezashite* (Enterprise Groups in Contemporary Japan: Focusing on an Analysis of Large Firms) (Tokyo: Toyo Shinposha, 1976).

holders (defined as those in the top twenty for a company) of Japan's largest firms, broken down by group membership.

The table indicates that share crossholdings are over 30 percent for all six groups, and in the range of 55–74 percent for the three zaibatsu groups. Percentages of shareholdings *across* groups, on the other hand, are small. Mitsui group companies, for example, hold only 1.7 percent of the shares of companies in the Mitsubishi group and in the Sumitomo group, in contrast to 55.2 percent of the shares of other Mitsui companies. Conversely, among their own shares, only 5.4 percent are held by Mitsubishi group companies and only 7.3 percent by Sumitomo companies.

In the process of holding each other's shares, mochiai becomes self-cancelling—a *kami no yaritori*, or paper exchange—thereby removing shares from open public trading. Offsetting shares constitute better than half of all holdings among group firms. Futatsugi has calculated these for companies in the three zaibatsu groups (excluding life insurance companies, whose shares cannot be held) and found them to account for 56 percent of Mitsunishi group companies' holdings, 57 percent of Mitsui's, and 68 percent of Sumitomo's.[19] In other words, in these groups between 56 percent and 68 percent of shares have corresponding shares held by the other firm. Specific patterns of crossholding are shown for the leading companies in the Sumitomo group in Figure 4–3.

The issue of why a self-cancelling shareholding system developed in Japan was well phrased by an executive in the Mitsui group over twenty years ago: "What's the use of owning two or three hundred shares in related companies? If we had the money, we would put it to better use in equipment or something else."[20] No answer was provided by this executive, but the question is a good one. By normal economic logic, borrowing heavily from financial institutions in order to use a significant portion of this to make equity investments in other firms does not make sense, for companies are paying interest on that borrowed capital. The reasons for share crossholdings seem to lie instead in their importance in shaping the qualitative relationships between firms. With the symbolic function that ownership implies, and its importance in linking firms in other ongoing transactions, share crossholdings among group companies create a structure of stable, mutual relationships among trading partners.

The overall structure of ownership for the six main intermarket *keiretsu* is shown in Table 4–4. Overall internalization to one's own

Figure 4-3. Stock Crossholdings of the Leading Companies in the Sumitomo (SMT) Group (*Top Ten Shareholdings Only*).

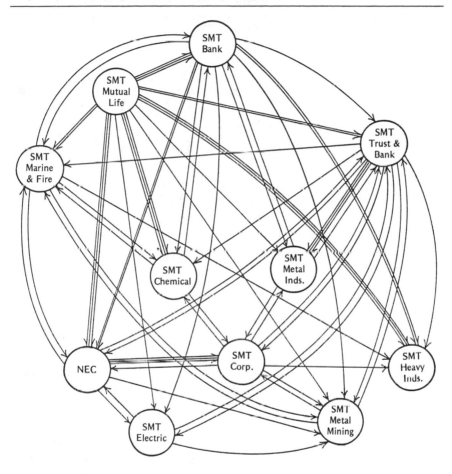

════════ 5% or more and leading shareholder

──────── 5% or more (not leading shareholder) or less than 5%
            and leading shareholder

────── One of top ten shareholders but less than 5%

Source: Data from *Industrial Groupings in Japan* (Tokyo: Dodwell Marketing Consultants, 1982).

Table 4-4. The Structure of Equity Networks in Former Zaibatsu and
Bank Groups.

	Zaibatsu Groups	Bank Groups	Total
Internalization	66%	43%	54%
Group bias factor	26X	7X	14X

Source: Calculated from data provided in Futatsugi, Yuusaku, *Gendai Nihon no Kigyo Shudan—Dai-Kigyo Bunseki o Mezashite* (Enterprise Groups in Contemporary Japan: Focusing on an Analysis of Large Firms) (Tokyo: Toyo Shinposha, 1976), p. 36, for seventy-one group companies. Top twenty shareholders only.

group is seen here to be even higher than for debt networks, particularly in the former zaibatsu groups. Group bias is also seen to be higher; zaibatsu firms are twenty-six times more likely to hold equity in each other than in firms in other groups, while the comparable figure for bank group firms is seven times. Once again, networks of interaction within the *keiretsu* are seen here to involve strong biases toward other firms within a company's own group.

The *Keiretsu* Structure of Trade in Intermediate Products

In addition to setting an organizing framework within which borrowed capital and corporate ownership networks are structured, the intermarket *keiretsu* also structure linkages within intermediate product markets, particularly through the group trading company, or *sogo shosha.* The *sogo shosha* are to the group's trading networks what banks are to its capital networks—the most centrally positioned firms, with direct linkages to most or all of the other companies in the group. Though not as important as in the past, they are nevertheless commonly a group company's leading overall supplier and customer, as well as an important organizer of small- and large-scale group projects. The general trading firm has been central in the historical development of the Japanese economy. By 1900 Mitsui Bussan alone handled about one-third of Japan's foreign trade.[21] Their emergence was closely linked to that of the *zaibatsu* themselves.

The general trading companies developed best when they were part of a zaibatsu. Those that were started independently of the zaibatsu either did not succeed or remained small. The zaibatsu was a system that provided them with ample capital and security as well as with room for initiative. And the name of the zaibatsu assured them also of qualified personnel because of the prestige and power the zaibatsu name involved.[22]

Even today, the *sogo shosha* are Japan's *sekai kigyo*, their "world corporations." They handle a significant portion of Japan's domestic trade,[23] and are the leading intermediary in international trade. In the mid-1970s they exported over 70 percent of all Japanese iron and steel products, and 70 percent of machinery products, and handled nearly half of machinery imports.[24]

Because of the central role of the trading firm in the group, patterns of group trade tend to reflect patterns of trade between the trading company and other companies in the group. Historical associations of group firms to each other through the group trading company have resulted in highly internalized transactions among some group companies. In the case of the Sumitomo group, many of its core operations derive directly from the group's historical position in copper mining. As a result, even with the postwar dissolution of the formal zaibatsu, historical trade patterns remained. *Oriental Economist* reported even in the late 1950s (July 1959) that Sumitomo Metal Mining (the direct descendent of Sumitomo's main Besshi mine) sold 60 percent of its copper output to Sumitomo Electric Industries and Sumitomo Metal Industries, while Sumitomo Electric filled 80 percent of its copper requirements with supplies originating from metal Mining.

There have been reports of the oncoming demise of the *sogo shosha* since the early 1960s, when Misonou Hitoshi published an influential article, "Is the Sun Setting on the Sogo Shosha?"[25] The most recent reports stem from the early 1980s when the Japanese business community began talking about "The Era of Winter," after the title of a bestseller at the time that predicted severe difficulties in the years ahead for the trading companies. As evidence of this, percentages of sales handled by the *sogo shosha* had declined by 10–20 percent in a number of major industries. But a revival seemed well underway by 1985, when sales of all major trading companies were up and four of the six leading *sogo shosha* reported record profits.[26]

Nevertheless, while reports of their demise appear exaggerated, the role of the trading firm is changing with the ongoing restructuring of Japan's economy away from heavy, industrial, and capital-inten-

Table 4–5. Share of Group Trade Conducted Through the Group Trading Company for Selected Industries in the Mitsubishi and Mitsui Groups.

	Sales (%)	Purchases (%)
Heavy Industries		
Mitsubishi Heavy Industries	55	27
Mitsubishi Oil	25	35
Mitsubishi Metals	22	38
Mitsubishi Chemicals	26	41
Mitsubishi Aluminum	75	100
Mitsui Shipbuilding	75	18
Mitsui Petrochemicals	65	50
Hokkaido Colliery (Coal)	68	55
Mitsui Metal Mining	33	31
Lighter, Component-Assembly Industries and Consumer Products		
Mitsubishi Electric	20	15
Nippon Kogaku (Nikon Cameras)	7	11
Kirin Beer	0.3	23
Toshiba	15	5
Sanki Electric	9	4
Nippon Flour Milling	28	1
Toyota Motors	1	1

Source: Data from Okumura, Hiroshi, *Shin–Nihon no Roku Dai–Kigyo Shudan* (A New View of Japan's Six Large Enterprise Groups) (Tokyo: Diamond, 1983).

sive products toward lighter, consumer, and knowledge-intensive industries. Estimates of the overall share of sales among the zaibatsu successor companies that gets channeled through the group trading firm are somewhere around 20–30 percent, but this varies considerably by industry.[27] The *sogo shosha*'s role as trading agent has historically been strongest in the area of heavy industries. Sumitomo Corporation, for example, relies on trade in metal products for 29 percent of its total sales, and on chemicals and fuels for 28 percent.[28] The proportion of group trade between the *sogo shosha* and group companies involved in heavy and industrial versus light and consumer product markets is shown for the Mitsubishi and Mitsui groups in Table 4-5. We find that the degree of internalization of group sales and purchases, through the group trading company, is over 20 percent in a variety of heavy industrial products, and in some cases over 50 percent.

These firms in addition carry on a portion of *direct* trade which does not involve the group trading company. The Japanese FTC reported this to be on the order of 16 percent overall.[29] In total, then, we may estimate that trade among firms in the same intermarket *keiretsu*, both direct and through the group trading company, averages perhaps 35–50 percent in heavy industrial sectors, less in consumer sectors.

Moreover, a significant share of each firm's purchases comes from its network of vertical *keiretsu* suppliers; for some core components, virtually all supplies come from captive satellites. These vertical suppliers, in contrast to the *sogo shosha*, are especially important in consumer industries like automobiles and consumer electronics. When we add to the intermarket *keiretsu* companies' trade with their vertical *keiretsu* affiliates, percentages of total *keiretsu*-based trade rise still further. A reasonable estimate of overall average internalization, including both *keiretsu* forms, is likely to surpass 50 percent of firms' total trade. By these estimates, over one-half of Japanese interfirm trade involves closely affiliated *keiretsu* partners, both intermarket and vertical.[30]

IMPLICATIONS OF THE *KEIRETSU* FOR UNDERSTANDING BARRIERS TO ENTRY IN THE JAPANESE MARKET

Japanese markets are constituted by alliances among financial, commercial, and industrial organizations in which the identity of those organizations is an important determinant of the actual flow of resources. As we have seen, the intermarket *keiretsu*'s presidents' council identifies core group membership and acts as a forum for interaction within the group. More significant, the *keiretsu* has internalized trade in debt, equity, and intermediate products within preferential trading relationships. Table 4–6 is a summary of earlier tables showing the effects of group membership on interfirm networks.

Patterns of international trade are based not only on exchange rates set by capital markets and legal barriers set by governments but also on the concrete relationships among the firms that actually make buying and selling decisions. To the extent that patterns of

Table 4-6. Intermarket *Keiretsu* Effects on Interfirm Networks—Summary Table.

	Debt	Equity	Intermediate Products
Internalization	21%	54%	35–45% (est.)
Group bias factor	6X	14X	N.A.

Note: N.A. = data not available.

industrial organization vary substantially across countries, so too will the purchasing decisions of firms in those countries vary in their sensitivity to economic, social, and political considerations. Densely linked and strongly preferential trading systems, such as that found in the Japanese *keiretsu*, are likely to be less sensitive to fluctuations in exchange rates or to government liberalization efforts than more arm's-length market ties. Allied firms, quite rationally, base their purchasing decisions on relationships in their entirety rather than on a transaction-specific pricing calculus. As a result of these structural differences in industrial organization, the rules of market access, even among nominally open economies, can have dramatically different results.

In this concluding section, we consider in turn the effects of Japan's peculiar organization of equity, debt, and product markets on the opportunities for foreign market entrants. While the discussion is focused on the effects of the intermarket *keiretsu*, we need to remember that this is only one of a variety of preferential trading patterns that make up the Japanese economy. Vertical *keiretsu* ties backward into component supply and forward into distribution are also important, particularly in consumer industries, as are other kinds of long-term reciprocal obligations.[31]

Trade in Banking Services

Preferential trade between Japanese firms and their creditors is most relevant to market entry by foreign banks. Biases toward own-group financial institutions, as we have seen, are strong in Japan (group bias averaged six times in Table 4-2), more than enough to at least partially offset whatever advantages in terms, financial tools, or services foreign banks may bring to the Japanese market. A company's main bank is not only a source of capital, it is also a source of business contacts and a source of security during economic downturns. At the margin, Japanese companies might look to foreign banks for loans, but fewer companies are relying on banks for capital than they used to as the ability to finance expansion through retained earnings and through other financial instruments has increased. For what business is needed, firms will continue to go to their long-standing creditors.

These creditors also serve as leading shareholders in the companies to which they lend, and are not prohibited by Glass-Steagall-like restrictions from acting on these interests. The barriers facing foreign banks in the Japanese market were stated nowhere more clearly than in the following observation by Igarashi Osamu, the financial vice president of Japan Air Lines: "We have 16 banks in our syndicate, each of which is a shareholder. . . . Therefore, we have to borrow from all 16 banks, and we could not think of borrowing from foreign banks."[32] Given views like the above, a direct result of the structure of interfirm alliances discussed in this chapter, it is unlikely that foreign banks will at any time soon gain anything more than a small fraction of the Japanese banking market.

Trade in Corporate Assets

The effects of *keiretsu* structures are even stronger on Japanese equity markets. Here the issue is the extent to which foreign investors have opportunities to acquire existing Japanese firms. Corporate takeovers of the kind now prevalent in the United States are virtually nonexistent in Japan. In part, this reflects the norms of the Japanese business community, which have established strong sanctions against offenders of the code of conduct, "though shalt not take over thy neighbor's company." Management and unions work together to expel outsiders in the philosophy of *jibun no shiro wa jibun de mamore* ("protect your own castle"). The colloquial term for takeover, *nottori*, is the same word used in Japanese to refer to an airline hijacking, with similar connotations.

Even more important to preventing acquisition by independent companies is the *keiretsu* structure of equity shareholdings. After all, if over one-half of a firm's top shareholder positions are controlled by fellow *keiretsu* members, as shown in Table 4-4, where are the access points for the foreign (or Japanese) interloper? An example of the ways in which the group rallies round to protect its own firms involves the Sumitomo group and its affiliated brewery, Asahi. In the mid-1970s, an investment group made up of Japanese doctors (and therefore independent of the conventions of the Japanese business community) had acquired about 30 percent of the shares of Asahi Breweries. Asahi's share of sales in the beer industry was declining and its overall performance had been poor. Asahi's main bank was Sumitomo, which arranged for Asahi Chemical (no relation) to pick up part of Asahi Breweries' operations. In addition, the bank sent down a number of its own executives to serve as officers in the company, including the new president of the company. Most important, it negotiated with the investment consortium to sell out its shares to the bank and to other "friendly" companies, including to other Sumitomo group members.

Japanese firms view the intentions of foreign firms with some suspicion. Foreign ownership of Japanese stock has increased substantially over the past two decades, and accounted for 5.1 percent total shareholdings in 1983, up from only 1.4 percent in 1961. Because of the tendency of Japanese institutional investors to hold onto their shares, foreigners, although holding only 5 percent of total shares, account for about 20 percent of all trading on the Tokyo Stock Exchange.[33] In 1969 Isuzu and General Motors announced that the latter would buy shares of the former. The Ministry of International Trade and Industry, under pressure, at this point raised the limit of foreign capital participation to 35 percent (from 25 percent) on the condition that a substantial portion of the shares be held by stable shareholders. An executive of Fuji Motors was reported to say at the time of Fuji's break with Isuzu Motors: "I think it is advisable for our company and Isuzu Motors to continue holding each other's shares in spite of their liquidation of ties, so that we can remain each other's stabilized shareholders. Also it is desirable that the automobile firm as a whole hold one another's shares regardless of group affiliations, *in order to defend native capital.*"[34] Since this time, Toyota and Nissan have been especially aggressive in buying shares of their supplier parts companies to preempt foreign corporations.

In 1971 the Finance Ministry revised the securities exchange to allow foreign takeovers of Japanese companies. However, despite this liberalization, there have been virtually no interfirm transactions in corporate assets involving foreign firms in Japan. In 1985, for example, a British–U.S. investment group attempted a hostile takeover of the Japanese company, Minebea. This attempt was defeated, however, when the investors found "Japanese" shareholders unwilling to sell their "shares." The market is in principal open but in reality internally regulated by the parties involved. In this way, market entry through acquisitions—an increasingly common strategy by Japanese firms overseas—while not entirely prevented, is nevertheless de facto considerably more difficult in Japan than in other "open" economies such as that of the United States and Britain.

Trade in Intermediate Products

A topic that has generated more heat than any other in Japan's external economic relationships is its international merchandise trade. That so little light has been generated at the same time results from a failure to fully understand the signal importance of the concrete, firm-level purchasing decisions which, in aggregate, determine a country's trade patterns. Intermediate product markets are often not fully competitive, and firms base their decisions on a host of factors, not all of which have to do with characteristics of the products themselves. Where characteristics of the trading relationship are important, changes in exchange rates and market liberalization efforts will have substantially less effect on trade than orthodox theory would suggest, since firms are concerned with more than simply discrete pricing decisions.

That is an important part of the reason why foreign market penetration into Japan has remained negligible in a wide variety of industrial markets—despite the ongoing reduction since the 1970s in formal regulatory and tariff barriers imposed by the Japanese government and despite the dramatic rise in the value of the yen since 1985. Whatever price reductions might be passed along to the Japanese buyer of foreign products are at least partially "absorbed" by the vertical channels through which these products must flow. Japanese firms are as interested in protecting their relationship with domestic suppliers as they are in passing along cost savings to others.

The main keepers of the gate, of course, are the *sogo shosha*. Handling two-thirds of Japan's international trade, these firms, as we have seen, are also central in the trading networks of their own *keiretsu.* Table 4–5 indicated that, at least in the case of Mitsui Bussan and Mitsubishi Shoji, trading companies handle anywhere from one-fifth to nearly all of the supplies for firms in industrial markets that are in their own *keiretsu. Keiretsu* firms in addition purchase somewhere around 16 percent of their supplies on average *directly* from other group firms. Thus, on average at least one-third and in many cases well over one-half of all trade among firms in industrial markets—steel, nonferrous metals, chemicals, industrial machinery—is constituted by affiliated firm within the same inter-market *keiretsu.* Even if we assume that the remainder of trade takes place at arm's length (much, in fact, takes place through *secondary* affiliates), this still means that a substantial portion of the Japanese economy in these sectors is organized through long-term relationships among firms tied both directly to each other and indirectly to the larger groups of which they are members. For firms in important consumer sectors like automobiles and consumer electronics, vertical *keiretsu* supplies are more important than the *sogo shosha.* The arguments concerning access to trade with these firms, nevertheless, remain the same, for these too are long-term relationships linked through complex equity and other interlocks.

CONCLUSION

Some have argued that the *keiretsu* structure in the Japanese economy is breaking down. While it is true that the requirements of new technologies has forced firms to forge alliances across group boundaries, and equally true that firms no longer need to rely on their main bank to the same extent as in the past for capital, it is not true that the *keiretsu* is a thing of the past. The *keiretsu* have never been entirely exclusive in their dealings and should not be expected to be so now. Group firms continue to cooperate in high-technology sectors. Each of the big six groups has formed cooperative projects in telecommunication information systems and the Mitsubishi group is even building its own satellite. Moreover, while company borrowings from group banks has been on the decline, overall internalization of equity shareholdings has been on the *rise*, in response to the ongoing liberalization of Japanese capital markets and the desire by group firms to protect themselves from the kind of "merger mania" found in the United States.[35]

The inroads now being made by companies from the newly industrializing economies of East Asia and by some European firms in Japanese markets, though impressive, must be placed in perspective. Products from the first have increased substantially the share of Japanese imports comprised of manufactured goods, but this has come largely in sectors out of which Japan is already moving (e.g., shipbuilding) and where added value is lowest (e.g., commodity steel and low-end textiles). European manufacturers, in contrast, have been most successful in sophisticated and name-brand luxury goods where domestic competition is minimal.

The competitive advantage of U.S. firms, in contrast, is often in precisely those high-value-added industrial and high-technology products in which *keiretsu* affiliations are most prevalent. The firms central in Japan's push into the "information industries," for example, are all formal members in at least one of the big-six intermarket *keiretsu*—NEC in Sumitomo, Toshiba in Mitsui; Fujitsu in Dai-Ichi Kangyo; Hitachi in Fuji, Sanwa, and Dai-Ichi Kangyo; and so forth. Each of these firms, known collectively as the JCMs (Japanese Computer Manufacturers), has been central in its own group as supplier of both hardware and telecommunications networking capabilities (for example, by linking affiliated firms through value-added networks, or VANs).

Japanese industry-promotion policies have long recognized these linkages. Government-sponsored cooperative projects have been careful to bring together where possible firms from each *keiretsu*. In the information industries, for example, projects such as the Fifth Generation Computer have included electronics firms from all of the six main groups, with the intention to promote research that allows these firms to better compete with their great corporate bête noire, IBM. Sophisticated foreign firms have also recognized the importance of interfirm affiliations in the Japanese market and incorporate these as part of their strategies in finding sales outlets and joint venture partners. IBM has been developing close ties with the Mitsubishi group in network services, through its relationships with Mitsubishi Electric, while AT&T has been doing the same with the Mitsui group, through its ties to Toshiba. (Japanese firms have, at least until recently, been technologically behind in this area.) Trade policy, too, must consider these linkages. National differences in industrial organization, even among nominally open economies, have consequences for actual patterns of trade.

NOTES

1. In Japanese, the terms *kigyo shudan* or *kigyo gruupu* are also used to refer to the groupings discussed below.

2. For an extensive survey of the intermarket *keiretsu*, see Michael L. Gerlach, "Business Alliances and the Strategy of the Japanese Firm," *California Management Review* (Fall 1987): 126–142, and *Alliance Capitalism: The Social Organization of Japanese Business* (Berkeley: University of California Press, forthcoming).

3. *Nihon Kigyo Shudan Bunseki* (Analysis of Japanese Enterprise Groups), vol. 2 (Tokyo: Sangyo Doko Chosa-Kai, 1980), pp. 25–31.

4. *Industrial Groupings in Japan* (Tokyo: Dodwell Marketing Consultants, 1982), pp. 380–85).

5. Kosei Torihiki Inkai (Japanese Federal Trade Commission), "Kigyo Shudan no Jittai ni Tsuite" (On the State of Enterprise Groups), 1983.

6. Industries that have little or no *keiretsu* participation are more likely to be newer and less central to core industrial operations (such as consumer industries)—what the Japanese call the "soft" industries. These include publishing, communications, and air travel, in which the *keiretsu* have no involvement, and the broad category of service industries, in which they constitute less than 5 percent of total sales.

7. In most cases where two or more companies are listed under the same category, they represent different area or product lines. For example, within the Mitsui group, Mitsui Bussan and Mitsukoshi are, respectively, a multinational trading company and a department store chain; Mitsui Construction is a large building firm, while Sanki Engineering specializes in equipment installation; and Mitsui Toatsu covers a broad spectrum of chemicals, but leaves petroleum-related products like polyethylene to Mitsui Petrochemicals.

8. By the early 1980s, the councils had grown to a size of 21 companies for the smallest, Sumitomo, 24 for Mitsui, 28 for Mitsubishi, 29 for Fuji, 40 for Sanwa, and 45 for Dai-Ichi Kangyo.

9. These records are not made available to the public, nor are they transmitted formally within the member firms. For this reason, information about the internal contents of the meetings and of their dynamics is by necessity secondhand and inferential. The discussion here comes from interviews with a number of executives involved in group councils, as well as from various press reports. The *Oriental Economist* has published periodic articles on the groups since the 1950s that discuss the *shacho-kai* in varying degrees of detail and plausibility. See also Okumura Hiroshi, *Shin-Nihon no Roku Dai-kigyo Shudan* (*A New View of Japan's Six Large Enterprise Groups*) (Tokyo: Diamond, 1983), pp. 90–105.

10. Henry Mintzberg, *Power in and around Organizations* (Englewood Cliffs, N.J.: Prentice-Hall, 1983), p. 667ff.

11. The formal board of directors in the modern Japanese corporation is a largely powerless institution that is ritually reenacted to conform to Japanese business law rather than for the true discipline of the firm or expression of external interests; Rodney Clark, *The Japanese Company* (New Haven, CT: Yale University Press, 1979). The *shacho-kai* exists within this power vacuum, providing a forum for the informal representation of companies' leading exchange partners—that is, the other members of the group.

12. Donald Palmer, "Broken Ties: Interlocking Directorates and Intercorporate Coordination," *Administrative Science Quarterly* 28 (1983): 40–55.

13. Anonymous quotations are from the author's notes from interviews carried out while the author lived in Japan, 1983–85.

14. Aoki Masahiko, "Aspects of the Japanese Firm," in M. Aoki (ed.), *The Economic Analysis of the Japanese Firm* (Amsterdam: North-Holland, 1984), pp. 10–11.

15. Clark, *The Japanese Company*, p. 86.

16. Aoki, "Aspects of the Japanese Firm."

17. Beth Mintz and Michael Schwartz, *The Power Structure of American Business* (Chicago: University of Chicago Press, 1985), p. 97.

18. Kosei Torihiki Inkai, "Kigyo Shudan no Jittai ni Tsuite."

19. Futatsugi, *Gendai Nihon no Kigyo Shudan*.

20. Quoted in *Oriental Economist*, March 1961.

21. Johannes Hirschmeier and Tsunehiko Yui, *The Development of Japanese Business* (London: George Allen and Unwin, 1975), p. 191.

22. Ibid., p. 192.

23. This has historically constituted nearly half of the *sogo shosha*'s business, though this share has been decreasing in recent years. The proportion of third-country trade (offshore transactions not directly involving Japan), on the other hand, has been increasing.

24. *Wall Street Journal*, July 18, 1983.

25. "Sogo Shosha wa Shayo de Aru-ka," *Mainichi Economist*, May 1961.

26. *Japan Times*, May 25, 1985.

27. Goto cites figures for overall trade moving between group companies and group *sogo shosha* of 30 percent (p. 57 in Goto Akira, "Business Groups in a Market Economy," *European Economic Review* (1982): 53–70). Somewhat lower figures are given in a study in 1977 by the Long-Term Credit Bank of Japan (cited in Okumura, *Shin-Nihon no Roku Dai-Kigyo Shudan*, p. 138). This study found that 28 percent of all sales and 27 percent of all purchases in the Mitsubishi group went to the group's trading firm, while the figures for Mitsui were 18 percent for sales to and 9 percent for purchases from the group trading firm in the Mitsui group. According to the same study, the *sogo shosha* appear less dependent on their groups than

vice-versa, as *sogo shosha* purchases from group companies constitute a little less than 20 percent of their total purchases, while sales to group companies account for only about 5–6 percent of their total sales.

28.   *Oriental Economist*, October 1981.

29.   Kosei Torihiki Iinkai, "Kigyo Shudan no Jittai ni Tsuite."

30.   Unfortunately, estimates of group bias are more difficult to make. The fine-grained level of data necessary for this kind of analysis is largely absent or proprietary. I would hazard to guess that group bias in trade in intermediates is less than in equity shares, and perhaps somewhere comparable to that in debt capital—that is, around six times.

31.   See Ronald Dore, *Flexible Rigidities* (Stanford, Calif.: Stanford University Press, 1985). Nor can the reader assume that these patterns are absent in other economies, including that of the United States. We are dealing here in a matter of degrees.

32.   Quoted in *The Economist*, August 22, 1987.

33.   *Business Week*, October 15, 1984.

34.   Quoted in Robert J. Ballon, Iwao Tomita, and Hajime Usami, *Financial Reporting in Japan* (Tokyo: Kodansha International, 1976), p. 22; italics added.

35.   See Gerlach, "Business Alliances and the Strategy of the Japanese Firm," and *Alliance Capitalism*.

▐▐▐ THE JAPANESE SYSTEM AT WORK
The Arguments Tested

5 MITI, MPT, AND THE TELECOM WARS
How Japan Makes Policy for High Technology

Chalmers Johnson

In his memoirs of postwar politics, Yoshida Shigeru, the great prime minister who presided over Japan's rise from the ashes, commented that, "the Occupation, with all the power and authority behind its operation, was hampered by its lack of knowledge of the people it had come to govern, and even more so, perhaps, by its generally happy ignorance of the amount of requisite knowledge it lacked."[1] More than thirty five years after the end of the Allied Occupation of Japan, the main issue has changed from America's ability to govern a defeated Japan to its ability to compete economically with a renascent Japan, but Yoshida's observation is still valid. During the 1980s American leaders vehemently declared on every possible occasion that no country was "more important" to them than Japan and that Japan was the "cornerstone" of their foreign policy in the Pacific.[2] And yet these same leaders demonstrated on equally numerous occasions that they had not a clue as to how Japan was governed.

During 1984 and 1985, frustrated by the issues of Japanese industrial policy and product certification procedures, the Americans attempted to make an issue out of the lack of "transparency" of the Japanese government—by which they meant that they did not know how policies affecting them were made within the Japanese government and that they wanted to be able to lobby the Japanese government at least as easily and effectively as Japanese were lobbying the U.S. government in Washington.[3] Equally to the point, the

177

Americans were mystified by the coincidence of a warm personal friendship between the president and the prime minister (President Reagan's and Prime Minister Nakasone's "Ron and Yasu" relationship) and the growth of the bilateral trade deficit to $50 billion, the figure for 1985. During the period of their special relationship, Ron and Yasu agreed on at least a half dozen market opening schemes that were supposed to redress the trade imbalance. Instead it got worse. Did this mean that it was useless and misleading to lobby the Japanese prime minister?

Such confusion and misunderstanding were by no means restricted to the Reagan and Nakasone administrations. In a major study of the negotiations during the late 1970s between Japan and the United States to open up the Japanese telephone monopoly to sales by American manufacturers, Timothy Curran concluded:

> The U.S. request for the inclusion of NTT [Nippon Telegraph and Telephone Company] under the code [signed in 1979 governing procurements by governments] assumed an ability on the part of the Japanese government to deliver the requested concessions. When the government did not deliver NTT concessions, U.S. officials believed Japan was deliberately being uncooperative.

Even after they got an agreement with Japan, the Americans never really figured out what had been the problem on the Japanese side or why the discussions were so acrimonious. This led Curran to conclude that the United States "must learn more about Japan—about the structure of power and influence within the Japanese government—and between the government and the public corporations."[4]

Five years after a supposed telecommunications agreement was reached between the two countries, the situation remained unchanged. By 1985 the bilateral trade deficit in telecommunications equipment had grown to $1.5 billion in Japan's favor, even though this is an area of high technology in which the Americans are pioneers and in which their equipment and networks are without equal. Most analysts have concluded that this deficit is likely to be permanent, regardless of any changes in the macroeconomic environment of the two countries such as currency exchange rates. Nonetheless, American trade negotiators were claiming in April 1985 that they had achieved virtually all of their goals in the telecommunications talks; and John J. McDonnell, Jr., vice president of the U.S. Electronics Industries Association for telecommunications, was quoted by the press as saying that "All of us are absolutely delighted" with the operations of the new, independent certification agency that replaced the old system under which NTT certified all equipment for use in Japan. McDonnell also added, however, that "I don't ever expect, in my lifetime, to see a positive balance in trade with Japan in telecommunications."[5]

Telecommunications was supposed to be the success story of the 1985 American effort at market opening in Japan, compared with timber products, medical equipment and pharmaceuticals, and electronics, on each of which the United States failed to make headway or else turned to the courts in antidumping suits. And yet, toward the end of 1985, Glen Fukushima, head of Japanese affairs in the Office of the U.S. Trade Representative, revealed, "We've encountered some serious difficulties, and because of this it's difficult for us to say now that telecommunications has shown the most significant progress." On the Japanese–American trade negotiations in general, Fukushima concluded, "we went around and around in this discussion, and it was quite evident that the role of the government [in Japan] was conceived of being very different, that the expectations the community had of the government were different, and that the fundamental notion of competition was also quite different in the two countries."[6]

In my personal experience as a scholar of the Japanese political economy, I have on occasion been approached by senior officials of American industries with a request that I help them in lobbying the Japanese Diet. I have always replied that although I am sympathetic to the idea of trying to get the message of American business across in Japan, it is foolish to attempt to lobby the Japanese Diet. No one, Japanese or foreigner, is interested in lobbying the Diet since policies are not initiated or decided there but only ratified and legalized. "Where, then, should we lobby?" I am asked. This chapter is an extended answer to that question.

What should Americans know in order to lobby the Japanese government? My answer is divided into two broad parts. The first concerns one of the most controversial subjects in contemporary Japanese studies—namely, who governs in Japan and how is the system of governance changing? Regardless of the many different answers given to these questions by Japanese and foreign analysts alike, all will agree that the components of the answer include bureaucracy, ruling party, faction, and what are called *zoku* (loosely translatable as members of tribes or caucuses). I shall attempt to describe each of these groups and how they relate to one another, particularly in the area of telecommunications. The second part of my answer takes the form of a case study of Japanese policymaking for one of the two or three most important high-technology industries—namely, telecommunications during what Japanese have come to call the telecom wars of 1983–85. Although the participants and battles of the telecom wars during the first half of the 1980s are fixed in time and place, the kinds of relationships they had are of continuing significance, and I am hopeful that such a cautionary tale will help put meat on the bones of my structural analysis.

JAPAN'S POLITICAL SYSTEM AND HOW IT IS CHANGING

During the first half of the 1980s, the Japanese government initiated and pursued many important official policies for the nation. These included the decision to end the century-old governmental monopoly in telecommunications services by reorganizing the Nippon Telegraph and Telephone Company as a joint stock company. English-speaking observers like to refer to this development as "privatization" even though, in fact, all shares of the new NTT are under the control of the government and only a portion of them are being sold to the public (none to foreigners) over a five-year period.[7] The government also undertook to rewrite its laws regulating the newly demonopolized telecommunications business, tried to force the interest rates on postal savings accounts down to the level of those authorized by the Ministry of Finance (MOF) for the commercial banks, established new organizations to support research and development in telecommunications and other high-technology industries, began to protect the property rights of authors and manufacturers of programs for computers, sheltered its domestic communications satellite industry from foreign competition so that it might one day become a viable exporter, negotiated with the Americans over what was euphemistically called "trade friction," and started to build digitalized telecommunications infrastructures for the eventual interconnection of "new media" equipment (video telephones, videotex terminals, two-way cable television, and so on). Each one of these initiatives was the occasion for a major battle in the telecom wars, as shown later in this chapter. The immediate problem is why the Japanese government, in part or as a whole, undertook these or any other public projects. What were the interests and motives of actors within the Japanese governmental process and how did they conflict?

It is necessary at the outset to reject most foreign analytical writing on this subject since it almost invariably projects onto Japan the experience of one or another foreign country or the ideological expectations of foreigners about what Japanese motivations should be. Thus, for example, when Charles L. Brown, the chairman of the American Telephone and Telegraph Company (AT&T), states that the telecommunications business everywhere is driven by "technological revolutions," by such things as microelectronics, the applications of light-wave physics to fiber optics, and software development, one may agree in very broad terms but the fact remains that almost none of this technology was developed in Japan and thus there were no endogenous technological imperatives that drove Japan to change its preexisting system.[8] Japan demonopolized the telecommunications business for good Japanese reasons, which have almost nothing to do with technology.

Similarly, Japan was not copying the example of the breakup of AT&T in the United States. AT&T was ordered by the U.S. courts to dismember itself before starting to connect computers with telephone networks, whereas Japan kept NTT intact but allows newcomers to try to compete with it. AT&T still buys most of its equipment from Western Electric, which it owns, whereas NTT has always depended on external sourcing. Japan was also not forced to change by American trade negotiators. The Americans were not so much interested in the legal status of NTT as in trying to get it to buy foreign products at least to the extent that it subsidized domestic exporters (until 1985 NTT paid Sumitomo Electric $1.50 per meter for cables while Sumitomo charged its American customers only 60 cents a meter).[9] When talking about Japanese motives, one must remember that Japan is one of the world's most intellectually isolated and inward-looking countries; it is always more preoccupied with domestic developments than with external events. This is not to say that technological developments or foreign pressures have no effect on Japan. It is rather to argue that such forces only supply opportunities and constraints that indirectly influence the primary motivations of domestic protagonists.[10] Who, then, are these domestic protagonists and what are their motives?

The first group is the official state bureaucracy. These are the officials of the central government ministries and agencies who since Japan's emergence as a modern state in the late nineteenth century have been the planners, engineers, and supervisors of Japan's economic and social development. This group is an inherent meritocracy of talent, educated in the best schools and universities in the country; and it is very much aware of and jealously protects its high prestige within the social system. In the postwar world from 1945 until approximately 1972, when Tanaka Kakuei became prime minister, the bureaucracy's monopoly of policymaking powers in Japan was virtually complete. The only areas where political rather than bureaucratic interests clearly prevailed were education, defense, and agricultural price supports.[11] Even after Tanaka began to change the system, most important policies still originate within a ministry or agency, not within the political or private sectors, although these policies may be extensively modified once the bureaucracy makes them public.

Of the three broad theories of bureaucratic behavior—that state bureaucrats attempt to serve (1) the public's interest, (2) the interests of their clients, or (3) their own interests—the evidence of Japan suggests that the last has the greatest explanatory power. In a famous study of the Ministry of Finance, John Campbell ranked the priorities of the ministry as it pursued its single most important task, that of drafting the national and investment budgets. First priority was "protection of the ministry's autonomy, elite status, and jurisdictional boundaries." This was put ahead of "pursuing correct fiscal policies for given economic conditions" (priority 2) and well ahead of "eliminating wasteful spending and obsolete programs" (priority 8).[12] Needless to say, the Ministry of Finance does not itself distinguish among serving the public's, its clients', or its own interests, presuming that the way to achieve the public's and its clients' interests is to ensure that its own needs are fulfilled. This is of course true of most official bureaucracies, from the U.S. Department of Defense to the Soviet Committee of State Security, and of all politicians.

The problem is that the interest of one agency of the government can and often does conflict with the interest of another agency, particularly in a government that has a vertically structured division of labor (tatewari-gyosei, as the Japanese put it) and is as pervasive as that of the Japanese capitalist developmental state.[13] In such a system the greatest threat to the security of a bureaucrat comes from other bureaucrats. The core of any bureaucratic interest becomes the protection of one's separate jurisdiction; and conflicts of jurisdiction (*nawabari arasoi*, or "conflicts over roped-off areas") are the most significant events in the lives of state bureaucrats. The resulting competition among bureaucrats may be a source of creativity and vitality or lead to irresponsibility and policy failures. The bureaucratic telecom wars elicited ingenuity and hard work from Japan's rival agencies, but Japan has also experienced some cases in which divided jurisdictions led to suboptimal results or to outright failure (for example, the new Tokyo International Airport or the atomic ship *Mutsu*).[14]

In the telecom wars, the two main bureaucratic actors were the Ministry of International Trade and Industry (MITI, Tsusho Sangyo-sho) and the Ministry of Posts and Telecommunications (MPT, Yusei-sho, literally, "Ministry of Postal Affairs" but since 1952, when NTT became a public corporation under MPT's jurisdiction, officially translated as "Ministry of Posts and Telecommunications"). Other agencies appeared on the battlefields as allies of one or the other side—the Ministry of Finance allied with MITI and the Agency of Cultural Affairs of the Ministry of Education allied with MPT— but generally speaking MITI and MPT were the chief protagonists and antagonists.

MITI SINCE THE "MIRACLE"

MITI's headquarters in Kasumigaseki, Tokyo, are located about fifty feet from the main office building of MPT, on the same city block, but the two are anything but friendly neighbors. After World War II, with the unification in 1949 of industrial development and trade administration, MITI emerged as the governmental sponsor and supervisor of high-speed economic growth. Given Japan's enormous success as a highly industrialized nation, MITI became what the press likes to call an "ultra-first-class bureaucracy" (*cho-ichiryu kancho*), staffed with some of the finest minds and best managerial talent in the country.[15] MITI today is more or less in the same class as the Ministry of Finance (in recent years it has attracted even better talent from the universities than MOF) and it is without question one of the nation's most valuable institutional assets.

But MITI has a serious problem. It is losing jurisdiction. MITI's historic task of protecting and nurturing Japanese industries until they could compete in any market in the world is over. Japan's big businesses no longer need MITI. Moreover, the slower growth of the Japanese economy since the first oil crisis of 1973 has meant that MITI's usual methods—home market protection, preferential supply of capital, import of foreign technology, "excessive" domestic competition, cartellization according to market share, and so forth—are no longer appropriate. For the decade and a half since the first oil shock and Japan's realization that it could ride out the crisis better than its competitors, MITI has been forced to think about its future role.[16] This is an activity in which MITI has acquired great experience and expertise.

Part of MITI's efforts have gone into refurbishing old sectors (for example, energy policy and measures for declining industries) and it continues to hone all its traditional skills such as administrative guidance, quasicovert measures to nullify the effects of publicly proclaimed "liberalizations," and industrial targeting. Even though poorly informed foreigners like to argue that administrative guidance, and even industrial policy itself, are things of the past, MITI's intervention during 1985 to prevent the import of gasoline refined abroad by Lion's Petroleum (there are no laws against importing gasoline) was one of the most blatant examples of administrative guidance.[17] Similarly, MITI's "temporary" laws for dealing with structurally recessed industries and its subsidies for medium and smaller industries are intended primarily to offset market openings, changes in exchange rates, and other developments that are disadvantageous to domestic industries. MITI is ingenious on these fronts.

But this cannot go on forever, and even MITI spokesmen have been unambiguous in saying so.[18] Even if the Americans do not crack down on Japan's huge export surplusses, the Chinese, Koreans, and Southeast Asians certainly will. Looking to the future, then, MITI sees two main prospects, one not very attractive but the other quite alluring. The unattractive option is that it might turn itself into a ministry of imports. This would require the ministry to lead the country from an almost totally supply-side-oriented economy to genuine demand stimulation. MITI could do this since it recognizes that anti-Japanese protectionism is probably the major potential threat to Japan's economic well-being. Moreover, as has been the case many times in the past, MITI understands that a crisis for the economy—the threat of protectionism—is not necessarily a crisis for MITI.[19] In the past such crises as postwar reconstruction, trade and capital liberalization, and the oil shocks merely gave MITI new leases on life. Even so, becoming a governmental agent for importers would be a comedown for MITI; and such a posture would make it vulnerable to charges of betraying national interests and of toadying to foreigners, a point all too well understood at MPT.[20]

Therefore, although MITI continues to toy with the idea of becoming an agency of Keynesian domestic demand management, its real thrust is toward the promotion of the high-technology industries of the future. What Americans rather lamely call the "postindustrial society" is identified more positively in Japan as the "information-ized society" (joho-ka shakai). MITI theorists and other Japanese futurologists note the increasing disconnections between modern manufacturing and the supplies of raw materials or labor. The raw materials of semiconductors and ceramic engines are virtually worthless in their natural state, and robots are not just replacing people on the production line but they are often more effective than people. Thus the society of the future may be dependent not on supplies of raw materials and cheap labor but on highly educated and skilled people who package and communicate information.[21] It will be a "service economy" but not in the sense that services will replace agriculture and manufacturing. Both the primary and secondary sectors will continue to be of central importance, but they will be largely automated and technology intensive. The key industries for this future economy, identified over and over again in Japanese technical and popular literature, will be telecommunications, new materials, and biotechnology.[22] In a world dominated by these industries Japan will no longer be a resource-poor, vulnerable trading nation living by its wits but one of the world's best endowed countries. It is on the basis of this vision that MITI vice minister Konaga has sought to put his ministry almost totally in charge of administering research and development for high-technology industries.[23]

Whether or not this vision of the future is valid, telecommunications is already one of the fastest growing industries on earth. Forecasts of demand for telecommunications services are virtually unlimited for at least two generations. In all of its many forms, including office automation, instantaneous transmission of data, and the diagnosis of malfunctions in human and man-made systems, telecommunications are probably the greatest single source of gains in productivity at work today. MITI's jurisdiction clearly includes the computer industry. The problem is, as MITI men like to say, "A computer without software is only a box, and a computer with soft-

ware is still only a computer. But a computer connected to a telephone circuit is something else again: it is a telecommunications network."[24] Unfortunately for MITI, telecommunications circuits are
clearly within MPT's jurisdiction. In order for MITI to usher in what
it has identified as its "third golden age" (the first was the heavy and
chemical industrialization of the 1950s and 1960s, followed by the
global victories in international trade of the late 1960s and 1970s),
it must overcome its rival and bring telecommunications under its
jurisdiction. Given MITI's history, talents, and high esprit de corps,
this should not have been too difficult a task. MITI may, however,
have underestimated its rival.

One of America's most seasoned analysts of Japanese politics,
Fukui Haruhiro, recently expressed surprise at an anomaly that
turned up in his data. While statistically analyzing the careers of
Japan's top political leaders, he confirmed that most of them had
served as head of MITI, MOF, and the foreign ministry, as well as
chief cabinet secretary, before becoming prime minister. The anomaly was that his data also showed that the third most common career
step to supreme political power was service as minister of Posts and
Telecommunications.[25] About the same time that Fukui was ponder-
ing this puzzle, Minowa Noboru, a member of the lower house of the
Diet from the Hokkaido First district, stalwart of the Tanaka faction
of the ruling Liberal Democratic party (LDP), and recently retired
as the last postal minister in the Suzuki cabinet, was saying in a
speech to his Hokkaido constituents, "Being postal minister is part
of the mandatory course to the prime ministership. There is no need
to mention it, but I, of course . . . (cough, cough)."[26]

For the elite bureaucrats of MITI and MOF, to the extent that
they think at all about it, MPT has been considered a "third-rate
business bureaucracy" (sanryu no gengyo kancho), utterly distinct
from their own "policy ministries" (seisaku kancho). What they overlook is that MPT always has been and still is a political powerhouse.
As the balance of power between bureaucrats and politicians began
to shift during and after the Tanaka era and as MPT bureaucrats began to imagine themselves recapturing some of the glory of their
prewar stronghold, the old Ministry of Communications (Teishin-
sho), MITI began to discover that it had taken on a tiger.

THE HISTORY OF MPT

It is important to recall that, in the wake of the Meiji Restoration of 1868, Japan's system of ministries and agencies came into being well before its political parties, constitution, or parliament. Differing from the United States, these ministries were not created to be "civil servants," or to provide regulation of private concerns, or to supply jobs for party loyalists, but rather to guide Japan's rapid forced development in order to forestall incipient colonization by Western imperialists. Japan's ministries were task-oriented mobilization and development agencies, and their criterion of success was advancing the wealth and power of Japan, as distinct from any particular group of Japanese. It is because of the ministries' sometimes overlapping jurisdictions, the bureaucratic competition among them, and their tendency to believe that the public can simply be manipulated from above, that Japanese political scientists have invented the concept of vertical administration

In the 1880s the Meiji oligarchs created the ancestors of MITI and MPT. In 1881 they set up the Ministry of Agriculture and Commerce, one of MITI's predecessors, to administer agriculture, commerce, and the postal service. Four years later they reorganized the whole government into the cabinet system that has lasted to this day. As part of that reorganization the leaders of the Restoration created the Ministry of Communications and coined the term *teishin* for it. The title of the Teishin-sho is made up of *tei* from *ekitei*, the feudal word for postal service, signifying the transfer of the service from Agriculture and Commerce to the new ministry, and *shin*, from *denshin*, meaning telegraph. The Ministry of Communications was destined to become one of Japan's superministries of development; during the 1930s it also became a cockpit of ultranationalism and militarism, one of the reasons that after the war the Allied Occupation wanted it broken up.

From its beginning the Ministry of Communications controlled mail, the telegraph, maritime shipping, and lighthouses. In 1891 it added telephones and electric power generation to its purvue. For exactly a century, from 1885 to 1985, the government supplied and monopolized all Japanese telecommunications. In 1892 the ministry also took charge of developing and administering the railroads, and in 1909 it was given supervision of hydroelectric power generation.

In 1916 the ministry added postal life insurance; in 1925 civil aviation and the aircraft industry; and in 1926 the postal annuity system. An attempt today to put the Ministry of Communications back together would involve merging MPT, NTT, the Ministry of Transportation, the Japanese National Railways, Japan Air Lines, MITI's Natural Resources and Energy Agency, and renationalizing the electric power industry. That obviously is not going to happen, but ambitious MPT bureaucrats still like to speak of "the revival of the great Ministry of Communications" (*Dai-teishin-sho no fukkatsu*) as one of their goals.[27] What they mean by this is not the literal recreation of the prewar ministry but the promotion of its grandchild, MPT, to the status of a "policy agency," on the same level as MITI and MOF in the Kasumigaseki pecking order.

The dismemberment of the Communications Ministry actually began during World War II and was completed by the occupation, but this "ancient" history is still relevant to the MITI-MPT rivalry forty years later. During the war the Ministry of Munitions, in MITI's lineage, obtained jurisdiction over electric power and the aviation industry, sectors that are still securely in MITI's bailiwick. During the war Communications also lost all control over transportation, the railroads having been taken away years earlier and put into a separate Ministry of Railroads. The Occupation continued this arrangement except that it created a new Ministry of Transportation to regulate the industry and spun off the government-owned railroad lines into a public corporation, the Japanese National Railways.

On June 1, 1949, at the height of General MacArthur's new policy of trying to get Japan back on its feet economically, the Japanese government in consultation with the Supreme Commander for the Allied Powers (SCAP) abolished the Ministry of Communications and replaced it with two new ministries: the Ministry of Postal Affairs (Yusei-sho), in charge of the mail and postal savings systems, and the Ministry of Telecommunications (Denki Tsushin-sho), in charge of rebuilding the telegraph and telephone systems. Three years later, just as the occupation was coming to an end, the Ministry of Telecommunications was transformed into a wholly government-owned public corporation, NTT, under the supervision of the Ministry of Postal Affairs. The model for NTT was the Japanese National Railways (JNR) except that NTT was an absolute government monopoly whereas the JNR was allowed privately owned rivals. Over time this difference turned the JNR into the greatest source of red ink in the Japanese budget, whereas NTT has always remained profitable.

From 1952 to 1985 MPT and NTT maintained a very peculiar relationship with each other. MPT, with 310,000 employees, was the largest agency of the central government, but virtually all of its staff were postal workers. Its officials were really the managers of a large delivery and banking business (the mail service, postal savings, and postal life insurance). NTT, by contrast, although nominally super-vised by MPT, actually outclassed it. When the Communications Min-istry had been divided in 1949, virtually all the engineers and other highly trained technicians had gone to the Telecommunications Min-istry and, in 1952, to NTT. MPT's supervision of NTT was therefore nominal, amounting to only two officials in the ministry's secretariat, one of whom was a technical expert detailed to MPT from NTT. MPT's real role was as liaison between NTT and the Diet, which had the legal power to approve the NTT budget and telephone rates.

During these public corporation years, NTT perpetuated and strengthened the relationships that the Communications Ministry had established during the 1920s with preferred suppliers of equip-ment. NTT did research in its laboratories, set specifications for what it wanted to buy, and bought all of its equipment from a group of civilian firms that came to be known as the "NTT Family." Until the late 1970s NTT was preoccupied with rebuilding the telephone system (Japan lost over half a million phones due to war damage; in Tokyo alone the drop from prewar days was from 200,000 to 16,000). The corporation bought everything it needed from domestic companies; and international competition never crossed its mind.

NTT's four largest suppliers were (1) NEC Corporation (Nippon Electric), founded in 1899, a member of the Sumitomo zaibatsu, and Japan's first joint-venture company (with Western Electric); (2) Fujitsu, established in 1915, derived from the Furukawa Electric Company of 1896, and allied with the Siemens Company of Ger-many; (3) Oki Electric, established in 1912 and associated for pur-poses of technology-transfer with British General Electric; and (4) Hitachi, founded in 1910, and independent of foreign connections. These firms maintained the most intimate personal, technical, re-search, and financial relationships with NTT. Until 1981, when the former president of Keidanren, Doko Toshio, sent his protégé, Shinto Hisashi, to NTT as president in order to reform it, the leaders of NTT were invariably bureaucrats from the old Communications Ministry with close ties to the "family" (see Table 5-1). Because of NTT's clout in the *zaikai* (the world of big business), it tended to regard MPT as merely its "Kasumigaseki branch office" (*Denden Kosha no Kasumigaseki shutchojo*). Perhaps more descriptive of their actual relationship, however, since MPT was still the legal superior, was the quip that MPT was a *gukei* (foolish elder brother) compared with NTT's *kentei* (clever younger brother).[28]

Even though MPT was regarded as only a "third-rate business bureaucracy" (to this day its staffers refer to it as "our company" rather than as "our ministry"), politicians have always liked it.[29] This was certainly true of the prewar Ministry of Communications, but even afrer the war politicians found it useful to serve as postal minister. Among the postwar politicians who occupied the post early in their careers, when it is most valuable, are faction leaders (all but one are also former prime ministers) Miki Takeo (1947–48), Sato Eisaku (1951–52), Tanaka Kakuei (1957–58), Suzuki Zenko (1960), and Komoto Toshio (1968–70). The postal ministry is attractive to politicians for three reasons: it directly controls a large number of votes; each year it places large orders for equipment (uniforms, bicycles, and so forth); and it runs what is today the world's largest financial institution, the postal savings system, which is popular with the public because it pays higher rates of interest than the banks. I shall delay discussing the last two reasons until we turn to the telecom wars directly, since they both figure importantly in those wars. But the first reason requires some explanation, since it is not too well known even to the Japanese public.

When referring to the bedrock on which an LDP Diet member's continued political existence depends, party officials often use the slogan *gunon, nittobi, kyokucho-san. Gunon* means the Gunjin Onkyu Renmei (Veterans' Pension League); *nittobi* is the Nihon Tobishoku Rengo (the Japan Construction Workers' Union); and *kyokucho-san* is a polite reference to the Tokutei Yubinkyokucho Kai (the Association of Special Postmasters).[30] It is the latter that concerns us here. There are in Japan about 23,000 post offices. Of these some 17,980 (in 1986) are "special post offices," meaning that they are local, family-owned, rural post offices, usually with no more than two or three employees. Back in the Meiji era, when the system was being set up, notable local families received franchises from the government to conduct mail and postal savings business; and these

Table 5-1. Presidents of Nippon Telegraph and Telephone Public
Corporation (Denden Kosha), 1952-85.

1952-58	
Kajii Takeshi	1887-1976. Graduate of Todai, doctorate in engineering, 1912. Communications Ministry, 1912-35. President of NEC and a director of Sumitomo until purged by the Occupation. On depurge, again president of NEC until assuming presidency of NTT. Postwar re-creator of the NTT "family" system. Father-in-law of Okita Saburo, special representative for trade negotiations, including NTT, in the Suzuki cabinet.
1958-65	
Ohashi Hachiro	1885-68. Graduate of Todai, political science, 1910. Communications Ministry, 1910-36 (vice minister). Wartime president of Japan Broadcasting Company (NHK). Chairman of NTT Management Committee until assuming presidency.
1965-77	
Yonezawa Shigeru	b. 1911. Graduate of Todai, engineering, 1933. Communications Ministry, 1933-49. 1952-77, NTT. Personal friend of Prime Minister Sato.
1977-81	
Akikusa Tokuji	b. 1909. Graduate of Tokyo Commercial University, 1934. 1934-81, prewar Kokusai Denshin Denwa (KDD, International Telegraph and Telephone), with service in Southeast Asia; to the Communications Ministry; to NTT. Appointed NTT president by Prime Minister Fukuda; both come from the same town in Gunma prefecture.
1981-85	
Shinto Hisashi	b. 1910. Graduate of Kyushu University, doctorate in marine engineering, 1934. 1934, joined Harima Shipyard as head of technical department; 1966, director, Toshiba Electric; 1972, president, Ishikawajima Harima Heavy Industries. Author of engineering books. Recipient of many awards from Ministry of Transportation for building supertankers.

franchises are often passed on from one generation to another.[31] MPT pays these private postmasters a commission on their sales of stamps and a bounty on their savings accounts over a certain amount. The Special Post Offices bring the nationwide postal savings system to remote areas and are both a cause and an effect of there being comparatively few branch banks in rural Japan.

These franchised postmasters constitute a powerful political interest group, primarily devoted to keeping the postal savings system out of the hands of the Ministry of Finance. Their main tool of influence is mobilization of the rural vote. On the basis of 400 post offices per constituency and 200 votes per post office, Horne calculates that postmasters control some 80,000 votes per district. That may overstate the case somewhat, but all commentators agree that to be named chairman of the party's Communications Section (Tsushin Bukai), a body to which we shall turn presently, is virtually to be guaranteed reelection and that the postmasters' help is critical for candidates from weak factions.[32] All of this means that MPT has many friends in political life who are quick to come to its aid when it needs a favor.

MPT's Rise in Status

MPT's status as a "foolish elder brother," even if beloved by politicians, began to change in the early 1980s for a series of interrelated reasons. First was the KDD scandal of 1979. KDD, or Kokusai Denshin Denwa Company (International Telegraph and Telephone), is the overseas equivalent of NTT. It was set up in 1953, a year after NTT, and is also a wholly government-owned public corporation under MPT's jurisdiction. It is much smaller than NTT (about 6,000 employees compared to NTT's 300,000 plus), since virtually all it does is to staff overseas offices and supply international operators for NTT's circuits.

In October 1979, two KDD employees were arrested at Narita airport while attempting to smuggle some ¥10 million worth of jewelry and other luxury items into the country without paying customs duties. The ensuing investigation revealed that for at least four years they and other KDD employees had been smuggling valuable goods into the country for KDD president Itano Manabu. Itano in turn passed out these items as corporate gifts to KDD board members, clients in southeast Asia, MPT minister Shirahama Nikichi (Ohira cabinet, 1978–80), and politicians of the LDP's postal caucus. During the Diet investigation of the affair, Koyama Moriya, chief secretary of MPT who was later vice minister during the telecom wars, became well known in political circles because he was frequently called to testify. He also became known to the press as "endless tape" because of his numerous, noncommital answers.[33]

Paradoxically, the KDD case contributed to an upgrading of MPT's status because it alerted the political world to the danger of corruption in organizations such as KDD and NTT. It also raised numerous questions about the excessive independence of the public corporations, their poor financial accountability, and the lack of effective supervision by the ministries, which use them as *amakudari* ("descent from heaven") landing spots for recently retired bureaucrats. Some politicians concluded that MPT had to be raised in status and given more policy responsibilities in order to ensure that nothing like the KDD case would recur. In subsequent years MITI would use the KDD case as evidence that MPT was too political and could not be trusted with so delicate and corruption-fraught a task as selling off the shares of the privatized NTT.[34] MPT's answer at the time of the KDD case and later was that in order for it better to supervise subordinate agencies it needed more clout.

Another reason for the change in MPT's status was NTT's involvement during 1978–80 in bitter trade friction with the United States. The issue was whether or not NTT's purchases of telecommunications equipment (worth over $3 billion per annum) were to be included in the liberalization of governmental procurements that Japan had agreed to in the so-called Tokyo Round of multilateral trade negotiations. The Americans did not target NTT from the start. All they asked was that Japan open up to international trade a share of its annual governmental purchases that was more or less equivalent to the share of American and Western European public procurements on which Japanese firms were free to bid. Whatever Japan's policy on this issue might have been, NTT quickly bungled the public relations aspects. After NTT president Akikusa was quoted to the effect that "the only thing NTT would buy from the United States was mops and buckets," many in the Japanese government recognized that NTT's engineers and "family" members could not be trusted with international negotiations.[35] MPT said that it could handle the matter better, but it needed new policymaking powers.

The third reason for the improvement in MPT's status was the launching during 1981 of the Second Provisional Commission for Administrative Reform (Rinji Gyosei Chosa Kai, abbreviated Rincho). The first such commission had existed during the 1960s, but it had failed both to stem the growth of government and to make it more efficient. By 1980 there were many reasons to try again. The Japanese National Railways were well on their way toward bankrupting the Japanese government if they were not reformed. The growing number of public corporations and other forms of "special legal entity" as retirement havens for bureaucrats had become unpopular with the public and had to be brought under control. And corruption cases, not just the one at KDD but in other agencies such as the Railroad Construction Public Corporation, had weakened the LDP at the polls. More important, however, was governmental indebtedness. During fiscal year 1980 the government issued bonds equivalent to U.S.$63 billion, which far exceeded governmental deficits that year for any other comparable country. Because of strong public resistance to tax increases, caused at least in part by the corruption scandals of 1979, the Japanese government was financing a third of its general account expenditures by bond issues and was forced to devote some 12 percent of the budget to debt service.[36]

Rincho was created to deal with what one expert member of the commission called the "failure of government."[37] It existed between March 1981 and March 1983 as the pet project of prime ministers Suzuki and Nakasone, who had enticed the most distinguished businessman in the country, Doko Toshio, recently retired president of Keidanren, to head it. One of the things the Rincho commission was determined to achieve was to get the government out of the railroad and telephone business by "privatizing" the JNR and NTT. As we shall see, it succeeded with NTT, at least on paper, but it required a major fight. Whatever its effects on governmental "reform," however, Rincho had major unintended consequences for MPT. If the nation really intended to privatize NTT, then MPT would need new legal powers to regulate it and any other firms that might enter the telecommunications business in competition with it. Because of Rincho, some farsighted bureaucrats at MPT began to envision a vast expansion of the ministry's jurisdiction and the real possibility of becoming a "policy agency."

Meanwhile, the winds of change began to blow in the summer of 1980. MPT minister Yamanouchi Ichiro, acting on the encouragement of his bureaucrats, proposed to the cabinet that the old two-man NTT supervisory office in the MPT secretariat be expanded and upgraded to a new "Communications Policy Bureau" (Tsushin Sei-saku Kyoku). The MITI minister, Tanaka Rokusuke (no relation to Tanaka Kakuei), one of the party's most powerful politicians, imme-diately objected. According to Tanaka, the idea was crazy. "Policy" was MITI's business, and it was unseemly to have a "policy bureau" in a ministry like MPT. Perhaps because Yamanouchi and Tanaka are both members of the Suzuki faction, Prime Minister Suzuki had to step in to settle the matter. He decided in favor of MPT. The new Communications Policy Bureau was charged with policy and super-vision of legislation concerning new media, planning for the "ad-vanced information society," research and development for telecom-munications, space communications, and international technical exchange and cooperation. Being chief of this bureau immediately became an indispensable step for a postal bureaucrat on the road to the vice ministership (the highest nonpolitical post in a ministry).[38]

Four years later, on July 5, 1984, in the midst of the telecom wars, MPT underwent a much more radical reorganization. It ac-quired three "policy bureaus," in addition to the three old postal "business" bureaus. The new structure, designed as much for warfare with MITI as for telecommunications administration, is as follows:

Minister
Vice Minister
Secretariat
Postal Affairs Bureau (Yumu Kyoku)
Postal Savings Bureau (Chokin Kyoku)
Post Office Life Insurance Bureau (Kan'i Hoken Kyoku)
Communications Policy Bureau (Tsushin Seisaku Kyoku)
Telecommunications Bureau (Denki Tsushin Kyoku)
Broadcast Administration Bureau (Hoso Gyosei Kyoku)

The new Telecommunications Bureau is responsible for the "promo-tion of the telecommunications industry" and supervision of NTT, KDD, and new entries into the business, while the Broadcast Admin-istration Bureau, the only bureau in MPT headed by a technical official (*gikan*), supervises the Japan Broadcasting Company (Nippon Hoso Kyokai, NHK), a public corporation set up in 1950. On the basis of this new organization, the then MPT vice minister, Morizumi Arinobu, said at a press conference on August 21, 1984, that MPT's

Table 5-2. The Leadership of MITI and MPT During the Telecom Wars.

MITI Ministers	MPT Ministers
First Nakasone Cabinet, 11/27/82–12/26/83	
11/27/82–6/10/83	
Yamanaka Sadanori	Higaki Tokutaro
(Nakasone faction, former PARC	(Nakasone faction, former vice
chairman, financial expert)	minister of agriculture)
6/10/83–12/26/83	
Uno Sosuke	
(Nakasone faction, former parliamentary vice minister of MITI)	
Second Nakasone Cabinet, 12/26/83–10/31/84	
Okonogi Hikosaburo	Okuda Keiwa
(Nakasone faction, member of Party	(Tanaka faction)
Executive Council)	
Third Nakasone Cabinet, 10/31/84–12/28/85	
Murata Keijiro	Sato Megumu
(Fukuda faction, former official of	(Tanaka faction, former official
the Ministry of Home Affairs)	of MPT, and member of the
	postal caucus)
Fourth Nakasone Cabinet, 12/28/85–7/23/86	
Watanabe Michio	Sato Bunsei
(Nakasone faction, former minister	(Nakasone faction)
of agriculture and of finance)	

MITI Vice Ministers	MPT Vice Ministers
October 1982–October 1984	July 1982–August 1984
Sugiyama Kazuo	Morizumi Arinobu
(b. 4/27. Todai law, entered MITI	(b. 8/24. Todai economics, entered
1952.) Deputy director of Machinery	MPT 1951.) Chief of Personnel Bureau,
and Information Industries Bureau,	to chief of Accounting Bureau, to
to chief of Secretariat, to chief of	chief of Postal Affairs Bureau, to chief
Industrial Policy Bureau, to vice	of Communications Policy Bureau, to
minister.	vice minister.
October 1984–June 1986	August 1984–June 1986
Konaga Keiichi	Koyama Moriya
(b. 12/30. Okayama University,	(b. 9/30. Todai law, entered MPT
entered MITI 1953.) Same career	1953.) Chief of Postal Life Insurance
path as Sugiyama, except personal	Bureau, to chief of Communications
secretary to former prime minister	Policy Bureau, to chief of Telecom-
Tanaka.	munications Bureau to vice minister.

officials had joined the ranks of "truly elite officialdom," and he expressed MPT's "determination to take the leadership in Japan's telecommunications industry for the advanced information society."[39] (See Table 5–2 for the political and administrative leadership of MPT and MITI during the telecom wars.)

Facing this parvenu postal bureaucracy was one of the great organizations of the Japanese developmental state. On the surface of it, MPT was hardly a match for MITI's Secretariat, seven bureaus (including the famous "Industrial Policy Bureau," the strategy center for Japan's rise to industrial preeminence), and four semiindependent agencies: the Natural Resources and Energy Agency, the Patent Agency, the Medium and Smaller Enterprises Agency, and the Agency for Industrial Science and Technology. But MITI has many responsibilities, and its attention is spread over a vast terrain. Concretely, MITI faced MPT not with twelve divisions but with only four battalions.[40] These are the four electronics and information sections (ka) in the Machinery and Information Industries Bureau.

These sections are unquestionably part of the MITI elite, and they are backed up by the Industrial Policy Bureau and the Agency for Industrial Science and Technology. Moreover, the career paths of recent MITI vice ministers always include service as deputy director of the Machinery and Information Industries Bureau. But four sections was still a small force to put in the field against MPT. The four sections were (1) the Electronics Policy Section, in charge of all legislation and legislative proposals for the microelectronics and information industries; (2) the Data Processing Promotion Section, in charge of all aspects of software, including its development, distribution, and protection; (3) the Electronics and Electrical Machinery Section, in charge of hardware, including computers, semiconductors, and telecommunications equipment; and (4) the Information Management Systems Development Section, newly created in July 1984 and charged with combining hardware and software into systems, including regional telecommunications infrastructure and the development of data bases.[41]

These forces—three new and three old bureaus on the MPT side versus four sections on the MITI side, with each array led by a politician minister and an actual commander-in-chief vice minister—were the main antagonists in the telecom wars. But they did not have the field to themselves. According to some analysts MITI and MPT were mere puppets for important political interests within the perpetually in power Liberal Democratic party. Others stress that the politicians were really only "cheering squads" (*oendan*) for the bureaucratic armies. Still others think that the involvement of politicians in bureaucratic turf struggles is like having control of the skies over a battlefield: good air cover for one's troops is indispensable, but it still can never replace the hard ground fighting necessary to seize terrain.[42] As this diversity of opinion suggests, the actual role of politicians in Japanese policymaking is ambiguous, complex, and changing. There is no question, however, but that the involvement of politicians is growing in importance and that in the telecom wars their interventions were often decisive.

THE PARTY IN POLICY-MAKING

"Where a decade ago," writes *The Economist*, "bureaucrats ran Japan and politicians stepped out of their way, now politicians are playing a steadily bigger role. This is happening at ministerial level as well as in parliament."[43] This generalization is true, but with at least three caveats. First, the Japanese system is structured so as inevitably to overstate the power and influence of the ruling party. The ruling party's actual role (*honne*, as the Japanese say) is always less than its pretended role (*tatemae*), but that is of course not to argue that it has no role at all.

Second, some of the most important policies in Japan are made through cabinet and ministerial ordinances, not through Diet-enacted legislation; and the ministries still have virtually complete control over the ordinance power. For example, implementation of the Telecommunications Business Law of 1984, a subject to which we shall return, required some seven cabinet orders and sixty-seven ministerial orders; and many substantive matters were left for decision to the Telecommunications Deliberation Council, appointed by MPT and without political (or, for that matter, foreign business) members.[44] Similarly, the extensive licensing, approving, and registering authority of the ministries, which can raise formidable nontariff barriers to trade if a ministry so intends, has declined slightly from the high-speed-growth era but is still very powerful. Third, it is true that politicians are playing a bigger role, but the critical question for an outsider who wants to influence politics is which politicians, and in which organizations. The role of the prime minister, for example, or of the opposition parties, is either unchanged or declining in importance since the early 1970s.

Formally speaking, the Diet (Kokkai, the assembly of elected representatives of the people) is the "highest organ of state power and shall be the sole law-making organ of the state" (Constitution of Japan, art. 41). The Diet, however, has never played a decisive role in policymaking. Legislation is deliberated and the influence of constituents and interest groups brought to bear in organizations outside the Diet; even the Diet's standing committees are not as important as the committees of the Liberal Democratic party in the actual shaping of laws. The Diet's most substantive real power is its ability, on occasion, to block passage of legislation. The length of the Japanese Diet session is unusually short compared to legislative sessions in other advanced democracies, and the number of hours and days devoted to deliberation is correspondingly short. This means that the opposition parties can delay or thwart passage of government bills simply by boycotting the proceedings.

There are many reasons for substantive Diet weakness, including the prewar history of imperial absolutism, the lack of staff support (each Diet member has only two staff assistants, one of whom is commonly a relative), and the intrinsic authority of the bureaucracy as a meritocracy of talent. But by far the most important reason that nothing very important ever occurs on the floor of the Diet is the existence of the Liberal Democratic party. Ever since its creation in 1955, the LDP has been continuously in power in both houses of the Diet. Sato and Matsuzaki cite three reasons for its unusually long reign: (1) the party has successfully absorbed various interest groups as Japanese society has changed and developed; (2) the party is being continuously reinvigorated by fierce internal competition among its factions; and (3) the LDP appeases the opposition parties in order to maintain the pretense of a multiparty parliamentary system.[45] Since the LDP is always in power, contributions of politicians to policymaking must go on within it if they are to occur at all.

For fifteen of the party's first seventeen years of existence (1957–72), its president (and therefore prime minister of the country) was a senior ex-bureaucrat. First came Kishi, a former vice minister of commerce and industry (MITI's immediate predecessor); then Ikeda, a former vice minister of finance; and then Sato, a former vice minister of transportation. During this period the party reigned, but the bureaucracy actually ruled, both directly and through the large number of senior bureaucrats who on retirement from public service were elected to the Diet as members of the LDP. During the 1980s 30 percent of all Diet members were still ex-bureaucrats, but it is the 1957–72 period that is most accurately characterized as one in which politicians "stepped out of the way" of bureaucrats getting the nation's public business done.

The party instead concentrated on politics. Shortly after its creation, the LDP split into four or five internal factions, which are actually miniparties that compete and combine in order temporarily to dominate the LDP itself. These factions are not primarily ideological groupings but alliances among Diet members to advance their own interests within the party. The goal of a faction is, minimally, political self-preservation (that is, reelection) and, maximally, to name the prime minister, who in turn has the power to name the members of his cabinet and the top party executive positions.

Theorists of democratic government in Japan have been highly critical of the party's factionalism, but it actually performs several important functions both for the party as an organization and for the political system. For the party, the factions are responsible for political recruitment (a new candidate simply does not have a chance in a multimember constituency without factional help), the collection and distribution of funds, handling constituents' petitions (appeals to the bureaucracy are often transmitted via the party), and the distribution of ministerial positions and party offices. For the political system, the factions make possible the long-term, stable reign of the LDP without at the same time eliciting the usual side effects of single-party dominance, such as isolation from the public, flagrant corruption, and presidents-for-life. During the first two postoccupation decades, the LDP gave Japan a political stability within which the bureaucracy actually developed the country, but it did so without the authoritarianism and degeneracy that characterized most other East Asian nations, communist and noncommunist alike, during the same period.

INTERNAL PARTY ORGANS FOR POLICY-MAKING

The bureaucracy may actually create the annual budgets and draft all laws, but the party still has the legal responsibility for passing them in the Diet. Therefore from the outset the party set up internal organs to approve, even if perfunctorily, what the bureaucracy told it to. The most important of these organs was (and is) the Policy Affairs Research Council (PARC, Seimu Chosa Kai, abbreviated in Japanese as Seichokai), the chairman of which is one of the four most important party positions after the presidency (the other three being vice president, secretary general, and chairman of the Executive Council). The PARC is in turn subdivided into an executive committee (Seicho Shingikai), which sends forward to the party's Executive Council its recommendations on substantive issues, some seventeen Sections (Bukai) that correspond to the ministries and the standing committees in each house of the Diet, and a large number of less formal investigative and special committees.

We may illustrate the internal structure of PARC by looking at the units that participated in the telecom wars. Backing MITI there was the Commerce and Industry Section (Shoko Bukai), members of which are normally also LDP members on the Commerce and Industry Standing Committees in each house of the Diet. Backing MPT was the Communications Section (Tsushin Bukai), which corresponds also to the Communications committees (Teishin Iinkai) in each house of the Diet. Each of these PARC sections had several influential subcommittees. In addition there were within PARC many special committees separate from the sections. Among these were the NTT Basic Problems Investigation Council (chaired by Kato Tsunetaro, former head of the lower house's Communications Committee), the NTT Business Affairs Subcommittee (chaired by Kameoka Takao of the Tanaka faction and vice chairman of the party's Executive Council), the Information Industry Investigation Council (chaired by Osada Yuji, a former vice minister of MPT who entered politics as part of the Tanaka faction), and the Telecommunications Circuits Subcommittee (chaired by Obuchi Keizo, a Tanaka faction member and deputy secretary general of the party). Figure 5–1 displays graphically the formal structure of policymaking in Japan since the founding of the LDP.

In the early days the PARC sections and the executive committee were the strongholds of ex-bureaucrats within the party, who usually supervised the very ministries from which they had just retired. Actually, little or no genuine supervision occurred. Section meetings were occasions for bureau or section chiefs from the appropriate ministry to lecture on the bills that they intended to introduce

Figure 5-1. The Japanese Legislative Process.

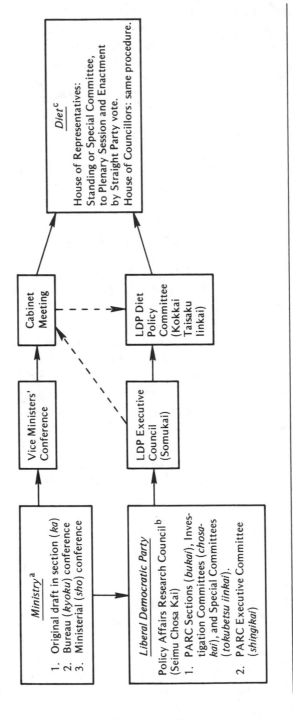

Diet[c]

House of Representatives:
Standing or Special Committee,
to Plenary Session and Enactment
by Straight Party vote.
House of Councillors: same procedure.

Cabinet Meeting

Vice Ministers' Conference

LDP Diet Policy Committee (Kokkai Taisaku Iinkai)

LDP Executive Council (Somukai)

Ministry[a]

1. Original draft in section (*ka*)
2. Bureau (*kyoku*) conference
3. Ministerial (*sho*) conference

Liberal Democratic Party

Policy Affairs Research Council[b] (Seimu Chosa Kai)

1. PARC Sections (*bukai*), Investigation Committees (*chosakai*), and Special Committees (*tokubetsu iinkai*).
2. PARC Executive Committee (*shingikai*)

a. All legislation, including the budget, originates in a ministry.

b. LDP Diet members from both houses belong to several committees.

c. Legislation is invariably broad in scope and short on detail. Concrete norms are supplied by cabinet orders, ministerial orders, and administrative guidance.

Sources: Murakawa Ichiro, *Seisaku kettei katei* (The Policy-making Process) (Tokyo: Kyoiku Sha, 1979), pp. 192–93; and Kawakita Takao, *Tsusan-Yusei senso* (The MITI-MPT Wars) (Tokyo: Kyoiku Sha, 1985), p. 87.

in the Diet during a current session.[46] LDP members were thus instructed on policy, but they did not in turn instruct.

In an analysis of the frequency of PARC meetings over time, Sato and Matsuzaki discovered that in the early years of the party, the executive committee met much more than any other subunit (162 times in 1956 but only 52 times in 1983). This suggests that during the late 1950s PARC spent most of its time ratifying ministerial plans but devoted little attention to studying them. During the 1960s the frequency of executive committee meetings declined, but the number of section and special committee meetings greatly increased. This suggests that the deliberations of PARC were becoming more specific and substantive. The executive committee became a place for the virtually automatic approval of section decisions.[47] Even the sections, however, were often too large and unwieldy for real analysis. The largest sections are agriculture and forestry with 117 members, construction with 108, and commerce and industry with 81. The smallest is science and technology with 17 members.[48] Over time some of the large sections have come to be dominated by their chairmen, vice chairmen, and members with more than ten years of service. Because of their longevity, such section leaders combine political influence with broad and accurate knowledge of the administrative fields in which they specialize. During the 1970s press and Diet insiders began to identify such people as *zoku* (caucus members) having one or another functional area of expertise.

Zoku should be distinguished from former bureaucrats who have entered politics. The latter are automatically understood to be specialists (*senmonka*) in the area of their previous service, but that does not make them *zoku*. *Zoku* are usually not ex-bureaucrats but pure politicians (what the Japanese call *tojin-ha*). They are veteran Diet members who have progressed in service through one or more of the following stages for a particular ministry: parliamentary vice minister, PARC section chairman or vice chairman, Diet standing committee chairman, and minister or director general. Diet members who are *zoku* are of course simultaneously members of a faction, and factions try to have a range of *zoku* among their members. But the interests of a *zoku* sometimes differ from those of a faction or a faction leader or, conversely, sometimes a faction will contain several conflicting *zoku*.[49]

Not all *zoku* are equal, however. Kawaguchi Hiroyuki ranks them into five grades. In the first rank is the "don" (in the sense not of

Don Quixote but of Don Corleone, the Mafia chieftain in the 1972 film *The Godfather*, which was very popular in Japan); second is a "boss" (*bosu*), one who has passed through all the stages from parliamentary vice minister to a cabinet or senior party post; third is the "elder" (*choro*), a politician who has served in most posts on the road to *zoku*hood but who will retire before making boss; fourth is "strongman" (*jitsuryokusha*), a Diet member who specializes in some subsection of a ministry's jurisdiction; and fifth is the ordinary *zoku*.[50] In approximately 1983 the commerce and industry *zoku* included one don, Tanaka Kakuei; three bosses, Nikaido Susumu (party vice president), Abe Shintaro (foreign minister and former MITI minister), and Tanaka Rokusuke (former MITI minister); three elders, Esaki Masumi, Sasaki Yoshitake, and Ogawa Heiji; three strongmen, and fourteen ordinary *zoku*. The postal *zoku* also had one don, Tanaka Kakuei; one absolute boss, Kanemaru Shin (secretary general of the party); a couple of elders, one in each house; two strongmen (both from the Tanaka faction); and twelve ordinary *zoku*. The question is whether these men made the policies that MITI and MPT executed, or whether they simply lobbied the ministries and ran interference for them.

THE CHANGING ROLES OF BUREAUCRATS AND POLITICIANS

Tanaka Kakuei, who became prime minister of Japan in 1972, was probably the most unusual figure to emerge in postwar Japanese politics.[51] Coming from a background of rural poverty and lacking even a university education, he nevertheless became a leader of the mainstream of the LDP made up of former elite bureaucrats. When he entered the first Kishi cabinet in 1957 as postal minister, he was the youngest politician in the cabinet since Ozaki Yukio in the Meiji era. During the high-speed growth of the Income Doubling Plan (early 1960s), Tanaka served for three terms in the critical post of finance minister, arguably the most important position in the government after the prime ministership. His last post before the prime ministership was the equally powerful position of MITI minister. In all of these positions he earned a reputation for mastery of the details of administration, something that was virtually unheard of at the time for ordinary politicians.

In 1972 Tanaka led a victorious insurgency against the bureaucratic old guard of the party, led by Fukuda Takeo, and emerged
as prime minister. His success came close to splitting the party for
the rest of the decade—something the Japanese call the "Kaku-Fuku
War," meaning the continuing struggle between the supporters of
Tanaka and the supporters of Fukuda. One of the effects of this
struggle was to elevate the party in relation to both the prime minister and the bureaucracy, since Tanaka represented a new order in
which bureaucrats were expected to pay some attention to what politicians asked them to do. The inner party struggle was exacerbated in
1974 by Tanaka's resignation as prime minister because of corruption charges and in 1976 by his arrest in the Lockheed bribery case.
Tanaka regarded these attacks on him as politically inspired and devoted himself to enlarging his faction as a defensive measure. By the
1980s he had succeeded so spectacularly that his faction had become
in fact a political machine. Tanaka remained the single most powerful political figure in the country until his severe cerebral hemorrhage
of February 27, 1985. He was also a central figure in the telecom
wars, in which he participated as a MITI *zoku*, a finance *zoku*, and a
postal *zoku*, the only person in the Diet with such varied bases of
influence.

Tanaka was not at war with the bureaucracy. On the contrary,
he was liked and respected by many of the officials who had worked
for him in MPT, MOF, and MITI. But he was committed to much
more effective party supervision of the bureaucracy than had existed
among his predecessors, if for no other reason than to check the decline in the party's popularity that long bureaucratic domination had
produced. One of the first things Tanaka did as prime minister was to
strengthen the research capabilities of the party secretary general's
office and to reassert PARC's role in investigating basic policy.[52] But
his intent was to make the party's voice heard within the bureaucracy, not to replace the bureaucracy as the initiator of policy. In
recognition of this fact, Sato rejects the dichotomy of *tokoseitei*
(party up, government down) that is frequently encountered in the
press in favor of what he calls the *jimin-kancho kongotai* (integrated
LDP-bureaucratic structure).[53] What happened during the 1970s was
a subtle shift of influence within the party from faction to PARC
section and then to *zoku*, a shift that had the effect outside the party
of ending the LDP's delegation of policy decisions to government
agencies. Under the integrated party-bureaucratic structure, the min-

istries began to consult with the *zoku* at every stage of policy formation; and young officials came to recognize for the first time that many politicians knew more about their ministries and functions than they themselves did.

Other forces contributed to this shift of influence. These included a deepening of social integration in Japan that accompanied successful economic growth; businesses and households needed the state less than in the past and therefore turned to it less. Slow growth after the oil shock of 1973 and the beginning, in the late 1970s, of genuine trade and capital liberalization also contributed to these trends. All segments of the bureaucracy had difficulty in adjusting to the changed sociopolitical environment and in the process engaged in intense jurisdictional conflicts with each other. Each such conflict tended to bring forth greater political intervention in what were previously regarded as purely bureaucratic affairs.[54] Despite all this, it must be stressed that the Japanese system remained one of bureaucratic initiative and near monopolization of expertise. Moreover, even the most senior *zoku* were sometimes hampered by the fact that industrial interest groups were often closer to the ministries than to the ruling party. Ministerial leaders were perfectly capable of using their industrial clients against a politician who went too far in asserting his interests.[55] In short, Japanese policymaking during the first half of the 1980s became more political and probably more democratic than it had been in the past, but it also became noticeably messier and much less efficient.

On the eve of the telecom wars, MPT possessed a stronger political base than MITI. Its *zoku*, concentrated in the Tanaka and Komoto factions, were powerful and united; and Tanaka himself, ever since he had served as MPT minister, had cultivated his own followers within the ministry and NTT. The MPT minister during the period of NTT's privatization, Sato Megumu, was himself a former MPT bureaucrat, a member of the Tanaka faction, and a postal *zoku*, in contrast to the MITI minister, who was a member of the Fukuda faction.[56] The press regarded MPT, together with the ministries of construction and finance, as "fiefs under the direct control of Tanaka Kakuei"; and Kawakita characterized the MPT as an "all-expenses-paid geisha of the Tanaka faction" (*Tanaka-ha marugakae*).[57]

Nonetheless, MITI was not politically defenseless, although it was much less public about cultivating its politicians than its rival. Konaga Keiichi, appointed MITI vice minister during 1984, was Tanaka's former personal secretary and ghostwriter for his 1972 book *Nihon retto kaizo ron* (A Plan to Remodel the Japanese Archipelago). This background probably influenced Konaga's selection as vice minister, since he comes from Okayama University rather than the more elitist Tokyo University.[58] In addition three top leaders of MITI during 1985 had served previously as personal secretaries to prime ministers (who are also, of course, faction leaders within the party). Fukukawa Shinji, chief of the Industrial Policy Bureau, was secretary to the late Prime Minister Ohira; Tanahashi Yuji, chief of the Machinery and Information Industries Bureau, had served Prime Minister Fukuda; and Iwasaki Hachio, chief of the Basic Industries Bureau, had served Prime Minister Nakasone.

During the summer of 1984, MITI used the inauguration of its new headquarters building to invite some hundred Diet members from the commerce and industry committees to the dedication ceremonies. MITI Minister Okonogi also cultivated the ministry's leading *zoku* after Tanaka himself—namely, party vice president and number 2 in command of the Tanaka faction, Nikaido Susumu. Before the summer was over MITI again played host to a meeting of former MITI ministers, including former prime ministers Kishi, Miki, and Tanaka, and the then current prime minister, Nakasone. The ministry denied that it was lining up political support, saying that the gathering was merely an opportunity for everyone to reminisce about old times. But some observers thought that MITI had learned a thing or two from MPT.

The telecom wars began in the autumn of 1981, when MITI successfully blocked an MPT-initiated bill that would have given MPT strong regulatory powers over computer-connected telecommunications circuits. They heated up during 1982 in the second VAN campaign, spread to new fronts during 1983 over the issues of providing legal protection for the writers of computer programs and the building of regional infrastructures for the "informationized" society of the future, and during 1984 and 1985 became a general conflagration with at least seven different battles going on simultaneously.

Even though each of the seven battles is interconnected with the others, I have separated them here for discussion and analysis. The seven are

1. Value-added networks and the fight over regulating the Japanese telecommunications industry
2. The "privatization" of NTT

3. Product standards and certification procedures
4. Protecting computer programs
5. Foreign satellites and space communications policy
6. Teletopias and "new media communities"
7. Controlling research and development in the telecommunications field

Before we can understand these battles, however, we have to explore the ancient enmity between MPT and the Ministry of Finance. Because of it MOF became a MITI ally in 1985 in the battle over research funding.

MPT, MOF, AND THE POSTAL SAVINGS SYSTEM

In 1875 Japan established a system whereby its citizens could save their money at post offices. Since the creation of the Ministry of Communications a decade later, the postal bureaucracy has always administered the system, which is one of the reasons why prewar politicians wanted to be communications minister: it gave them control over the investment of people's savings, a trust that on occasion they abused. In the postwar era the postal savings system is much more strictly controlled than it was before the war. One reason that being postal minister is still popular with postwar politicians is that the postal savings system is popular with the people. The Postal Savings Law of 1947 specifically requires MPT to consider the "well-being of the saver" in setting interest rates, which utterly distinguishes the post offices from the banks.[59] The post offices normally pay a better rate of interest than the banks, and the post offices usually raise their rates in periods of high inflation in order to keep saving attractive.

The postwar postal savings system has been fabulously successful and is the institutional linchpin of Japan's high savings rate, which has allowed the country to fund its industrialization more cheaply than virtually any of its competitors. During the last quarter of 1985 the system's assets topped ¥100 trillion (or $555.5 billion at ¥180 to U.S.$1), giving the system greater financial strength than any of the Japanese commercial banks, which are among the world's largest (Dai-Ichi Kangyo Bank has assets in the ¥25 trillion range, whereas Fuji, Sumitomo, Mitsubishi, and Sanwa banks all fall into the ¥15–20 trillion range). The postal savings system is the primary source of funds for Japan's Fiscal Investment and Loan Program (FILP), a plan set up in 1953 for governmental investments in industrial development, research, public housing, and infrastructure. Because of the strength of the postal savings system, the FILP continues to be one of Japan's most powerful instruments of official industrial policy.

The Ministry of Finance is not opposed to the postal savings system, only to the way it is run. MOF is the government's financier, and as a player in the market it is the nation's largest borrower. Since the first oil shock Japan has radically increased its reliance on fund-raising through the issuance of bonds (the volume of national bonds went from 11.3 percent of general account expenditures in fiscal 1974 to 31.3 percent in fiscal 1978). All of these bonds are underwritten by the banking system. MOF has a strong financial reason for wanting to keep domestic interest rates low in order to reduce its own debt service charges. But low interest rates also strongly depress the banks' profits. The banks could be more profitable if they had the business that small savers give to the post offices, but they cannot attract them with interest rates lower than those offered by MPT. Thus, since MOF and the banks do not want to raise their own interest rates, they would like to get control of the postal savings system in order to lower its rates.

This problem is exacerbated by the issue of tax fraud. Postwar Japan created several programs to encourage saving as part of its overall industrial policy. One of these is the *maruyu yokin* system (tax-exempt deposits), which makes the interest on the first ¥3 million in any savings account tax exempt. In addition, up to ¥3 million can be invested tax free in government bonds, and salaried workers can bank up to ¥5 million in a tax-free pension plan. Aside from this so-called *maruyu* system, any individual can deposit up to ¥3 million in a postal savings account without paying taxes on the earned interest; and another ¥500,000 can be deposited in a special post office account reserved for the purchase of a home. Many people in Japan open any number of different *maruyu* and postal savings accounts, often in the names of every member of the family and sometimes using invented names, at banks and post offices all over the country. During 1985 MOF declared that it had discovered an all time high of ¥950 billion in illegal *maruyu* accounts, but it cannot audit the post offices since MPT absolutely refuses to give it access.[60]

Bitter clashes between MOF and MPT over this issue occurred in 1971–72, 1975, 1977, 1980–82, and 1984, with MPT always emerging victorious. Politicians invariably side with MPT, but they must do so discreetly because MOF makes its case not in terms of the banks' profit margins or its own desire to reduce the costs of government debt but in terms of the need to raise additional revenue and to stop tax cheating. This is a serious issue of public policy, and politicians must be responsive to it. However, there is also a suspicion that politicians themselves are among the heaviest users of the post offices to hide money tax-free.[61]

In March 1980 the Diet enacted a law that would have ended at least the tax fraud aspects of the problem by issuing to every saver a so-called Green Card for his or her identity when making deposits. This was intended to end the use of multiple *maruyu* and postal accounts as ways of evading taxes. Given the failure during 1979 of Prime Minister Ohira's attempt to raise taxes, the Green Card system would have produced some badly needed new revenues. However, even though the law was passed, it was never implemented. This blockage of implementation is said to be one of the postal *zoku*'s greatest victories. Led by Kanemaru Shin, who created his own Diet members' league to deal with the matter (the Yusei Jigyo Konwakai, or Postal Business Discussion Group), the postal *zoku* intimidated MOF into not implementing the law. The final decision on the matter, including a determination to keep postal and banking interest rates unintegrated, was made within the Tanaka faction, between Kanemaru of the postal *zoku* and Finance Minister Takeshita Noboru of the finance *zoku*, without any involvement of the two ministries.[62] MOF, however, has never forgiven MPT for its recourse to powerful *zoku* in order to protect its bureaucratic turf. Thus, when in 1985, MPT came up with a great new idea on how to spend the dividends from the shares of the newly privatized NTT, MOF allied with MITI to help frustrate MPT's plans.

THE VAN CAMPAIGNS

The Japanese break down the general concept of telecommunications into three broad types. First is direct, unprocessed communication, as in a telephone. Second is communication between a computer terminal and a data processing center, as in an automatic teller machine at a bank (what the Japanese call a cash dispenser). Third is a value-added network (VAN, *fuka-kachi tsushin*), which is a combination of the first and second types. A VAN is a network in which information from computers of one type is communicated to computers of another type, the data being processed in the transmission and becoming thereby "value-added." A VAN is the electronic equivalent of a system of simultaneous translation from one language to another. The standard example is a Japanese travel agency's computer with its ability to communicate with the reservations computers of ten or more companies, including JAL, JNR, the Japan Travel Bureau, private railroads, other airlines, and numerous hotel chains. Banking systems and supermarkets are heavy users of VANs. Until 1982 it was illegal in Japan to connect a computer to the telephone lines without the explicit permission of NTT.

During 1981 it became apparent to the new Communications Policy Bureau of MPT that demand for different kinds of VANs was outstripping NTT's ability to meet it. Therefore it proposed new legislation that would both legalize enhanced use of VANs and make absolutely clear MPT's responsibility for regulating this growing business. Entitled the Value-added Data Communications Bill, it incorporated draconian licensing and approval requirements and put harsh limits on the degree to which foreign firms or domestic firms with high degrees of foreign capital (such as IBM Japan) could participate.[63]

MITI opposed the proposed law because MPT appeared to be infringing on its turf, both by seeking to regulate computer-based communications (computers are in MITI's bailiwick) and by presuming to regulate foreign commerce (which MITI also likes to think of as its exclusive preserve). MITI publicly and stridently opposed MPT's draft law, using as a pretext for its attack the reports of the recently created Provisional Commission for Administrative Reform (Rincho), which called on the government to reduce, not add to, its required licenses and approvals. MITI won this battle and MPT withdrew its bill. In light of later events this contretemps became known as the first (there were two more) VAN campaign.

During 1982 MPT renewed its efforts by arguing that as a matter of national security it had to regulate foreign VANs coming into Japan. The ministry successfully scared the political world with the specters of IBM and AT&T (the U.S. dismantling of which was imminent and which the Japanese wrongly interpreted as an act of American rationality and competitiveness) taking over Japan's entire telecommunications industry. In light of Rincho's simultaneous advocacy of the privatization of NTT, which MPT and the postal *zoku* initially opposed, the possibility of an "invasion of foreign capital" was somewhat more plausible than usual. However, MITI countered MPT by arguing that the VAN business should be completely liberalized. It reasoned to itself that if VANs were opened up to competition, then MITI could advance into this terrain and bring it under control via its influence over the computer and microelectronics industries. Publicly MITI defended its position in terms of the threat of foreign protectionism if the Japanese domestic market remained closed.

In October 1982 the LDP intervened to try to settle this dispute. It took to the Diet and passed a revision of the Public Telecommunications Law of 1953 liberalizing VANs only for medium and smaller enterprises. The party was unable to resolve how much regulation large-scale VANs required or how much foreign penetration was acceptable. The LDP made clear that its revision to the country's basic electric communication law was an expedient to meet the needs of small businesses, and it asked the bureaucracy to undertake a total reform of the basic legislation in order to deal with the bigger issues. Reform was required if for no other reason than the fact that the government was also beginning to discuss the privatization of NTT.

The postal ministry spent 1983 drafting three new laws. These are, first, a new Telecommunications Business Bill to replace the old basic law of 1953 in order to deal with large-scale VANs, the regulation of foreigners, the setting of technical standards after NTT was privatized, and many other matters. Second was the Nippon Denshin Denwa Kabushiki Kaisha Bill, transforming NTT into a private company under Japan's Civil Code; and third was an omnibus bill to revise and adjust all other laws made obsolete by the passage of the first two bills. A hint of the ministry's plans came in May, when it published the 1983 edition of its annual "Communications White Paper" or annual report. In it MPT identified as one of Japan's greatest needs the protection of the secrecy of communications, which in turn it said required the "coordination" (*chosei*) and "stabilization" (*antei*) of all forms of telecommunications. (The terms *chosei* and *antei* when used by Japanese bureaucrats are invariably euphemisms for control.) MITI reacted with fury to this trial balloon, saying that white papers are places to report activities, not to advocate policies; and it demanded that MPT correct its own white paper. However, the *Nihon keizai* newspaper thought that MITI's manner on this issue was arrogant and high-handed.[64]

In February 1984 MPT unveiled to the press the first drafts of its three new laws, and for the next year and a half the Japanese political, bureaucratic, and industrial worlds seemed to talk of nothing else. The heart of the Telecommunications Business Bill was its treatment of VANs. The original MPT draft divided the telecommunications business into two broad classes and then further subdivided the second class. Class I telecommunications businesses were defined as common carriers, like NTT, that install their own circuits, either land lines or via satellite transmission. Under the new law, ownership of such class I carriers is totally prohibited to foreigners or to Japanese firms that are more than one-third controlled by foreigners. The law also requires that such class I firms be licensed by MPT and that the ministry approve their rates.

Class II telecommunications businesses are those that offer large-scale VAN services over circuits leased from a class I carrier. They are further subdivided into special class II firms and general class II firms. Under the original draft, special class IIs are firms that exceed certain narrow technical specifications that the ministry supplies through ministerial ordinances or that offer any form of international service between Japan and one or more foreign countries. Foreigners are prohibited from engaging in special class II business, and all of them must be licensed by MPT. All other VANs are general class IIs, which are open to foreign ownership and need only "register" with MPT. These complex distinctions were invented specifically to keep IBM and AT&T out of Japan.[65]

The U.S. government was interested in this law. It had been deeply frustrated by its agreement of December 1980 with NTT to open up the Japanese market to American telecommunications sales; and it saw in MPT's definition of a special type II business a new Japanese nontariff barrier to trade. MITI agreed, since it recognized that if the bill passed in its original form, MPT would dominate the telecommunications field through its licensing powers. Even the requirement that general type II businesses had only to register would not have deceived an experienced MITI official. An old Japanese bureaucratic trick is refusing to accept unsatisfactory reports, thereby making an activity that requires reporting illegal. In all formal written applications or notifications to Japanese ministries, filing of the report is the end of a complex process. The applicant or reporter is expected to negotiate in advance concerning how to fill out the forms. When the actual written report is filed, it is usually accepted. If a ministry intends to reject an applicant or a report, it will do so verbally during the preliminary negotiations.[66] On these and other grounds U.S. trade negotiators and MITI protested the terms of the new Telecommunications Business Law.

MPT's response was predictable. It accused MITI of selling out to the Americans, of using the issue of trade friction to advance its own bureaucratic interests, and of being agents of "national dishonor" (*kokujoku mono*).[67] It is useful to recognize that for both MITI and MPT, the United States was not so much an independent player as a counter to be used in their domestic struggle. U.S. pressure on Japan was never decisive unless it happened to coincide with the interests of a major domestic player, in which case it could be quite effective. The Americans were usually ineffective because they typically did not know what was going on within the Japanese government and made their protests only to the foreign ministry or the prime minister. As one of the few Japanese linguists among the U.S. trade officials at the time of these negotiations said to Michael Berger,

> The real battle isn't between the Americans and the Japanese. This [telecommunications struggle] is a gigantic turf fight between the Ministry of Posts and Telecommunications and the Ministry of International Trade and Industry. We Americans are like a little terrier, yipping at the heels of two giants. Every once in a while we get their attention, and they toss us a bone.[68]

The Telecommunications Law was, of course, the kind of issue in which the LDP would have to get involved. Following MPT's announcement of its laws in February 1984, Keidanren endorsed them the following month. At the same time, the United States warned that restrictions on foreign participation in class II businesses appeared to be a *prima facie* violation of the Organization for Economic Cooperation and Development code on capital liberalization. The prime minister said at a meeting of the lower house's budget committee that foreign participation in VANs would have to be liberalized, but NTT President Shinto vowed that, "Even with the liberalization of VANs, we are confident of defeating foreign capital."[69] On March 16 the PARC Communications section and its postal-*zoku*-dominated subcommittees approved the draft Telecommunications bill; but five days later, after a massive MITI counteroffensive, the PARC Executive Committee made some major changes in the law. It opened all forms of class II VANs to foreign participation; and it changed MPT's powers over special class IIs from "license" to "report" and over general class IIs from "report" to "notify."

On April 4, 1984, the four top leaders of the LDP met with MITI and MPT officials and endorsed the version advanced by the PARC Executive Committee. In the LDP's view it had given the MPT a victory, even though it had taken away a few things the ministry had wanted. MITI saw a victory of sorts in the weakening of MPT's licensing powers; and the Americans took the removal of restrictions against foreigners as a victory for their low-key trade negotiations. Most external observers regarded the final outcome as a clear victory for MPT, which is also the way the ministry saw it. After the LDP leaders had endorsed the draft law, the ministry held a party on the eleventh floor of its headquarters building. According to the press, the postal bureaucrats boisterously proclaimed, "At long last MPT has won."[70]

The battle was not yet over, however. Because of delays by the opposition parties and the intervention of PARC chairman Fujio Masayuki (Fukuda faction, former labor minister in the Suzuki cabinet), none of the three MPT bills had been passed when the Diet session ended on August 8, 1984. Fujio had sought a delay because he did not want Prime Minister Nakasone to take credit for passage in the forthcoming party presidential election campaign, and Nakasone himself was not too sorry to postpone the vote because some of the postal *zoku* were still not in favor of the NTT privatization bill. Since many postal *zoku* were concentrated in the Tanaka faction and since Nakasone could not be reelected without the support of that faction, Nakasone clearly preferred privatizing NTT after he had been reelected. On October 30, 1984, Nakasone was reelected to a second term as LDP president, and the three laws were finally passed without fanfare on December 20, 1984. They came into effect on April 1, 1985.

THE "PRIVATIZATION" OF NTT

The Nippon Telegraph and Telephone Public Corporation had long had a reputation for low productivity, resembling more a typical government agency than a corporation, even a public one. With 1984 sales in the ¥2.3 trillion range ($23.8 billion at ¥200 to U.S.$1) and some 320,000 employees, each worker produced only ¥14.8 million for the company, compared with ¥40 million for Japan Steel employees and around ¥20 million at the private railroads. Government auditors concluded that NTT had at least 100,000 surplus workers, and noted that they only worked a thirty-seven hour week.[71] It was to deal with these and other problems that Doko Toshio, the chairman of Rincho, sent his trusted subordinate, Shinto Hisashi, to NTT as president. (Shinto was president of Ishikawajima-Harima Heavy Industries, a firm founded by Doko and headed by him for twenty years until he became president of Keidanren.) Both Doko and Shinto had become alarmed by NTT's seeming inability to handle the international competition that the Americans offered it during 1978–80; and they were worried that NTT might become as great a drain on the treasury as the JNR (which was then losing some $20 million a day).[72] Their plan was to turn NTT into a private company.

Shinto was not popular at NTT. Internally the company had long been dominated by a group of technicians who much preferred that NTT remain a state-managed monopoly. Others opposed to Shinto and to privatization were the NTT "family" firms, led by NEC, and the LDP's postal *zoku*, who feared that if MPT and NTT were separated, they would lose control over one or both. In addition to members of Rincho, the Americans and MITI favored privatization, the latter opportunistically (and erroneously) believing that privatization would weaken MPT.

U.S. pressure was an important background influence in this case. In mid-February 1983, U.S. Trade Representative William Brock complained in Tokyo that despite the three-year "NTT Procurement Procedures Agreement" of December 1980, during the previous year NTT bought only $11.6 million worth of U.S. products out of a total procurement of $2.9 billion. He threatened not to renew the agreement when it expired at the end of 1983. The Japanese got the message. Just before President Reagan's visit to Tokyo in November 1983, NTT placed orders in the United States for several one-time-only but big ticket items (a supercomputer, for example). The Americans were mollified and in January they renewed the agreement for another three years. Nonetheless, in 1984, U.S. telecommunications sales to NTT amounted to only $130 million, whereas Japanese sales in the United States, spurred by the break-up of

AT&T, surged to over $2 billion. For the Americans, a privatized NTT could not make things much worse than they already were, although there was concern over whether a private NTT would continue to honor the agreement of January 1984, which of course covered only purchases by governmental agencies.

The deadlock between those wanting privatization of NTT and those opposed was broken by a group of creative MPT bureaucrats. The more they thought about it, the more they saw in a privatized NTT a way of *expanding* the minsitry's jurisdiction. Led by Telecommunications Bureau chief Koyama, these officials reasoned that they could write the law in such a way as to keep NTT under their jurisdiction while simultaneously expanding their coverage to include the new class I carriers who were petitioning the ministry to go into business in competition with NTT. Similarly, privatizing NTT would mean that MPT would have to take over the functions that NTT had previously performed, including setting telephone rates, determining product standards and certification procedures, and supervising research in telecommunications. Old hands at MPT were also not sorry to turn the tables on NTT's proud engineers, who had long lorded it over the mere postal workers.

With this new conception of their task, Koyama and his colleagues set out to convince the LDP's *zoku.* They had several good arguments. As the country's largest single enterprise, a private NTT would be a much better source of political contributions than a public corporation. The actual sales of NTT's shares would produce a bonanza of cash for the Japanese treasury. And competition might serve to strengthen NTT. Even more important to the eventual outcome of the NTT case was the involvement of Tanaka Kakuei himself. In its original draft of the NTT law, MPT proposed that the government hold 50 percent of the shares of a private NTT in perpetuity. Tanaka's concern was with the distribution of profits from the dividends and from the sales of NTT shares. The potential amounts of money were enormous. By selling some proportion of NTT shares and collecting dividends on those that it retained, the government might generate at least $8 billion in extra-budget funds. MPT wanted to control these funds, whereas MOF wanted to use them to reduce the national debt. Tanaka was the "don" of the postal *zoku*, but he was also first and foremost an expert on public finance. He favored the MOF's position on this issue, even though most of his followers supported MPT.[73]

Together with his close supporter and number 1 postal *zoku* Kane-maru, Tanaka worked out a formula containing these points: (1) NTT would become a private company on April 1, 1985; (2) MOF would sell two-thirds of its shares to the public (but not to foreigners) and it would do so over a five-year period in order not to disrupt the securities markets, using the proceeds to help retire the national debt; and (3) the dividends on the remaining one-third would be used to fund a new telecommunications research facility. This last item was necessary to placate the NTT-family firms, which were worried about losing their research cartels under a privatized NTT.[74] Nonetheless, setting up this new research organ produced one of the bitterest battles between MITI and MPT.

The Tanaka-Kanemaru formula became the contents of the law passed in December 1984. In April 1985 NTT emerged as a new joint stock company. In January 1986 the private NTT even entered into a joint venture with IBM to create a new network service that can transmit and receive voice, character, and image messages. Deafening howls of outrage were heard from the old family firms, even though they continued to supply the majority of NTT's purchases.[75] MPT seemed unperturbed by these developments, knowing at least that NTT was not going to embarrass it by becoming a second JNR. Also, during March 1986, MOF announced its intention to sell the first batch of NTT shares, some 1.95 million of them. The ministry said that based on a net assets per share calculation of ¥213,210, the government stood to make ¥415.8 billion on this sale alone ($2.3 billion at ¥180 = U.S.$1). There is actually every reason to believe that MOF will eventually receive substantially more than the price based on net assets per share.[76] The Dai-Ichi Kangyo Bank was so interested in these lucrative goings on that it established a new department exclusively to handle NTT shares and said that it planned to hire a couple of NTT *amakudari* (descent-from-heaven) retirees to help advise it on the business.[77]

PRODUCT STANDARDS AND CERTIFICATION PROCEDURES

Michael Aho and Jonathan Aronson, in a study done for the Council on Foreign Relations, argue:

> The Japanese government clearly devises rules that inhibit imports and promote exports. . . . Japanese procedures and standards are often designed to

exhaust all but the largest and most determined foreign firms wishing to sell in Japan. Today, on a percentage basis, Japan imports fewer manufactured products from industrial and developing countries than it did ten or twenty years ago.[78]

The standards for telecommunications imports, which were set by NTT and its family firms until the Telecommunications Business Law of 1984 transferred them to MPT, seem an apt illustration of this point.

The new law requires that MPT use a "designated approval agency" to certify the acceptability of what NTT calls "consumer provided equipment" and what the Americans call "interconnect equipment" (everything from PBXs to computers). According to the new law, this "designated approval agency" must be a not-for-profit foundation as defined under article 34 of the Japanese Civil Code (a *zaidan hojin*). This requirement alone makes it structurally impossible for laboratories outside of Japan to be designated as approval agencies by MPT. Moreover, on March 30, 1984, several months before the Telecommunications Business Law was even passed, NEC, Fujitsu, Hitachi, Oki, and other companies set up the "Telecommunications Terminal Equipment Inspection Association" (a *zaidan hojin*), capitalized at ¥150 million, in order to serve as the "designated approval agency" whenever MPT got around to designating it. There are no other such agencies. The foundation itself had no staff, only a board of directors, since it borrows its technical personnel and testing equipment from NTT's Engineering Bureau.[79]

The officers of this new approval agency are Akiyama Toru, a former official of the old Ministry of Communications and a former vice minister of transportation; Kashiwagi Teruhiko, a former employee of the Ministry of Communications and of NTT from 1942 to 1970; and Asanuma Isao, a former NTT director of engineering for Kanagawa prefecture (capital, Yokohama). Director Asanuma was quoted by the press as saying that "the association does not intend to accept U.S.-generated technical data." He also indicated that he had no plans to include foreign companies as contributors to the foundation and that technical standards would be distributed only to "friendly companies."[80] The foundation opened its offices for business in October 1984 in preparation for NTT's privatization the following April.

According to the Telecommunications Business Law, the technical standards themselves are to be set by the Telecommunications Deliberation Council, appointed by and attached to MPT. This council was created on October 1, 1982, by cabinet order and is composed of some twenty prominent citizens appointed for two-year terms by the Minister of Posts and Telecommunications. Prior to 1985 there were no foreign members nor any with a foreign institutional connection.[81]

Needless to say, the few alert Americans charged with watching such developments were not pleased by what they saw. MITI, too, thought that maybe MPT was being a little unsubtle in these arrangements and believed that it might embarrass its rival politically. MPT seemed determined to humiliate Prime Minister Nakasone, who in his January 1985 meeting with President Reagan had specifically promised to get rid of these kinds of nontariff barriers to trade in the telecommunications field. The Americans charged the Japanese with violating the GATT code on standards, which Japan signed in 1979 and which came into effect on January 1, 1980. This code states (art. 2.1) that the "parties shall ensure that technical regulations and standards are not prepared, adopted, or applied with a view to creating obstacles to international trade."[82] Since the law setting up Japan's new system for telecommunications had already been passed, MPT claimed that it could not do anything about that. Interest therefore turned to how MPT would implement the law through its ministerial ordinances. Reagan sent his aide Gaston Sigur to Tokyo to plead with Nakasone for some improvement in Japanese-American trade in telecommunications products, which then stood at 10 to 1 in Japan's favor. MPT's answer to this pressure was to produce petitions from consumers' groups saying that the Americans were trying to sell Japan television sets one could not see and telephones one could not properly hear.[83]

A part of the problem is that in Japan standards setting and product certification are a governmental responsibility, whereas in the United States they are largely left to the insurance companies and their Underwriters' Laboratories. Japanese consumers by no means believe that in enforcing high standards their government is acting to restrict trade or violate international agreements. They think that foreigners should meet Japanese standards of quality and performance, just as Japanese must meet the United States admittedly less stringent standards. Nonetheless, MPT determined that it could not win this battle, and while retaining its apparatus of a foundation and a deliberation council, began to compromise. In negotiations between vice minister Koyama and undersecretary of commerce Lionel Ulmer, Koyama started progressively to lower the number and stringency of MPT-set standards. He also agreed to add two members to the Telecommunications Deliberation Council from foreign-connected firms in Japan and to appoint experts from AT&T International, Nippon Philips, IBM Japan, Nippon UNIVAC, Fuji Xerox, and Nippon Motorola to its board of technical advisers.[84] The Americans declared themselves to be satisfied even though MITI charged, probably accurately, that these MPT concessions were only cosmetic.

PROTECTING COMPUTER PROGRAMS

The battle over protecting computer programs was confusing to foreigners because MITI, which they had begun to think of as "liberal," came down hard on the protectionist side; and MPT advocated what might appear at first glance as the free trade solution. Of course neither ministry is protectionist or liberal; each of their positions changes in accordance with the dictates of the bureaucratic struggle for survival. Computer software was probably MITI's best opportunity to make real inroads against MPT, and the fact that it lost this battle was probably its most bitter defeat. MITI was also highly self-righteous about software, believing that NTT engineers did not understand how important it was to the future of the Japanese computer industry.[85] It is true that not until April 1985 did NTT's Telecommunications Laboratory set up a unit devoted exclusively to software production—the Software Production Technical Research Laboratory (Sofutouea Seisan Gijutsu Kenkyujo), located in Yokosuka.

As background to the software battle, one must recall the 1982 industrial espionage scandal in which Hitachi was caught red-handed in California trying to steal the operating secrets of a new IBM computer. As details of the case unfolded, MITI and the Japanese public became painfully aware that the software and operating systems in Hitachi and Fujitsu computers were basically copies of IBM products, for which Hitachi and Fujitsu subsequently agreed to pay IBM millions of dollars. The scandal revealed Japan's weakness in software, compared with the United States; and it also made clear that by building IBM-compatible machines, Japanese firms were being tempted into industrial espionage against IBM. Far too much time was being spent in Japanese laboratories on "reverse engineering," that is, taking apart someone else's product to find out how it works, instead of on independent development of new products. MITI's position on software thus reflected its concern to acquire legally the software that Japan needed from abroad and to avoid a repetition of Hitachi's humiliation.

Until January 1, 1986, there was no protection in Japan for computer software; and foreign programs were routinely pirated and rented or sold to personal computer owners. In early 1983 the Cultural Affairs Agency (Bunka-cho) of the Ministry of Education, which is legally responsible for administering Japan's copyright law, asked its Copyright Deliberation Council (Chosakuken Shingikai), an advisory body of twenty leaders from the book, film, recording, and university worlds, to look into the matter. The council proposed that Japan protect computer software by copyrighting it, meaning that for some fifty years the authors of computer programs could take legal action against unauthorized copying. Such protection is powerful but also rather narrow. As Edwin Whatley notes, "Copyright protects only the form in which a work is expressed rather than the ideas or concepts which it embodies. Thus, copyright offers strong protection primarily against direct copying of a work and none against works employing the same concepts, so long as they are expressed in a sufficiently different manner."[86]

Unlike the copyright is the patent, which covers both the form and the concepts involved in a work but which, being more comprehensive, is offered for a much shorter period of time. MITI, which viewed the protection issue from the point of view of Japan's computer makers, advocated patent protection (at first for ten years but extended to fifteen in the ministry's draft law).[87] This approach was itself controversial, since the United States protects computer programs under the copyright laws; but it was what MITI further proposed that set off a storm of protests. MITI's bill stipulated that anyone could use a program so long as a fee was paid; and in cases where the parties could not agree on the fee, a MITI-appointed panel of experts would arbitrate and set one. Most important, MITI's proposed law further required that the holders of software patents license their operating systems to Japanese computer manufacturers, again for an arbitrated fee if the two parties failed to agree.

In early 1984 MITI and the Cultural Affairs Agency unveiled their respective draft laws, setting off what was probably the nastiest fire fight in the telecom wars. The United States and IBM backed the Cultural Affairs Agency, although IBM-Japan did so more quietly since it would still have to work in Japan however this issue was decided. Fujitsu and the other makers of IBM-compatible computers strongly favored MITI's position. They feared that under copyright IBM would gain exceptional rights in Japan, whereas IBM feared that MITI was trying to continue its old policy of the early 1960s of forcing IBM to license its patent rights to Japanese as the price of being allowed to do business in Japan. Some press observers, who remembered the IBM sting operation against Hitachi in California, thought that MITI was merely trying to get even. In February 1984, while locked in battle with MITI over the VAN law, MPT also entered the fray, strongly endorsing the Cultural Affairs Agency's bill.

MITI was eventually defeated. American pressure helped the Cultural Affairs Agency and MPT. The U.S. Congress introduced reciprocity legislation to stop sales in the American market of the products of countries that failed to protect American intellectual property rights. The Americans also pointed out that in UNESCO the Japanese have always strongly opposed all requests by Third World nations for the compulsory licensing of patents. In April 1985 the LDP finally took the Cultural Affairs Agency's draft, modified somewhat to reflect MITI's concerns, to the Diet, where it was passed on June 7 and came into effect on January 1, 1986. The law gives copyright protection to computer programs, defined as "arrangements of commands to make computers function and to obtain functioning results," for fifty years.

SATELLITES AND SPACE COMMUNICATIONS POLICY

On February 4, 1983, Japan launched its first commercial communications satellite at a cost some three times greater than similar or more effective satellites that could be purchased in the United States. The project was under the direction of the Science and Technology Agency, attached to the prime minister's office, and strongly backed by Keidanren. As the single most powerful association in the country for expressing the views of big business, Keidanren mirrored the divisions within the telecommunications industry over satellites. Its two main leaders, known as the "two Kobayashis," were the chairmen of the two leading NTT "family" firms. First was Kobayashi Taiyu, chairman of Fujitsu, who headed Keidanren's committee on data processing and favored buying Japan's satellites abroad. Second was Kobayashi Koji, chairman of NEC, who headed Keidanren's Space Activities Promotion Council and favored the national production of communications satellites. When in July 1983, Kobayashi Koji's committee recommended the national development of large (2–4 ton) communications satellites rather than buying them from the United States, Japan's satellite program became a serious issue in Japanese-American trade friction and a skirmish in the telecom wars.

There is no doubt that Japan's decision to build communications satellites with public money is an unambiguous example of targeting and of industrial policy. The Japanese government refused even to discuss with the United States the possibility of buying better and cheaper satellites from abroad, saying that it was a matter of national security, even though Keidanren had already made clear that Japan intended to start exporting them to North America and Western Europe by the 1990s. Given that Japan's share of imports in the U.S. domestic market for telecommunications products had grown from 3 percent in 1978 to 11 percent in 1983 and that fully one-third of Japan's total production was exported, the Americans were outraged. As one of them put it:

> Imagine that seven or eight years ago, just before the video tape recorder industry reached takeoff position, if Sony had come to the U.S. with its first VTR machine and we had said to them: "Sorry, Sony. It's true we don't produce this type of product in the U.S., but our technicians are working on it. In fact, we hope to be able to satisfy our own domestic market in another four or five years so your application for an import permit is rejected." ... This is essentially what has happened to the sale of American communications satellites in Japan. In fact, it is the stated policy of Japan not to buy advanced technology produced abroad until Japanese products are competitive.[88]

American pressure on Japan and on Keidanren ultimately forced the government to modify its position. It continues to prohibit sales of foreign satellites to government agencies but no longer prohibits Japanese civilians from buying them. Nonetheless, when in 1985 two consortia of big trading companies, Mitsui Trading and Ito Chu on the one hand and Mitsubishi Trading and Mitsubishi Electric on the other, applied to become class I telecommunications carriers, MPT refused to allocate frequencies to Hughes Aircraft or any other American satellites that they proposed to buy. The ministry ultimately backed down only when Keidanren reversed itself and decided to join one of the satellite consortia that were being formed.

Meanwhile, MITI was being made nervous by these goings on. It criticized MPT and the Science and Technology Agency for contributing to trade friction, but it also set up its own internal advisory organ, called the "Space Utilization Research and Examination Committee." The purpose of the committee is to help MITI try to take over space development from the Science and Technology Agency and to shift the emphasis in Japan's space program from science to industry. The Japanese government continues to work to develop a national communications satellite capacity, and one suspects that MITI is merely getting ready to assume jurisdiction when the nation starts exporting.

TELETOPIAS AND NEW MEDIA COMMUNITIES

Nobody of course really knows what the "informationized" society of the future will look like, but the Japanese are taking no chances. It is possible that telecommunications will require an investment in facilities and infrastructure equal to the investment in railroads in the late 19th century. During 1984 NTT was already using figures of from ¥30 to ¥100 trillion for its Information Network System (INS) alone. Towns and prefectures certainly wanted to make sure that their localities were included in whichever ministry's plan became national policy. For this reason the Diet Members' League for New Media, created in the autumn of 1983 by Kanemaru Shin and Sato Moriyoshi (both belong to the Tanaka faction) immediately attracted some 220 members.[89]

MITI was the first to air its proposal. On July 26, 1983, it unveiled a plan to build some eleven (later cut to eight) "new media communities," that is, towns around the country designated as test sites for digitalized, multimedia networks and new equipment. (Note that both MITI and MPT use English to market their offerings—*nyu media komyuniti* is MITI's term and *teletopia* is MPT's. Japanese commonly use English as the language of fashion and advertising, just as French is used in English-speaking countries.) MITI justified its choice of specific communities in terms of their diversity—textile regions, high-technology areas, resorts, and so forth—but it also took care to include Nagaoka, the capital city of Tanaka Kakuei's district in Niigata prefecture.[90]

MPT was astounded by this MITI announcement, and Telecommunications Bureau chief Koyama scurried to the postal *zoku* to complain that MITI was infringing on its turf. The *zoku* told him to speed up his own announcement, and in August MPT duly published its list of some twenty cities it planned to designate as teletopias. This meant that NTT would install in them its advanced INS system and supply them with its new character and pattern telephone access information network (CAPTAIN) videotex telephones. Neither INS nor CAPTAIN was as yet available in the summer of 1983 (full-scale testing began only in November 1984 at Mitaka, a suburb of Tokyo adjacent to the main NTT laboratory), and many thought that MPT's first announcement was merely designed to head off MITI. Nonetheless, since MPT has NTT on its side, it could probably deliver on its plans sooner than MITI, and cities all over the country began petitioning their Diet members to get themselves included as future teletopias.[91]

In late 1984 MITI and MPT both sent to the LDP bills that would provide funds to build the new media communities and teletopias. They also flooded the press with propaganda about the wonders of the informationized society of the future. The party, however, scrapped both bills simply because they were too expensive (MITI's actually passed but in a watered down version that provided only small-scale funding to test the collaborative use of computers in industries). Meanwhile, the Ministry of Construction decided that both MITI and MPT were infringing on *its* jurisdiction and produced its own bill to build new telecommunications networks along the national highways. Not to be outdone, in November 1984, the Ministry of Transportation got interested in laying optical fiber cables along the JNR right-of-ways and going into business as a class I common carrier in competition with NTT and other new entries.

As a result of this bureaucratic free-for-all, the party hedged for more than a year. During this time MOF made clear to the politicians that they certainly could not afford all four ministries' proposals and very probably could not afford any of them. Finally, on February 28, 1986, the Nakasone cabinet approved a compromise bill, one that incorporated the LDP's newly discovered concept of "vitality." *Baitaritei*, an example of Japanese-created English that does not exist in English (so-called *wasei eigo*), does not mean "vitality" in Japanese but rather governmental incentives for private sector initiatives. It is a code word for leaving a public matter to the private sector, as for example in the LDP Executive Council report of July 16, 1985: "The stimulation of domestic demand by actively promoting private vitality which is not dependent on government spending is the best policy to be adopted."[92] As Ronald Dore notes, "the [Japanese] language lends itself to pompous neologisms" (he had "informationized society" in mind), and vitality is certainly one of them.[93]

The cabinet proposal of February 1986 combines the infrastructure plans of all four ministries. It offers a 13 percent special investment tax credit in the first year to private firms that come in on designated projects, and it also exempts them from property and land sales taxes. Additional funding is provided by concessionary loans from the Japan Development Bank, a government agency that invests postal savings through the Fiscal Investment and Loan Program. The areas designated for investment are (1) facilities for high-technology research and development and for training technicians; (2) telecommunications infrastructure (MPT); (3) information oriented-society infrastructure (MITI); (4) facilities for telecommunications research and development for joint use by public and private enterprises; (5) facilities for international fairs and conferences; and (6) projects to upgrade harbors and port terminals.[94] Thus, in the teletopias case, the party seems temporarily to have solved interministerial conflict through an omnibus pork barrel bill that gives something to everybody.

PROMOTING TELECOMMUNICATIONS RESEARCH

The centerpiece of MITI's policy for fiscal 1985 was a new agency under its control to promote and help finance the high-technology industries of the future—specifically, telecommunications, new ceramics, biotechnology, and microelectronics. If MITI could occupy the high ground of high-tech R&D, it had a good chance of ushering in its until then elusive "third golden age." In order to get such a new agency approved by the Budget Bureau of the Ministry of Finance and the General Affairs Agency of the prime minister's office, however, it had to do two things. It had to find an agency under its control to abolish before the General Affairs Agency would allow a new one to be created; and it had to find an off-budget way of financing its new project, given the generally flat budgets of the mid-1980s imposed by MOF and Prime Minister Nakasone. To meet the first requirement, MITI offered up for sacrifice its old Foreign Trade Training Institute (this being one area in which Japanese assuredly do not need further education); and it proposed to fund the new agency through low-interest loans from the Japan Development Bank and through "private vitality."

As it turned out, MPT also wanted to fund a new organ to facilitate telecommunications research. With the privatization of NTT, the government's major telecom research institutes had passed into private industry; and MPT needed some kind of public agency to fund and keep alive the research cartels of the NTT "family" firms. MPT did not have the required agency to sacrifice in order to create a new one, but it had something just as valuable—lots of money. MPT believed that it controlled the dividends on one-third of NTT's shares, and it now proposed to use these funds to finance joint public-private telecommunications research.

Unhappily for MPT, the Ministry of Finance took the view that "at a time of great stress in national finance, to leave a third of the NTT shares—which is the joint property of the people—under the monopoly of a single ministry is scandalous."[95] Instead, MOF proposed, in cooperation with MITI, to revive the almost moribund Industrial Investment Special Account with NTT dividends, plus funds derived from the privatization of the government's tobacco monopoly. The Industrial Investment Special Account was an unconsolidated, earmarked account dating from the 1950s and early 1960s, when it was used as an instrument of industrial policy. Its funds had not been replenished for many years, however, when MOF and MITI urged reviving it to fund high-technology research. Needless to say, this proposal would have removed MPT from having any control over the NTT dividends, since all special accounts are under MOF's jurisdiction.

This three-ministry dispute went to the LDP for arbitration. Party secretary general Kanemaru devised a solution and then sold it to his own faction (Tanaka's), which ensured its passage in the Diet. Kanemaru accepted MOF's financing formula. He proposed that the new Basic Technological Research Promotion Center (Kiban Gijutsu Kenkyu Sokushin Senta) be supplied with start-up capital from three sources. First, it would receive ¥6 billion from the Industrial Investment Special Account, which would itself be restored to life in the manner MOF had proposed. Second, it would accept a ¥3 billion loan from the Japan Development Bank. Third, the private sector would contribute some ¥4.5–5 billion. In addition, Kanemaru authorized the new center to create joint research projects with two or more private companies, for which an additional ¥2 billion of working capital would be supplied from the Industrial Investment Special Account. Finally, he gave the center still another ¥2 billion from the Industrial Investment Special Account for research loans to private firms for risky projects (they do not have to repay the loans if the projects fail). NTT dividends should amount to at least ¥20 billion per annum, which is more than enough to fund all of these sub-accounts and still build up the special account for the future.

Since MITI was supplying the sacrificial agency and MPT (indirectly) the money, Kanemaru gave them both jurisdiction in administering the new center. This decision produced one of the classic encounters of the telecom wars. On December 18, 1984, in MOF's press club room on the second floor of the MOF building, MITI Minister Murata and MPT Minister Sato gathered for a press conference. They had just completed final negotiations over the fiscal 1985 budget with Finance Minister Takeshita, in which the main issue was MOF's approval of the Basic Technological Research Promotion Center. Murata opened: "With regard to the center, it has been decided that both the Ministry of International Trade and Industry and the Ministry of Posts and Telecommunications will be involved, but MITI will take the upper hand." Sato then stepped forward, interrupted, and said, "This project is absolutely under the joint jurisdiction of both MITI and MPT. MITI is not playing any leading role."[96] The next day every newspaper in the country reported the "blood feud" between MITI and MPT. Incidentally, Murata and Sato are close friends; they were both born in 1924, both graduated from the law department of Kyoto University, both served as bureaucrats before entering politics, and both were first elected in 1969.

The Basic Technology Research Facilitation Law, setting up and funding the center, passed the Diet on June 15, 1985. Because the center was partly funded by the private sector and was thus an example of "vitality," the government insisted that its chairman had to be a civilian. It asked the venerable president of Keidanren, Inayama Yoshihiro, eighty-one years old in 1985 and an official in MITI's predecessor ministry during the 1930s, to find one. He first asked Iwata Kazuo, the former chairman of Toshiba, but MPT rejected him for being "too close to MITI." Inayama then tried Shindo Sadakazu, chairman of Mitsubishi Electric, but MITI turned him down as a "member of the NTT family." Inayama finally went to Hiraiwa Gaishi, the respected chairman of Tokyo Electric Power, and when he declined, decided to take the post himself.[97]

Serving under Inayama are the chosen agents from the three concerned ministries. The chairman of the board is Saito Taichi (MITI 1945–75), whose last position in the government was as director of the Medium and Smaller Enterprises Agency. Managing Director is Koizumi Tadayuki (MOF 1948–81), whose last position in the Finance Ministry was as chief of the Customs Department in the National Tax Agency. Deputy Managing Director is Takanaka Masaru, former head of MPT's Postal Savings Bureau. In his inaugural remarks to his colleagues when the center opened on October 1, 1985, Saito said, "Although this is a motley group drawn from such diverse sources as MITI, MPT, and MOF, and the private sector, we must not fall into disarray but hang together as one and try to advance the cause of research in basic technology. We must forget who our parents are and just work together."[98]

So was launched Japan's latest bureaucratic effort to achieve scientific and technological preeminence in the industries of the future. The new center was given a big send-off on July 29, 1985, at the New Otani Hotel, Tokyo. Chairman Inayama brought out some fifty-five "*zaikai* all stars" to pledge their support, including NTT president Shinto, Ishihara Takashi of the Japan Automobile Industry Association, Hagura Nobuya of the National Banking Association, and Morita Akio of the Japan Electronic Machinery Association (and head of Sony). The center is a typical Japanese hybrid: the product of bureaucratic competition, funded from public but not tax monies, and incorporating private sector supervision and participation. And yet it is also likely to be more effective than anything Japan's competitors will put together.

CONCLUSION

As the telecom wars amply demonstrated, lobbying is a common occurrence in Japanese public life. During 1984, at the height of the battles over VANs and the privatization of NTT, representatives of domestic computer manufacturers paid virtually daily calls on the leading postal *zoku*.[99] Hitachi, Toshiba, Mitsubishi Electric, and Matsushita are the fourth, fifth, seventh, and eighth largest political donors in the country (first, second, third, and sixth are Nissan, Japan Steel, Mitsubishi Heavy Industries, and Sumitomo Bank). No other industry has as many contributors of funds to the LDP in the top ten as the electrical manufacturers.[100]

What do the cases of policymaking in the telecommunications industry that we have touched on here suggest about the knowledge needed by a person who wants to lobby the Japanese government? First, the potential lobbyist must know which ministry or ministries has jurisdiction over his or her problem and then find out everything it is possible to know about that organization, including its history, personnel cliques, postretirement patterns, scandals, and so forth. This is precisely the kind of information that any Japanese manufacturer or marketing organization compiles all the time. The major Japanese daily newspapers, for example, routinely print on page 2 details of personnel shifts within the ministries and agencies of the central government. It would be unheard of to read such information in the *New York Times* or the *Washington Post* on, say, the Department of Commerce, but in Tokyo it is important news. The Japanese press reports on who is in charge of what section throughout the Japanese executive branch because its readers need and want that information.

Second, the potential lobbyist should have an intimate understanding of the organization and personnel of the Liberal Democratic party and keep up to date on *zoku* and their activities. It is obvious that until 1985 Tanaka Kakuei was the single most useful person in Japan to try to influence. It is also obvious that as a consequence of the Lockheed case and the way in which it was made public by a committee of the U.S. Senate, Tanaka was not open to appeals from American sources. But as a result of serious illness, his political life is now over. There will probably not again soon be a Japanese politician as powerful and as effective as Tanaka, but this only means that persons interested in what the Japanese government may decide cannot afford to neglect any LDP faction or group of *zoku*.

Information on Japanese politics is not hard to acquire. Official, academic, and journalistic writing on Japanese public affairs is voluminous; and Japanese officials do not mind being interviewed. Like officials everywhere, secrecy is their most powerful weapon, but they also hope to learn as much from a good interview as they put out. The problem is that to keep up with what is going on in Japan, the analyst must be on the ground in Tokyo, just as the lobbyist of the U.S. government must be in daily touch with Washington, D.C. There is no substitute for on-site data collection, conversation, interviews, and analysis. Businessmen, government officials, and other foreigners who want to get over their message in Japan and who do not have their own agents in Tokyo would be well advised to abandon the effort. A short trip by, for example, a U.S. government official or congressman will be not only ineffective but genuinely misleading, since the Japanese are skilled in letting foreigners *think* they have actually accomplished something. Attempting to influence Japan requires professional levels of linguistic and area studies knowledge. It is high time that foreign nations that are dissatisfied with Japanese governmental policies began to match their rhetoric with some expertise.

NOTES

1. Yoshida Shigeru, *The Yoshida Memoirs* (Cambridge, Mass.: Houghton Mifflin, 1962), p. 128. Note that Japanese names are given in the Japanese manner, family name followed by given name.

2. "No Country More Important" is the English-language title of an influential book published in both English and Japanese by the U.S. ambassador to Japan during the late 1970s and early 1980s, Mike Mansfield. See Mansfield, *Nihon hodo juyo na kuni wa nai* (No Country Is More Important Than Japan) (Tokyo: Simul Press, 1980, 1984). For the idea of Japan as the "cornerstone" of U.S. policy in Asia, see U.S. Department of State, "U.S.-Japanese Relations," *Gist*, January 1986, p. 1.

3. On the origins of the transparency issue, see Chalmers Johnson, "The Institutional Foundations of Japanese Industrial Policy," in Claude E. Barfield and William A. Schambra, eds., *The Politics of Industrial Policy* (Washington, D.C.: American Enterprise Institute, 1986), pp. 192–95.

4. Timothy J. Curran, "Politics and High Technology: The NTT Case," in I.M. Destler and Sato Hideo, eds., *Coping with U.S.-Japanese Economic Conflicts* (Lexington, Mass.: D.C. Heath, 1982), p. 236.

5. Sam Jameson, "Japan's Trade Image Improves in Some Areas," *Los Angeles Times*, April 21, 1986.

6. Glen S. Fukushima, "The U.S.-Japan Trade Conflict: A View from Washington," *International House of Japan Bulletin* 6: 2 (Spring 1986): 7–11.

7. On "privatization," see *The Economist*, December 21, 1985, pp. 71–74.

8. Charles L. Brown, "The Dynamics of Information Technology, Enterprise, and Public Policy," *International House of Japan Bulletin* 6: 1 (Winter 1986): 1–3.

9. *The Economist*, March 30, 1985, p. 81.

10. On the relatively slight influence of "foreign financial and corporate institutions, and of foreign governments, on the policymaking process in the Japanese financial markets," see James Horne, *Japan's Financial Markets: Conflict and Consensus in Policymaking* (Sydney, Australia: George Allen and Unwin, 1985), p. 22.

11. Kawaguchi Hiroyuki, "Jiminto habatsu to kanryo: 'zoku' no rankingu" (LDP Factions and the Bureaucracy: Rankings of *zoku*), *Gekkan kankai* 9 (November 1983): 95.

12. John Creighton Campbell, *Contemporary Japanese Budget Politics* (Berkeley: University of California Press, 1977), p. 111.

13. *Kankai* (Bureaucratic World) Editorial Board, comp., "Yusei vs. Tsusan zenmen senso no naimaku" (Inside Story of the All-out War Between MPT and MITI), *Gekkan kankai* 9 (November 1983): 137. On the concept "vertical administration," see Albert M. Craig, "Functional and Dysfunctional Aspects of Government Bureaucracy," in Ezra F. Vogel, ed., *Modern Japanese Organization and Decision-making* (Berkeley: University of California Press, 1975), p. 11 ff. On the concept "capitalist developmental state," see Chalmers Johnson, *MITI and the Japanese Miracle* (Stanford, Calif.: Stanford University Press, 1982), p. 17 ff.

14. On bureaucratic competion, see Chalmers Johnson, *Japan's Public Policy Companies* (Washington, D.C.: American Enterprise Institute, 1978), p. 147.

15. Kawakita Takao, *Tsusan-Yusei senso* (The MITI–MPT Wars) (Tokyo: Kyoiku Sha, 1985), pp. 56–57. On the idea that MOF is also a "super-elite bureaucracy," see Jin Ikko, *Okura kanryo: cho-erito shudan no jinmyaku to yabo* (MOF Bureaucrats: The Cliques and Intrigues of a Super-elite Group) (Tokyo: Kodansha, 1982), p. 19 *et passim*.

16. *Gekkan kankai* (November 1983): 132–41.

17. For the opinion that "industrial development policies have become less important to Japanese economic development as the Japanese economy itself has grown and matured," see Jimmy W. Wheeler, Merit E. Janow, and Thomas Pepper, *Japanese Industrial Development Policies in the 1980s* (Croton-on-Hudson, N.Y.: Hudson Institute, 1982), p. xxi, s.v. pars. 1, 5–8. Interestingly enough, this report was commissioned and paid for by the U.S. Department of State. It has been reprinted and distributed commercially as *The Competition: Dealing with Japan* (New York: Praeger, 1985). On the Lion's Petroleum case, see Kawakita, *Tsusan-Yusei senso*, p. 99; and *Japan Law Letter*, March 1985, p. 28. On MITI's targeting of and measures for the semiconductor industry, see Shimura Yukio,

IC sangyo no himitsu (Secrets of the Integrated Circuit Industry) (Tokyo: Chobunsha, 1981), p. 45 *et passim.*

18.	See, in particular, Amaya Naohiro (former deputy vice minister of MITI), *"Saka no ue no kumo"* to *"saka no shita no numa"* ("The Beautiful Clouds of the Up-slope" and "The Swamp at the End of the Downslope") (Tokyo: Tsusho Sangyo Chosa Kai, 1985). This book includes Amaya's English-language essay, "A Note on MITI's Industrial Policy," presented to the Aspen Institute, August 28, 1984.

19.	Kodama Fumio, "Policy Innovation at MITI," *Japan Echo* 11: 2 (Summer 1984): 67–69. This article is a translation of Kodama's "Tsusan-sho ni yoru kiseki wa futatabi kanoka" (Can the MITI-made Miracle Occur Again?), *Chuo koron*, March 1983, pp. 139–47.

20.	In early 1986, after All Nippon Airways, Japan's leading domestic airline, decided to buy Boeing 767-300s as its next mainstay aircraft, the *Nihon keizai shimbun* reported charges that MITI had become "America's good friend" and "America's lackey." However, some analysts recognized in MITI's proimport drive "a facade for expanding the ministry's influence over domestic firms." The *Nihon keizai* wrote: "The drive to cut the surplus is a good opportunity for MITI to recover its old iron grip on domestic industries which it lost in the process of Japan's trade liberalization. MITI plans to intervene in domestic industries as 'an emergency measure' and maintain that intervention for a long time." *Japan Economic Journal* (January 25, 1986): 1, 5. In the summer of 1985 MITI also discussed and then shelved as too controversial a draft "Overseas Investment Facilitation Law." This bill stipulated that firms whose exports exceeded MITI-set limits would be obligated to shift some of their production offshore. The draft law would have given MITI strong powers of control over export-oriented industries, particularly the electronics and telecommunications industries that do not have MITI-administered quantitative controls over exports such as exist in the automobile industry.

21.	For a Japanese analysis along these lines, see Kumon Shumpei, "Japan Faces Its Future: The Political-Economics of Administrative Reform," *Journal of Japanese Studies* 10: 1 (Winter 1984): 143–65, particularly 160. Cf. Peter F. Drucker, "The Changed World Economy," *Foreign Affairs* 64: 4 (Spring 1986): 768–91. In Japanese, see Sangyo Kozo Shingikai Sogo Bukai Kikaku Shoiinkai (Industrial Structure Council, Coordination Division, Planning Subcommittee), comp., *21-seiki sangyo shakai no kihon kozo (an)* (The Basic Structure of Industrial Society in the 21st Century; Draft) (Tokyo: Sangyo Kozo Shingikai, May 26, 1986), 104 pp.

22.	See, for example, Kawakita, *Tsusan-Yusei senso*, pp. 60–61. Cf. National Research Council, National Academy of Sciences, *High-technology Ceramics in Japan* (Washington, D.C.: National Academy Press, 1984).

23.	Konaga Keiichi, "Tsusan-sho no shin senryaku: tekunoraibaru Beikoku to no kyoso" (MITI's New Strategy: Competition with Our Technorival,

America), *Next* (December 1984): 48–53. (Note that many new Japanese magazines use English words or phrases for their titles, including *Focus, This Is, Trigger, Voice,* and several others. *Next* is such a magazine.)

24. Kawakita, *Tsusan-Yusei senso*, pp. 61–62.

25. Fukui Haruhiro, "The Liberal Democratic Party Revisited: Continuity and Change in the Party's Structure and Performance," *Journal of Japanese Studies* 10: 2 (Summer 1984), 409–11 and n. 25.

26. *Gekkan kankai* (November 1983): 133.

27. Kawakita, *Tsusan-yusei senso*, p. 62. Also see Shin Yusei Mondai Kenkyukai (New Postal Ministry Problems Study Group), *Yusei-sho no gyakushu* (The Postal Ministry's Counterattack) (Tokyo: Bijinesu Sha, 1986).

28. Kawakita, ibid., p. 73.

29. "The Business-minded Ministry: MPT," *Journal of Japanese Trade and Industry* 5: 2 (March–April 1986): 30. (Note that this magazine is published by a MITI-affiliated organization.)

30. See Watanabe Tsuneo, Miyazaki Yoshimasa, and Iijima Kiyoshi, eds., *Seiji no joshiki daihyakka* (Practical Political Encyclopedia) (Tokyo: Kodansha, 1983), p. 255, s.v. Yusei-zoku.

31. "100-cho-en banku, yucho" (Postal Savings, the ¥100 Trillion Bank), *Nihon keizai shumbun*, January 29, 1986. (My thanks to Barry Keehn for drawing my attention to this article.)

32. Journalists' Roundtable, "'Tsushin kakumei' ni ugomeku seiji riken" (Political Vested Interests Squirm Under the 'Telecom Revolution'), *Ekonomisuto* 62 (April 17, 1984): 25; Horne, *Japan's Financial Markets*, pp. 132–33; Inoguchi Takashi and Iwai Tomoaki, "Jiminto rieki yudo no seiji-keizaigaku" (The Political Economy of Guidance of the LDP by Special Interests), *Chuo koron*, March 1985, p. 160; and "Dissolution of NTT," *Zaikai tembo*, September 1984 (trans. Foreign Broadcast Information Service [FBIS], *Japan Report*, JPRS–JAR–84–017, November 14, 1984, p. 56). An interesting case of a direct connection between the special post offices and MPT is that of Hirose Masao. He went from being postmaster of his family's post office in Kyushu to the Diet as a representative of the Oita First district and on to service as postal minister in the third Sato cabinet (1971–72). Hirose's post office had been part of his family's business for three generations. See Noda Keizai Kenkyujo, comp. *Seiji to sono gunzo* (Politics and Political Groups) (Tokyo: Noda Keizai Kenkyujo, 1975), p. 275.

33. Kawakami Noriyasu, "Kankai jinmyaku chiri: Yusei-sho" (Geography of Bureaucratic Personnel Relations: Ministry of Posts and Telecommunications), *Gekkan kankai* 11 (February 1985) (trans. American Embassy, Tokyo, *Summaries of Selected Japanese Magazines*, April 1985, p. 6); and *Japan Times Weekly*, October 20, 1979, p. 10; October 27, 1979, p. 2; November 3, 1979, p. 9; November 10, 1979, p. 2; November 17, 1979, p. 1; and November 24, 1979, p. 1.

34. Ouchi Takao, "Yusei vs. Tsusan: hateshi-naki arasoi" (MPT vs. MITI: A Struggle Without End), *Gekkan kankai* 10 (June 1984): 142.

35. Quoted by Curran, "Politics and High Technology," p. 201.

36. James Elliott, "The 1981 Administrative Reform in Japan," *Asian Survey* 23: 6 (June 1983): 765. On the first Provisional Commission for Administrative Reform and related matters, see Chalmers Johnson, "Japan: Who Governs? An Essay on Official Bureaucracy," *Journal of Japanese Studies* 2: 1 (Autumn 1975): 1–28.

37. Kumon, "Japan Faces Its Future," p. 153.

38. Gotoda Teruo, "Nihon ni okeru kodo gijutsu hatten no kanryo kiko no taito to sangyo seisaku no saihensei" (The Emergence of a Bureaucratic Apparatus for the Development of High-technology in Japan and the Reorganization of Industrial Policy), *Himeji Gakuin kiyo* (Himeji University Bulletin), no. 13 (1985), p. 142.

39. 21-seiki Kigyo Kenkyu Group (Industries of the 21st Century Study Group), *Nyu media no shihaisha* (Managers of the New Media) (Tokyo: Yamate Shobo, 1984), pp. 202–4. Also see "Yusei-sho kambu shokuin" (Roster of MPT Leaders), *Shukan yomiuri*, January 1, 1985, pp. 158–68; and Jihyo-sha, comp., *Yusei-sho meikan* (Ministry of Posts and Telecommunications Directory) (Tokyo: Jihyo-sha, 1986).

40. Kawakita, *Tsusan-Yusei senso*, p. 69. It should be noted that the use of military metaphors is not exclusive with Kawakita but is common for virtually all Japanese writers on this subject. Other examples include "Terekomu uozu sokanzu" (Chart of the Telecom Wars), *Konpyutopia*, June 1985; and Nikkei Bijinesu, ed., *Sekai terekomu senso* (The Global Telecom War) (Tokyo: Nihon Keizai Shimbun Sha, 1984).

41. For the Japanese names of the first three sections, see Johnson, *MITI and the Japanese Miracle*, p. 338. The name of the new Information Management Systems Development Section is Joho Shori Shisutemu Kaihatsu-ka.

42. For the view that politicians dominate the bureaucracy, see Takahashi Yoshiyuki, "Jiminto habatsu to kanryo: 'Tanaka shihai' no nouhau" (LDP Factions and the Bureaucracy: The Knowhow of the "Tanaka Domination"), *Gekkan kankai* 9 (June 1983): 114–24; Editorial, "'Minko-kantei' e no tenkan" (The Switch to "Civilians Up, Bureaucrats Down"), *Next* (December 1984): 47; and Kawakita, *Tsusan-Yusei senso*, p. 91. For the "cheering squad" view, see *Gekkan kankai* (November 1983): 140; and "Seme no Yusei, shiren no Denden" (MPT on the Attack, NTT on Trial), *Nihon keizai shimbun*, October 22, 1984 For the theory of politicians-as-air-cover, see Kawakita, ibid., p. 72; and Inoguchi and Iwai (they use the metaphor of artillery rather than air power), *Chuo koron* (March 1985), p. 160.

43. *The Economist*, May 3, 1986, p. 13.

44. Peter E. Fuchs, "Regulatory Reform and Japan's Telecommunications Revolution," in Program on U.S.-Japan Relations, ed., *U.S.-Japan Rela-*

tions: New Attitudes for a New Era (Cambridge, Mass.: Center for International Affairs, Harvard University, 1984), p. 136.

45. Sato Seizaburo and Matsuzaki Tetsuhisa, "Jiminto chochoki seiken no kaibo" (Autopsy on the Super-long-term Reign of the LDP), *Chuo koron*, November 1984, p. 95. Also see Sato and Matsuzaki, *Jiminto seiken* (The Political Regime of the LDP) (Tokyo: Chuo Koron Sha, 1986) with their outstanding compilation of data on all postwar cabinets, pp. 294–337.

46. Sato and Matsuzaki, *Chuo koron*, November 1984, p. 89; and Kawakita, *Tsusan-Yusei senso*, p. 88. The most important study of PARC is Nihon Keizai Shimbun, ed., *Jiminto seichokai* (The LDP's Policy Affairs Research Council) (Tokyo: Nihon Keizai Shimbun Sha, 1983), which includes a valuable commentary on the role of PARC by former Prime Minister Tanaka Kakuei, pp. 194–208.

47. Sato and Matsuzaki, *Chuo koron*, November 1984, p. 90.

48. Inoguchi and Iwai, *Chuo koron*, March 1985, pp. 138–39.

49. The relationship between faction and *zoku* is perhaps best captured in Tanaka Kakuei's metaphor of the faction as a "general hospital." According to Tanaka, his own faction, which is by far the largest within the LDP, was like a first-rate hospital—one staffed by qualified specialists in all medical fields and equipped with the best possible facilities (that is, bureaucratic connections). As a result the Tanaka faction could cope with any type of "illness"—for example, a constituent's petition (*chinjo*), a faction member's need for funds, a businessman's need for access to the bureaucracy, or a trade association's desire to see some market-opening scheme delayed. In short, what this good general hospital had was a comprehensive array of *zoku*. See Joho Kenkyujo, ed., *Tanaka Kakuei* (Tokyo: Deta Hausu, 1983), p. 139. On *zoku*, also see the articles by Masuzoe Yoichi in *Sankei shimbun*, July 30 and August 2, 1984; *Seiji no joshiki daihyakka*, pp. 205, 215, 227, 235, 245, 255; Inoguchi Takashi, "Nihon seiji no zahyojiku kaeru boeki masatsu" (Trade Friction Changes the Axes of Japanese Politics), *Ekonomisuto* (March 25, 1986): 34–41; and Yuasa Hiroshi, *Kokkai "giin zoku"* (The Diet's "Tribes") (Tokyo: Kyoiku Sha, 1986).

50. Kawaguchi, *Gekkan kankai* (November 1983), p. 96.

51. See Chalmers Johnson, "Tanaka Kakuei, Structural Corruption, and the Advent of Machine Politics in Japan," *Journal of Japanese Studies* 12: 1 (Winter 1986): 1–28.

52. Murakawa Ichiro, *Seisaku kettei katei* (The Policy-making Process) (Tokyo: Kyoiku Sha, 1979), p. 15; and Takahashi, "Jiminto habatsu to kanryo," p. 115.

53. Sato and Matsuzaki, *Chuo koron*, November 1984, p. 74.

54. LDP leaders have long observed that conflicts of jurisdiction within the bureaucracy provide opportunities for the party to assert and enlarge its

authority. See Journalists' Roundtable, *Ekonomisuto* (April 17, 1984): 24.

55.   Horne notes (in *Japan's Financial Markets*) many cases in which the Federation of Bankers' Associations and the city banks were closer to and more influential with MOF than with the LDP (for example, pp. 107-11, 129). Also see Sato and Matsuzaki, *Chuo koron*, November 1984, p. 91.

56.   See "Jushoku iincho no 'teishin seppo'" (The Head Priest's "Sermon on Communications") [interview with Sato Megumu, then chairman of the House of Representatives' Standing Committee on Communications], *Gekkan kankai* 9 (May 1983): 102-8 [the title alludes to Sato's background as the descendant of Buddhist priests] ; and Sato Megumu [then Minister of Posts and Telecommunications], "Iza homban: 'Tsushin jiyuka' jidai" (Lights! Camera! Action! The "Liberalized Telecommunications" Era), *Gekkan kankai* 11 (May 1985): 64-74.

57.   Kawaguchi, *Gekkan kankai* (November 1983), pp. 105-6; and Kawakita, *Tsusan-Yusei senso*, p. 71.

58.   Koita Hashijiro, *Seikai orai*, October 1985 (trans. FBIS, *Japan Report*, JPRS-JAR-86-005, March 27, 1986, p. 40).

59.   Horne, *Japan's Financial Markets*, p. 120.

60.   Michael Korver, "Developments in Japanese Finance," *Japan Economic Journal* (May 17, 1986): 5; and Jin Ikko, *Okura kanryo*, pp. 189-201.

61.   Horne, *Japan's Financial Markets*, pp. 137-39.

62.   *Gekkan kankai*, November 1983, pp. 105-6, 132-33; *Japan Law Letter*, May 1985, p. 11, and March 1986, p. 7; Kawakami, in *Summaries of Selected Japanese Magazines*, April 1985, p. 3; and Takahashi, "Jiminto habatsu to kanryo," pp. 121-22.

63.   Kawakita, *Tsusan-Yusei senso*, pp. 136-37.

64,   *Nihon keizai shimbun*, May 10, 1983; and *Gekkan kankai*, November 1983, pp. 135-36.

65.   Ouchi, *Gekkan kankai* (June 1984), p. 140; *NTToptics*, no. 11 (Summer 1985): 2; and *Zaibai tembo*, August 1984 (trans. FBIS, *Japan Report*, JPRS-JAR-84-017, November 14, 1984, pp. 32-35). For the text of the Telecommunications Business Law in English, see *Japan Law Letter*, February 1985, pp. 19-30, and March 1985, pp. 14-23.

66.   See Mark E. Foster, "Telecommunications Equipment Standards and Certification Procedures for Japan" (unpublished paper, Foreign Commercial Service, U.S. Department of Commerce, Tokyo, October 1984), p. 12 (permission to cite obtained from the author). Also see Foster, "A Guide to Mandatory Technical Standards and Product Certification Procedures Under Japan's Electrical Appliance Law" (unpublished paper, same source and date).

67.   Ouchi, *Gekkan kankai* (June 1984), p. 138.

68.   *Business Week*, March 11, 1985, p. 67.

69. *Zaikai tembo*, August 1984 (trans. FBIS, *Japan Report*, JPRS-JAR-84-017, November 14, 1984, p. 34).

70. Gotoda, *Himeji Gakuin kiyo*, p. 145; *Japan Law Letter*, May 1984, p. 64; and *Nihon keizai shimbun*, April 6, 1984.

71. Kawakita, *Tsusan-Yusei senso*, p. 75; Ohashi Ikuo (MPT official), "The Effects of Telecommunications Deregulation," in Program on U.S.-Japan Relations, ed., *U.S.-Japan: Towards a New Equilibrium* (Cambridge, Mass.: Center for International Affairs, Harvard University, 1983), p. 91; and *Zaikai tembo*, August 1984 (trans. FBIS, *Japan Report*, JPRS-JAR-84-017, November 14, 1984, p. 24).

72. *The Economist*, December 21, 1985, p. 74.

73. Gotoda, *Himeji Gakuin kiyo*, pp. 146–47; Kawakami, in *Summaries of Selected Japanese Magazines*, April 1985, p. 6; Kawakita, *Tsusan-Yusei senso*, pp. 78–82; and Takahashi, "Jiminto habatsu to kanryo," pp. 121–22.

74. Journalists' Roundtable, *Ekonomisuto* (April 17, 1984): 26.

75. *NTToptics*, no. 14 (Spring 1986): 3; *Journal of Japanese Trade and Industry* 5: 2 (March–April 1986): 29; *Japan Times Weekly*, October 19, 1985, and January 11, 1986.

76. *Japan Law Letter*, March 1986, p. 13.

77. Ouchi, *Gekkan kankai* (June 1984), p. 145.

78. C. Michael Aho and Jonathan David Aronson, *Trade Talks: America Better Listen* (New York: Council on Foreign Relations, 1985), p. 85.

79. Foster, "Telecommunications," p. 25 and appendix.

80. *Denkei shimbun*, April 16, 1984 (quoted in *ibid.*).

81. General Affairs Agency (Somu-cho), ed., *Shingikai soran* (General Survey of Deliberation Councils (Tokyo: Okura-sho Insatsu-kyoku, 1984), pp. 402–3, s.v. Denki Tsushin Shingikai.

82. Foster, "A Guide to Mandatory Technical Standards," appendix O.

83. Kawakita, *Tsusan-Yusei senso*, pp. 42–44.

84. Japanese Telecommunications Association, *New Era of Telecommunications in Japan* 1 (1985): 3–4; Sam Jameson, "Japan: Rules Eased on Telecommunications," *Los Angeles Times*, April 4, 1985; Sam Jameson, "Japan Moves to Keep Its Promises to U.S.," *Los Angeles Times*, April 9, 1985; and William C. Rempel and Sam Jameson, "Japan Phone Market: Patience vs. Pressure," *Los Angeles Times*, April 21, 1985.

85. *Gekkan kankai*, November 1983, p. 140.

86. Edwin Whatley, "Legal Protection of Software," in Program on U.S.-Japan Relations, ed., *U.S.-Japan Relations: New Attitudes for a New Era* (Cambridge, Mass.: Center for International Affairs, Harvard University, 1984), pp. 146–47.

87. For an outline of the MITI draft law, see *Japan Law Letter*, April 1984, pp. 74–77.

88. *Asian Wall Street Journal*, October 3, 1984, p. 10. Also see *Japan Law Letter*, November 1984, pp. 15–17.

89. "Shin Denden: Nihon ichi no kyodai kigyo" (New NTT: Japan's Biggest Enterprise), *Za 21* (PHP Kenkyujo), March 1985, pp. 42–43; and *Nihon keizai shimbun*, October 22, 1984.

90. See the map of all new media communities and teletopias in Kawakita, *Tsusan-Yusei senso*, pp. 148–49. For background, see Richard J. Samuels, *The Politics of Regional Policy in Japan* (Princeton, N.J.: Princeton University Press, 1983).

91. For the networks, capabilities, and vast array of equipment involved in the INS experiment at Mitaka, see the issue devoted to the launching of INS of *Denki tsushin gyomu* (Telecommunications Business), no. 416 (November 1984), pp. 4–34. This is the monthly journal of NTT.

92. "Report on Concrete Measures for Activation of Private Vitality," *Seisaku tokuho*, August 10, 1985 (trans. FBIS, *Japan Report*, JPRS–JAR–85–024, December 1, 1985, pp. 34–64). For further explanations of "vitality," see "MITI's Six Important Projects for 1986," *Jihyo*, December 1985 (trans. FBIS, *Japan Report*, JPRS–JAR–86–002, January 24, 1986, pp. 79–85); and *Tsusan-sho koho* (MITI Gazette), August 1, 1985, pp. 1–2.

93. Ronald Dore, *A Case Study of Technology Forecasting in Japan: The Next Generation Base Technologies Development Program* (London: Technology Change Centre, October 1983), p. 7.

94. *Japan Economic Journal*, March 8, 1986, pp. 3, 8.

95. Kawakita, *Tsusan-Yusei senso*, p. 157.

96. "Shoten: Kiban Gijutsu Kenkyu Sokushin Senta ga hassoku" (Focus: Start of the Basic Technological Research Promotion Center), *Trigger*, December 1985, p. 10; and Kawakita, *Tsusan-Yusei senso*, p. 153.

97. *Trigger*, December 1985, p. 10.

98. Ibid., p. 11.

99. *Zaikai tembo*, September 1984 (trans. FBIS, *Japan Report*, JPRS–JAR–84–017, November 14, 1984, p. 57).

100. Nihon Keizai Shimbun, *Jiminto seichokai*, pp. 230–34.

6 WEAK LINKS, STRONG BONDS
U.S.-Japanese Competition in Semiconductor Production Equipment

Jay S. Stowsky

Continued innovation and successful competition in the semiconductor industry depend increasingly on technological and market leadership in semiconductor production equipment. Advances in semiconductor devices proceed hand in hand with advances in chip processing capabilities. Still, little attention has been paid to the equipment sector in press and policy discussions, even though U.S. firms are losing market share there even faster than they lost it in the chip industry, dropping from an 85 percent share of the world market in 1978 to barely 50 percent in 1987 (see Figure 6-1).

The scope of the competitive problem—whether the problem will be confined to the relatively small $5-6 billion equipment market or magnified to include the entire half-trillion dollar market for final electronic systems—depends on the nature of the technical linkages between semiconductor equipment development and prowess in semiconductor production. If those technical linkages are sufficiently loose, then purchases of foreign equipment can substitute for interactive equipment development on the part of U.S. semiconductor firms and their domestic equipment suppliers. As this study argues, however, equipment development and manufacturing prowess are tightly linked, representing a capability embodied in people and organized in firms, but not readily tradable across national boundaries. A failure to capture the benefits of such technical linkages domestically

Figure 6-1. Semiconductor Manufacturing Equipment World Market Share (*Percentage of World Shipments*).

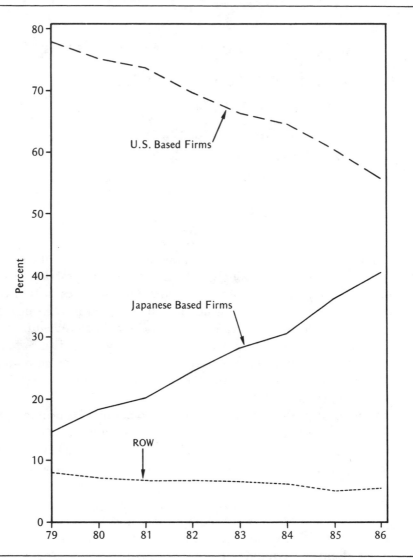

Sources: 1979–85, VLSI Research, Inc.; 1986, authors' estimate. Thomas R. Howell, William A. Noellert, Janet H. MacLaughlin, Alan Wm. Wolff, *The Microelectronics Race: The Impact of Government Policy on International Competition* (Boulder, Colo.: Westview Press, 1988).

will not be compensated by the purchase of advanced production equipment from abroad.

The strategic value of organizational linkages between semiconductor makers and their equipment suppliers increases with the technical linkages between successful semiconductor manufacturing and the know-how gained through managing the process of equipment development. The major thesis of this chapter is that, with regard to both the generation of learning in production and the appropriation of economic returns from such learning, the U.S. semiconductor equipment and device industries are structurally disadvantaged relative to the Japanese. The Japanese have evolved an industrial model that combines higher levels of concentration of both chip and equipment suppliers with quasiintegration between them, whereas the American industry is characterized by levels of concentration that by comparison, are too low *and* excessive vertical disintegration (that is, an absence of mechanisms to coordinate their learning and investment processes).

The sensitivity of the semiconductor production process creates a particular pattern of learning by using. The yield of useable chips may be as low as 5 percent when a new chip design or a new piece of equipment is first put into production; over time, the yield will typically rise sharply as trial-and-error methods improve production conditions. Specifically, the necessity of finely calibrated temperature and vibration levels, split-second timing, elimination of dust, and close attention to the density of chemical solutions often involves adjusting or "tweaking" a given piece of production equipment.

The development of production equipment prior to its implementation in wafer fabrication is itself a type of job shop operation. Highly skilled technicians and engineers tinker with complex parts and subassemblies—electronic measuring devices, optical apparatus, gas and vacuum control equipment—fine-tuning here, reconfiguring there, focusing their efforts on meeting each customer's particular technical specifications. The overriding competitive consideration is not cost, but performance—getting the equipment to perform properly at the user's wafer fabrication facility.[2]

In the United States, equipment development and implementation are most often separate processes. They occur in different locations under the control of different firms. Equipment is brought fully assembled to the customer's wafer fabrication facility, where it is "tweaked" until it works. In contrast, the Japanese typically conflate the two-stage process of development and implementation, building the equipment on site in a clean room under the supervision of the semiconductor producer. This enables both chip and equipment producers to exploit the technical synergies inherent in the two stages; the learning is ongoing and shared.

The fragmented structure of the U.S. equipment and device industries impedes this process of synergistic learning by using in production, and purchases of Japanese production equipment will not serve as adequate substitutes for that process. Only the interactive development of manufacturing equipment by U.S. semiconductor producers and their domestic equipment suppliers can generate, for U.S. firms, the sort of disembodied technological know-how that characterizes the Japanese industry. And it is only through such interactive development that American firms can hope to capture the lion's share of economic returns to domestic technological expertise. If U.S. semiconductor equipment producers are allowed to fail, U.S. semiconductor producers, including large in-house producers like IBM and AT&T, will either have to bear the expense of building their own equipment (an expense that will be reflected in higher prices for their final products) or they will be forced to turn to their Japanese competitors' affiliated equipment suppliers for the latest manufacturing technology. Either choice leaves American electronics firms extremely vulnerable in international competition.

EVOLUTION OF THE INDUSTRY IN THE UNITED STATES

During the early days of semiconductor manufacturing, device makers built their own production equipment by modifying or reconfiguring general purpose machinery and instruments. Electronic measuring devices, optical apparatus, and gas and vacuum control equipment were purchased from established suppliers of analytical and scientific equipment. However, the development of integrated circuits (ICs) in 1958 and the subsequent development of the planar process for manufacturing them created a demand for an entirely new class of semiconductor production equipment: machines designed to conduct precise layer-by-layer deposition and diffusion processes in silicon and instruments built to ensure the correct alignment of circuit patterns between the layers.

By making higher volume batch production feasible, the planar process cleared a technical path for the commercial manufacture of integrated circuits. Government procurement through NASA and the Pentagon provided both Fairchild and Texas Instruments with an initial, successful demonstration market for ICs, expanding production volumes and pushing U.S. firms down the learning curve earlier and faster than their foreign competitors. The quest for higher production yields and more consistent performance spurred the continued development of production equipment dedicated specifically to the manufacture of semiconductor devices. This was reflected in the scope of government procurement. The air force's December 1960 award to Texas Instruments included $2.1 million to support the development of "production processes and special equipment dedicated to the fabrication of ICs in bulk quantities." It was reflected too in the appearance of a small set of independent, specialized equipment suppliers, including Materials Research, GCA, Kulicke and Soffa, and Thermco.

The impact of this early government procurement on the structure of the new U.S. semiconductor industry grew out of the interaction of that highly technologically sophisticated demand with several institutional and environmental factors that were unique to the United States. Chief among these were the ready availability of venture capital, the high mobility of technical personnel between firms, liberal licensing policies by pioneering semiconductor firms, and most important, antitrust constraints on potential entry by electronics giants IBM and AT&T into the open market for semiconductor devices. In combination, these factors contributed to a uniquely dynamic competitive environment or "social structure of innovation" that was unusually conducive to entrepreneurial ventures. Unlike integrated circuit production in Europe and Japan, which was dominated by large, vertically integrated electronic systems manufacturers, IC production in the United States came to be dominated by a set of independent "merchant" firms whose primary business was the manufacture and open market sale of semiconductor devices. Large organizations like universities and corporate research laboratories came to function as incubators for technological innovations that were then exploited and commercialized by small entrepreneurial companies with backing from venture capitalists.

As the 1960s progressed, conditions for continued innovation and growth became less tied to government support. Indeed, they were becoming internalized in the competitive structure of the industry itself. Growing competition among merchant firms and between the merchants and older electronics houses—RCA, Sylvania, Motorola, Raytheon, Westinghouse—pushed the pace of product and process innovation; each new round of competition lowered the cost and improved the performance of integrated circuits, sparking the interest of computer and telecommunications equipment producers and accelerating the diffusion of IC technology throughout the domestic economy. Diffusion was facilitated also by the rapid circulation of technical and managerial personnel, as well as by both formal and informal exchanges of information among manufacturers, suppliers, and vendors. Indeed, requests for information following a series of public seminars given by Motorola in 1963 eventually made that company one of the first open-market vendors of semiconductor production equipment.

The small size and financial vulnerability of the newer merchants, combined with the rapid pace and growing expense of technological advance in circuit design, continued to encourage specialization in both products and production processes. The biggest chip producers— IBM, Fairchild, Texas Instruments, AT&T—continued to build production equipment in-house. By the mid-1960s, however, high growth rates and recurrent cash flow crises among the merchant start-ups meant they had to search for other firms with which to share the costs of financing and manufacturing increasingly expensive production equipment. Both independent equipment start-ups and large, established analytical and scientific equipment firms came forward to fill the void.

A technologically dynamic, entrepreneurial and often antagonistic competitive environment, fueled by venture capital, biased the innovative process in equipment start-ups toward new product creation and away from the more interactive process of manufacturing process improvement.[3] As in the device sector, new equipment ventures were often started by defecting executives from chip houses or other equipment firms. This fact, by itself, militated against the development of detailed, highly personalized interchanges between device firms and their equipment suppliers. Technical knowledge was highly prized; but no firm could be sure that it alone would reap the benefits of that knowledge in the marketplace. Until the development of the microprocessor in 1971, the most important innovations in the semiconductor device industry were process innovations, not product innovations; device makers were understandably reluctant to share proprietary information with equipment suppliers that might go on to disseminate that information to the competition. Second, with the important exception of microlithography equipment, many technicians and engineers possessed the expertise necessary to put together a working piece of semiconductor production equipment. Once they had bought a new machine, semiconductor firms could, and often did, modify and reconfigure the equipment themselves, performing the integration, service, and maintenance functions that would otherwise make up the highest value-added portions of the equipment makers' business. Merchant equipment firms could not benefit, then, from any monopoly of scarce technical or engineering skills. Their task was rather to create exciting new products and to convince equipment buyers that it was in their competitive interest to buy them.

By the end of the 1960s, the relatively low entry costs associated with semiconductor equipment manufacturing began to attract a set of larger companies that had previously produced scientific instruments or manufacturing equipment for older generation electron tubes. New divisions of established firms positioned themselves, often by acquiring struggling start-ups, to share or shoulder the development costs of capital goods that most merchant chip producers could not afford to develop internally. Economies of scale in marketing, combined with some limited scale economies at the product R&D level, underwrote the emergence of a relatively stable set of larger equipment firms, including Varian, General Signal, and the persistent market leader, Perkin-Elmer. Organizational size and product diversity fed financial stability; expanded resources soon translated into expanded internal R&D and expanded product lines. Each new generational crisis brought with it a new crop of innovative start-ups. Some succeeded on their own, others failed, and many were acquired by the larger firms, still seeking to diversify their product lines in order to take advantage of scale economies in marketing and development.

By the early 1970s, a separate semiconductor equipment industry had emerged in the United States, benefiting from the exploding demand for semiconductors and the growing internal resources of the large equipment firms. Major proprietary product innovations began to emerge from the equipment firms themselves, such as Perkin-Elmer's Micralign projection aligner in 1973 (initially developed with support from the U.S. Air Force) and GCA's direct wafer stepper in 1978. The relationship between chip and equipment firms began to shift with the cost and complexity of semiconductor equipment; as equipment development costs soared, big-money transactions combined with the equipment makers' growing technical sophistication to give them some real clout with the semiconductor merchants.

Still, most semiconductor equipment manufacturers remained small, undercapitalized and highly vulnerable to the economic and technological fortunes of the device sector. Their characteristic lack of communication with their major customers showed when the device makers' fortunes soured, for the first time, in the midseventies. Quick to double order in boom times, the device makers moved even faster to cancel during the bust. Still smarting from the shock, equipment makers were slow to respond to new orders from chip makers during the 1977–78 recovery, and the enormous order backlogs and stretched-out delivery schedules that resulted just exacerbated the antagonism and mistrust that already existed between them.[4] Long delivery lags, combined with normal delays due to distance and poor communications, also badly weakened the stronghold that U.S. equipment manufacturers had quietly established in the Japanese market, just as Japanese equipment suppliers were gearing up to support the coming assault by Japanese chipmakers on the high-volume market for semiconductor memories.

The U.S. equipment industry continued to exhibit considerable competitive strengths. A large pool of mobile, entrepreneurial talent formed a solid base for continuous technological innovation; the ready availability of venture capital financing accelerated the translation of innovative ideas into marketable products. Moreover, the independence of semiconductor equipment firms enabled them— indeed, *required* them—to sell their most advanced machines to all potential users, a practice that led routinely to the rapid diffusion of state-of-the-art production equipment throughout the world. As long as all of the equipment firms were American, these strengths tended to hide a host of potentially serious competitive weaknesses that also derived from the U.S. industry's fragmented institutional structure. The most serious of these involved the lack of any mechanisms to coordinate learning and investment processes between users and producers of semiconductor production equipment.

The entrepreneurial environment biased the innovative strategies of U.S. equipment suppliers, who emphasized development of state-of-the-art equipment (proprietary product development) rather than the constant modification and refinement of existing machines. In foreign markets, as well, marketing targeted sales of new equipment rather than upgrading the existing stock; marketing in Japan, for example, was generally organized around the establishment of joint ventures for sales and technical support rather than the formation of wholly owned manufacturing subsidiaries located close to Japanese chip making facilities. The vulnerabilities of this strategy in a context of relatively free technology transfer among the advanced industrial countries remained hidden as long as U.S. equipment firms dominated the international market and continued to control the development of new production technology.

EVOLUTION OF THE INDUSTRY IN JAPAN

Japanese semiconductor device and equipment makers recognized their dependence on American technology early on and, with considerable assistance from the Japanese Ministry of International Trade and Industry (MITI) and Nippon Telephone and Telegraph (NTT), Japan's quasipublic telecommunications monopoly, they organized themselves to turn this apparent weakness into a source of competitive advantage. Through marketing agreements and joint ventures, Japanese firms initially emphasized the rapid acquisition and adaptation of semiconductor production equipment developed in the United States. Subsequently, a government-orchestrated R&D program, the very-large-scale integration (VLSI) project, underwrote the cooperative development and diffusion of an indigenous technology base. Throughout both periods, government policy and the familial characteristics of Japanese business structure worked in concert to insulate domestic producers from foreign competition.

Until the late 1970s, Japanese markets for semiconductor fabrication and test equipment were almost entirely supplied by U.S. firms via marketing agreements with affiliated companies of Japan's giant trading firms or of the combined semiconductor-computer manufacturers. The most important of these was TEL, which, unlike its domestic rivals, began in 1963 as an independent trading company specializing in semiconductor production equipment. The network of bank-centered business alliances (*keiretsu*) that characterize Japanese corporate structure provided an ideal institutional context for close collaboration between semiconductor device makers and their fledgling equipment suppliers (see Table 6-1). *Keiretsu* ties stabilized business relationships, improved interfirm information flows, and provided a financial and planning environment conducive to aggressive, long-term growth policies.

Throughout the period of technological catch-up, most Japanese equipment and device firms were intent on simply keeping up with American advances in semiconductor design and manufacturing. Only in the area of semiconductor assembly equipment did Japanese firms provide any hint of an indigenous capacity for technological innovation. Constrained by government policy and the domestic industry's strongly interlinked structure, Japanese chip makers chose not to follow the typical American merchant strategy of moving labor-intensive assembly operations offshore to some low-wage export platform. Relatively high Japanese wages subsequently created a demand in Japan for sophisticated, automated semiconductor assembly equipment, a demand that could not be adequately met by American assembly equipment firms whose products were geared to the more labor-intensive processes of the U.S. offshore operations. In this instance, Japanese firms stepped in to fill the void; once America's technological lead in assembly equipment vanished, so did American domination of the Japanese market, a portent of things to come. In short order, Japan's Disco (dicing saws) and Shinkawa (automatic wire bonders) were able to expand their overseas sales as well, penetrating the U.S. market for the first time in 1975 and 1976, respectively.

Most Japanese equipment firms remained engaged in the importation, marketing, and maintenance of foreign-produced machines. Unlike their American counterparts, fueled by the demands of an expanding computer sector and fired up by the entrepreneurial drive of the semiconductor merchants, Japanese equipment firms (with the exception of producers of assembly equipment) faced no dynamic expanding demand for products more sophisticated than the ones they were currently marketing. Through the early 1970s, Japanese semiconductor firms remained substantially dependent on the production of discrete circuits for consumer electronics products; significant basic research was being carried out in government and NTT laboratories, but was not on par with spending by U.S. firms. By the end of the 1970s, demands from America's rapidly expanding computer sector were accelerating the pace of semiconductor innovation,

Table 6-1. Vertical Integration of Japanese Semiconductor Producers—Upstream Sectors.

Equipment Sector	Hitachi	Fujitsu	NEC	Toshiba	Mitsubishi	Matsushita
Lithography	Hitachi			Toshiba	Nikon Machine	JOEL
Diffusion	Kokusai				JOEL	ULVAC
Ion Implant	Kokusai					ULVAC
Deposition	Kokusai		Anelva	Tokuda-Seisakusho	JOEL	ULVAC
Etch	Kokusai		Anelva; Kaijo Denki	Tokuda-Seisakusho		
Test		Takeda-Riken*	Ando-Electric		Nippon Kogaku	
Assembly	Shinkawa		Kaijo Denki	Toshiba-Seiki		

Source: U.S. Department of Commerce, A Competitive Assessment of the U.S. Semiconductor Manufacturing Equipment Industry, March 1985.
*Now Advantest.

and Japan's semiconductor-computer firms were lagging farther and farther behind.

It was at this point that officials of the Japanese government stepped in. Between 1971 and 1975, a series of coordinated, government-subsidized R&D efforts cartelized the Japanese semiconductor industry and worked with the shifting composition of consumer demand to change the nature of semiconductor production in Japan. The proportion of total semiconductor production accounted for by integrated circuits rose from 27 to 42 percent. Nevertheless, concerted government-industry efforts to develop LSI technology did not come fast enough to promote the efforts of Japanese computer firms to break into the LSI-based computer market. In mid-1975, MITI and NTT agreed to unite parts of their separate LSI research and development projects into a joint program aimed at developing the next generation of device technology, VLSI.

The VLSI project resulted in about 1,000 patents between 1976 and 1979. Between one-third and one-half of the project's funds were used to purchase advanced U.S. production equipment. Some of this equipment was clearly used for the production of semiconductor prototypes, but much was simply dismantled and analyzed by manufacturing technicians in an effort to fabricate production equipment capable of equal or superior performance. Japanese equipment makers were also able to benefit from a slowdown in the pace of new product innovation during the late 1970s, a fact that played into Japanese strengths, well honed during many years of adopting and adapting American technology, at improving and extending the life of existing equipment.

Most important, the VLSI project provided an institutional context in which semiconductor device and equipment firms could work together to organize a production system geared toward the constant introduction and refinement of new manufacturing techniques. Because it was understood that involvement in the project would provide all major firms in the industry with a common technical base, competition between semiconductor firms would have to center on improving quality or lowering costs through constant refinement of the manufacturing process. Semiconductor firms thus had a clear strategic incentive to cooperate closely with their equipment suppliers.

In the context of the VLSI project, overall development costs were shared. Equipment needs were jointly defined by device and equipment firms, with chip producers using their own prototype wafer fabrication lines as development laboratories for the equipment producers' systems integration and quality improvement efforts. Experiential knowledge built up during the equipment development process thus accrued directly to the *users* of the equipment; the development process typically proceeded under the direction of the very production engineers who would be responsible, ultimately, for implementing the new equipment into production at the chip maker's wafer fab. Not surprisingly, the familiarity of manufacturing engineers with their equipment enabled them to achieve higher yields without constant resort to state-of-the-art technology. Cooperating firms, NTT, and MITI's electrical labs also provided a large, guaranteed internal market that enabled equipment firms to generate learning out of relatively large production runs.

By 1980 the VLSI project had resulted in the development of an indigenous semiconductor technology base in Japan. Japanese semiconductor firms had decided (correctly, as it turned out) that economies of scale would be crucial to the success of the aggressive market-penetration pricing strategies they adopted to enter the world's high-volume semiconductor memory markets. Thus, despite a massive recession in 1981–82, Japanese semiconductor firms continued to invest heavily in the construction of huge, increasingly automated wafer fabrication facilities, investments enabled by the firm's close ties to patient Japanese banks. Consequently, while the U.S. market for semiconductor equipment grew only 10 percent between 1980 and 1982, the Japanese market exploded, growing a phenomenal 66 percent (see Figure 6-2). U.S. equipment firms, mostly dependent on Japanese trading firms for feedback on the Japanese market, were caught unprepared; lacking their Japanese counterparts' special financial ties, they would have been unprepared, in any event, to invest in gearing up production during such a severe recession. As delivery delays lengthened, Japanese semiconductor producers switched rapidly to their domestic equipment suppliers, and the U.S. share of Japanese equipment markets declined rapidly for every category of equipment. By the mid-1980s, Japanese firms had locked up nearly three-quarters of their domestic equipment market.

On the eve of its entry into international competition, the Japanese equipment industry exhibited several competitive strengths, all flowing from the characteristically close relationship between user and producer. First, device makers most often took the lead in pro-

Figure 6–2. Japanese Semiconductor Production Equipment Demand (*$ millions*).

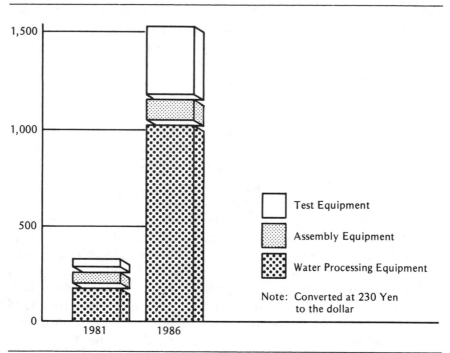

Source: *Electronic News* supplement, March 7, 1983, p. 5.

moting or introducing new equipment into the manufacturing process. So, rather than emphasizing new product development, Japanese equipment firms were focused on the interactive introduction of new equipment or, more often, the making of incremental improvements in the operation of existing equipment. Manufacturing engineers and scientists employed by the device makers worked closely and routinely with their equipment suppliers to adapt equipment to the actual production environment in which it was expected to operate, prior to marketing the product. While financial and ownership ties among semiconductor device and equipment firms provided a larger pool of investment capital than that available to independent equipment producers in the United States, government-orchestrated research programs (see Table 6-2) and the protected domestic mar-

Table 6-2. MITI-Sponsored Joint Research and Development Projects in Microelectronics.

Project	MITI VLSI	Opto Electronics	Super Computer	New Function Elements	SORTEC[b]	Optoelectronic Devices[b]	Fifth Generation Computer
Time Frame	1975–77	1979–86	1981–89	1981–90	1986–96	1986–96	1981–91
Technological Focus	VLSI manufacturing	Optical semiconductors	High-speed devices	VLSI device and process	Synchrotron lithography	Optical semiconductors	VLSI logic
Government Funding[a] ($ million)	112	80	135	140	62	42	NA
Participants	NEC Hitachi Fujitsu Toshiba Mitsubishi	NEC Hitachi Fujitsu Toshiba Mitsubishi Oki Sumitomo	NEC Hitachi Fujitsu Toshiba Mitsubishi Oki Sharp	NEC Hitachi Fujitsu Toshiba Mitsubishi Oki Sharp Sanyo Sumitomo Matsushita	NEC Hitachi Fujitsu Toshiba Mitsubishi Oki Sharp Sanyo Sumitomo Nippon Sheet Glass Matsushita Nippon Kogaku	NEC Hitachi Fujitsu Toshiba Mitsubishi Oki Sharp Sanyo Sumitomo Nippon Sheet Glass Fujikura	NEC Hitachi Fujitsu Toshiba Mitsubishi Oki Sharp

Sources: Nihon Keizai (May 6 and May 26, 1986); U.S. Embassy, Tokyo.
a. Yen:dollar conversion average for the period.
b. Funded through Japan Key Technology Center.

ket provided an insulated base within which Japanese firms could reach scale economies, improve quality, reduce costs below world levels, then enter competition with U.S. and European firms.

The Japanese industry was not without its weaknesses. Venture capital was scarce, and start-ups were difficult to establish, discouraging the entrepreneurial pursuit of new product ideas. Information about some types of innovative advances diffused less quickly than in the U.S. context; because of their very close ties to particular semiconductor producers, equipment firms were generally not in a position to benefit from exposure to technological advances made by their domestic competitors outside the context of a government-sponsored cooperative project. Domestic market options were limited for the same reason, since semiconductor producers were likely to be wary of purchasing equipment from firms affiliated with one of their competitors. Still, as the 1980s progressed, the new market and technological environment seemed to play into characteristic Japanese strengths—heavy capital investment, mass production, and marketing—while simultaneously exposing the U.S. industry's comparative weaknesses.

INTERNATIONAL COMPETITION IN SEMICONDUCTOR PRODUCTION EQUIPMENT: A COMPARISON OF STRATEGY AND STRUCTURE IN THE UNITED STATES AND JAPAN

Between 1975 and 1985, Japanese equipment suppliers captured their home market. U.S. firms supplied nearly 80 percent of that market in 1975 and barely 25 percent ten years later. The Japanese benefited most from close ties between native chip and equipment producers and from the Japanese government's capacity to orchestrate cooperative R&D projects involving all the major firms in the industry. They benefited also from some fortuitous economic and technological developments. One was the emergence of a high-volume commodity product market, in the form of dynamic random access memories; another was the shift from large-scale to very-large-scale integration. Both developments favored the typical strengths of large, integrated firms (capital investment, mass production, and marketing).

Japanese semiconductor device and equipment producers began to compete internationally in the late 1970s, just when escalating capital costs were beginning to outstrip the ability of each new generation of chip sales to pay for each new generation of production equipment. The wafer fab that cost about $100,000 in 1954 cost nearly $1 million by 1977. The Japanese responded, in part, by choosing competitive strategies aimed at maximizing market share in the commodity memory segment. Subsequent U.S. losses in world markets for standard, commodity products like dynamic random access memories (DRAMs) undermined the competitive position of the American equipment sector.

U.S. losses in commodity chip markets diminished the ability and willingness of U.S. semiconductor producers to invest in long-term cooperative R&D and began to shift the chief source of demand for leading-edge production equipment from the United States to Japan. Expenditures for semiconductor equipment in Japan pulled ahead of U.S. expenditures in 1983 (see Figure 6-3). By the beginning of 1987, Japan's demand for fabrication equipment (excluding test and assembly) stood at about 35 percent of the world total (as compared to 23 percent in 1979); equivalent demand in the United States had shrunk from 67 percent to 57 percent during the same period.

Keiretsu ties continued to provide a more patient pool of capital for Japanese equipment producers while their relatively isolated U.S. counterparts were left to scour the trade press and the tea leaves to figure out what their customers anticipated investing in next. U.S. equipment producers continued to build heavily during the 1981–82 recession so as to avoid the long delivery times that had cost them so dearly during the 1978 recovery. Unfortunately for them, U.S. chip producers were busy responding to Japanese successes in the commodity memory market by shifting to smaller batch production of more complex chips. Equipment makers that had built up large inventories soon found themselves stuck with large stocks of machines that were suddenly technologically obsolete.[5]

Ironically, it was sales to the booming Japanese equipment market that kept many U.S. equipment firms afloat during the early 1980s. While the chip boom of 1984 encouraged several new U.S. equipment start-ups and a host of ambitious expansion plans, the Japanese kept busy consolidating their home market advantage and building extensive sales and distribution networks in the United States. As the chip boom crested on real and anticipated sales of personal com-

Figure 6–3. The Growth of Equipment Sales in Japan.

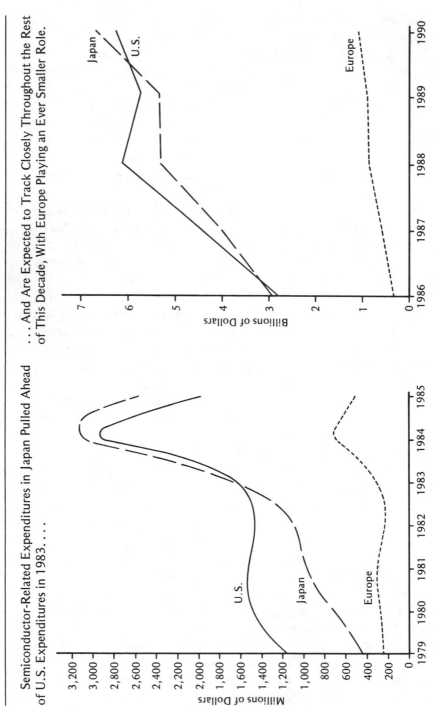

Semiconductor-Related Expenditures in Japan Pulled Ahead of U.S. Expenditures in 1983. . . .

. . . And Are Expected to Track Closely Throughout the Rest of This Decade, With Europe Playing an Ever Smaller Role.

Source: *Electronic News* supplement, March 10, 1986, p. 3.

puters, however, few American firms had close enough ties to the Japanese market to know that it would not be available to bail U.S. equipment firms out of the next slump.

The historic slump that finally came in 1985 gave better financed Japanese equipment firms the opening they needed to enter the U.S. market. Despite Japan's smaller share of the worldwide semiconductor market in 1985, the Japanese were able to spend 12 percent more for capital equipment that year than did U.S. firms. Capital spending by Japanese chip makers amounted to 31 percent of the value of production in 1985; equivalent spending by U.S. firms amounted to just 21 percent.

By 1986, when chip producers were buying equipment only for R&D and advanced prototype production, Japanese firms were in a good position to seize U.S. and European markets for leading-edge optical lithography and automatic test equipment (see Table 6–3). It is surely no accident that the first and strongest Japanese equipment companies in the U.S. market were Nikon (in wafer steppers) and Advantest (in automatic test equipment, ATE). Each competes in a market whose cutting-edge products are honed on the mass produc tion of semiconductor memories. By examining the competitive evolution of wafer steppers and ATE, we can gain a clearer understanding of the ways in which structural differences between the U.S. and Japanese equipment industries affect competitive outcomes.

Microlithographic Equipment

Microlithography is the process by which circuit designs are "printed" onto successive layers of a silicon or gallium arsenide wafer. Microlithographic equipment includes contact/proximity and scan projection aligners, and step-and-repeat aligners or "steppers." Newer lithography equipment utilizes electron beam or x-ray energy sources. E-beam equipment, especially, is used increasingly in the production of custom (application-specific) chips and any chip designs characterized by submicron line-widths. Altogether, microlithography is the largest wafer processing equipment segment, accounting for over 36 percent of sales (see Figure 6–4).

Competition in the microlithography segment has been characterized by a regular series of shifts from one technological generation

Table 6-3. Semiconductor Manufacturing Equipment Market Sizes and Competitive Positions of Vendors.

Companies	Wafer Steppers	Other Photo-lithography Products	PVD (Sput-tering)	Diffusion and LPCVD	Plasma Enhanced CVD
Anelva (J)			XXX	X	
Applied Materials				X	X
Advanced Semi Materials	X			XX	XXXX
Canon (J)	X	XXX			
Eaton		X		X	
GCA	XX				
Gemini Research					
General Signal	XX			X	
Hitachi (J)	X	X	X	X	X
KLA Instruments					
Kokusai (J)			X	XX	X
Kulicke & Soffa					
Lam Research					
Lasertech/NJS (J)					
Machine Tech			X	X	
Nikon	XXX	X			
Perkin-Elmer	XX	XXX	X		
Shinkawa (J)					
Silicon Valley Group				X	
Ulvac (J)			XX	X	
Varian			XXX	X	X
Other [b]	X	X	XX	XXX	XX
Market sizes ($ Millions)					
1984	$539	$478	$299	$366	$83
1986	308	429	261	361	73
1989	571	598	353	619	134

Key: (J)   Japanese Supplier
      X   Minor Producer
      XX   Secondary Producer
      XXX   Leading Producer
      XXXX   Dominant Producer

Table 6-3. continued

Epitaxial CVD	Ion Implantation	Etching	Resist Processing	Mask/ Wafer Inspection[a]	Assembly Equipment
		XX			
XXXX	XX	XXX			
X					XX
			X		
	XXX		X		
		X	XX		
XXX					
		X	XX		XX
	X	X	X		X
				XXXX	
X		X			
					XXX
		XX		XX	
			XX		
				XX	
		X			
					XXX
			XXX		
	X				
X	XXX	X			
X	XX	XX	XXX	X	XX
$163	$344	$554	$196	$ 94	$808
145	142	507	143	119	458
234	462	794	268	190	881

a. Includes only wafer inspection equipment that use pattern recognition technology such as the KLA 2020).

b. Competitive impact of companies not listed above.

Source: Market sizes, VLSI Research Competitive Analysis, Michael J. Stark, "Asian Semiconductor Equipment Overview" (San Francisco: Robertson, Colman & Stephens, February 5, 1987).

Figure 6-4. The Semiconductor Manufacturing Equipment Market (*Worldwide Sales, $ Millions*).

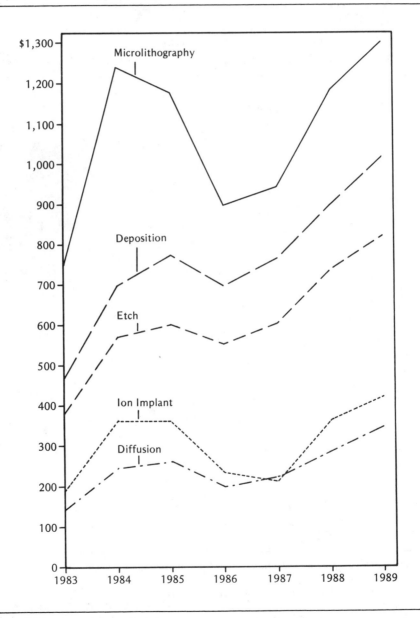

Source: *Electronic News*, January 4, 1988, p. 22.

to the next. Each shift has been associated, historically, with a shift to a new market leader. Until 1985, however, all of the leaders were U.S. firms. Kulicke and Soffa's contact aligner dominated the industry in the 1960s, followed by Perkin-Elmer's Micralign projection mask aligner, introduced in 1973, and GCA's wafer stepper, introduced in 1978. The market leader in the late 1980s was Japan's Nikon, but should Nikon be displaced within five years as its predecessors have been, it will likely be displaced by Canon (another Japanese firm), or ASM, which is partially owned by the Dutch electronics giant, Philips. A GCA comeback is possible, but unlikely. The company still suffers from its lack of strong strategic and financial ties to a multibillion dollar parent company, the same deficiency that sped the company's loss of the worldwide stepper market in the first place.

GCA accounted for 73 percent of the 240 wafer steppers installed during 1981. It was that same year that Nikon and Canon emerged from the VLSI project, specifically the MITI laboratories. They emerged with strong ties to Japanese semiconductor producers who were just then poised to beat their U.S. counterparts by seizing 70 percent of the emerging market for 64K DRAMs. Nikon and Canon benefited greatly from that seizure, which shifted the cutting-edge equipment market (and resources for continued innovation) directly to Japan. By the end of 1984, the Japanese stepper market was bigger than its U.S. counterpart; some 55 percent of the 1,088 units sold that year went to Japan, meaning that Japanese chip producers bought more steppers that year than the rest of the world combined. In addition, Nikon and Canon benefited from their ability to coordinate their initial entry into international competition; the Japanese giants did not compete at first, Nikon concentrating on steppers while Canon concentrated on the still-lucrative market for projection aligners.

GCA did not have strong strategic or financial ties to any of its big customers, in the United States or Japan. Caught short by the equipment demand surge in early 1981, GCA gave delivery priority to its U.S. customers, enabling Nikon to snatch away its big Japanese NEC and Toshiba accounts. Characteristically, GCA responded by forming a joint venture with Sumitomo to provide technical and marketing support for its stepper in Japan; the company was apparently unaware, or unconcerned, about Sumitomo's *keiretsu* ties to NEC.

Meanwhile, Nikon equipment builders were busy honing their production skills in NEC semiconductor plants.

GCA fought back from the serious recession of 1981–82 due in large part to the existence of its large installed base in the United States; most U.S. equipment operators had been trained on GCA steppers and were not flexibly skilled enough then to experiment on a large scale with competing products. While Nikon was thus quietly laying the groundwork for U.S. stepper sales by first establishing a strong American support and service network, GCA managers set out to diversify. With no clear signals from its customers as to what the near-term demand for equipment would actually be, GCA launched, then abandoned, several new equipment projects—a deposition system, an ion implanter, a dry-etch system, an electron-beam project. The company even attempted to compete at the low end of the stepper market with Ultratech, a unit of General Signal, though by 1985, most low-end applications in 2- or 3-micron chip production had shifted to Japan.

The diversification attempts diverted GCA's attention from its primary stepper business, and the lack of close ties to customers meant that GCA could not anticipate the severity of the slump that was to materialize in 1985. GCA geared up to sell between 500 and 600 steppers that year (at $1 million a piece) and ended up selling barely 100; the company lost $94 million. Overproduction combined with the lack of long-term financial support from customers to stall the development of the company's newest product, the high-end Model 8000; despite GCA's cancellation of its low-end Model 5000, the financial drain was already too great. Major suppliers began to cancel deliveries, including Zeiss, GCA's lens maker; Nikon makes its own lenses and would never face a similar problem. Nikon sold 145 steppers in 1985 compared to GCA's 115, and GCA was left to contemplate a partial sale to Sumitomo (read NEC) to stave off bankruptcy. The company was finally bought by General Signal in early 1988, where it will share the stepper business with its erstwhile competitor, Ultratech.

Automatic Test Equipment.   The story of U.S. losses in the ATE segment is rather similar to the story of GCA's loss to Nikon and Canon in the market for wafer steppers. Fairchild's test equipment division (now Sentry) dominated the Japanese and U.S. tester market through the 1970s, but its lead was already slipping when

France's Schlumberger purchased the company in 1979. Fairchild's unique position among American firms as an integrated chip and equipment producer did not mask its lack of close ties to customers in Japan, where tester producers Advantest and Ando were both owned, in part, by giant integrated chip and systems producers. Fujitsu owns 21 percent of Advantest (formerly Takeda Riken), and Ando Electric is 51 percent owned by NEC.[6]

Fairchild's hold began to slip as soon as Advantest emerged from the VLSI project (the NTT labs) in 1979 with the most sophisticated memory device tester on the market. The 100 MHz tester was ahead of its time, but it helped to establish the company's technological reputation. Moreover, Advantest (and Ando) were both benefiting from their ties to Fujitsu and NEC. Japan's share of the worldwide market for memory testers grew with its share of the worldwide market for memory devices; its tester share jumped from about 30 percent in 1978 to approximately 45 percent in 1985. Hitachi, by then the world's leading DRAM producer, became a major Advantest customer, though by 1985 it was preparing to market a memory tester of its own. Like Nikon and Canon in the lithographic equipment market, Advantest and Ando benefited also from their capacity to coordinate market entry. Advantest initially targeted high-end memory testers while Ando pursued a broad-based position in logic, memory, and eventually, VLSI logic testers. By 1986 Advantest and Ando had locked up about 80 percent of the Japanese market, with Advantest alone accounting for over 50 percent.

Relationships between U.S. tester makers and their domestic chip producing customers, meanwhile, continued to be short term and arm's length. Tester makers were slow to develop higher capacity equipment without financial commitments from chip firms; chip producers were typically loathe to share proprietary chip prototypes with tester makers who needed the prototypes in order to design the next generation of testers. Chip producers most often responded to the resulting delays in tester development by developing test equipment of their own in-house, further undermining the capacity of independent tester makers to engage in long-term R&D.

In the early 1980s Fairchild/Sentry's financial problems contributed to further delays of its own VLSI tester, providing an opening for venture-capital-backed start-ups like Megatest and Semiconductor Test Solutions, and other American firms, like GenRad, Teradyne, LTX/Trillium, and Textronix to target pieces of Fairchild's disintegrating market. But the Japanese ATE makers were in the strongest position to capture market share, operating as they did from their secure domestic base. Targeting former Fairchild customers, Advantest doubled its U.S. sales between 1984 and 1985; by the beginning of 1987, exports accounted for about 40 percent of Advantest's total sales. Meanwhile, Ando pursued a strategy of following its parent NEC to production sites overseas. Of the U.S. firms, Teradyne is in the strongest position, and it is the *only* U.S. firm attempting to compete in the market for next-generation megabit memory testers. But even Teradyne, an independent, relatively undiversified $400 million company, has its hands full competing with Japanese tester producers owned in part or in whole by the very companies most likely to dominate the world's markets for megabit memory chips.

Other Processing Equipment.   U.S. firms still dominate markets for other processing equipment, but that lead is precarious (see Table 6–4). The deposition equipment segment accounts for about 27 percent of overall sales and includes chemical vapor and physical sputtering deposition equipment and epitaxial growth equipment, all of which are becoming more important with the transition to VLSI and ULSI (ultra large scale integration) multilayer integrated circuits. Deposition equipment is used to deposit or develop materials with different electronic properties onto the surface of the semiconductor wafer. Diffusion furnaces and ion implantation equipment are used to impart additional electronic properties through the addition of selected impurities; together equipment sales in these categories account for an additional 16 percent of total sales. Etch and stip equipment is used to develop the circuit designs projected onto the wafer surface during microlithography and accounts for 21 percent of wafer processing equipment sales.

The U.S. lead in these segments is precarious because the structural characteristics that have advantaged Japanese firms in higher volume equipment segments are beginning to advantage them in these segments as well. In segment after segment, government-assisted R&D, *keiretsu* ties, and joint ventures with cash-starved U.S. equipment firms enable Japanese firms to catch up technologically, diminish access ro the growing Japanese market, then compete directly with American firms in Europe and in the United States. As a result of these efforts, and the lack of anything comparable so far in the

Table 6-4. Status and Trends of U.S. Semiconductor Technology Relative to Japan.

	U.S. Lag			Parity With Japan	U.S. Lead		
	Substantial	Clear	Slight		Slight	Clear	Substantial
Silicon Products							
DRAMs		<	•				
SRAMs		<	•				
EPROMs				<	•		
Microprocessors					<•		
Custom, Semicustom Logic				•	<	•	
Bipolar		<					
Nonsilicon Products							
Memory			<		•		
Logic			<				•
Linear					•<		
Optoelectronics	<		•				
Heterostructures		<	•				
Materials							
Silicon			<	•			
Gallium Arsenide		<			•		
Processing Equipment							
Lithography							
Optical				<			
E-Beam					<	•	
X-Ray				<	•		
Ion Implantation Technology					<•		
Chemical Vapor Deposition				•<			
Deposition, Diffusion, Other				<	•		
Energy-Assisted Processing*			<				
Assembly				•<			
Packaging		<•					
Test				<	•		
CAD				<		•	
CAM			<		•		

Key: *N/A in 1979-80; • U.S. Position 1979-80 (IQ); < U.S. Position 1986-87 (IQ).
Source: U.S. Government InterAgency Working Group on Semiconductor Technology.

United States, Japanese vendors are poised to become major suppliers of deposition and etch equipment in the 1990s.

Despite American leadership in technology and in the world market, Japanese semiconductor makers typically foster their own equipment suppliers, which are then able to lock up their home market. NEC's Anelva held on to between 60 and 70 percent of Japan's dry etch market in 1981; its market share slipped a bit by 1984, but the slack was taken up by another Japanese supplier, Hitachi. Yet the Japanese subsidiary of America's Applied Materials, the world market and technological leader in dry-etch systems, held onto only 22 percent of the Japanese market in 1984, just as its Japanese competitors were busy readying their initial assault on the U.S. market.

In ion implantation equipment, where the Nova Systems subsidiary of America's Eaton Corporation holds a clear market and technological lead, substantial Japanese market share has been captured by Ulvac, a Matsushita affiliate that developed its own ion implanters in cooperation with NTT Labs during the VLSI project. Nova's high-current systems still lead the market even in Japan, but they are sold there by Sumitomo.

Varian continues to be the leading producer of sputtering equipment worldwide, but faces increasingly stiff competition from Anelva, the NEC affiliate that actually began life as a joint venture between NEC and Varian. Varian is currently involved in a joint R&D project sponsored by the NTT Labs in Japan, where its equipment will be sold by Tokyo Electron Ltd. These joint ventures are attractive in the short run to cash-starved U.S. equipment suppliers: they provide financial support and some guarantee of a small foothold in the Japanese market. But they also transfer technology to Japanese *users* of the equipment, who can easily turn around and share the know-how with their own affiliated equipment suppliers.

Clearly, the most successful foreign firms in the Japanese market have been those that have been able to open wholly owned Japanese subsidiaries. These include Teradyne, the tester maker discussed earlier, ASM, the Philips subsidiary and world market leader for plasma-enhanced chemical vapor deposition reactors, and Applied Materials, the world leader in dry-etch and epitaxy equipment and a competitor in the deposition and ion implantation markets. The Japanese government, seeking access to technological leadership wherever it exists, loaned Applied Materials $3.4 million in 1985. (The British government, incidentally, helped Applied Materials raise nearly $6 million for the development of its ion implanter in Britain, in return for the use of British R&D personnel.)

Emerging Technologies

As ominous as these trends are for U.S. firms, worse may be in store judging from comparisons of ongoing U.S. and Japanese efforts to commercialize important new process technologies. Japan is already considered to be leading in the development of microwave plasma processing, laser-assisted processing, compound semiconductor processing, and 3-D device structures. Japanese firms are concentrating especially on the development of more efficient focused ion beam systems and high-throughput electron beam systems and are making a substantial commitment to x-ray lithography.[7]

Initially, opportunities in the electron beam market called forth a typically contentious group of a half dozen American suppliers, undercapitalized and overcommitted. In Japan, three larger firms came forward—Hitachi, Toshiba, and JEOL (an affiliate of Matsushita); after first acquiring E-beam technology from American suppliers, these firms created protected internal markets in which to learn about and further develop the technology, then came out with proprietary systems of their own. Today JEOL dominates the market for E-beam equipment; only one U.S. firm, Perkin Elmer, now even markets an E-beam system. Perkin Elmer's system, unlike JEOL's, is for mask and reticle making, not direct writing of circuit patterns. The company benefited from its participation in the Pentagon's very-high-speed integrated circuit (VHSIC) program, which paid for 40 percent of the system's development costs, but suffered as performance problems with the company's AEBLE 150 were traced, in part, to contamination in the defense plant where the equipment was first tried out. At least, Perkin Elmer remains in the market; the other five U.S. entrants had abandoned the E-beam market by mid-1985, writing off losses in excess of $100 million.

In the area of x-ray lithography, still thought to be a decade away from large-scale commercialization, U.S. firms appear to have lost the initiative to Japan, and to Siemens and Philips, working together in West Germany. German firms have already announced the commercial availability of both superconducting x-ray synchrotrons and x-ray steppers; a consortium including Siemens, Philips, Telefunken, and Eurosil is conducting development work on an even more powerful x-ray source. Similarly, MITI and MPT are cosponsoring a consortium of thirteen Japanese electronics firms aimed at developing an x-ray system based on an advanced synchrotron source. NTT also has its own ongoing synchrotron project, involving Hitachi, Toshiba, and Mitsubishi.

In the United States, such a project is not yet underway, although the Departments of Energy and Defense have been competing for congressional approval to create one. IBM is the only American firm experimenting with a synchrotron source (thought to be capable of superior resolution down to the less than 0.1 micron range as compared to the conventional x-ray source used by Perkin Elmer and the plasma source used by Hampshire Systems). By some estimates, Japan and the Europeans have a two- or three-year lead over the United States in advanced synchrotron radiation development, due mainly to government-sponsored efforts. By contrast, the synchrotron at the University of Wisconsin at Madison was not even made available to industry researchers until late in 1985 and had to contend with some serious bureaucratic bickering before being guaranteed continuing financial support by the National Science Foundation in May 1986.

CREATING ADVANTAGE: POLICIES AND PROSPECTS

The U.S. semiconductor industry has so far advanced two major political responses to the competitive dilemma it faces in the late 1980s. The first has been to lobby for trade legislation to ensure greater access to the Japanese market; the second has been to promote the idea of a billion-dollar, government-assisted R&D and chip manufacturing consortium (Sematech). True to form, the American chip industry was slow to consult its equipment suppliers in the process of drafting these responses. Since the U.S. government calculates fair market value on the basis of costs incurred by Japanese firms when producing chips for export to the United States, U.S. equipment producers have contended that the semiconductor trade agreement reached in 1986 creates an incentive for Japanese firms to stretch the usable life of older equipment to produce chips in older plants, thus further reducing the size of the potential equipment market. In addition, to the extent that Japanese chip makers respond to the pact by building chip manufacturing facilities in the United States, the pact may simply create new U.S. business for Japanese equipment suppliers, who often follow their chip-making patrons across the Pacific to their new U.S. production sites.

As for Sematech, planning for the consortium has already proved to be a useful vehicle for building cooperative relationships between semiconductor firms faced with a formidable competitive challenge that none of them can meet alone. But Sematech will not be sufficient to solve the industry's competitive problem either if it is viewed merely as a technical fix. Despite Japan's growing technological prowess, its primary advantage has always derived from the interactive process of equipment development and the efficiency with which the equipment was used and incrementally improved. Indeed, Japanese chip makers typically endure only half as much downtime as U.S. semiconductor firms on the same U.S. made machines. The evidence so far indicates that Sematech has not yet taken this lesson to heart; equipment producers were integrated into the consortium only as an afterthought.

Priority for participation in Sematech will be given to equipment vendors who already work with IBM and AT&T, due to the provision of chips by the two electronics giants as development vehicles for the consortium's Austin facility. Because participation by non–U.S. firms such as Nikon and ASM is prohibited, Sematech's orders for lithography equipment are virtually certain to be placed with GCA.[8] Chemical vapor deposition equipment is expected to be supplied by Tegal and Applied Materials, which will also provide etchers, along with Plasma-Therm. Ion implanters are likely to come from Eaton's Nova Systems, while diffusion furnaces will be purchased from Bruce and Thermco. Teradyne is most likely to provide automatic test equipment while Kulicke and Soffa will provide automatic wire bonders and dicing saws for assembly.

Equipment used during Sematech's first phase will be provided off the shelf, with equipment suppliers building customized equipment for phase 2. Custom equipment will be funded in part by Sematech and in part by the equipment vendors themselves, but Sematech participants will have a right of first refusal on any production equipment developed specifically for Sematech. Nevertheless, vendors will be restricted for an as-yet-unspecified period of time from offering equipment modified for use in Sematech for sale to other chip-makers.

The role of the Defense Advanced Research Projects Agency (DARPA) as the primary vehicle for government support of the manufacturing consortium suggests the importance, also, of assessing the potential pitfalls of military support for commercial technological development. The requirements of civilian and military users increasingly diverge; in fact, in the late 1970s, VHSIC grew out of the Pentagon's frustration with commercial chip producers who were refusing to provide the custom devices desired by the military. That divergence continues ten years later. Concerned about the time it might take to adapt military devices for further civilian development, Sematech officials bypassed VHSIC-generated devices and chose the commercially developed IBM 4-MB DRAM and AT&T 64-K static random access memory (SRAM) as development vehicles for the consortium. They did this even though the commercial devices have feature sizes larger (0.7 micron) than the VHSIC devices Sematech could have used in working down to the submicron level.

Military procurement and R&D funding are not likely to play the same role in the 1980s and 1990s as they played in the late 1950s, when purchases by NASA and the Pentagon clearly promoted the commercialization of integrated circuits. Negotiations between Sematech and DARPA have already encountered difficulties over DARPA's desire to push forward to x-ray lithography (which would compete for public funds with a megaproject being promoted by the U.S. Department of Energy) and to fund Sematech activities on a project-by-project basis. Moreover, because Defense Department involvement in Sematech has been justified on the basis of national security concerns over the potential loss of an indigenous microelectronics industry, doubts have been raised about the Pentagon's capacity to resist classifying or restricting access to Sematech-developed production equipment created under military auspices. Experience suggests, in any event, that the Pentagon should simply fund Sematech with no strings attached, except for a guarantee that the Pentagon can farm Sematech-developed equipment out to its own network of defense contractors, where it can be retrofitted to serve the Pentagon's purposes.[9]

The challenge then is for American semiconductor equipment and device producers to evolve some of the mechanisms that enable the Japanese industry to coordinate and gain access to learning and investment funds without losing the particular advantage that the fragmented U.S. industry has provided in terms of spurring constant product innovation and rapid technological diffusion. Something like Sematech is a necessary ingredient, along with closer ties to Korean and European customers and improved access to the Japanese market, but the most important item on the agenda is the development of closer technological and strategic ties between U.S. semiconductor firms and their domestic equipment suppliers. To this end, electronics producers in the United States should take a closer look at the network of semimarket, semiownership ties that characterize the relationships of their Japanese counterparts. Quasi-integration of this type seems to avoid the rigidities of classic vertical integration by forcing equipment firms to compete against outside vendors for a substantial share of the parent firm's business; on the other hand, it also enables small, undercapitalized firms to avoid the financial and strategic uncertainties of a pure market relationship. Both types of uncertainty must be avoided if the synergistic processes of manufacturing and product innovation are to go forward, and if domestic firms, and the domestic economy, are to capture the economic benefits of the knowledge they create.

NOTES

1. Sections of this chapter are based on BRIE Working Paper 27 "The Weakest Link: Semiconductor Production Equipment, Linkages, and the Limits to International Trade" (August 1987) by Jay S. Stowsky. Funds for the research on which this work is based were provided by the U.S. Office of Technology Assessment, Berkeley Roundtable on the International Economy, and the Carnegie Corporation of New York.
2. This is not to say, of course, that cost is irrelevant.
3. On this and related points, see the work of Richard Florida and Martin Kenney, particularly "Venture Capital-Financed Innovation and Technological Change in the U.S.," Working Paper 87-28, Carnegie Mellon School of Urban and Public Affairs, October 1987; "Venture Capital and High Technology Entrepreneurship: Technology, Financial-Oriented, and Hybrid Complexes," Working Paper 87-27, Carnegie Mellon School of Urban and Public Affairs, October 1987; and "Social Institutions and Economic Restructuring: Response and Adaptation to Technological Change in the U.S. and Japan," Working Paper 87-31, Carnegie Mellon School of Urban and Public Affairs, November 1987.
4. In addition, short product life cycles in both the device and equipment sectors mean that it is normally unwise, in any event, for equipment producers to build up substantial inventories. With technical progress so dramatic, the

useful life of most capital equipment is typically projected to last five years or less.

5. A distinction needs to be drawn between new generations of existing types of equipment (projection aligners, wafer steppers) and movement toward the use of new types of equipment (E-beam, x-ray) for lithography. Both classes of equipment are significantly more expensive to build than the machines they are replacing, and the more general move toward the production of smaller-batch ASICs raises *per-chip costs* for all capital equipment. For the most part, producers of all sorts of chips (commodity, semicustom, custom) are moving to new generations of lithography equipment in order to achieve clarity at narrower line-widths. As of 1988, most chip producers use a mix-and-match method, employing projection aligners for line-widths of above about 2.5 microns and wafer steppers between 1 and 2.5 microns. Use of new equipment—E-beam equipment for mask-making and/or direct writing—at the submicron level is increasing, though not yet typical. X-ray equipment for even smaller line-widths is experimental at this point.

6. It is interesting to note that, although Fairchild was both an equipment maker and a chip maker for a time, this apparent "integration" did not serve as the kind of close link we postulate to be so responsible for Japanese success. The point to remember is this: the capacity to take strategic (i.e., technical and financial) advantage of ownership ties between a chip maker and equipment maker is only a *potential* capacity; it will remain merely "potential" unless and until the firm's managers do something to actively exploit the advantage implicit in those links.

7. Influential technological assessments include the "Report of the Defense Science Board Task Force on Defense Semiconductor Dependency," Office of the Undersecretary of Defense for Acquisition, Washington, D.C., February 1987; National Materials Advisory Board to the National Science Foundation, *Advanced Processing of Electronic Materials in the U.S. and Japan* (Washington, D.C.: National Academy Press, 1986); and "JTECH: Panel Report on Opto- and Microelectronics," Science Applications International Corporation, La Jolla, Calif., May 1985.

8. The dire straits in which GCA and the entire lithography segment of the U.S. industry currently find themselves can be most dramatically illustrated, perhaps, by the fact that Sematech will be forced to use Nikon steppers (supplied by IBM) during its first phase. "Two Nikon Steppers Set for Sematech," *Electronic News*, September 26, 1981, p. 1.

9. For a more extended analysis of the Pentagon's R&D programs and their impact on the competitiveness of participating firms, see Jay S. Stowsky, "Beating Our Plowshares into Double-edged Swords: The Impact of Pentagon Policies on the Commercialization of Advanced Technologies," Working Paper 17, Berkeley Roundtable on the International Economy, University of California, Berkeley, April 1986.

7 DEFENSE PRODUCTION AND INDUSTRIAL DEVELOPMENT
The Case of Japanese Aircraft[1]

Richard J. Samuels
Benjamin C. Whipple

Japanese industry and government have targeted aerospace as one of three key technologies for the twenty-first century. In its famous 1970 Vision, the Ministry of International Trade and Industry (MITI) elevated aerospace as the equal of nuclear power and the information industry, a status reaffirmed in 1980. Coveted for its technological linkages with a wide range of high-value-added industries and its potential to lift prominent firms out of declining sectors, aerospace enjoys considerable public support. By the early 1980s, formal government subsidies for commercial jet engine development were nearly equal to those for computer research and greater than those for telecommunications, energy, and "next-generation base technologies."[2] By the late 1980s, MITI had supported a decade of commercial collaboration with leading Western aerospace firms. Some scholars and the press have suggested that this support, like that for steel, machinery, and electronics before it, will transform commercial aerospace into the next Japanese export success. Others are more pessimistic.[3]

But this debate misses a critical point, for the aerospace industry is unlike any other in one very important respect: it has been created and sustained by the military and its derivative air and space programs, not by commercial markets for civilian products. Commercial aviation is a large and expanding business, but it has played a minor role in the development of the manufacturing enterprise that enables it. Accordingly, an analytic focus restricted to commercial aviation overlooks essential characteristics of the aerospace industrial development process. In Japan as elsewhere, military production will predominate for the foreseeable future.

The military side of Japan's aerospace sector merits attention for another reason. The global transformation of the industry's primary activities—from bending metal to integrating advanced materials, microelectronics, computers, telecommunications, and high technology in general—has converged with growing Japanese strength in these fields, and with long-developed strengths in small-lot precision manufacturing and quality control. Domestic and overseas military markets now present major opportunities for Japanese firms to profit from the extended application of technologies originally developed for commercial purposes. Such opportunities for dual use are especially prevalent in electronics but exist for a broad spectrum of manufacturing industries. The Japanese call this technology transfer "spin-on," emphasizing the difference from the experience elsewhere, in which technology has historically "spun *off*" from military to civilian applications. Commercial technology is now vital to all Western military aerospace industries. The U.S. Department of Defense and MITI both have expressed intense interest in the technology base of the Japanese commercial electronics and materials industries.

Japan's military aerospace industry arms the nation, serves as the bellwether for commercial aerospace, and provides an important new market for the application of civilian high technology. For these reasons, among others to be explored below, Japan's military aerospace sector is growing in size and importance. As it grows, Japan must juggle the conflicting imperatives of commercial opportunity, international relations, and the legacy of demilitarization. This chapter explores the evolving linkages between military production, industrial development, and Japanese strategies in aerospace.

THE BACKGROUND

Aerospace emerged from a World War II alliance among the military, the scientific community, and the aviation, electronics, and instrumentation industries. Airliners and space programs have attracted more attention in the intervening decades, but military production remains the core activity. Commercial production is secondary and rests firmly on a military-industrial infrastructure. American aerospace, by far the world's largest, most diversified and commercialized national industry, typically sells over 60 percent of output to the Department of Defense and a significant fraction of the remainder to other government agencies and foreign military establishments. The Japan Defense Agency (JDA) procures over 80 percent of Japanese output, in a market where the largest domestic producer of jet engines has never sold one for commercial use. Military production dominates the European aircraft industry despite the Airbus project. Over the last twenty years, military aircraft production has overwhelmed civilian production worldwide by a margin greater than two to one. Only five of twenty-two aircraft manufacturers have survived in postwar commercial markets, and only one does more business with the airlines than with the armed forces. Both foreign experience and Japan's own industrial development suggest that Japan cannot afford to nurture commercial aerospace apart from military production.[4]

It could have been otherwise had Japan's planners succeeded, for they have tried repeatedly to participate in the postwar commercial aircraft business. The first major effort attempted to establish an independent presence via design and production of the YS-11, Japan's first and thus far only indigenous commercial aircraft. Government and industry initiated the YS-11 project in 1957 with the creation of the Nippon Aircraft Manufacturing Company, a "national policy company" (*kokusaku gaisha*).[5] This project engaged all of Japan's heavy industrial and related components manufacturers in a consortium in which the state assumed 50 percent of the equity and guaranteed full subsidization of development costs. By most accounts this formula also guaranteed that there was little incentive for market analysis or cost reduction. While acclaimed as a technological success, fewer than 200 planes were sold, two-thirds to domestic airlines, which would have bought more had it not been for severe production delays. The program ultimately suffered losses four times its capitalization and when it wound down in the early 1970s, the planners retreated from their independent approach to consider less ambitious strategies for commercial aviation.

By 1980 government and industry had swapped indigenous development for international collaboration and allied themselves strategically with the Boeing Commercial Airplane Company and with the International Aero Engines (IAE) consortium led by Rolls-Royce and Pratt and Whitney.[6] But despite a successful and historically unprecedented junior partnership in the development and production of Boeing's 767, the collaborative strategy is succeeding slowly, at best. Even measured in devalued dollars, the Japanese commercial aircraft business remains about one-fortieth the size of its U.S. counterpart, and accounts for merely 0.04 percent of Japanese manufacturing value. Indeed, after a decade of subsidized cooperation, the total value of Japanese commercial aircraft production remains less than 2 percent of the sales of Toyota Motors. Nor has international cooperation been profitable. Slow sales of the 767 have forced Japanese firms to produce at one-third the planned rate and spread tooling costs over far fewer units than anticipated. The high yen and dollar-denominated contracts have forced them to supply parts at a loss for Boeing's 747 as well as for the 767.[7] To make matters worse, the crown jewel of collaboration was snatched away in late 1987 when Boeing dramatically cut back the successor to the 767, the 7J7 co-development project. The 7J7 (the letter "J" standing for Japan) was the largest and most promising component of the collaborative strategy; its effective cancellation after years of planning has reopened debate over appropriate strategies for the Japanese commercial airframe business.

Similarly, problems at the IAE consortium do not bode well for Japanese engine manufacturers. The consortium's slow-selling V2500 engine repeatedly failed development tests and resumed progress toward government certification only after the temporary substitution of old technology in a key subsystem from Rolls-Royce. IAE will need to recertify the V2500 when the production model is ready and will deliver engines late and below specification. In 1987 IAE angered an important airline customer and lost credibility throughout the industry when it announced the Superfan V2500 derivative, committed to an ambitous development schedule, and then cancelled the project within four months, stating that the Superfan had never been a definite product. The airline eventually cancelled its V2500 orders altogether, and another followed suit. IAE is resolving the technical problems slowly, but costly delays, combined with tough competition and the organizational awkwardness of a five-nation consortium with two leaders, have made future profits improbable and the future of IAE itself problematic. At best, the V2500 will be runner-up in a market segment led by the General Electric and Snecma consortium and is unlikely to recover development costs. At worst, the leaders will tire of IAE's problems and pursue alternate strategies to maintain their status as full-line producers, a real if apparently diminishing possibility. In any case, the Japanese participants long ago delivered their relatively low technology subsystems, and with major events beyond their control, are learning what they can about international sales and support.[8] They are also learning about the vulnerabilities associated with junior partnerships in international consortia.

Between the troubles at IAE and the demise of the 7J7, the collaborative strategy once intended to drive commercial aerospace into the next century is beginning to appear little more satisfactory than the autonomous approach of the YS-11 era. Once again, and despite persistence and flexibility, Japanese policymakers and industrialists have proved unable to replicate in commercial aviation their success in other industries. Is this failure inevitable, overdetermined by a long list of adverse market conditions that Japan cannot surmount and that MITI's policies often exacerbate? Such conditions discussed in the literature include a small and possibly misshapen home market, lack of domestic competition, the strong position of Western technology suppliers, overdependence on low-growth military coproduction, a ban on weapons exports, lack of experience with design, systems integration, and international sales and support, and other factors.[9] The pernicious effects of many of these problems can be seen in the preceding examples.

It is true that Japan's aerospace industry faces fundamental problems. But these problems and their solutions are less determined by market forces per se than by political forces flowing from Japanese attitudes about how and how much to best provide for national security. Traditional reluctance to invest in the defense industry and a ban on military exports surely have stunted the development of Japanese aerospace. Most analyses acknowledge this and stop there, suggesting that these political limitations place a "natural cap" on the industry; Mowery and Rosenberg, for example, argue that "any growth in the aircraft market must perforce come from an expansion of the commercial aircraft market."[10] To the contrary, the Japanese perceive the benefits of this business to be so compelling, and their perceptions are converging so rapidly with other strategic and technological developments, that a significant recalculation of Japanese defense industrial policy is not only far more probable than permanent weakness in aerospace, but indeed, is already underway.

A NEW STRATEGY FOR JAPANESE AEROSPACE

The weakness of Japanese aerospace is best understood as the obverse of the general economic benefits conferred by postwar demilitarization. By the end of the Pacific War, the military had come to play a major role in Japan's heavy industrial development, consuming a large fraction of domestic output and presiding over a large and technically advanced aircraft sector.[11] Under Occupation orders, the military and its budget vanished and the aircraft industry disappeared for seven crucial years while the West entered the jet age. Despite nominal rearmament starting in 1954, the military has played a trivial role in the postwar Japanese economy. Demilitarization, imposed by the Occupation and later enabled by U.S. security guarantees, became the centerpiece of postwar security policy. A popular antimilitarist political consensus, enshrined in the ambiguous Article Nine of Japan's Constitution, combined with exceptional opportunities in world markets for commercial goods, made possible a temporary limit on spending for "self-defense" forces of 1 percent of gross national product (1976–87). Military procurement has been carefully supervised by MITI, and the military industry is formally forbidden to export.[12] These restrictions undoubtedly contributed to commercial competitiveness overall but undermined Japan's efforts to compete in aerospace. This trade-off was quite a happy one for most of the postwar period; the formal budget limit in effect between 1976 and 1987 had been a reality since the mid-1960s, and the export ban went unchallenged while heavy industry prospered in commercial markets.

In the 1980s, however, a realignment of political and economic forces has brought a recalculation of defense policy, which in turn has stimulated a fundamental change in Japan's overall approach to aerospace industrial development and in the scale and scope of the industry itself. The defense budget and the fraction spent on aerospace have grown steadily over the past decade, a period of austerity for other government agencies. The ban on weapons transfers, always open to interpretation, is eroding as an obstacle to the export of dual-use aircraft and aerospace technology. Military aerospace, including expanded production at the major electronics firms, is fast becoming the primary beneficiary of an evolving Japanese national security regime. In turn, this regime benefits from a gold mine of domestic high technology, originally developed for civilian purposes but now available to supplement and gradually supplant the imported results of U.S. military research and development.

Aerospace industry sales measured in yen have more than doubled and have become increasingly important to the diversified companies that participate and increasingly attractive to those that do not. At industry leader Mitsubishi Heavy Industries (MHI), aerospace sales grew by 50 percent between 1983 and 1985 alone, catapulting the business from last to second among seven divisions.[13] Aerospace and defense production have undergone similarly vertiginous growth at Ishikawajima-Harima Heavy Industries (IHI) and Kawasaki Heavy Industries (KHI). Technological competence, managerial experience, and facilities for research, development, and manufacturing have all improved substantially. A minor portion of the growth in sales and capability has been funded by commercial projects and somewhat more by the ambitious Japanese space program, but the lion's share has come from a defense buildup that has already spanned several administrations and that will continue at least into the 1990s. The 1 percent of GNP limit ended with the fiscal 1988 budget, but its demise was preordained by programs begun in the late 1970s and its importance had diminished regardless. Japan's emergence as an economic giant means that 1 percent of GNP now supports a defense budget comparable to that of West Germany or France, each spending three times as much when expressed as a percentage of GNP. Japan now ranks second in military spending among nonnuclear powers.

The shift toward aerospace industrial development via increased defense production is best seen as part of a larger, nascent Japanese industrial policy and national security strategy stimulated in large part by a perceived decline in U.S. hegemony and the realignment of power in the international political economy. Necessary preconditions were established in the 1970s, when expensive oil, slow growth, and increased competition from newly industrializing countries (NICs) sparked widespread agreement within the industrial and economic policy bureaucracies and the private sector that a strong presence in high-technology industries was essential to Japan's future economic success. Government and industry launched major efforts in computers, materials science, semiconductors, mechatronics (robotics and electronics), and other high-value-added fields, many of which would later contribute to "spin-on" competitiveness in aerospace even when more direct strategies proved disappointing. At the same time, the U.S. retreat from Southeast Asia, the growth of Soviet power throughout the region, Japan's emerging economic strength, and, most of all, U.S. exhortations to "burden-share," converged to create compelling reasons for a Japanese military buildup. Economic pressure from the NICs, political pressure from the United States, and, at least until the 1988 Gorbachev initiative, military pressure from the Soviet Union, have only intensified in the years since.

Whatever the extent of external pressures, legitimate defense needs, or available technology, considerable antipathy toward the military remains firmly embedded in Japanese society. The pacifist legacy of the Pacific War has led to a curious situation for defense planners. Former Prime Minister Nakasone's previous service as director-general of the Defense Agency notwithstanding, there is no evidence that the military have regained either sufficient political influence to bring about such a change in policy, or sufficient political respectability to be given a larger share of scarce public funds, financed with deficits, to spend as they see fit. Although the situation has begun to change as career officials assume key Japanese Defense Agency posts, many are still held by officials seconded from other ministries, especially MITI.[14] In a sense, though, this change is irrelevant, for one of the most interesting and unusual aspects of the buildup is that it could not have been started or sustained without MITI's firm support.

MITI officials have always been aware of the link between military and commercial aerospace, and the depth of their previous commitment to an exclusively civilian strategy can be overstated; as the name of its Aircraft and Ordnance Bureau implies, MITI oversees the military production that dominates the industry. As a result of such long-standing involvement and the bleak near-term outlook for commercial projects in the late 1970s, MITI endorsed stepped up military production as a more timely, controllable and realistic means of aerospace industrial development, as well as a fruitful way to help the electronics industry move from consumer to capital goods.[15] MITI officials have steadily supported the defense buildup and worked closely with the JDA and the private firms to ensure that the defense budget is advancing strategic industrial goals as well as strategic military ones. It is likely, moreover, that the latest disarray in commercial strategy stemming from the demise of the 7J7 and the problems at IAE will renew the relative importance of military efforts in MITI's policy portfolio.

MITI's involvement in the growth of the military aerospace industry has created a novel situation, for it has been standard historical practice for nations to foster civilian industrial development in pursuit of military advantage, not the other way around. It is not the case that the defense buildup is somehow a Trojan horse for commercial strategy, although it is clear that some civilian leaders support it for this reason. Nor have Japanese planners replaced their goal of building a competitive commercial aerospace industry with that of creating a military industrial complex; plans are already being made for a new Japanese-led transport consortium to fill the void left by the 7J7, a next-generation transport engine is under development, and commercial aspirations remain very much alive.[16] Finally, Japanese planners do not seem to be expecting military R&D to spin-off commercial technology to the extent that it did in the United States thirty years ago; they are convinced that far more technology will be spun on than off.[17] With increased defense procurement, and ultimately with overseas sales, however, Japan is likely to fund the military-industrial infrastructure that has been an historical precondition for success in commercial aerospace, an infrastructure that today is built upon dual-use technologies, already a Japanese strength. For the first time, Japan is preparing to spin-off and spin-on technology and products simultaneously.

This first was suggested openly in an influential report to the vice-minister for International Trade and Industry in mid-1988. After establishing that Japan is a peaceful country that will continue to adhere strictly to its three principles on weapons exports, this report clearly addresses the rationale for participation in dual-use technology transfer and joint weapons development with the United States:

> although patterns of technology diffusion related to dual-use technologies are changing, one can see that there are not a few cases of the effective diffusion of "key technologies" from military to civilian sectors. In order not to lag behind the West in international competitiveness in the future, it is undoubtedly necessary to participate as appropriate in the military sector through close contact with top rank Western firms. Most advanced technologies are already dual-use.[18]

The report then continues by noting how sensitive a matter such an advance into the defense industry is for Japan.

However sensitive, increased defense production is proving to be a versatile and effective strategy for both industrial development and national security. It satisfies multiple needs and interests and has become the basis for a new and active domestic political coalition, a coalition that joins influential subgroups in the industrial, foreign, and economic policy bureaucracies and the defense establishment with an increasing number of important private firms. After identifying the industrial base of this coalition in the next section, we will explore its actions in the specific case of Japan's single largest procurement program of the 1990s, the FS-X next-generation fighter plane.

THE AEROSPACE INDUSTRIAL BASE

The four heavy industrial companies that dominate the Japanese aerospace industry have been strong proponents of increased defense production. Mitsubishi Heavy Industries (MHI), Kawasaki Heavy Industries (KHI), Fuji Heavy Industries (FHI), and Ishikawajima-Harima Heavy Industries (IHI) were all central participants in the first stages of economic recovery, manufacturing ships, cars, electrical equipment, and other capital goods that led Japan's industrialization through the 1960s. They were then big losers from the first oil shock and the end of high growth. Along with textile and steel firms, they were also among the first to be threatened by producers in the NICs. By the mid-1970s they clearly needed new business, and for historical and economic reasons they looked quite naturally to aerospace. At the time, however, commercial opportunities were actually contracting as YS-11 production wound down without a successor project. The firms and their many stakeholders developed a strong interest in increased defense production, and raised their collective voices in support. The influential Federation of Economic Organizations, Keidanren, began insisting through its Defense Industries Production Committee that the JDA do more for the domestic defense industry.[19]

The military aircraft business is by no means new to these four firms. They have engaged in different parts of the business together and separately since its national introduction in the early part of the century. In the prewar period all airplane manufacturing was done by single firms, there was little or no standardization of parts or specifications, and productivity was low. A wartime consolidation ordered by the military was incomplete, handicapped by opposition from the firms. As late as 1944 there were twelve independent airframe producers and seven engine manufacturers. The U.S. Occupation then banned all aircraft manufacturing and broke up the major manufacturers into smaller, more benign enterprises.[20] The result was a dispersion of engineering talent and the refocusing of manufacturing activities. When the ban was lifted in 1952, the rest of the world was already in the jet age, while the thinning ranks of Japanese aircraft engineers had been designing bicycles and fire extinguishers.

The industry was revived first by repair and maintenance, then by offshore procurement, and later by co-production agreements with the U.S. military, and has never overcome its financial dependence on military production.[21] The handful of commercial projects, including the YS-11 and components for Boeing, have been produced alongside warplanes and military engines in plants surviving from the prewar era, often with machine tools and other equipment paid for by the Japan Defense Agency.[22] The technological spillovers from military licensing also have been considerable.[23] According to Hall and Johnson:

In a very short period—largely as a result of skillful importation of technology—the Japanese acquired a small but capable and profitable aerospace industry. A key element in this accomplishment was the Japanese government's sponsorship of military aircraft co-production programs.[24]

Aircraft production is organized as divisions of the heavy industrial companies and until recently provided only a small portion of their total revenue. Despite Hall and Johnson's optimistic assessment, in the 1950s and 1960s, these divisions were less profitable than Japanese firms overall, than other manufacturing firms, and than other divisions within the firms, and were viewed internally as poor cousins. In the 1970s the business collapsed. In the 1980s, however, it has been revived once again by military production, and the prospect of sustained higher defense spending and increased emphasis on domestic technology have turned the business into an important and prestigious growth sector, offsetting precipitous declines in such areas as shipbuilding and petrochemical plant construction. Defense production has provided an almost natural path for the migration of human and capital resources; the transition from sophisticated heavy machinery to military aricraft is not seamless, but it is quite straightforward compared with the steel firms' moves into silicon wafers and theme parts.[25]

The heavy industrial firms making airframes and engines are the biggest but not the only players in the Japanese aerospace industry, nor are they the only beneficiaries of the buildup. Mitsubishi Electric, Nissan, Toshiba, NEC, and Hitachi produce avionics, propulsion, missiles, and military communication systems, all prime areas for spin-on and all of which have boomed. There are also many smaller component firms, and although most of their increasing output goes to the JDA as well, they have enjoyed brisk growth in overseas commercial sales since the mid-1980s. Overall, the industry comprises nearly 200 firms, three-quarters of which are members of the Society of Japanese Aerospace Industries (SJAC), the major industry association.[26]

MAKING MILITARY AIRCRAFT

Product and Process

Modern jet fighters are remarkably complex, high-performance machines. The largest weigh up to 20 tons empty and the most powerful carry more than their own weight in fuel and armament. They travel at altitudes ranging from 100 feet to 10 miles at speeds exceeding 1,500 miles per hour, and execute maneuvers that will cause the pilot to black out before reaching the limits of the airframe. Their avionics meld together a bewildering array of electronic, electromechanical, and optoelectronic equipment that must function in an environment of extreme temperature, shock, vibration, g-forces, and in the worst case, electromagnetic pulse.[27] Although many nations now produce low-performance tactical aircraft, those with the technological, managerial, and financial wherewithal to design and deploy top-of-the-line fighters form an exclusive club, and they pay dearly for membership. The amount typically spent by the United States simply for fighter-related R&D has historically exceeded the sales of the entire Japanese aerospace industry.

The design and manufacturing processes for these sophisticated machines are equally complex and demanding. Like all aerospace final products, fighters require long lead times and high R&D expenditures, both absolutely and relative to manufacturing costs. Each is an intricate assembly of subsystems—structure, propulsion, avionics, and armaments—and each subsystem in turn is an intricate assembly of components, many of which push the limits of the technologies involved. The low-rate manufacturing process is both capital and labor intensive and depends on elaborate facilities, highly skilled artisans, and slow learning curves. Figure 7–1 illustrates the value-added chain, in which millions of parts are designed, manufactured, and built up into final products. The multiyear multibillion-dollar process is essentially the same for all aerospace vehicles, although some lack life support or armaments.

Aerospace systems integration deserves special mention. Systems integration is not only, as pictured, one of the last links in the value chain where all subsystems and components must be made to fit and work together, but is also a metaphor for the management process in its entirety. Subsystems cannot easily be integrated at the tail end if the interface was not properly specified up front or if inevitable in-process design changes have not been properly managed. Integration problems are magnified by concurrent development and production, multiple organizational boundaries, sheer complexity, and the need to insulate the overall program from delays and difficulties at the subsystem level. With its blend of stiff technical and managerial requirements, systems integration is the most challenging aspect of aerospace production, and given the infrequency of full-scale production programs, also the hardest set of skills to develop. A stable set of partners is a critical requirement.

Industrial Organization

The intricate value-added chain is reflected in an industrial division of labor that varies from country to country. In the United States, the traditional structure has been a pyramid with a dozen or so large "prime contracting" firms competing at the top, mostly corporate combinations of the original aircraft makers. With few exceptions, these firms specialize in aerospace production and their fortunes rise and fall accordingly. In a typical program, the winning prime contractor does system R&D, manufactures most of the main structures, and performs final assembly, integration, and testing; the remaining

Figure 7-1.   The Value-Added Chain in Aerospace.

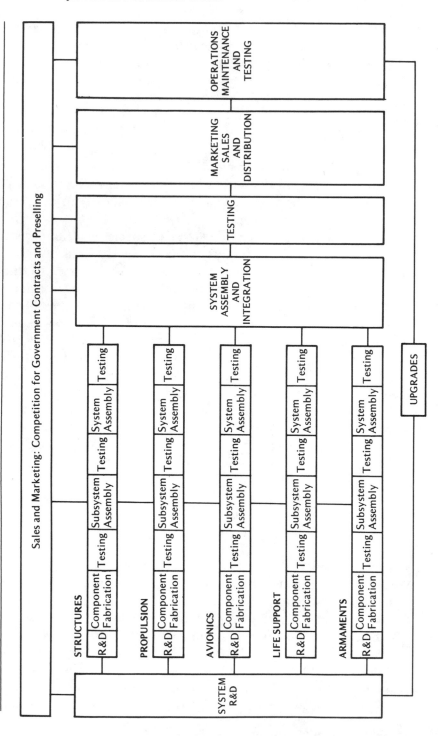

40–70 percent by value is subcontracted directly or as "government-furnished equipment." Contracts for the major subsystems are shared among other primes and a larger number of subsystem manufacturers, which in turn let out work to thousands of small component fabricators and machine shops. The general structure of European aerospace is quite similar, although intra-European consortia generally assume the role played in the United States by prime contractors, national firms serve as the main subcontractors, and a large but diminishing number of designs and components come from the United States. Both industries (and their government customers) rely heavily on exports to lower unit costs.[28]

The industrial structure of Japanese aerospace production is very different. The industry is organized as divisions of diversified companies, which in turn are affiliated with important *keiretsu*, the finance-centered business groups descended from the prewar zaibatsu trusts. As a result, aerospace is more closely linked to other industrial sectors, both within the firms and within the *keiretsu*. Presumably, this closer linkage promotes both the identification of multiple use technologies and their intersectoral transfer, by reducing the organizational boundaries over which opportunities must be perceived and through which technologies must pass.[29]

The industry is far more concentrated than in the United States, with three firms controlling over 90 percent of the prime contract market. Mitsubishi alone has almost half, Kawasaki and IHI about one-quarter each. Fuji Heavy Industries accounts for much of the rest, giving the "big four" essentially complete responsibility for Japanese aircraft production. Extensive vertical integration within these companies and other historic ties lead to a different pattern of subcontracting than is common in the West; often other *keiretsu* members are major beneficiaries. Mitsubishi Electric (MELCO), for example, is the leading supplier of avionics, while Mitsubishi Precision, created in 1962 by MHI, MELCO, Mitsubishi Trading, the Mitsubishi Bank, and U.S. General Precision, is a leading supplier of instrumentation.[30]

Relatedly, the industry is also far more openly collusive than in the United States. The Japanese describe it as a sort of "friendship club" (*nakayoshi kurabu*) built within a "village society" (*mura shakai*), and based upon "mutual knowledge" (*tsuka*).[31] The central purpose of the First Aircraft Industry Promotion Law of 1954 was to cartelize the industry with inducements to interfirm cooperation, and the law and its successors have been very successful in this regard.[32] From the Japan Jet Engine Consortium established in July 1953 to the "Orient Express" hypersonic plane project now on the drawing boards, every MITI, STA, and JDA program has been divided up such that the big four participate significantly in each one, regardless of which among them has been designated military prime contractor or commercial consortium leader.

Collaboration often begins with research and development, and nearly every project combines several firms that would otherwise (and elsewhere) likely be competitors. Participating firms often protect proprietary information, yet the extent of their collaboration and the stability of the partnerships are extraordinary by U.S. standards. A prominent example is collaboration in new materials conducted under the aegis of MITI's Agency for Industrial Science and Technology Program for "Research for Basic Technologies for the Future Industries." This program supports the R&D Institute of Metals and Composites for Future Industries, which consigns a significant portion of its research support to aerospace firms for work on metal and polymer matrices, and carbon fibers. Additionally, SJAC (with MITI support) has successfully diffused metal bending and processing technologies to its members.[33] The big four (in collaboration with thirty-three other firms) are jointly developing a quiet, fuel-efficient, low-pollution, all-Japanese "Advanced Turboprop" engine with funding from the government's Key Technology Center. Here, too, they are collaboratively focused upon new materials, process technologies, design, and optics problems.[34] The same players are simultaneously engaged in the Japan Aero Engines joint venture with the IAE to build the V2500 engine for large commercial aircraft. These firms again join to form the Japanese consortium participating with Boeing in its 767 and 7J7 aircraft, in military projects such as the T-2 and XT-4 trainers, the FS-X, and, of course, the ill-fated YS-11. In short, the division of labor has been remarkably stable; after thirty years of carefully orchestrated work sharing, coordinated investment strategies, and managed competition among the leading firms, all backed by extensive state support, are prominent features of the industry.

Finally, the Japanese industry has historically lacked independent capability in key segments of the value chain, notably systems-level R&D and design, systems integration, and international sales and support. The industry's mainstay has been licensed co-production of

U.S. warplanes, for which R&D has been long since completed, for which all systems integration problems have already been solved, and for which export sales are out of the question. Co-production, even with steadily increasing local content, is equivalent to following a script; Japanese officials often deplore co-production as a transfer of know-how but not "know-why." As we will see, however, Japan has made considerable progress in remedying these deficiencies during the 1980s and is poised to take advantage of and to continue this progress. One senior industry leader described how Japanese firms now approach licensed co-production by using the metaphor of a hand-me-down garment: "First you put it on, then you grow out of it."[35]

The Next Generation

The transformation of aerospace from metal bending to integrating multiple advanced technologies continues to recast the production of military aircraft. The industrial requirements of the fighter business have changed radically in the last decade due to a revolution in design made possible by cumulative advance in materials and electronics, and made urgent by the proliferation of precision-guided anti-aircraft munitions. The old school of design, stressing size and speed, reached its peak in the early 1970s with the F-15, a very large and very fast all-metal airplane with mechanical controls and instruments, and with radar and radios essentially bolted in.[36] The F-16 and F-18, dating from the mid-1970s, blend old and new technology and are best considered transitional aircraft. The next generation, still in the R&D stage, makes extensive use of a broad range of new technologies: composite structural materials for lighter weight, lower observability, and more streamlined shapes; "fly-by-wire," in which mechanical controls are replaced by computer-controlled actuators, and software algorithms actually fly the plane; miniaturized, more sophisticated and more tightly coupled sensors, displays, and avionics, now tied directly into the computerized flight control system; and the odd-looking control surfaces, unstable aerodynamics, and extreme agility made possible by fly-by-wire, known as control configured vehicles (CCV).[37] The confluence of these new technologies will bring higher performance and "survivability" to the next generation of fighters.

The changing technology has already brought new skill requirements and much higher costs and complexity to the aircraft development process, and structural change to the industry. European
firms and governments are struggling to form a consortium to succeed the Panavia organization of the F-15 era, and U.S. prime contractors have been forced into unprecedented alliances to spread
costs and risks that the Department of Defense is no longer willing
to absorb. To accommodate the next generation within the declining
defense budgets of the latter day Reagan administration, DOD began insisting that former arch rivals collaborate on the dwindling
number of new major projects and assume much of the cost of competitive development without the guarantee of a future monopoly.
Both next-generation fighter projects, the navy's Advanced Tactical
Aircraft and the air force's Advanced Tactical Fighter, are being developed in this manner. At least one and perhaps two or three U.S.
producers are likely to quit the tactical aircraft business, and others
may disappear through merger and divestiture.[38] Those that remain
will participate in either teamed production of new aircraft or in the
growing market for more affordable programs to retrofit new technologies into existing aircraft.

How might these disruptive changes affect Japanese ambitions? It
is tempting to argue that they can only increase the competitive
advantage of experienced U.S. firms serving the enormous U.S. market, thus raising the threshold and rendering any Japanese fighter
project somewhat quixotic. They may have precisely the opposite
effect, as the specific requirements of the next generation make vir-
tues of the distinctive technological, organizational, and managerial
characteristics of Japanese industry. Technologically, Japan is on the
leading edge in advanced materials, microelectronics, and other relevant areas, a potential advantage that the spin-on strategy deliberately exploits. Organizationally, since much of the new technology
originates in other industries, Japanese aerospace's tighter intersectoral links should assist its identification and transfer. Managerially,
Japanese firms have thirty years of experience with interfirm cooperation, while it is a brave new world for their U.S. counterparts. Finally, it should be noted that Japan will move toward the next generation via an upgrade program, albeit an extensive one, that combines the benefits of new technology with the economic advantage
of starting from an existing aircraft. The transitional and widely

acclaimed F-16, which they have chosen for the FS-X project, is an ideal platform.

THE CASE OF THE FS-X

The Requirement

Under the "roles and missions" philosophy that guided defense cooperation between the United States and Japan in the 1980s, Tokyo agreed to assume primary responsibility for protecting Japan's territory, airspace, coastal waters, and sea-lanes out to 1,000 miles.[39] Expanded airpower is necessary to meet these objectives, as illustrated by former Prime Minister Nakasone's vow to make Japan an "unsinkable aircraft carrier." The current structure of Japanese airpower shows the legacy of dependence on U.S. aerospace: of thirty-six types of aircraft deployed by the three Japanese services, nine are imported, sixteen co-produced, and among the remaining eleven are several direct copies of low-technology U.S. aircraft. The Japan Air Self Defense Force (JASDF) currently flies three different fighters, and two of them, the F-4J and F-15J, were designed by McDonnell Douglas and co-produced by a consortium led by MHI. The F-1 close support aircraft, the first and thus far only postwar Japanese fighter, was designed and built by the MHI consortium without formal Western assistance, but like the other two it is powered by engines produced under license by IHI.

The F-1, which first flew in 1977, is much smaller, slower, and less capable than the F-4 and F-15, designed in the late 1950s and 1960s respectively.[40] The production run of eighty or so ended in 1983, by which time JASDF was already concerned about technical obsolescence in the avionics, metal fatigue in the airframe, and the stiffer requirements posed by new "roles and missions" responsibilities and the buildup of Soviet power in the region. The JDA decided to accelerate replacing the F-1 and thus was born the formal requirement for the Fighter-Support/Experimental (FS-X). Some of the F-4Js would also need replacement later in the decade, and although this issue was not explicitly linked to the FS-X procurement, the two could not be disentangled.

The need for new aircraft was uncontroversial, but settling the specifics immediately gave rise to a domestic debate, a debate best understood in its institutional, international, and historical context. Defense production in the United States is settled by the Department of Defense and Congress, with muted complaints from the Office of Management and Budget, occasional intervention by the president, and constant lobbying by industry. In Japan, proposals originate within JDA, are passed on for MITI's modifications and approval, and attract considerable attention from the ministries of finance and foreign affairs. The JDA has been traditionally unconcerned with the commercial implications of its procurement plans, but naturally prefers domestic production to simplify maintenance and repair. MITI's participation, however, injects a clearly articulated industrial policy component that favors domestic content and industrial development for reasons only partially related to defense. MITI's position is strongly supported by and is often set in cooperation with the heavy industrial companies. The powerful Finance Ministry predictably favors least-cost solutions, while the Ministry of Foreign Affairs (MOFA) serves to remind all that the United States (and Japan's neighbors) are keenly interested in Japanese defense procurement.

The Domestic Debate: Initial Positions

There were few surprises at the outset of the FS-X debate in the early 1980s, although both MITI and the JDA were internally divided. Private industry, the JDA's Technical Research and Development Institute (TRDI) and Air Staff Office, and MITI's Aircraft and Ordnance Office, were the most active proponents of domestic development, while MITI's Trade Bureau and JDA budget officials were opposed. Finance and Foreign Ministry officials concerned with budgets and U.S.-Japanese relations were reported to be cautious or opposed. The other ministries were united in opposition and were joined by Japan's perennial opposition parties.[41]

Early arguments that the time had come for Japan to design an advanced aircraft were strengthened by clear indications that the United States was adopting a tougher stance on technology transfer. Regarding the F-1, Japan had originally sought to co-produce an American plane but was turned down because DOD felt that they could persuade Japan to buy one instead; when JDA then sought to license avionics technology for their domestic program, DOD turned them down again.[42] The contrast between F-4J co-production in the

1970s and the F-15J program just getting underway was also instructive. In the F-4 program, as in the F-104 program of the 1960s, the United States had adopted a very liberal attitude toward technology transfer and work sharing, and Japanese content and aerospace know-how rose accordingly. Many more restrictions were applied to the F-15 program. The most advanced 40 percent of the aircraft was to be perpetually imported "black boxes," and DOD refused to release a sensitive electronics warfare system in any form; meanwhile the U.S. Congress was complaining that the program was overly generous.

Proponents also argued that with Western aerospace industries about to incorporate major technological advances in a new generation of fighters, and with the FS-X slated to be the only major new procurement program for a decade, Japan would fall hopelessly behind if it settled for restricted co-production of an existing aircraft. TRDI issued a report concluding that domestic development was within the technical grasp of Japanese industry, while MHI invoked the experimental TRDI/Mitsubishi T-2 control configured vehicle as additional evidence that Japanese industry could go it alone. The solemn remarks of MHI president Suenaga Soichiro were typical: "If a foreign type is applied, there will remain no opportunity for new development in this century, and our development capability will be far behind international levels. A national design is necessary by all means."[43]

In the early 1980s, however, this position was a minority viewpoint even within JDA and MITI. There were few reasons to believe that Japan had the technological or budgetary resources to design and build a competitive fighter. There were many reasons to believe that she did not, including the unsatisfactory F-1, the new generation getting underway in the West, technical problems and delays in the T2 CCV project, and the fiscal austerity then crimping all budgets save defense. The high cost of such a project generated particular opposition, and although the Japanese government has always been willing to pay a co-production premium for jobs and technology transfer, the proposed FS-X project entailed a different magnitude of expense.[44] Given the uncertain success and high cost of a fighter development program spread over the short production run of a plane needed in limited quantities and unavailable for export, budget officials in JDA, MITI, and especially the Ministry of Finance viewed domestic development as a good way to pay more and buy less.

These officials were already quarreling over the cost of the military buildup, and the domestic option received little initial support and generated much opposition.

Officials at the MOFA and MITI expressed additional concern at the predictably negative reaction of the United States, still the ultimate guarantor of Japan's defense and its largest trading partner. Aerospace was one of the few industries where the United States ran a consistent surplus, and it had become a traditional means of alleviating trade tension. When U.S. policymakers expressed alarm over the widening deficit in the late 1970s, MITI and the Economic Planning Agency acted to defuse the situation by subsidizing the purchase of unneeded U.S. transports for lease in the world market.[45] In 1978, acting under pressure from the MOFA, the JDA agreed to reduce further the Japanese content in the upcoming F-15J program.[46] With the trade surplus expanding rapidly in the early 1980s, officials concerned with U.S. relations were reviving the transport leasing program and viewed the proposal for a domestic fighter as a step in the wrong direction.

Given the breadth and depth of opposition, it was apparent that a foreign design would be selected if the FS-X decision was made on schedule in 1984; indeed, JDA procurement officials earmarked funds in the 1981–86 five-year plan to buy twenty-four aircraft and solicited bids from the West.[47] Moreover, the FS-X timetable rested on an assumption of co-production or outright purchase and did not allow enough time for indigenous development even if the decision was favorable: the F-1s were to be replaced late in the 1980s, but a domestic aircraft could not be available before the end of the decade at the earliest. From the FS-X advocates' perspective, delay was imperative.

Strategic Delay

Technical and structural obsolescence were driving the need for near-term replacement of the fighters. JASDF, TRDI, and MHI came up with an inexpensive solution known as the Service Life Extension Program (SLEP). Ironically, both the idea dn the technology were imported from the United States, where SLEPs are common practice. The JDA had begun investigating them in the mid-1970s with an eye to the future of their F-4 fleet. In 1981 a team of engineers from

TRDI and MHI was dispatched to the United States to study U.S. methods for reinforcing high stress areas on airframes. In 1982 MHI was awarded a contract to reinforce and refit a single F-4J with advanced avionics and armaments, extending its useful life well into the 1990s. In 1984 the five Western firms that had submitted FS-X proposals were told that consideration of foreign aircraft had been dropped for the time being in favor of an F-1 SLEP, and the modified F-1 would last another five years. In early 1986 MHI was awarded a $400 million contract to update 100 F-4Js.[48]

But the SLEP strategy was much more than a technological "quick fix." By extending the service life of the F-1 by four years, the Japanese were giving domestic producers breathing space to get their own FS-X program up and running:

> Time for producing a domestic FS-X was thereby ensured. . . . These four years provide a golden opportunity for domestic development because the powerful rivals of a domestic FS-X will have become obsolete by the mid-1990s.[49]

> The JDA, mindful of the need to nurture a domestic aircraft industry, had been set all along on using the FS-X procurement as an opportunity for the development of a new fighter plane. . . . A domestic plane would put Japanese manufacturers in the driver's seat, help nurture their capabilities, and ultimately assist our future needs. . . . Postponement will tilt the scale in favor of domestic development.[50]

The SLEP strategy was a resounding success because it offered something to all parties. Budget officials at JDA and the Finance Ministry were delighted because it delayed funding new aircraft years into the future. The United States and MOFA were mollified temporarily, for much of the F-4J contract was slated for American avionics, and because in a separate decision, the length of the F-15J production run was extended. MHI got a substantial contract and experience with integrating digital avionics, while JASDF got uninterrupted deployment. More important, the SLEP contracts gave Japanese industry additional time to prepare, and perhaps most important, deployment rescheduled into the 1990s winnowed the field of potential competitors. Western planes designed in the 1970s would be technically obsolete.

Despite the window of opportunity opened by SLEP, however, convincing the critics that a Japanese FS-X was viable remained a challenging task; if the aerospace coalition was to prevail when the decision reappeared on the agenda, they had to overcome widespread and well-founded skepticism about the level of domestic technology and the lack of aerospace experience.

Technology Development

JDA began funding next-generation fighter studies in the late 1970s, primarily to identify requisite technologies. On the basis of their findings, TRDI focused attention, efforts, and funding on advanced metallurgy, composite materials, stealth technology, advanced avionics, and CCV. One aspect of these efforts was a traditional quest for American technology, despite increasing U.S. reticence. In the case of the F-15, the JDA was able to overcome or at least reduce this reluctance by bargaining and persistence: "Among the items initially withheld were some that were open to reconsideration as passage of time made them less sensitive. The JDA pursued DOD on this list every year for the first 5–6 years of the program and eventually got everything short of what was firmly "non-negotiable."[51]

In an important break from past practice, however, TRDI emphasized the creation of indigenous expertise in the key technologies and took advantage of the higher defense budgets to step up funding in its own laboratories and at the major aerospace and electronics firms. A noteworthy feature of the ensuing domestic development program was the manner in which contracts were conceived and organized in close correspondence with the value-added chain (Table 7–1). Numerous small contracts were let for component development in each of the six aerospace subsectors. A smaller number of subsystem contracts, even fewer system contracts, and only one full-scale development and production program were awarded. Each contract, whatever its type or magnitude, was focused on some aspect of the larger issue of technological and industrial capability, and all were scheduled to show results by 1986.[52]

Strategic Systems Integration

While the proliferation of smaller contracts was targeted at improving indigenous capabilities in specific segments of the value chain, the fewer but larger contracts aimed along the full length of the chain—at

Table 7-1. Japanese Military Aircraft Programs in the 1980s.

Aerospace Materials	Avionics	Complete Systems
Advanced metallurgy	ALQ-7 airborne jamming system	*Prototypes*
Composite fabrication techniques	ALQ-8 electronic warfare system	C1-ECM
Heavy aluminum plates	Attitude/heading reference system	Q-STOL[a]
Metal/polymer matrixes	Automatic flight management system	T2-CCV
Radar-absorbing materials	Cockpit systems and displays	
	Digital engine control system	*Upgrades*
Generic Technologies	Fiber optic aircraft data bus	F-1 SLEP
Aerodynamic research	Fire control system	F-4 SLEP
CAD/CAM	Flight computer	XSH-60J
Next-generation fighter studies	Fly-by-wire control system	
Test facilities	Phased array radar	*Coproduction*
	Radar warning system	AH-1S
Aircraft Propulsion	Search radar	CH-47J
FJR-710[a]		F-15J
XF-3	*Aircraft Armament*	P-3C
	ASM-1 missile	SH-3BJ
	ASM-2 missile	UH-1H
	AAM-3 missile	
	Radar guided missile	*Production*
		XT-4

a. National Aerospace Laboratory.

systems integration—deserve special mention. Two of the contract types, upgrade programs and prototypes, replicate in miniature important aspects of the systems integration experience provided by a full-scale program but with lower costs and in less time. The F-4J SLEP, in which MHI rebuilt the planes from scratch and installed and integrated a completely new (though mostly American) avionics suite, thus provided benefits extending beyond deferred replacement. TRDI followed up the SLEP with the XSH-60J program, in which two American helicopters were bought "green" and fitted with mostly Japanese avionics. Eleven advanced systems were joined together in the aircraft, which JDA called "a platform for national capability development," and which domestic firms and TRDI planned and executed, though with substantial Western assistance.[53] In a program that combined the development of key technologies with systems integration experience, MHI was awarded the contract to convert a jet trainer into a prototype CCV.

While work on advanced components, upgrades, and prototypes narrowed the gap in technology and experience, it did not address the criticism that Japanese industry completely lacked experience managing the development and production of a completely new aircraft: even the three major postwar "domestic" designs relied on imported or co-produced engines, avionics and other major subsystems.[54] The FS-X advocates were proposing to undertake a multi-year project involving billions of dollars, multiple organizations, thousands of highly skilled people and countless risks. Cost overruns, schedule slippage and technical problems are endemic, and the demands on management are high. Systems integration skills in the narrower sense are necessary but not sufficient; there is no substitute for experience managing the full process.

The JDA responded to these concerns with design and production of the supersonic XT-4 jet trainer. Trainers are smaller, simpler, and much less expensive than fighters, so the decision to pursue national development was relatively uncontroversial; the program first appeared in the budget as an $8 million item, and received only token resistance from MOFA bureaucrats, who suggested foreign engines to appease trading partners. But overseas firms were formally excluded in 1980. The consortium awarded this project was by now familiar: KHI would take the lead as prime contractor responsible for 40 percent of the airframe. MHI and FHI were each allotted 30 percent, and IHI would provide its XF3 engine. In all, 43 firms are participating in the project and will build 200 aircraft. This is the first Japanese aircraft to use carbon fiber on a large scale and to use all Japanese aluminum plates, and the first to employ large-scale use of computer-aided design and manufacturing. It is also the first aircraft project in which the engine and the body development proceeded in parallel. No plane of the postwar period has been composed so exclusively of Japanese technology and components.[55]

The challenge of XT-4 development was more managerial than technical, as it replicated in miniature all aspects of an FS-X program, but with less demanding technology. A tight schedule, small budget, and almost equal participation by the three major firms intensified the demand for skillful management at every link in the value-added chain. Despite their inexperience, Japanese managers proved their ability to meet these demands when the first plane rolled out a month early and on budget, an exceedingly rare event in aerospace. Equally unusual, the XT-4 reportedly met all specifications during flight testing and entered production on schedule in 1986.[56] The complete success of the project contributed greatly to the increasing self-confidence and domestic credibility of the Japanese aerospace community, leading one U.S. official at the time to note "peacock-like tails over Mitsubishi and the others."[57]

The FS-X Decision: Trade and Technology

Although the FS-X ultimately became a trade issue, it was first and foremost a controversial domestic decision with an uncertain outcome. Japanese FS-X advocates were poorly received in the domestic arena when they first presented their case in the early 1980s. If they had not been able to delay the decision for several years, their defeat would have been certain. When the decision reappeared on the agenda later in the decade, however, they achieved many of their goals despite intense U.S. pressure to "buy American." Ironically, this same U.S. pressure rallied support for domestic production as an assertion of national sovereignty.

Five developments in the interim tipped the balance. First and foremost, an industrial strategy carefully crafted to develop and demonstrate the requisite technical and managerial skills came to fruition; the Japanese aerospace industry circa 1988 can cite specific accomplishments and argue credibly that it is now prepared for the

FS-X, something it simply could not do earlier in the decade. Second, the delay allowed the coalition to redefine the FS-X as a possible replacement for two or perhaps even three different aircraft types instead of the original one, paving the way for an economically feasible development program. Third, by rescheduling deployment from 1986 to 1997, the coalition could argue persuasively that unmodified American aircraft designed in the early 1970s would be obsolete when deployed. Fourth, a consensus emerged within industry and government that dual-use technology ought to be recognized and nurtured as such.

Finally, external events also played a role: renewed difficulties in shipbuilding and the collapse of the Middle Eastern construction business intensified the heavy industrial companies' need to diversify and the government's desire to help them do so. Simultaneously, growing frustration with the 7J7 and IAE junior partnerships undoubtedly was undermining the perceived wisdom of international collaboration in commercial programs, at least as a junior partner, and was helping the "hard-liners" make their case for domestic development. When the FS-X decision was finally made, domestic opposition to domestic development had largely withered away, and only U.S. pressure, amplified by the Toshiba incident, remained a significant obstacle.

In October 1987 Director-General Kurihara Yuko of the Japan Defense Agency announced that Japan would forgo domestic development of the FS-X and instead spend $6 billion procuring a "lightly modified" American aircraft. The decision was widely interpreted as a conciliatory gesture by the departing Nakasone administration, as an unambiguous victory for the United States, and as vindication of the intense pressure applied by U.S. congressmen and negotiators. U.S. officials praised the Prime Minister and Kurihara for realizing that given U.S. strength in aerospace, the $60 billion trade deficit and concern about the "interoperability" of Japanese and U.S. military forces, a "buy American" policy was appropriate. Senator John Danforth of Missouri, who had focused congressional attention on the issue and who earlier warned Japan not to throw "large amounts of gasoline on the already raging fires of protectionism," accepted the announcement as a sign that Japan was "serious about improving trade relations."[58]

Kurihara's announcement came as a surprise to many who had been following the dispute, because the decision overrode strong opposition from a coalition of officials within the Japanese defense establishment, MITI, the heavy industrial companies, the Keidanren and the Diet. Since the late 1970s, this coalition had been laying the groundwork for an all-Japanese FS-X, and they had become increasingly confident that their views would prevail. Given their careful preparations and growing influence, it had appeared unlikely that the United States could exert sufficient pressure to win such a victory, especially since excessive pressure ran the risk of being counterproductive rather than countervailing. As it became apparent that some sort of compromise was likely, the leading Japanese business daily editorialized that the lame duck Nakasone administration was too weak to resist U.S. pressures and that the emerging "government, LDP and industry stance" was that the decision should be left to its successor.[59]

As the general framework for FS-X co-development was subsequently worked out, the project was portrayed as less and less of a U.S. victory in the American press, yet as more and more of one in the Japanese press.[60] Neither portrayal is correct, and both fail to capture the essential significance of the Memorandum of Understanding approved eight months after the announcement. The SX-3, as the plane is now called, will be an extensively modified F-16 with a high level of Japanese content and technology. The fuselage and the engine will remain generally unchanged, but the wing, the avionics, and the armaments will be largely Japanese. Japan will lead the project, with a roughly 60–40 split of the development and production work. Given its strong resemblance to original proposals for an "all domestic" aircraft, which itself rested on a base of borrowed American technology, the SX-3 is clearly not an unambiguous U.S. victory.[61] Nor is it an unambiguous defeat. The 60–40 split is a genuine compromise negotiated under intense and conflicting pressures on both sides.

At the heart of this compromise is a set of rules for technology transfer that acknowledge Japan's rise as a technological power of the first rank and that are likely to become a model for future agreements. In exchange for access to some of the U.S. aerospace industry's most sophisticated technology, the Japanese have agreed to return any improvements they make at no charge and without being asked, and to make available any original Japanese technology used in the program if it is specifically requested and paid for.[62] They have also agreed, in a separate but closely linked issue, to make an exception to Japanese patent law and permit U.S. firms to have military patents held confidentially at JDA instead of openly at MITI.[63] In effect, the United States is betting that Japanese firms can improve U.S. military aerospace technology by spinning-on commercial manufacturing and electronics expertise, that U.S. firms will learn and exploit these improvements, and that the interests of both countries will be served by such an arrangement.

Rather than a victory or defeat for either country, the FS-X agreement is simply a reflection of the shifting terms of trade in advanced technology, a shift noted by Yamamoto Masashi, Director-General of JDA's Equipment Bureau and one-time Deputy Director-General of MITI's Machinery and Information Industries Bureau:

> I want you to regard it as a "fusion of high technologies." At the final stage, the U.S. side was extremely co-operative, and Japan was able to negotiate on an equal footing, for the first time, in regard to defense technology. . . . It is true that the gaps in the field of aircraft are big, but as a result of Japan's having shown to what extent it will be able to do things through the use of elemental technology, such as onboard equipment, and partial systems, we have been able to elicit the positive co-operation of U.S. manufacturers concerned. I think that this is epoch making.[64]

A U.S. Defense Department official who participated in these negotiations agreed, pointing out that

> The Japanese made it very clear that the American side needed to recognize the world had changed considerably. . . . When we proposed yet another co-production project, the Japanese calmly urged us not to be so "nostalgic." They insisted that the era of co-development is upon us.[65]

The $6 billion SX-3 co-development project will develop and test Japan's ability to lead the redesign, manufacture, and systems integration of a world-class jet fighter, one of the most technologically sophisticated products ever devised, and one considerably more demanding in many respects than a commercial transport. Although not the total victory sought by advocates of domestic development, SX-3 co-development will give the Japanese aerospace industry a powerful technological and financial boost. It provides a formal structure for access to American expertise in areas where Japan lags. It will give a generation of Japanese aerospace engineers design experience with high-performance aircraft. And it will provide a massive capital inflow to underwrite continued expansion of the aerospace industrial infrastructure, including the base of dual-use technology, production equipment, and skilled employment in the plants where military and commercial production take place in tandem. It is very different from the co-production model that it replaces, and it will unquestionably advance Japan's long-range plans to compete effectively in world aerospace markets.

CONCLUSION

We do not suggest that revitalization and growth of the defense industry is a unanimous goal of Japanese leaders, uncontested in domestic bureaucratic or democratic politics, or that it is uninfluenced by external events, particularly conflicting pressures from the United States. To the contrary, we have shown how the subject is highly controversial both domestically and in the larger context of U.S.–Japanese relations. Our analysis of the different organizations involved in the case of the FS-X reveals many different interests and agendas. No consensus for rearmament is apt to emerge suddenly. Most important, we certainly do not suggest an impending resurgence of Japanese militarism, a different matter altogether.

We do argue, however, that increased defense production has emerged in the 1980s as a new strategy for aerospace industrial development, that it has emerged because it is a versatile and effective strategy that satisfies the needs and interests of numerous influential groups, and that it has become the basis for a sturdy political coalition. Convinced that aerospace can help revitalize the troubled heavy industry sector and spread high-technology benefits throughout the economy, frustrated in attempts to develop commercial aircraft, anxious to capitalize on new opportunities to exploit domestic technology, and continually pressured by the United States to rearm more vigorously, Japanese policymakers in the 1980s have turned to military spending as a mechanism for industrial development.

The Japan Committee for Economic Development (Keizai Doyukai) made the case for this strategy a decade ago, when it recognized that single domestic markets are never large enough to sustain national production. Their report argues that even then Japanese fighter aircraft were technologically, but not economically competitive because of export constraints. Low-cost "efficient mass production" was possible only through government procurement. The link between civilian and military production was stated explicitly:

> Generally, the dependence upon military aircraft production is high in developing countries and is low in countries with a well developed aerospace industry. In this sense, Japan is clearly a latecomer, as our aircraft industry is nurtured by the high capital costs and technological requirements of military demand that, in turn, establish the base for an advance into civilian areas.[66]

Naito Ichiro, the former head of the JDA's Technical Research and Development Institute, echoed this by pointing out: "Once demand for fighter aircraft exceeds 300 units it will be possible to establish a mass production system (that eventually) will enable us to gain sight of the civil aircraft market."[67] Morikawa Hiroshi, the executive director of the Keidanren Defense Production Committee, has linked the specific case of the FS-X to the current problems in commercial aircraft development: "We have no alternative but to pin our hopes on the FS-X, given the current lack of progress in plans to jointly develop civilian aircraft."[68]

Industrial development is the key variable because competitiveness is central to Japan's definition of national security. In large measure due to U.S. security guarantees, postwar Japan has measured national security far more by industrial strength than by military power. While quietly questioning the capabilities and commitment of the declining U.S. hegemony, Japanese planners continue to build their future upon the foundation of high-value-added industrial technologies. Aerospace, with the added attraction of military application, is considered vitally important. This importance remains undiminished by past setbacks and continuing difficulties in efforts to develop a competitive presence.

The report of a MITI advisory commission in 1986, when the 7J7 still appeared promising, indicates that MITI was well aware of the obstacles but undeterred. The report introduced its recommendations for increased public support of aerospace by highlighting derivative technological benefits, and went on to discuss the problem:

> Every nation is avidly promoting its aerospace sector in order to strengthen its technology base. . . . The strengthening of the Western European and the U.S. aerospace oligopoly in large and medium sized planes, combined with the emergence of a light aircraft industry in the developing countries, means that if a Japanese aircraft industry is to survive, it will have to escape through a very narrow gate.[69]

Figure 7-2. Technology Diffusion to Other Industries from Aerospace Technologies.

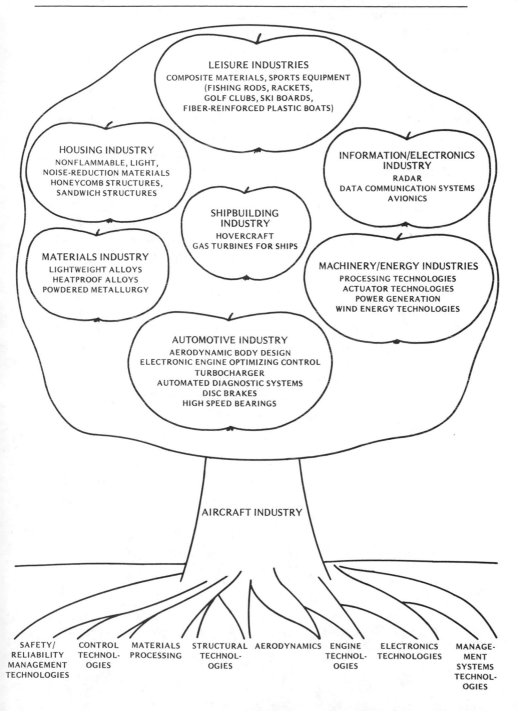

LEISURE INDUSTRIES
COMPOSITE MATERIALS, SPORTS EQUIPMENT
(FISHING RODS, RACKETS,
GOLF CLUBS, SKI BOARDS,
FIBER-REINFORCED PLASTIC BOATS)

HOUSING INDUSTRY
NONFLAMMABLE, LIGHT,
NOISE-REDUCTION MATERIALS
HONEYCOMB STRUCTURES,
SANDWICH STRUCTURES

INFORMATION/ELECTRONICS
INDUSTRY
RADAR
DATA COMMUNICATION SYSTEMS
AVIONICS

SHIPBUILDING
INDUSTRY
HOVERCRAFT
GAS TURBINES FOR SHIPS

MATERIALS INDUSTRY
LIGHTWEIGHT ALLOYS
HEATPROOF ALLOYS
POWDERED METALLURGY

MACHINERY/ENERGY INDUSTRIES
PROCESSING TECHNOLOGIES
ACTUATOR TECHNOLOGIES
POWER GENERATION
WIND ENERGY TECHNOLOGIES

AUTOMOTIVE INDUSTRY
AERODYNAMIC BODY DESIGN
ELECTRONIC ENGINE OPTIMIZING CONTROL
TURBOCHARGER
AUTOMATED DIAGNOSTIC SYSTEMS
DISC BRAKES
HIGH SPEED BEARINGS

AIRCRAFT INDUSTRY

SAFETY/
RELIABILITY
MANAGEMENT
TECHNOLOGIES

CONTROL
TECHNOL-
OGIES

MATERIALS
PROCESSING

STRUCTURAL
TECHNOL-
OGIES

AERODYNAMICS

ENGINE
TECHNOL-
OGIES

ELECTRONICS
TECHNOLOGIES

MANAGE-
MENT
SYSTEMS
TECHNOL-
OGIES

This MITI report, the first proposing the International Aircraft Development Fund, stressed two fundamental benefits of a healthy aerospace sector: (1) economic expansion and (2) enhanced national security through technological independence and sophistication. Japan's goal was clearly to make its aircraft industry equal to the rest of the world's by the early part of the next century, and in so doing, contribute to the economy in every related area. These relationships are commonly embodied in the metaphor of a tree that provides the technologies and the products (from roots to fruits) that will sustain Japan into the twenty-first century (Figure 7-2).

Beneath the hyperbole and simplicity, this metaphor reveals a way of thinking about how success or failure in aerospace has profound implications for the future of Japanese industry. The perceived benefits extend well beyond creating new business for the heavy industrial companies. They extend past the explicit linkages between avionics and electronics, systems design and computer science, "space-age plastics" and ceramics and alloys that will never leave the ground. They extend past the multitude of other opportunities for spinning technologies off and on among military and commercial aerospace and the rest of the industrial economy. In this vision, machinery, housing, automotive, leisure, and service industries are each linked systematically to a healthy and active aerospace sector. The benefits are commercial and technological.[70] But they cannot be divorced from their implications for Japanese national security. Nor, we insist, will they be derived entirely from commercial projects. We expect a vibrant military aerospace program, revolving on an axis of indigenous dual-use technology, to help push the Japanese commercial aircraft industry through the "narrow gate," to what policy planners and industrialists believe will be greener and safer pastures.

NOTES

1. The authors would like to acknowledge the thoughtful critiques of a draft of this chapter provided by Michael Chinworth, Ellen Frost, Tom Gros, David Mowery, Paul Rubin, Gregg Rubinstein, and Bud Shank. The remaining mistakes are, of course, our own.
2. These refer only to *hojokin* loans. Data are from Table 12-3 in Wakasugi Ryohei, *Gijutsu Kakushin to Kenkyu Kaihatsu no Keizai Bunseki* (Tokyo: Toyo Keizai, 1986).

3. For a typical press account, see *Aerospace America* (March 1987), which claimed (with some alarm) that in each major case of aerospace technology licensing from American to Japanese firms, licensing was phased out in favor of independent projects as the Japanese firms developed their own design and integration skills.

    For an optimistic analysis, see Orit Frenkel, "Flying High: A Case Study of Japanese Industrial Policy," *Journal of Policy Analysis and Management* 3, no. 3 (1984): 406–20.

    For scholarly pessimism, see David Mowery, *Alliance Politics and Economics* (Cambridge, Mass.: Ballinger, 1987); Thomas Roehl, "Emerging Sources of Foreign Competition in the Commercial Aircraft Manufacturing Industry: The Japanese Aircraft Industry," Report to the United States Department of Transportation, June 1985; and Thomas Roehl and J. Frederick Truitt, "Japanese Industrial Policy in Aircraft Manufacturing," *International Marketing Review* (Summer 1987): 21–32.

4. To put the Western jetliner business into market perspective, consider that as of 1984, $180 billion in total postwar sales had yielded an estimated net loss of $40 billion, without counting the costs of essential research, development, and manufacturing facilities spun off from military programs. Three of the total twenty-nine jet transports designed and built have passed break-even; the Boeing Corporation, which makes all three, is just now beginning to reap net positive returns from thirty years of activity, after being launched into the business by military production and sustained through many bad years by government contracts. The Airbus consortium among European military firms is quite unlikely ever to recover its sponsors' full investments, even disregarding the time value of money. For an excellent summary, see Wolfgang and Christopher Demisch, "The Jetliner Business," First Boston Research Special Report, AE1991, October 5, 1984.

5. For details on this form of industrial organization, see Chalmers Johnson, *Japan's Public Policy Companies* (Washington, D.C.: American Enterprise Institute, 1978) and Richard J. Samuels, *The Business of the Japanese State: Energy Markets in Comparative and Historical Perspective* (Ithaca, N.Y.: Cornell University Press, 1987).

6. In order to facilitate this shift, the Aircraft Industry Promotion Act was revised in April 1986. The legal objective was changed from "promotion of domestic production" to "promotion of joint international development" of aircraft. Symbolically, this revision also abolished the already moribund Nippon Aircraft Manufacturing Company, maker of the YS-11. See *Tsusan Koho*, February 1986. A new public corporation was also established. This "International Aircraft Development Fund" was designed to make funds available to Japanese manufacturers despite severe budgetary constraints imposed by the Ministry of Finance and despite foreign

pressures to eliminate "targeting." The result was a creative financing package that supports only joint international ventures through off-budget financing and that establishes a permanent "kitty" for the aircraft makers.

7.   *Wall Street Journal*, February 17, 1988.

8.   The Japanese press continued to run positive puff pieces on the progress of the IAE long after IAE's ongoing problems have been chronicled in the Western press. Compare, for example, the *Asahi Shimbun*, June 26, 1988, with *Aviation Week*, June 3, 1985, July 7, 1986, February 16, 1987, March 16, 1987, April 13, 1987, May 25, 1987, and November 9, 1987.

9.   There are several studies in English that identify and discuss these problems. See, for example, Mowery, *Alliance Politics and Economics*; Roehl and Truitt, "Japanese Industrial Policy in Aircraft Manufacturing"; David C. Mowery and Nathan Rosenberg, "The Japanese Commercial Aircraft Industry since 1945; Government Policy, Technical Development, and Industrial Structure," Occasional Paper of the Northeast Asia–United States Forum on International Policy, 1985; and Frenkel, "Flying High." For an optimistic view by a leading Japanese bank, see Long Term Credit Bank of Japan, ed., "The Japanese Aircraft Industry: Entering a Period of Progress Spurred by International Joint Development," May 1986. For MITI's view, see Kokuki Kogyo Shingikai, Kokuki Kogyo Bukai, ed., "Kokuki Kogyo no Tomen suru Kihon Mondai to Seifu Hojo no Arikata ni Tsuite–Chukan Hokoku" (The Current State of Government Assistance and Basic Problems in the Aircraft Industry—A Midterm Report) (Tokyo: MITI, 1985).

10. David Mowery and Nathan Rosenberg, "Commercial Aircraft: Cooperation and Competition Between the U.S. and Japan," *California Management Review* 27, no. 4 (Summer 1985): 77.

11. Japanese aircraft technology was considerable in this period. A Japanese plane, the *Kamikaze-go* set a world flight distance record in 1938, and Japanese firms were building experimental jet engines and aircraft by the end of the war. For a study of the wartime aircraft industry structure, see Asajima Shoichi, "Senji Taiseiki no Nakajima Hikoki" (The Nakajima Aircraft Company During the Wartime Period) *Keieishi Gaku* 20, no. 3 (1985).

12. This "ban" was actually a 1967 reinforcement of a 1949 Export Trade Control Order prohibiting foreign sales of arms. Fearing a domestic backlash against its cooperation with the U.S. military in Vietnam, Prime Minister Sato Eisaku's Cabinet put forth the "Three Principles," proscribing sales to Communist countries, countries at war, and those apt to engage in international disputes. In 1976 Prime Minister Miki extended this to weapons technology as well. In 1981 the United States requested a revision allowing it to import Japanese military technology, and in 1983 Prime Minister Nakasone granted its wish. See Reinhard Drifte, *Arms Production*

in Japan: The Military Applications of Civilian Technologies (Boulder, Colo.: Westview Press, 1986).

13. Mitsubishi Handbook, 1986. 1985 sales of the Aircraft and Special Vehicles Division surpassed 314 billion yen, second only to Power Systems. This does not include automobiles, which were spun off into the Mitsubishi Motor Corporation in 1970.

    Other signals of Japan's shifting calculus on the defense-industrial linkage include the 1983 technology transfer agreement and participation by Japanese firms in the U.S. Strategic Defense Initiative. (For details on the negotiations concerning Japanese industrial participation in SDI, see Michael W. Chinworth, "Japan's Defense Policies in the Post–One Percent Era," Japan Economic Institute Report May 8, 1987.) There is also public debate underway concerning the production of "light carriers" that would simultaneously revive ship production and help Japan fulfill its commitment to defend the 1,000 mile sea-lanes. Internally, there is the transformation of corporate charters, such as Komatsu's entry into the missile business in 1987 and Ishikawajima-Harima Heavy Industries' new division in 1988 devoted entirely to weapons systems. (See the *Japan Economic Journal*, December 19, 1987 and *Aviation Week*, March 14, 1988.)

14. In 1988, for the first time, top positions in JDA were given to career JDA officials; the top career position in the JDA was given to Nishihiro Seiki, and the top post within the JDA's Technical Research and Development Institute was given to Tsutsui Ryozo. The position of JDA Equipment Bureau Chief (procurement) has been a virtual MITI monopoly.

15. In the mid-1970s, the full dimensions and costs of YS-11 failure were readily apparent to officials of MITI's Aircraft and Ordnance Bureau and their superiors. The commercial aircraft strategy was in disarray, as was the Japanese budget. The Ministry of Finance made it quite clear that the government could not afford to sponsor a follow-on program similar in scale and scope to the YS-11, and MITI planners knew that no such program would emerge without their sponsorship. Officials articulated the new strategy of international collaboration and arranged two new consortia (one for airframes and one for engines), but most of the decade passed without a clear definition of their purpose: negotiations with Boeing began in 1973 but did not yield the 767 agreement until 1978, and the engine consortium idled along from 1971 until it joined with Rolls-Royce in 1979. Between 1972 and 1977, hours worked in the aerospace industry declined by two-thirds. See *Aviation Week*, March 21, 1977.

16. The Japanese press continues to report on possibilities for civilian aircraft projects. Some, such as the "follow-on" to the YS-11, have been championed by the Transportation Ministry and by MITI, which is now subsidizing feasibility studies. The reported goal is to eliminate dependence upon foreign manufacturers in the long run. Other projects mentioned are

helicopter engine cooperation with MBB of West Germany, commuter planes with China, and hypersonic transports with the United States. See the *Nihon Keizai Shimbun*, April 14, 1988, May 9, 1988, and May 7, 1988.

17.   The more general point about the declining importance of "spillover" from military to commercial aircraft is made by Mowery in *Alliance Politics and Economics*, pp. 48–49.

18.   Tsushosangyosho Daijin Kanbo, ed., *Nippon no Sentaku* (Japan's Choices) (Tokyo: MITI, June 1988), p. 116.

19.   More recently this has included demands that the JDA expand its procurement program and broaden its definition of defense items to include so-called rear support expenses such as communications, fuel, and other items. See *Asahi Shimbun*, April 12, 1985. Also see Drifte, *Arms Production in Japan.*

20.   The aircraft division of Mitsubishi Heavy Industry, which had built 17,000 aircraft and 54,000 engines, for example, was broken up into three firms that focused upon auto bodies, internal combustion engines, scooters, and agricultural equipment. Nakajima Hikoki, which ultimately became Fuji Heavy Industries, was divided by SCAP into twelve firms. Kawasaki became a manufacturer of fire extinguishers, textile machinery, and bus bodies. See Kuno Masao and Paul Rubin, "Japanese Aerospace—Aiming for the Twenty-First Century," *Aerospace Japan* (July 1984–February 1986); and in the original, see Kuno Masao, *Nihon no Kokuki Uchu Sangyo* (The Japanese Aerospace Industry) (Tokyo: Daiyamondo, 1984). Also see the postwar history produced by the Society of Japanese Aerospace Companies, *Nihon no Koku Uchu Kogyo Sengoshi* 1987). Note that in 1952, as soon as restrictions were removed with the end of the Occupation, the MHI firms, the KHI firms, and the FHI firms were all reconsolidated. Note also that the key players in the prewar aircraft industry returned as the presidents and senior managing directors of these companies. Also see the detailed company histories, such as Fuji Juko, ed., *Fuji Jukogyo Sanju Nen Shi* (The Thirty Year History of Fuji Heavy Industries) (Tokyo: Fuji Heavy Industries, July 1984).

21.   In all, nineteen different U.S. military aircraft have been produced under license by Japanese firms. Japan's first postwar aircraft export was Toyo Koku's licensed version of the U.S. Fletcher FD-26 trainer/attack plane sold to Cambodia and Vietnam in the late 1950s; Japan's first export of aircraft technology was a license for "wave-suppressing sonar" sold to Grumman in the 1970s. In the entire postwar period, the value of commercial production surpassed military only at the height of the YS-11 program and quickly returned to its traditional level of about 20 percent of output.

22.   Interview with Civilian Aircraft Corporation official, Tokyo, June 20, 1988.

23. FHI manufactures the main wing spars and horizontal stabilizers of the P-3, the landing gear of the F-15, the entire UH1B helicopter, and the main wing cowling of the B-767 in the same plant. Interview with an official of the Society of Japanese Aerospace Companies, Tokyo, June 10, 1987; and interview with a U.S. Department of Defense official, Tokyo, June 11, 1987.

A direct example is the landing gear for the commercial YS-11, which was adopted from the co-produced KHI/Lockheed P2V-7 aircraft. This example is drawn from Frenkel, "Flying High."

24. G.R. Hall and R.E. Johnson, "Transfers of United States Aerospace Technology to Japan," p. 315 in R. Vernon, ed., *The Technology Factor in International Trade* (New York: National Bureau of Economic Research, 1970), pp. 305–63. Mowery, *Alliance Politics and Economics*, p. 56; and Roehl and Truitt, "Japanese Industrial Policy in Aircraft Manufacturing," p. 26 disagree, arguing that licensing and co-production has not provided Japanese or any other firms the design experience necessary for an independent aircraft industrial base. Hall and Johnson go on to argue, however, that "co-production increased the rate, amount, and kinds of technological information provided the Japanese by several orders of magnitude," including even manufacturing "art" embodied in translated "blackbooks" of shop foreman (pp. 316–17).

25. For a (now slightly dated) introduction to the Japanese defense industry, see Tomiyama Kazuo, *Nihon no Boei Sangyo* (Japan's Defense Industries) (Tokyo: Toyo Keizai, 1979). Also see Asahi Shimbun Shakaibu, ed., *Heiki Sangyo* (The Weapons Industry) (Tokyo: Asahi Shimbunsha, 1986). News reports are often revealing as well. Consider the following pair of stories in the same newspaper on the same day: The first article describes how KHI has begun a "large scale" transfer of personnel from shipbuilding to aircraft due to the recession in the dockyards. The second story reports that KHI has announced the use of industrial robots for its aircraft manufacturing operations. See the *Nikkei Sangyo Shimbun*, June 18, 1986.

26. For a useful overview of the industry, see Kuno and Rubin, "Japanese Aerospace." The Society of Japanese Aerospace Companies now publishes annually a detailed membership list and statistical abstract in English called "The Aerospace Industry in Japan." Additionally, the *Nikkei Sangyo Shimbun* and the *Nikkan Kogyo Shimbun* provide detailed coverage of these businesses.

27. Electromagnetic pulse (EMP), the intense burst of energy released by the atmospheric detonation of nuclear weapons, is a major concern for designers of military electronic systems.

28. See Jacques S. Gansler, *The Defense Industry* (Cambridge, Mass.: MIT Press, 1980) for a discussion of U.S. defense industrial structure.

29. It must be noted, however, that *keiretsu* affiliation is not a reliable predictor of technological linkage in Japan. Firms increasingly are seeking

R&D partners from *outside* their own *keiretsu* group. See R.J. Samuels "Research Collaboration in Japan," Working Paper 87–02, MIT-Japan Science and Technology Program, April 1987 for a more systematic analysis.

30. Tomiyama Kazuo, "Revival and Growth of Japan's Defense Industry," *Japanese Economic Studies* 9, no. 4 (Summer 1981): 3–51.

31. These descriptions were provided in a series of interviews with senior industry leaders, government officials, and officials of the Society of Japanese Aerospace Companies, June 1988.

32. MITI long has favored this strategy for most industrial sectors but has been generally unable to enforce it. One famous case is MITI's attempt to keep Honda out of automobile production. See Samuels, *The Business of the Japanese State*, for a fuller explanation of the relationship between the politics of oligopoly and industrial policy in Japan. In any case, MITI encountered little opposition in aerospace, most likely because the government procures four-fifths or more of industry output.

33. For a full list of SJAC-sponsored projects (many of which also attract MITI support), see the SJAC yearbook, *Koku Uchu Kogyo Nenkan*. See also *Nikkei Aerospace*, September 29, 1986.

34. The firms participating in this consortium justify their cooperation by reference to the need to "confront Western manufacturers" (MHI), to "expand the Japanese share" of world markets (IHI), or to "compete with Western firms" (FHI). Each clearly links this project to its broader technology strategy.

35. Interview, June 22, 1988, Tokyo.

36. The F-15, like all fighters, has been upgraded continuously since its introduction. More recent models incorporate some composite materials and are fitted with advanced avionics.

37. The flight characteristics of a control-configured aircraft are closer to those of a flying saucer than of a traditional airplane. With computerized manipulation of canards, winglets, and other novel control surfaces, a CCV can change altitude and flight path without changing "attitude," the direction the vehicle is pointing. The advantages for aerial combat and defensive maneuvering are significant.

38. This is certainly the prevailing view among Wall Street aerospace analysts. See, for example, *Aviation Week*, February 22, 1987 and *Wall Street Journal*, October 31, 1986.

39. These new responsibilities were formally recognized in a 1981 joint communiqué signed after talks between then Prime Minister Suzuki and President Reagan. For discussion of the U.S.-Japan defense relationship, see Gregg A. Rubinstein, "U.S.-Japan Security Relations: A Maturing Partnership," (unpublished paper), October 26, 1987; and Michael W. Chinworth, "The Trade-Defense Linkage," Japan Economic Institute Report, no. 35A, September 18, 1987.

40. The F-1 is actually a reworked version of MHI's T-2 trainer, which in turn is closely though informally modeled on the Anglo-French Jaguar, with which it shares the French Aldour engine.

41. *Asahi Shimbun*, April 16, 1985; *Aviation Week*, March 12, 1984, March 18, 1985, September 30, 1985.

42. The plane in question was Northrop's F-5E. The story of the Defense Department's refusal to release it is from personal correspondence from a former defense official, May 18, 1988.

43. *Aviation Week*, March 18, 1985.

44. The co-production premium for the F-15 is about $2 billion. However, Hall and Johnson, "Transfers of United States Aerospace Technology to Japan," argue that Japan coproduced the F104 in the 1960s for 10 percent less than the cost of outright purchase, with the savings accounted for by lower labor costs.

45. *Aviation Week*, January 16, 1978.

46. *Aviation Week*, November 23, 1981.

47. Initial candidates for the FS-X discussed in the Japanese press included the General Dynamics F-16, the Panavia Tornado, the Harrier of British Aerospace, and the McDonnell Douglas F-4. Much later, the McDonnell Douglas F-18 was actively discussed, but was denigrated in the press as inferior.

48. The Japanese press tied the delay to the midterm elections in the United States. There was apparently some hope that a more congenial Congress would reduce the pressure on Japan for co-production or outright purchase. See *Nikkei Aerospace*, September 29, 1986; *Aviation Week*, March 3, 1980, January 1, 1981, March 18, 1985, March 10, 1986.

49. *Airworld*, December 1985. See also the *Asahi Shimbun*, April 16, 1985, which suggested that the JDA and MHI were moving secretly in this direction and were making every effort to shield the SLEP strategy from public debate and from the Japanese Diet in particular.

50. *Nikkei Aerospace*, September 29, 1986.

51. Personal correspondence from a former defense official, May 18, 1988. See also "U.S. Military Coproduction Agreements Assist Japan in Developing Its Civilian Aircraft Industry," U.S. General Accounting Office, Washington, D.C., 1980.

52. *Aviation Week*, March 9, 1981 and March 10, 1986.

53. *Aviation Week*, March 18, 1985.

54. These were the C-1 of KHI, the F-1 of MHI, and the YS-11.

55. For a brief but detailed overview, see *Nikkei Aerospace*, May 13, 1985, pp. 1–6. The development of this aluminum plate capability is another example of public/private cooperation to meet industrial goals. Alcoa Aluminum had been the sole source to MHI/KHI of polished aluminum sheets for the B-767 but could not deliver on time for the T-4. MHI/KHI

encouraged MITI and SJAC to establish the Advanced Aerospace Technology Development Center. Kobe Steel and Furukawa Aluminum acquired the technology, invested in special equipment for processing it, and began deliveries in 1984. See Kuno and Rubin, "Japanese Aerospace."

56. The USAF/Fairchild T-46 jet trainer, the U.S. counterpart of the XT-4, ran into such cost, schedule, and quality problems that the U.S. Air Force cancelled it.

57. *Wall Street Journal*, April 23, 1986. As noted above, KHI was the prime contractor on this project.

58. Danforth quoted in the *Wall Street Journal*, March 16, 1987 and October 12, 1987. The corporate headquarters of the two U.S. firms that competed to supply the FS-X are in St. Louis. McDonnell Douglas is one of Missouri's largest employers, while General Dynamics' production facilities are located in Fort Worth, Texas. McDonnell Douglas was heavily favored to win the competition: the Japanese had always insisted that the FS-X, which will spend much of its time over water, have two engines, and both of McDonnell Douglas's candidates (the F-15 and F-18) do. General Dynamics's F-16 does not, and General Dynamics discouraged such a major modification.

A team of engineers visited the United States shortly before the decision and returned to Japan endorsing the F-15, but their advice was ignored; the F-16 was selected in a last minute reversal. The official reason given was cost, but the F-15 was already in production at MHI and the strong yen made all U.S. fighters a relative bargain. One reason may be that the fly-by-wire F-16 offered more opportunities to learn than the F-15 and was more amenable to extensive modification; by these criteria, however, the fly-by-wire F-18 was the natural choice. A modification of this argument would be that Japanese planners, having worked with McDonnell Douglas on coproduction of the F-4 and F-15, felt that they could learn more by switching partners. There has even been speculation that the JDA's surprise move was influenced by a desire to punish Danforth, sometimes known as "the senator from McDonnell Douglas," for the heavy-handed pressure and outright threats he made prior to the decision.

59. "Nakasone Cannot Fight U.S. on FSX Development," *Nihon Keizai Shimbun*, reprinted in *Japan Economic Journal*, July 25, 1987.

60. Vociferous criticism of the arrangement in the Japanese press indicates that the FS-X coalition may have used the "humiliation factor" to rally support for a tough stance in negotiations over program leadership. For example, Keidanren Defense Production Committee Executive Director Morikawa Hiroshi said at the time of the October agreement "Now that our original FS-X development plan has been completely abandoned, our concern is how Japan can take the initiative in the joint project." Similarly, the *Nihon Keizai Shimbun* editorialized that the United States had "jeopardized Japanese national sovereignty," and said, "We hope that the

Defense Agency will spare no words in securing a leadership role to ensure that the program is as fruitful for Japan as possible." (Both citations are from the *Japan Economic Journal*, October 17, 1987, p. 27.) The *Asahi Jaanaru*, July 1, 1988, went even further in its story on the "U.S.-Japan High Tech Air War," asking if "Japanese industries, that have finally achieved their independence, can escape from the evil influence of techno-nationalism that was born in Nazi Germany and nurtured in the United States."

61. Although the SX-3 is clearly not the all-new, all-domestic aircraft sought by the FS-X coalition, the comparison is potentially misleading. In discussing the agreement's benefits for Japanese industry, JDA defense policy bureau chief Nishihiro Seiki remarked: "Japanese fighter contractors wouldn't have any real future as long as they merely dreamed of developing their own FS-X. Their blueprint for domestic development was essentially not better than a copy of an American fighter plane." Quoted in *Japan Economic Journal*, October 17, 1987, p. 3.

62. Neither the "flowback" provision nor access upon request to original Japanese technology is unique to the SX-3 deal or new in U.S.-Japan defense technology agreements. Flowback has been negotiated in previous deals, but never on the scale of the SX-3. Access on request to Japanese military technology, as defined by Japanese companies, was agreed to in 1983, but there have been few transfers under its terms. The SX-3 is the first major test of the 1983 agreement. There will be little room for ambiguity as to which technologies are covered, although much debate is likely as to which category they belong in.

DOD interest in acquiring Japanese technology has been growing since the 1970s. In 1980 the DOD and the JDA established a Systems and Technology Forum to discuss the coordination of defense technology transfers, and in 1981 the United States proposed a looser interpretation of the "Three Principles" governing military exports. This met with firm opposition from MITI, other government agencies, and the opposition parties. Prime Minister Suzuki avoided the issue, but in early 1983, Prime Minister Nakasone agreed to take the political heat and approved the transfer of military technology to the United States. An Exchange of Notes in November established an intergovernmental channel for reviewing requests and assisting the transfer.

For a complete account of these discussions, see Gregg Rubinstein, "Emerging Bonds of U.S.-Japanese Defense Technology Cooperation," *Strategic Review* (Winter 1987). For the Defense Science Board's evaluation of Japanese dual-use technologies, see the *Report of the Defense Science Board Task Force on Industry-to-Industry International Armaments Cooperation—Phase Two—Japan* (Washington, D.C.: U.S. Government Printing Office, June 1984).

In a more recent, but predictable development, Japanese firms are beginning to test the limits (and the reach) of MITI policy by acquiring defense production capabilities abroad. The first such case involved Minebea, a bearing manufacturer, and was reported in the *Nihon Keizai Shimbun*, July 12, 1988.

63. The 1951 Patent Secrecy Law discourages U.S. companies holding patents with Pentagon classification from registering them in countries that will not keep them secret. A number of countries, including Australia, France, Norway, Turkey, and the United Kingdom, have since signed separate agreements to establish procedures for processing secrecy order patent applications. The Japanese Diet ratified such a treaty in 1956, but the Japanese government failed to take measures to implement the agreement. Thirty-two years later the changes were made in order to accommodate the formally unrelated FS-X and the SDI cooperative projects. *Wall Street Journal*, February 24, 1988. The weekly, *Asahi Jaanaru*, July 1, 1988, has argued this is part of an American "Nazi-style patent strategy."

64. Interviewed by *Nihon Keizai Shimbun*, October 25, 1987.

65. Interview, U.S. Defense Department official, Tokyo, June 26, 1988.

66. Keizai Doyukai, ed., "21 seki e no Sangyo Kozo Bijiyon o Mitomete," (Demanding a Vision for the 21st Century) Tokyo, June 1979, p. 71.

67. Interview in the *Shukan Posuto*, October 9, 1987.

68. Quoted in *Asahi Jaanaru*, July 1, 1988.

69. Kokuki Kogyo Shingikai, Kokuki Kogyo Bukai, ed., "Kokuki Kogyo no Tomen suru Kihon Mondai to Seifu Hojo no Arikata ni Tsuite (Chukan Hokoku)," pp. 1-2.

70. This way of thinking about technology linkages is also articulated in Keizai Doyukai, "21 seki e no Sangyo Kozo Bijiyon o Mitomete," pp. 69, 85–89.

INDEX

ABOUT THE EDITORS

Chalmers Johnson is a professor of Asian studies within the Graduate School of International Relations and Pacific Studies at the University of California, San Diego. He is the former Walter and Elise Haas Professor of Asian Studies and former chairman of the Center for Chinese Studies, both at the University of California, Berkeley. He received his A.B., M.A., and Ph.D. degrees in economics and political science from the University of California, Berkeley. He has written extensively on East Asian political economy, revolution, and social movements, including *Peasant Nationalism and Communist Power, An Instance of Treason, Revolutionary Change, Conspiracy at Matsukawa, Autopsy on People's War, Japan's Public Policy Companies*, and *MITI and the Japanese Miracle*.

Laura D'Andrea Tyson is director of research at the Berkeley Roundtable on the International Economy (BRIE) and a professor of economics, both at the University of California, Berkeley. She received her Ph.D. in economics from the Massachusetts Institute of Technology. She has written books and articles on the economics of competitiveness, including *American Industry in International Competition* (with John Zysman), *The Dynamics of Trade and Employment* (with William T. Dickens and John Zysman), "Competitiveness" (in Martin K. Starr, *Global Competition*), and "The Economic Black Hole" (with Lester Thurow, in *Foreign Policy*). She has also written on the economies of Eastern Europe, including *Power, Purpose and Collective Choice* (with Ellen Commisso).

John Zysman is co-director of the Berkeley Roundtable on the International Economy (BRIE) and a professor of political science, both at the University of California, Berkeley. He received his Ph.D. in political science from the Massachusetts Institute of Technology. His major publications include *Manufacturing Matters* (with Stephen S. Cohen), *Government, Markets and Growth, American Industry in International Competition* (with Laura Tyson), and *The Dynamics of Trade and Employment* (with William T. Dickens and Laura D'Andrea Tyson).

ABOUT THE CONTRIBUTORS

Stephen S. Cohen is a professor of planning and co-director of the Berkeley Roundtable on the International Economy (BRIE), both at the University of California, Berkeley. He has directed numerous interdisciplinary research projects on technology and production organization and on American competitiveness. He is the author of *Manufacturing Matters* (with John Zysman), *Modern Capitalist Planning: The French Model*, and "Corporate Lessons from the Trade Disaster" (with John Zysman).

Giovanni Dosi is a professor of applied economics at the University of Rome, "La Sapienza," and a visiting research fellow at the Science Policy Research Unit (SPRU), University of Sussex. He has written extensively on technical change, industrial evolution and international trade, including *Technical Change and Industrial Transformation, Technical Change and Economic Theory* (with C. Freeman, R. Nelson, G. Silverberg and L. Soete), and *The Economics of Technical Change and International Trade* (with K. Pavitt and L. Soete).

Michael Gerlach is an assistant professor of business administration at the University of California, Berkeley. He received his Ph.D. in organizational behavior from Yale University and has carried out research in Japan under the sponsorship of both the Henry Luce Foundation and the Japan Foundation. His current interest is in the com-

331

parative organization of inter-firm relationships in Japan and the United States. He is the author of *Alliance Capitalism: The Social Organization of Japanese Business* (forthcoming).

Richard J. Samuels is director of the MIT-Japan Science and Technology Program and an associate professor of political science, both at the Massachusetts Institute of Technology. He received his Ph.D. in political science from MIT. He is an appointed member of the Joint Committee on Japanese Studies of the American Council of Learned Societies, and the Social Science Research Council. He has written numerous books, including *The Business of the Japanese State: Energy Markets in Comparative and Historical Perspective*, and *The Politics of Regional Policy in Japan: Localities Inc?*

Jay S. Stowsky is a research fellow at the Berkeley Roundtable on the International Economy (BRIE) and a doctoral candidate in the Department of City and Regional Planning, both at the University of California, Berkeley. He received his Master's degree in public policy from the John F. Kennedy School of Government, Harvard University. He is the author of several studies of the relationship between high-technology sectors and economic development, including "Beating Our Plowshares into Double-Edged Swords: The Impact of Pentagon Policies on the Commercialization of Advanced Technologies," and "The Weakest Link: Semiconductor Production Equipment, Linkages, and the Limits to International Trade."

Benjamin C. Whipple is a doctoral candidate in the Department of Corporate Strategy and Policy at the Sloan School of Management, Massachusetts Institute of Technology. He received his B.A. in political science and history from Swarthmore College.